THAILAND

Thailand

A Short History

DAVID K. WYATT

Yale University Press
New Haven and London

Designed by James J. Johnson
and set in Baskerville Roman by
Asco Trade Typesetting Ltd., Hong Kong.
Printed in the United States of America by
Edwards Brothers, Inc., Ann Arbor, Michigan.

Library of Congress Cataloging in Publication Data

Wyatt, David K.
  Thailand: a short history.

  Bibliography: p.
  Includes index.
  1. Thailand—History. I. Title.
DS571.W92   1984   959.3   83–25953
ISBN 0–300–03054–1

10 9 8 7 6 5 4 3 2

Contents

Illustrations

Maps

Tables

Preface

The presentation of the history of Thailand to the Western reader began in the 1840s, when American missionaries, helped by the soon-to-be King Mongkut, contributed a series of articles on the history of Siam to a Hong Kong newspaper. In the century and a half since then, few have followed their lead. The only general history of the kingdom is W. A. R. Wood's *A History of Siam*, first published in 1926 and subsequently reissued only in Bangkok without revisions. Thailand deserves better. Its long history as the only country of Southeast Asia to escape colonial rule in the nineteenth and twentieth centuries demands thoughtful consideration, and its long tradition of independence and development provides a useful case study to compare with the history of its neighbors. Most of all, however, Thailand's history is worth studying simply because it "is there," certainly as much so as the histories of Indonesia and Vietnam, for example.

To try to encompass several thousand years in a few hundred pages is rather like trying to capture the essence of a sculpture in a single photograph. Most of the pages of this book might quite easily be expanded several dozen times over with the work of several generations of scholars. This book, however, is directed primarily to the general reader, those who develop some interest in Thailand for whatever reason, and the beginning student. For this audience an extensive scholarly apparatus, with dense clouds of footnote references to Thai sources and arcane tomes, would be both superfluous and confusing. Serious students of Thailand will either recognize the sources from which I have worked or be guided to them by the "Suggestions for Further Reading" at the end of the volume. I trust that, by aiming this history at the general reader, my specialist colleagues will not feel that I have abandoned them.

One of my friends suggested that I might have done better to structure the book differently, to write separate chapters dealing with economic questions in each time period and so forth. Had I done so, this book would have run on for many times its present length. I chose instead to weave, as artfully as my skills allow, what I think is a wide variety of themes through what is basically a chronological framework. Topical concerns arise only when it seems necessary to deal with them; and the lowly Thai peasant farmer, I am afraid, emerges from the shadows only here and there over the many centuries with which we deal.

Kings, on the other hand, are on nearly every page, and I might quite justly be accused of displaying a royal bias, certainly through the period down to 1932. Kings function in the narrative in this way for several reasons. First, until the end of the absolute monarchy, the royal reign was a real unit of time. Individual rulers, because they had so much power, immediately and materially affected the lives of their subjects, whether directly or indirectly. As long as their individual personalities affected people's lives, I have had to concern myself with them. Second, I have the impression that readers expect to see kings through most of Thai history, and someone interested, for example, in finding out about Mongkut's reign would at least be disappointed if I had not given him the few pages he has here. Third, in the short compass of this book, political history has proven to be the least readily reduceable—I had to cut out the poets Si Prat and Sunthon Phu and Lady Phum, but I could not avoid talking about their sovereigns and patrons at some length.

I trust that the many deficiencies that remain in this book will detract only from my good name, not from the names of those on whom I have relied in writing it. Over the past twenty years I have continually picked up ideas, information, suggestions, and even inspiration from a host of friends and acquaintances. A special few proved to be ready sources of assistance, even those I see only at three- or five-year intervals. The late Dr. Kachorn Sukhabanij was among the first of these, a good friend and a good man to argue with. Tri Amatyakul, Praphat Trinarong, and Kullasap Gesmankit were always helpful, and the indefatigable Mrs. Kullasap, now head of the National Library, continues to be a model of courtesy and helpfulness. A. Thomas Kirsch, Charles Keyes, and Lauriston Sharp have, I hope, given me some anthropological sensitivities. Nidhi Aeusrivongse has been a superb correspondent and a valued source of intellectual stimulation. A few were generous enough to allow me to read their unpublished manuscripts, and I am especially grateful to the late Chester Gorman in this regard.

I have learned most from my graduate students, primarily but not exclusively those who have worked in the field of Thai history. Their theses and dissertations are in a prominent position on my study shelves, partly because I am proud of them but mainly because I use them so often; and most of them are listed in the bibliography of this volume. These include the alumni of three institutions where I have had the privilege of teaching: the School of Oriental and African Studies of the University of London, the University of Michigan, and Cornell University. When one talks and argues with others, week after week and year after year, it becomes difficult to remember who first came up with what idea or suggested a new way of looking at a complicated phenomenon. I am indebted to them all.

A handful of people took the time and trouble to read and comment on part or all of the manuscript. Anthony Diller was especially helpful on linguistic matters and Hiram Woodward and Lorraine Gesick on some points of early history. The most helpful critics of the entire manuscript were Craig J. Reynolds, Nidhi Aeusrivongse, Benjamin A. Batson, and the Yale University Press's anonymous reader, whom I would love to be able to write a book good enough to satisfy. It is not their fault that this book is not better than it is.

Work on the book was begun under the tenure of a Senior Fellowship from the National Endowment for the Humanities in 1973–74, and I am grateful for their support, as well as for the continuing assistance of the Cornell University Southeast Asia Program, the Department of History, and the University Libraries' John M. Echols Collection on Southeast Asia.

Procuring illustrations proved much more difficult than I had imagined it would be. Three old friends were especially helpful: Mrs. Kullasap Gesmankit, acting for the National Library of Thailand and the Fine Arts Department; Penelope Van Esterik, and William L. Bradley. The maps were skillfully drawn to my specifications by Stephanie Voss. Douglas, Andrew, and James Wyatt repeatedly rescued me from the arcane perversities of the computer, while writing software that will serve me for years. And I am especially grateful to the Cornell Savoyards for the staff of life, and to a few good friends for their encouragement, constancy, and smiles.

DAVID K. WYATT

Ithaca, New York
October 1983

Editorial Note

Romanization

Throughout this work, the Thai Royal Academy's "General System of Phonetic Transcription" is used to romanize Thai names and words, and a similar phonetic system is used for Lao. Diacritics have been held to an absolute minimum, maintaining only *ü* (for the Royal Academy's *ư*), thus blurring the distinctions between *o*, *œ*, and *ǫ*. Personal names and titles are romanized following the preferences of the individuals concerned, when known; thus King Chulalongkorn and Prince Devawongse (not Čhulalongkon and Thewawong). Geographical nomenclature usually follows the standardized forms of the U.S. Board on Geographic Names, as employed, for example, on the maps of the National Geographic Society.

The aspirated consonants *p*, *t*, and *k* are written *ph*, *th*, and *kh*, but they are not pronounced as they would be in English. Thus, Thai *phon* is like English *cornpone*, not *telephone*, and Thai *that* is pronounced *tut*, not *that*.

Names, Ranks, and Titles

Surnames are a twentieth-century innovation in Thailand, and Thai usually are referred to by their given name, not their surname—even in telephone directories. Sarit Thanarat thus is referred to as Prime Minister Sarit, not Prime Minister Thanarat.

In premodern times, various terms were used to denote royalty. The oldest are such terms as *chao* (Shan *sao*), *khun*, and *thao*. Modern Thai royalty is governed by a rule of declining descent, by the terms of which each successive generation diminishes one degree in status, until members of the sixth generation are commoners. The children and grandchildren of kings, termed *chao fa* or *phra ong chao*, and *mom chao*, are usually referred to as princes and princesses. The next two generations are not. They are *mom ratchawong* (*M.R.W.* or *M.R.*) and *mom luang* (*M.L.*).

Ranks and titles were conferred on the bureaucratic and military nobility until the end of the absolute monarchy in 1932, a rank and title usually being associated with an office. The *chaophraya* were highest on the list, the equivalents of cabinet ministers, generals, and the governors of the most important provincial cities. On a descending scale came *phraya*, *phra*, *luang*, and *khun*. While individuals usually were referred to by their ranks and titles, the individual's personal, given name was written after it to distinguish him from others with the same rank and title; thus, *Chaophraya* Yommarat (Pan, surname Sukhum) was distinguished from *Chaophraya* Yommarat (Thong-in).

Many who were conferred titles under the absolute monarchy perpetuated those titles as surnames, for example, Phibunsongkhram and Wichitwathakan.

Money and Measures

The only unit of Thai currency referred to in this study is the *baht*. It was valued at eight baht to the pound sterling before 1880 and ten baht through the 1880s; then followed a period of fluctuating rates that stabilized around thirteen baht in the World War I period and dropped to eleven baht until World War II. Since World War II, it has remained constant at around twenty to the U.S. dollar.

The only unit of Thai measure used here is the *picul*, equivalent to about 60 kilograms or 132 pounds.

The *rai*, a measure of land area, is equivalent to about 0.16 hectares, or 0.4 acres.

Chronology

All dates have been expressed in Western terms, converted from the complicated Thai luni-solar calendar. The key to their conversion is a series of tables in Roger Billard, "Les cycles chronologiques chinois dans les inscriptions Thaïs," *Bulletin de l'Ecole français d'Extrême-Orient* 51 (1963): 403–31, which give the Julian or Gregorian equivalent of the Thai New Year.

THAILAND

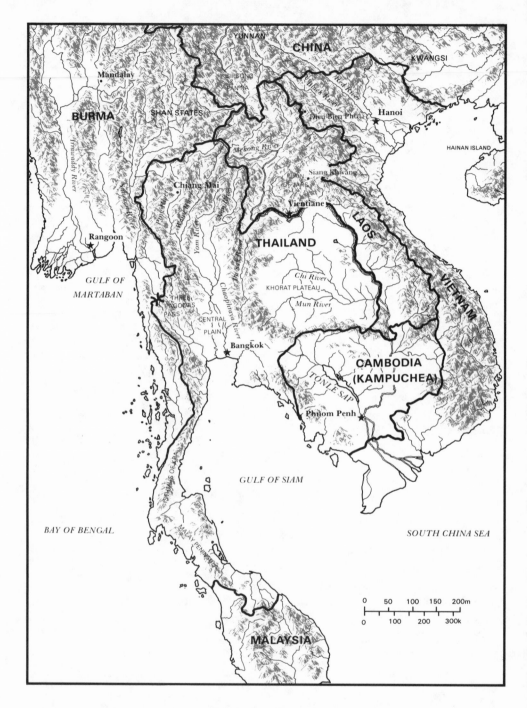

Thailand and its neighbors: physical geography.

I

The Beginnings of Tai History

The people of modern Thailand are as varied as the populations of many nations of the world. They come in all shapes and sizes, complexions and statures, and include farmers and computer programmers, soldiers and bus drivers, merchants and students, princes and monks. Virtually all would, when asked, call themselves "Thai" and, in using this term, would imply a definition primarily political: they are "Thai" as citizens of Thailand, subjects of the Thai king. If pressed, they might extend their definition further, to give the term a cultural and linguistic sense, and be "Thai" as a speaker of the Thai language and a participant in Thai culture. All the things that make up "Thai" identity, however, have developed only slowly through many centuries, and none of the things to which the modern Thai now refers—political, cultural, linguistic— existed in its present form until relatively recently.

Indeed, the people who brought the core elements of the contemporary Thai identity to what is now Thailand did not even arrive in that central portion of the Indochinese peninsula until a thousand or so years ago. These were people for whom we had best reserve the word *Tai*, a cultural and linguistic term used to denote the various Tai peoples in general, peoples sharing a common linguistic and cultural identity which in historic times has become differentiated into a large number of separate identities. The modern Thai may or may not be descended by blood from the late-arriving Tai. He or she may instead be the descendant of still earlier Mon or Khmer inhabitants of the region, or of much later Chinese or Indian immigrants. Only over many centuries has a "Thai" culture, a civilization and identity, emerged as the product of interaction between Tai and indigenous and immigrant cultures.

In attempting to trace the history of Thailand, we must primarily be concerned with people, with culture, and with society, and only secondarily with their environment. The course of Thai history is complex because the

I

historical experience of the Tai and Thai has taken place over and through a series of changing environments—environments that are as much social and cultural as they are geographical. To begin at the beginning, then, we examine in this chapter the Tai people and their experience outside the territory of modern Thailand prior to the eleventh century; only later will we ask what sort of world they entered on spilling into the Chaophraya River basin.

The Tai peoples today are widely spread over several million square kilometers of the southeastern corner of the great land mass of Asia. Their most visible representatives are the Thai (or Siamese) of Thailand, of whom there are 27 to 30 million. Many others who speak related Tai languages and recognize themselves as Tai call their own ethnic and linguistic groups by other names. Of these, there are more than 20 million Lao, most of whom live in northeastern Thailand, with only about 2.5 million in Laos. In northeastern Burma live approximately 3 million Shans. There are numerous other Tai groups scattered through the uplands of northern Southeast Asia and south China. These fall into two groupings. The first includes the Lü of Yunnan province, China, and the various upland Tai—the Black Tai, White Tai, and Red Tai, for example—of Laos and northern Vietnam. Together these number perhaps another 2.5 million. The second group, strongly influenced by Chinese culture and located to the east, is most prominently represented by the Chuang people of the Chinese provinces of Kwangsi and Kweichow, numbering around 18 million; but this group also includes such peoples as the Nung of northern Vietnam, perhaps 400,000 in number. Adding smaller, more isolated groups in north-eastern India and the Chinese island of Hainan, we arrive at a total of about 70 million people, a linguistic and cultural group comparable in numbers to the French or Germans.

The most obvious characteristic that serves to identify the Tai as a separate people is their language. The relationship between the Tai family of languages and the neighboring languages of East and Southeast Asia has not been definitely established, and it is not yet possible to speak of Tai languages as belonging with any certainty to any larger linguistic grouping like "Romance languages" or "Indo-European languages." The relationships among the Tai languages themselves, however, are relatively clear, even to the point that there is some degree of mutual intelligibility among speakers of Lao, Siamese, and Shan, for example. No such striking relationships exist, however, among Tai languages and such neighboring tongues as Burmese, Cambodian, Vietnamese, or Chinese.

Generally speaking, the Tai languages are monosyllabic and tonal. This means that, barring borrowings from neighboring polysyllabic languages, the basic vocabulary of any Tai language or dialect is made up of single syllables. Over a long course of development, early Tai languages lost many of the consonants that helped distinguish words one from another, leaving tone as the distinguishing feature instead. Thus *maa*, "to come," spoken in Siamese Tai with a level tone of voice, is distinguished from *máa* (high tone), "horse," and *mǎa* (rising tone), "dog." The number of tones, which can be as many as nine, varies from one Tai dialect or language to another; most varieties have from five to seven. There is also a good deal of vowel and consonant variation, rather regular in the southern Tai-speaking areas but much less so to the north. For all its variation, however, the basic language, with its grammatical structure and vocabulary, is common to all the Tai groups.[1]

The cultural identity of the Tai is not so easily defined, for the Tai share a great deal of their culture, their style of life and patterns of behavior, with other Southeast Asian peoples, though this culture is markedly different from the cultures of India and China. Both the cultural and the linguistic origins of the Tai peoples seem best to be explained by reference to the existence in prehistoric times of a Southeast Asian cultural pool, or heartland, located perhaps in the extreme northern portions of Southeast Asia and in central and southern China.

As long as forty thousand years ago, the progenitors of Southeast Asian peoples were inhabiting relatively permanent sites through much of that region. They hunted and gathered their food from the streams and forests, using many of the sorts of wooden and bamboo tools still in use in Southeast Asia. With stone choppers and knives, they fashioned such tools as the blowpipe, the bow and arrow, animal and fish traps, and baskets. By ten to twenty thousand years ago, they had begun to engage in agriculture, cultivating peas and beans and domesticating such animals as the chicken. It was only around ten thousand years ago that the individual ethnic groups of Southeast Asia began to be differentiated, linguistically and culturally, over the broad span of territory from the Yangtse Valley of central China to the islands of the Indonesian Archipelago. This process of differentiation and separation, however, took place on the basis of a common culture formed over the preceding thirty millennia. Here we have the technological core of Southeast Asian civilization, together with much of its culture. Swine, cattle, and fowl were domesticated and rice was cultivated; and Southeast Asians invented the outrigger canoe, enabling navigation to be undertaken as far afield as Japan, Melanesia, India, and even Madagascar. Sophisticated metallurgy also developed in Southeast Asia as early as anywhere in the world. Copper and bronze working is attested by the excavation at a site in what is now northeastern Thailand of a mold in which bronze axes were cast, dating back to more than five thousand years ago. There was also ironworking in the same region around three thousand years ago and a considerable pottery-making technology.

It is not unreasonable to suppose that by two thousand years ago the

Ban Chiang painted vessel, late period.
Private collection, Bangkok.

peoples of Southeast Asia shared a common, distinctive, and advanced civilization. Like their neighbors, the Tai conducted subsistence agriculture based on
the cultivation of rice, supplemented by fishing and the gathering of forest
products. They lived as nuclear families in small villages, among which there
was regular communication and some trade in such items as metal tools,
pottery, and salt. Because the region was underpopulated, manpower was
highly valued and women enjoyed a relatively high social status, certainly by
contrast with the low social and economic status of Chinese and Indian women.
In determining inheritance, for example, equal value was accorded the maternal and paternal lines, and sons and daughters usually received equal shares of
their parents' estates. Throughout the region, folk beliefs were remarkably
consistent. The world was regarded as being peopled with good and evil spirits
that had the power to aid or harm humans and thus had to be propitiated by
ceremonies or offerings of food. Women frequently were believed to have a

special power to mediate between mankind and the spirit world, and were called upon to heal the sick or change unfavorable weather. Nature and the world were regarded as unpredictable and hostile forces with which humans had to cope as best they could.

The earliest Chinese references to the Tai peoples are consistent with this picture that anthropologists and archeologists have given us of prehistoric Southeast Asian culture. Tai whom the Chinese encountered were always referred to as inhabitants of the valleys and lowlands, rather than of the hillsides and uplands, and usually were reported as having an economy based on wet-rice cultivation. Many Tai groups considered cattle (or buffalo) as significant, often more as a measure of status and wealth or for their use in ritual than for their usefulness as a draft animal. Tai always were reported as having lived in houses raised on piles above the ground, in contrast to their Chinese and Vietnamese neighbors. Young people customarily were allowed free choice of marriage partners and were given wide sexual license in an annual spring festival. Tattooing, associated with the passage to adulthood, was widely practiced among men, and a form of poison-doll sorcery was apparently widespread among them.

These Tai to whom the Chinese referred under a wide variety of names were at various times scattered over much of south and southwest China in the early centuries A.D., and in the preceding millennia they may have been located well to the north. We know, however, little about their earliest history in organized groups or states. There is no clear evidence that there was any Tai "state" prior to the early centuries A.D., and certainly none with any discernible relationship to the Tai states that began to appear in northern Southeast Asia late in the first millennium A.D. The most plausible connection that can be drawn between the early cultural and linguistic mosaic of the first millennium B.C. and that of the later Tai states derives from linguistic hypotheses about the evolution of the Tai languages. These are still controversial theories, but a consensus seems to be emerging among linguists that on some points bears striking resemblances to Tai legendary accounts of their own origins. This is further reinforced by what little is known of the earliest history of the geographical areas concerned.

By the last centuries of the first millennium B.C., we must presume that the major linguistic and cultural families of the peoples that we regard as Southeast Asian had become differentiated, and to some extent physically separated, from one another. The peoples of island Southeast Asia, from the Philippines to the Malay Peninsula, spoke Malayo-Polynesian (Austronesian) languages, while Austroasiatic languages, such as Mon and Khmer (Cambodian), were spoken in the central and southern portions of the Indochinese peninsula from lower

Burma to the Mekong Delta of southern Vietnam. The Burmese were located in northern Burma and southwestern China, while the Vietnamese lived along the coasts of what is now northern Vietnam and southeastern China. Caught between the Vietnamese and Khmer speakers was a pocket of Malayo-Polynesian–speaking Chams in central and southern Vietnam.

At about the same time there existed a large and fairly homogeneous population in the inland river valleys of extreme southeastern China, in the present-day provinces of Kweichow and Kwangsi, speaking what we might call "Proto Tai" languages. These people lived under mounting demographic, economic, and political pressure from their neighbors, the Vietnamese and the Han Chinese to their north and east. As populations grew and groups became isolated from one another, the languages they spoke began to diverge. The dispersal of the Proto Tai, perhaps in the earliest centuries of the Christian Era, must have been precipitated by Imperial China's expansion along the south China coast to the Red River delta of what is now northern Vietnam. This Chinese expansion probably coincided with, and undoubtedly hastened, a southwestward movement of some Tai speakers into the upland portions of what is now northern Vietnam and perhaps also into extreme northeastern Laos. When, in the first few centuries A.D., the Chinese and Vietnamese gradually tightened their administrative and military control and moved northwestward up the Red River valley, they in effect divided the early Tai into two major groups. Those remaining to the north and northeast of the Red River valley, such as the Chuang people of Kwangsi and the Tho and Nung of Vietnam, developed separately both in their language and, under the influence of the Chinese and Vietnamese, in their culture.

The second, southern Tai group probably should be localized in the valley of the Black River and extreme northeastern Laos and neighboring portions of China around the fifth to eighth centuries A.D. This Tai group, whom we can notionally associate with the region of Dien Bien Phu (Müang Thaeng), was the ancestor of all the Tai peoples of Laos, Thailand, Burma, northeastern India, and southern Yunnan—the Lao, Siamese, Shans, and upland Tai. In what to them was a new geographical, cultural, and political environment, their concerns, habits, and ideas came to be oriented in new directions. They were increasingly isolated from their kinsmen to the north, to the point ultimately even of forgetting their kinship with them. In the centuries to come, perhaps between the seventh century and the thirteenth, they were to spread seven hundred to one thousand miles to the west and the south. Yet all of them, as we shall see, preserved in their folk memories and traditions a sense of their common descent which is borne out by their linguistic affiliation.

The Tai Village and Müang

Piecing together the information we have, almost entirely from the reports of their neighbors, we can construct a composite picture of Tai life in the first millennium A.D. At its base was the farming household, probably composed of a simple nuclear family. The labor of all family members was utilized in eking out a bare subsistence, growing rice and vegetables, tending cattle and domestic animals, fishing in nearby streams and hunting in the forest, and weaving cloth or fashioning implements. A dozen or two such households would share their labor at harvest time, or when repairing a bridge or building a house, their efforts being coordinated by an informal council of the village elders, who also resolved disputes and arranged communal festivals.

Such villages could not sustain themselves in perfect isolation. These rural Tai were dependent to some degree on trade, for salt or metal, for example; and alone they were highly vulnerable in time of war. For almost all the Tai peoples, the *müang* was the primary unit of social and political organization above the simple village level. *Müang* is a term that defies translation, for it denotes as much personal as spatial relationships. When it is used in ancient chronicles to refer to a principality, it can mean both the town located at the hub of a network of interrelated villages and also the totality of town and villages which was ruled by a single *chao*, "lord." We can imagine that such müang originally arose out of a set of political, economic, and social interrelationships. Under dangerous circumstances, such as those pertaining in the uplands of northern Vietnam in the first centuries A.D. when Chinese and Vietnamese sought to extend their administrative control, Tai villages banded together for mutual defense under the leadership of the most powerful village or family, whose resources might enable it to arm and supply troops. In return for such protection, participating villages rendered labor service to their chao, or paid him quantities of local produce or handicrafts.

It needs to be stressed that this was a mutually beneficial relationship. It would have been natural for müang centers, though initially villages not much larger than those around them, to have been more prosperous and powerful than surrounding villages, and that these advantages grew over time. We can also suppose that this organization of upland Tai society might have been regarded as advantageous to the imperial powers, such as Vietnam and China, who preferred dealing with a limited number of müang rather than a virtually limitless number of villages. Vietnamese and Chinese alike adopted the practice of recognizing Tai chao as the leaders of their communities, either as enemies or as allies or tributaries. In return for their recognition of Chinese supremacy and the annual rendering of tribute, a Tai chao was left alone to preside over the life of a relatively isolated and (from the viewpoint of nearby Chinese officials) unimportant community. Again, this was yet another level of mutually advantageous relationship by which rural Tai communities, already beginning to be integrated among themselves, were at least loosely tied into a larger world outside.

There was also another world nearer at hand. It is clear that, from the earliest times, the Tai were never the sole inhabitants of the interior uplands. Their rice agriculture kept them for the most part to the lower-lying valleys, while the hills above them were inhabited by other peoples of a variety of ethnic and linguistic stocks. From a very early time, Tai chao established relationships with such neighboring groups, employing them as slaves and menial laborers and taking on their chiefs as "vassals," just as the Tai themselves were "vassals" of the Chinese rulers. Such patterns are significant both in the immediate context of their upland existence in early centuries and as an early stage in the development among upland Tai peoples of political skills and patterns that later became part of their "technology" of state building.

Over time, we can imagine how the structure of the upland Tai müang might gradually have evolved and become more elaborate. The successful müang defended itself militarily or diplomatically against neighboring müang, rude hill peoples, and major states like China and Vietnam. It maintained order in its own region and imposed some system of justice to punish malefactors and settle intervillage disputes, for example, concerning land or water rights or cattle thefts. It provided an economic framework within which exchanges of produce and manufactures could take place; and it certainly must have benefited from the payment of tax obligations, whether in labor or in kind, by villages in return for security and order. Müang ruling families could be supported in a style at least one level above that of the surrounding villages. Strengthened both by their local political and economic power and by the prestige gained through successful dealings with hill peoples and the outside world, ruling families could maintain themselves for generations. A chao built up his own administrative apparatus for collecting tax revenues and settling legal complaints. He regularized the succession to his office, often by appointing his heir (usually, but not always, his eldest son) to a high administrative position so the young man could familiarize himself with and control the networks of personal relationships upon which the structure of the müang depended.

As much as anything else, the Tai müang was an instrument for the efficient use of manpower in a region where land was plentiful in relation to labor and agricultural technology. This was a world in many ways insecure, where such wealth as cattle or precious metals or reserves of grain might disappear overnight in a bandit raid or in warfare. Security, wealth, and life all depended upon the relations among individuals and families that provided for durable and effective leadership and order. Although müang society was hierarchical, it must be emphasized that the patron-client relationship, the ruler/ruled dichotomy, was not nearly as one-sided as it may appear. Each party to the relationship clearly needed the other. Pushed to a confrontation, the chao could rely upon superior force, but the village farmer could resort to flight to the surrounding wilderness or to a neighboring müang eager to gain his labor. Such extreme recourses were avoided on both sides in favor of mutual accommodation and compromise.

During the first millennium of the Christian Era, the population of the Tai communities of upland, interior Southeast Asia apparently steadily increased. Under the prevailing ecological and political conditions, it was natural that there should have been a slow expansion of this population in a western and southwestern direction. The coastal lowlands to the east and northeast were controlled and densely settled by well-organized and powerful Chinese and Vietnamese states. The upland river valleys to the west and southwest, in northern Laos and southern Yunnan, were only sparsely populated by ab-original Austronesian and Austroasiatic-speaking populations, the ancestors of today's hill peoples, whose technology, weapons, and social and political or-ganization ill-equipped them for successful competition with the Tai.

The early chronicles of Tai groups, extending from Laos to northeastern India, are filled with stories of demographic and political movement and expansion. The patterns of movement they depict are remarkably consistent. Characteristically, a ruler would gather together the men of his müang and form them into a military expedition, usually under the leadership of one of his sons. They would conquer, or simply colonize, a distant region and settle it with families from the parent müang, who would "turn the forest into rice-fields" and settle in organized communities ruled by the young prince. The ruler might organize such campaigns for a whole succession of his sons, giving each a principality of his own to rule while enhancing the power of the parent müang. Sons might thus be sent out in order of their seniority, leaving the youngest son to inherit the domains of his father. In northern Vietnam and Laos, where this movement must have occurred, the mountain valleys suitable for rice cultiva-tion are extremely small and narrow, and are separated by difficult, moun-tainous territory. Thus the demographic and political center of gravity of the Tai population could have moved fairly rapidly, and usually in the same general direction, to the west and southwest. Upon their father's death, brothers would have found it difficult to hold together their principalities, and they may not have been able easily to defend themselves against Chinese or Vietnamese attempts to bring them under control. Moreover, once his father had died and his own sons came of age, a prince frequently would wish to provide for them as he himself had been provided for. In this fashion might chains of Tai principalities slowly have stretched across the northern reaches of Indochina.

What is perhaps a folk memory of this early expansion of the Tai is conveyed by such origin legends as the Khun Borom story told by the Lao and echoed in the folklore of their neighbors. According to this story, early in the earth's history mankind was uncivilized, rude, and brutal, and not yet settled to agriculture. Man's ingratitude to the Heavenly Spirit so angered the chief of the gods that he unloosed an enormous flood upon the earth from which only three chiefs escaped, Khun Khan, Khun Khek, and Khun Pu Lang Song. They made submission to the chief of the gods and remained with him in heaven until the floods subsided. At that time, they returned to earth with a buffalo, which helped them lay out rice fields in the great plain around Dien Bien Phu and then died. From the nostrils of the dead buffalo there grew an enormous plant bearing gourds or pumpkins from which there soon came loud noises. When the gourds were pierced, mankind came pouring out to populate the earth. The Lao explain that those who came out of the gourds through holes made with a red-hot poker are the dark-skinned aboriginal populations, and those who came through the holes made with a chisel were the lighter-skinned Lao.

With the assistance of the chief of the gods, Khun Khan, Khun Khek, and Khun Pu Lang Song taught the Tai (and only the Tai, presumably) to build houses and practice rice culture, and to observe proper conduct and ritual. The population soon grew so numerous that it required assistance in governing. So the chief of the gods sent to earth his own son, Khun Borom, who arrived on earth accompanied by courtiers and teachers, tools, and the useful and fine arts. After a prosperous reign of twenty-five years, Khun Borom appointed his seven sons to rule over the Tai world—the eldest to Luang Prabang, and the others to Siang Khwang, Lavo-Ayudhya, Chiang Mai, the Sipsong Pan Na (of southern Yunnan), Hamsavati (the Mon state of Pegu in lower Burma), and a region apparently in north-central Vietnam (Nghe-an province?). One version of this tale from Siang Khwang dates this event in A.D. 698.

For all their anachronisms and inconsistencies, the various versions of the Khun Borom legend shed important light on the early history of the Tai. Many of the states to which they refer were founded only centuries later, whereas the archeological record would date Tai culture much earlier. Nonetheless, the legends convey an important sense of group identity and kinship, of commonality of culture and language, and of the spatial relationship among widely scattered Tai groups that is echoed in the findings of modern scholarship. A combination of linguistic and fragmentary documentary evidence suggests that

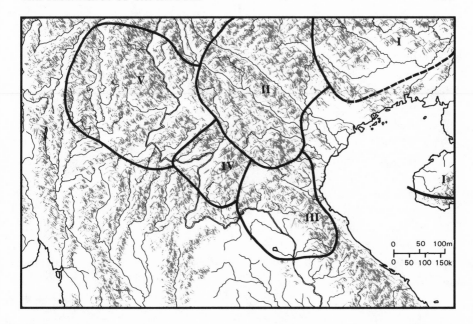

Hypothetical reconstruction of the differentiation of the Tai languages by the eighth century A.D.

   I. Northern group, ancestor of Chuang, etc.
  II. Upland Tai group, ancestor of Black, Red, White, etc. Tai
 III. Siang Khwang group, ancestor of Central Thai (Siamese)
  IV. Lao group, ancestor of Lao and Sukhothai languages
   V. Western group, ancestor of Shan, Ahom, Lü, etc. languages

some such split and dispersion of Tai peoples did occur between the eighth and eleventh or twelfth centuries along geographical lines consistent with the legends. We note that, although Khun Borom is said to have come to earth in the Dien Bien Phu region, none of his sons was left to rule there, and that the upland Tai world of what is now northern Vietnam is omitted from the lists of lands over which his sons were sent to rule. The Black Tai, White Tai, Red Tai, and similar groups must have been separated from the parent tongue of the Lao and Siamese languages extremely early, and from such northwestern languages as Shan, Ahom, Lü, and Northern Thai (Tai Yuan) between, say, the eighth and eleventh centuries.

   Postulating first from the linguistic arguments, let us suppose that around the eighth century A.D. the Tai world already was extended across much of northern Southeast Asia, differentiated into five linguistic groups. First, the northern groups left behind in China were evolving into the ancestors of the present Chuang group. Second, there remained another grouping of upland Tai peoples in northern Vietnam, the ancestors of the Black, White, and Red Tai. Third, another grouping of Tai peoples must have been localized somewhere in northeastern Laos and adjacent portions of Vietnam, the ancestors of the Tai of Siang Khwang and of Siamese Ayudhya. A fourth group may have been located in northern Laos, perhaps in the vicinity of Luang Prabang. A final, fifth group was certainly located to the west of them, in extreme northern Thailand and adjacent portions of Laos, Yunnan, and Burma. Differentiation of the groups is required by linguistic considerations, which hold that related dialects underwent some of the same changes at the same time, whereas others that lack features that may then have developed must by that time have been located elsewhere. Obviously, we cannot locate linguistic groups in specific localities at precise dates in the distant past. But given the present-day distribution of dialects and the natural routes of communication, we can make reasonable guesses as to the regions where various groups were located during broad spans of time.

Leaving aside the question of which Tai dialects were spoken in which regions, how can we know that speakers of any Tai language might have inhabited the regions specified at such an early date? How do we know they were not much further north by the eighth century, perhaps in Yunnan? Since the turn of the present century, many have argued that the Tai peoples entered Southeast Asia only in the thirteenth century, and that prior to that time they had formed the population of the powerful state of Nan-chao in Yunnan. When the Mongols conquered Yunnan in 1253, the argument runs, the Tai dispersed. Both to deal with this argument and to consider the environment in which the early Tai peoples developed their culture and institutions, it is necessary to take up the "Nan-chao question," and to depict, as fully as the evidence allows, the world in which the Tai peoples lived during a critically important epoch in their history.

Nan-chao

Largely owing to their desire to open land communication with India, the Chinese moved to gain control over what is now the province of Yunnan during the Han dynasty, especially in the second century A.D., when even western Yunnan was absorbed into the empire. The Chinese found there a bewildering assortment of peoples they called "barbarians" (*man*), some of whom adopted Chinese civilization. One such local ruling family, who intermarried with Chinese administrators or colonists, was the Ts'uan family, centered in the region extending southward from Kun-ming to the present Vietnamese frontier. They gradually became the hereditary governors of the province after the fall of the Han in the third century A.D. This southeastern portion of Yunnan appears to have been inhabited by a mixture of Tai and Miao-Yao peoples. The western and southwestern portions of the province were for the most part dominated by people the Chinese termed *Wu-man*, "black barbarians," dark-skinned peoples speaking Tibeto-Burman languages akin to those of the Lolo and Lahu peoples who still inhabit the region. It was the Wu-man of western Yunnan who in the seventh century formed the nucleus around which the state of Nan-chao was formed.

Under the T'ang dynasty, the Chinese in the first half of the seventh century had controlled about half of Yunnan, their rule extending as far west as the Mekong River. By the latter half of the century, however, the Chinese were put on the defensive by an expanding Tibet which threatened their south-western frontiers in Yunnan and Szechuan. Abandoning attempts at direct ad-ministration in the region after 713, the Chinese tried to maintain their frontier security through alliances with local principalities, negotiated by Chinese officials in Szechuan. One such ally was P'i-lo-ko, the ruler (chao) of Meng-she, one of six small principalities around Ta-li Lake in western Yunnan. With Chinese encouragement, P'i-lo-ko united these six small states under his rule in the 730s and in 738 gained recognition from the Chinese court as "Prince of Yunnan." Relations between China and the "Southern Prince (Nan-chao)" remained friendly through the 740s but rapidly deteriorated in the following decade under P'i-lo-ko's son, Ko-lo-feng, owing perhaps to Chinese concern over Nan-chao's growing power in Yunnan and certainly to the political meddling of Chinese border officials. Four Chinese armies were sent against Nan-chao between 752 and 754, each time defeated by Ko-lo-feng's forces. Nan-chao then extended its control over all of eastern Yunnan and even western Kweichow. Once T'ang China was preoccupied with rebellion, Chinese pressure on Nan-chao eased, and the foundations of the new empire in the southwest were firmly built with the establishment of a secondary capital at present-day Kun-ming in 764 and the full elaboration of Nan-chao's administration.

The most extensive contemporary account of Nan-chao, the *Man shu* (written by a Chinese official in the 860s), depicts a well-organized, quasi-military state, ruling over an enormous variety of ethnic groups. The king of Nan-chao presided over a court and administration similar to those of China, with six "boards," like ministries, in charge of war, population and revenue, the reception of foreign guests, punishment, works, and assemblies. Additional boards treated offenses against the public order and military planning. There are indications, however, that the power and status of the boards was exceeded

14   THE BEGINNINGS OF TAI HISTORY

by twelve "great generals," who "every day. . . have audience with the *Nan-chao* and deliberate on [public] affairs," and six "pure and just officials" who seem to have served as the privy councillors of the king.[2] The administration rested upon a hierarchy of officials under the central control of the boards and "great generals." This ranged from the officer in charge of a hundred households to the governor in charge of ten thousand households, each of whom was granted land in proportion to his rank. Male householders paid annually a tax of two pecks of rice and in addition were liable for call to military service. The army had its attractions for rural lads, who practiced their skills "whenever there is a break in agricultural work." Men passing various tests of skill and endurance for the cavalry and infantry could be promoted and were liberally rewarded. Each year in the late autumn the Board of War would issue the call for men to muster for the military tests and maneuvers; and Nan-chao armies were proficient, powerful, well-disciplined, and effective on the field of battle for several centuries.

From the middle of the eighth century to the end of the ninth, Nan-chao was a major power in the affairs of northern Southeast Asia and south China. Its armies maintained pressure on the Pyu kingdom of central Burma through most of this period; attacked what is now southern Burma and northern Thailand in the early ninth century; mounted an expedition against Khmer Chen-la, which is reported to have gone "as far as the seashore," probably in the ninth century; and sent repeated expeditions against the Chinese Protectorate of An-nam (northern Vietnam) between 846 and 866. Thereafter, Nan-chao's power receded before Chinese revival, newly independent Vietnam (from 939), and new developments that began to reshape northern Southeast Asia.

The significance of Nan-chao for Tai history is not due to the identity of its rulers, who especially during this period were certainly not Tai. The chao of Nan-chao followed the patronymic linkage system in choosing their names, the first syllable of each ruler's name being the same as the last syllable of his father's name—thus, P'i-lo-ko, Ko-lo-feng, Feng-chia-i, I-mou-hsün, and so on—a pattern common among the Lolo and other Tibeto-Burman groups but unknown among the Tai. Moreover, the lists of Nan-chao words mentioned by Fan Ch'o are identifiable as Lolo and untraceable as Tai. No Tai legend or chronicle mentions Nan-chao or any of its rulers, but nineteenth-century Lolo chiefs in central Yunnan traced their ancestry back to the Nan-chao ruling house. The significance of Nan-chao for Tai history therefore must be sought in its effects upon the Tai peoples living in the southern and eastern portions of its empire and along its periphery.

The most obvious effects of the rise of Nan-chao's power in Yunnan were the natural consequences of bringing a large tract of northern Southeast Asia under a centralized administrative control. Nan-chao's move into Burma (and perhaps even into northeastern India) opened lines of overland communications between India and China. This undoubtedly had beneficial economic effects, but probably at least as important were its intellectual and cultural consequences. Nan-chao, like T'ang China and Chinese An-nam, became a Buddhist state and must have contributed to the spread of Buddhism in the region it dominated, as well as to the more diffuse acculturation of the region to the Indian arts and sciences.

In assessing the political impact of nan-chao on the Tai in the eighth and ninth centuries, it is difficult to distinguish between the conditions that facilitated the expansion of both the Tai and Nan-chao and the conditions that Nan-chao uniquely created for the Tai environment. That is, did Nan-chao and Tai expansion stem from the same conditions? Or did Nan-chao create conditions favorable to the spread of the Tai? There are no answers to these questions. The least that can be said is that the rise of Nan-chao effectively blocked the northern portion of inland Southeast Asia from direct contact with China. At the same time, the power of Nan-chao, extending over a wide area, facilitated the overland trade between China and India and presumably also stimulated local trade in northern Southeast Asia. In what must have been an environment of some economic opportunity, local princes must also have grasped what could appear as political opportunities. By submitting to or allying themselves with Nan-chao, they could gain a powerful benefactor or protector and use that relationship against their neighbors. They would also have sought to imitate some of the administrative and military features of the Nan-chao kingdom, which in that day would have been fashionable. Even those Tai chao who did not fall directly under the hegemony of the rulers of Nan-chao might have been pressed to mobilize their manpower, perhaps organizing it by the tens-hundreds-thousands method of Nan-chao, in order to defend themselves. Nan-chao probably was not the first state of major proportions to intrude upon the Tai world, and it certainly was not the last. But it was the first major state to become involved in the interior uplands of mainland Southeast Asia, that is, the regions that are now the Shan states of Burma, northern Thailand and Laos, and northwestern Vietnam. In the centuries immediately following Nan-chao's heyday in the eighth and ninth centuries, however, the pressure was to come from the south, from very different sorts of major empires.

Mainland Southeast Asia in the Ninth and Tenth Centuries

The surviving records concerning Nan-chao mention nothing that can be taken as Tai states in upland Southeast Asia in the ninth and tenth centuries. They do, however, identify most of the states that were to be the southern neighbors

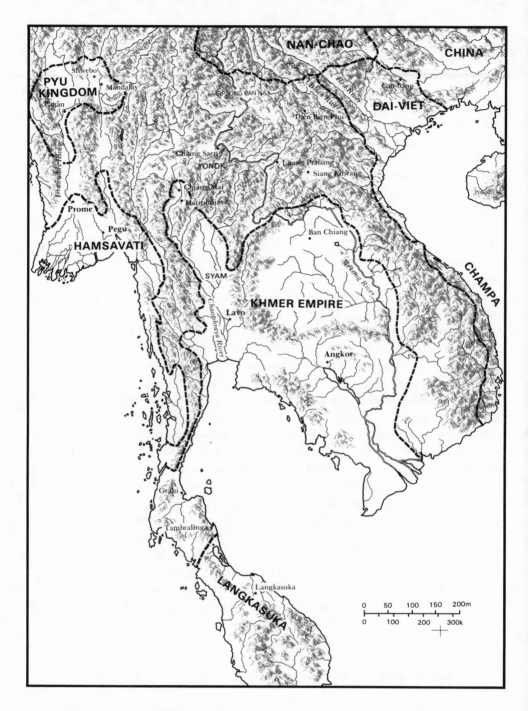

Mainland Southeast Asia in the late tenth century, showing major empires. (After G. Maspero, "La géographie politique de l'Indochine aux environs de 960 A.D.," *Etudes asiatiques* (Paris, 1925), vol. 2.

and rivals of the Tai in the ensuing centuries, states that were to make critically important contributions to the formation of Tai civilization. These included, from east to west, a Vietnamese state centered in the Red River valley and delta of northern Vietnam; the kingdom of Champa, on the coast of central Vietnam; the Khmer Empire of Angkor; the kingdoms of central and northern Thailand; and the Mon and Pyu kingdoms of Burma. For the most part these were states facing toward the sea, forming a ring around the Tai in the uplands. Particularly from the beginning of the ninth century they grew in power and territorial extent, and the Tai increasingly became involved in their lives and their politics.

The situation in northern Vietnam in the tenth and eleventh centuries probably was typical of the Tai situation in that period over a broader region. The Vietnamese state that became independent of Chinese administration and control in 939 was based on the coastal plain and the Red River delta. It was flanked in all directions by major empires: China to the north, Nan-chao to the northwest, and Champa and Angkorian Cambodia to the south and southwest. The upland zones separating the Vietnamese from their rivals were inhabited by third parties, especially Tai peoples; and successive Vietnamese rulers took pains to impress upon them the kingdom's power and to gain at least their neutrality, if not their active support. They were not always successful. A Nung chief in the Cao-bang region of the extreme north revolted and formed an independent kingdom in 1038, and he and his son kept both the Vietnamese and the Chinese court at war for fifteen years. That revolt revealed both the extent to which some of the upland groups were behaving politically in the patterns set by their lowland neighbors and the dangers they could pose to the major powers. The Vietnamese mounted a major diplomatic effort on their northern frontiers, entering into alliances with local chiefs, alliances that were sealed by bestowing Vietnamese "princesses" upon them.

Champa by the ninth and tenth centuries was fighting for its existence against the encroachments of its powerful neighbors. It had been able briefly to threaten both Chinese An-nam (i.e., Vietnam) and Cambodia at the beginning of the ninth century, but in a few decades it was on the defensive against both, its territory reduced to an ever-shrinking slice of the central coast of Vietnam. It definitely had overland communications with the middle Mekong and what is now southern Laos and northeastern Thailand; and it must have been through such connections, involving trade and warfare, that Tai, *Syam*, slaves reached Champa, to be mentioned in an inscription of 1050.

Of all the empires of the region it was the Khmer Empire, centered in the Angkor region, that was expanding most rapidly during this period, beginning with the accession of Jayavarman II in about 802. During two centuries, he and his successors, particularly Yaśovarman I (r. 889–900) constructed an empire that dwarfed all its rivals. From a heartland that included both the core of Cambodia, centered on the Tonle Sap, and the southern half of the Khorat Plateau, it expanded outward in all directions. To the east it controlled the Mekong Delta and pushed against the Chams on the Vietnam coast. To the north it extended at least as far as the Vientiane Plain, and even exerted some influence (perhaps by an occasional military expedition) in the regions of Luang Prabang and Chiang Saen, and through the latter into the region called the Sipsong Pan Na, bordering on Nan-chao. To the west and northwest it took control over the lower valley of the Chaophraya River in Thailand and extended its suzerainty over the Mon kingdom of Haripuñjaya, near present-day Chiang Mai. Yaśovarman I even established a strong presence on the Malay Peninsula, where Khmer royalty may have ruled over communities of Khmer settlers or military garrisons at Grahi and Tambralinga. It is worthy of note that the Khmers as a result of this expansion controlled virtually every route of communications and trade in the central core of the Indochinese peninsula, whether these were links between producing hinterlands and the sea or transit routes for the great east-west trade between India and China. The effect of this power was at least in part to deprive potential rivals of income and strength, gaining these for themselves.

To the west, in what is now Burma, in the ninth and tenth centuries there was no great single empire. The strong military pressure from Nan-chao, which began in the mid-eighth century and was maintained until the middle of the ninth, had diminished. The Pyu state, centered on Prome (and later the Shwebo area in the north), had collapsed, and into their commanding position in the Irrawaddy valley the Burmans were moving. The Burmans, based on the irrigated rice lands of the Mandalay region, established a small new state centered on Pagân in the mid-ninth century. On the coast, at the head of the Gulf of Martaban, a new Mon kingdom was rising at Pegu around the same time in the wake of another Nan-chao invasion around 835. Neither of these states appears to have been at all concerned with the upland valleys in what were later to be called the Shan states.

Finally, Nan-chao after the middle of the ninth century seems to have confined its military and political energies to its heartland in southwestern China, after decades of exhausting warfare in Burma, Vietnam, and Szechuan that ended with a peace treaty with China in the 880s. The state fell into some political instability, with thirteen kings in the next 120 years, none of whom appears to have taken an active interest in the region to the south.

During the ninth and tenth centuries, we must envision the Tai peoples as living in the largely untroubled reaches of upland Southeast Asia, in the spaces between the major states that surrounded them on all sides. Because we know that Nan-chao earlier had driven through this region in military expeditions against various Burma states, Cambodian Chen-la, and Vietnam, and because there is some evidence of Angkorian interest in the same region during this period, we can assume that the Tai at this time were not isolated either politically or culturally. Perhaps like the Pyu and Burmans, various Tai groups had been impressed into Nan-chao armies and had seen military service far from their homes. Tai probably were taken as war captives and slaves by the parties to these conflicts, and some may have traveled for trade, or on religious pilgrimages, to distant capitals. The Tai had begun to become a part of Southeast Asian history, but they had as yet no history of their own. This would come only when they formed their own kingdoms and empires.

2

The Tai and the Classical Empires, A.D. 1000–1200

In all of Tai history, perhaps no period is as tantalizingly dark and unknown as the eleventh and twelfth centuries. By the end of this period, early in the thirteenth century, we know a great deal about where the Tai groups were, what they were doing, the lives they led, and the ideas they held. We can only assume that their experience in the two centuries immediately preceding this one must have been critically important for them. Unfortunately, neither their own accounts nor the records of their neighbors tell us very much about that experience.

For the major, lowland civilizations of mainland Southeast Asia, the eleventh and twelfth centuries were the golden age of the classical Indianized empires, the period when they constructed their greatest monuments and left numerous stone inscriptions attesting to the high state of their learning. This was the great age of Angkor and Pagán; the age of Suryavarman I, Suryavarman II, Jayavarman VII, Anorahta, and Kyanzittha; the age of Angkor Vat, Angkor Thom, the Bayon, and the myriad temples of Pagán. Angkorian and Pagán civilization, moreover, was not simply an elite phenomenon, localized in capitals or provincial centers remote from the lives of ordinary people. It spread far out over the countryside to at least touch upon, and in some areas to penetrate, the outlying regions that we presume to have been inhabited by groups of Tai. Considering the classical civilizations of the eleventh and twelfth centuries with the Tai peoples in mind, we can come to some appreciation of the circumstances of their Indianization and their acculturation into the civilization of lowland Southeast Asia.

Even on the contemporary map there is a sharp dividing line between those Tai who underwent Indianization and those who did not, between Buddhist and non-Buddhist Tai, between those whose languages incorporated words taken from Sanskrit and Pali and those whose did not. It would appear that the same line separates those who fell under the sway of Angkorian and Pagân civilization in the eleventh and twelfth centuries from those who remained outside their reach.

Dvaravati

The basis of a Buddhist civilization in central Southeast Asia was laid between the sixth and ninth centuries. During that period, there developed in central and northeastern Thailand a distinctive Buddhist culture complex associated with the Mon people and with the name *Dvaravati*. Little is known of its history, its geographical extent, or even the location of its capital, if there was a single capital. Many of its inscriptions, however, were in the Mon language; and it is supposed that Dvaravati arose, more as a civilization than as an empire, to capitalize on the overland trade between the Gulf of Martaban and the Gulf of Siam (via the Three Pagodas Pass) late in the sixth century. Characteristically Dvaravati sites are clustered most densely, and date the furthest back in time, along the fringes of the Central Plain of Thailand. Those to the west—sites in the vicinity of Nakhon Pathom and Suphanburi—are particularly well known, and it is at Nakhon Pathom that a coin bearing the inscription "Lord of Dvaravati" was found, the only local evidence of the name of that state.

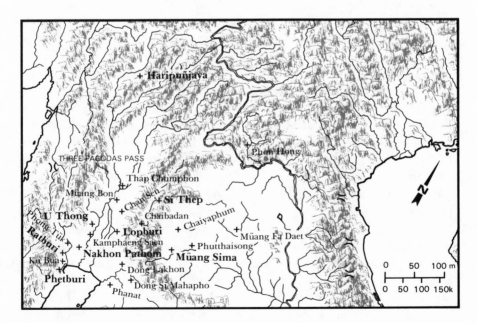

Main Dvaravati sites.

The dispersal of Dvaravati sites, and the nature of the objects uncovered at them, provides considerable information concerning Dvaravati civilization. The central group of Dvaravati sites rings the edges of Thailand's Central Plain, extending outward along what must have been the overland trade routes westward to Burma and eastward to Cambodia, northward up the Chaophraya River valley toward the Chiang Mai region and up the Pa Sak River valley toward northern Laos, and northeastward toward the Khorat Plateau. This particular configuration of sites suggests a commercial orientation; and the discovery of items foreign to Southeast Asia—beads, coins, lamps, and even imported statuary—indicates their foreign connections, important both economically and culturally. The northeastern group of Dvaravati sites extends across the Khorat Plateau from Müang Sima (Nakhon Ratchasima) at least as far as Müang Fa Daet in Kalasin province, and probably onward to Phon Hong on the northern fringe of the Vientiane Plain, where a characteristically Dvaravati Buddha image has been found. It is tempting to suppose that these sites lay on an overland route connecting the Gulf of Siam with northern Vietnam. Finally, a small northern group of sites, centered around Lamphun and Chiang Mai, traditionally is thought to have been founded in the eighth century as an offshoot of the major Dvaravati center at Lopburi. These northern sites might be interpreted as involving the overland trade between the Chaophraya valley and Yunnan.

Common to virtually all these sites, including even the one at Müang Fa Daet, are inscriptions in the Mon language, towns (usually circular or ovoid in plan) fortified by earthen ramparts and moats, and abundant Buddhist remains, including religious buildings and Buddhist statuary, sculpture, and votive tablets. The Mon inscriptions are singularly uninformative on the political history of the region, which must be inferred from other evidence. The fortified towns often included within their walls as much as ten square kilometers, suggesting extensive populations. These town dwellers probably lived off the labors of the surrounding rural people and were involved in a carrying trade in metals, spices, forest products, and textiles. They supported extensive religious establishments, usually but not always Buddhist. Their religious life probably was refreshed from time to time by contacts with India through traveling monks and the importation of such things as sacred scriptures and works of art. Dvaravati Buddhist sculpture, hewn from local rock by indigenous sculptors or fashioned in terra-cotta or stucco, is especially distinctive. Stone Buddhas seated in the European fashion are well known and were widely distributed. Less common were the carved stones placed to mark the boundaries of the sacred precincts of monasteries, particularly fine examples of which come from Müang Fa Daet. Few Dvaravati sites are lacking in large numbers of

Buddhist monastery boundary stone (*sima*) of the Dvaravati
period (sixth to ninth centuries, A.D.) from Müang Fa Daet,
Kalasin province.

small clay votive tablets bearing an image of the Buddha, sometimes inscribed
with a Pali religious formula in Mon script. These archeological remains attest
to the presence, over a wide area of what is now Thailand and portions of Laos,
of an extensive, populous, and prosperous Buddhist civilization. Perhaps deriving partly from its ethnic and linguistic identity as Mon, Dvaravati's civilization had distinctive qualities of its own that sharply contrasted with those of
the neighboring Khmer.

     Of perhaps more immediate relevance to the history of the Tai, who were
living on the fringes of Dvaravati and probably were beginning to become
involved in its life, is the fact that during the Dvaravati period certain patterns
of relationships between the local regions of central Southeast Asia became well
established. Though these may have antedated Dvaravati, it was during the
period of its flourishing that regular contacts were established between the head

of the Gulf of Siam and the upper Mekong (via Chiang Mai and Lamphun) and the middle Mekong region (via the Khorat Plateau), perhaps extending onward to Yunnan, Champa, and Vietnam.

Two examples will serve to suggest the importance of these relations. First, according to traditions embodied in the chronicles of northern Thailand, the state of Haripuñjaya was founded at Lamphun by a number of holy men, former Buddhist monks with connections in Lopburi, far to the south, on February 19, A.D. 661. (This date is clearly spurious, and scholars are inclined to date the event in the early ninth century.) They turned to the Buddhist ruler of Lopburi to provide them with a ruler. He sent them his daughter, Camadevi, who arrived in Haripuñjaya with a large retinue of Mons and established a dynasty that lasted until the middle of the eleventh century. Both during the rule of this Mon dynasty and afterwards, Lopburi continued to serve Haripuñjaya and the north as a cultural and religious center to which Buddhist monks went for training and study and with which some commercial and political relations presumably were maintained.

Another case, in this instance documented by art objects, concerns Laos. Both on the northern edge of the Vientiane Plain and far to the north in Luang Prabang, the earliest Buddhist statuary yet discovered there, dating from the eleventh and twelfth centuries, is closely related in style and iconographic details to the Buddhist sculpture of Lopburi and Phimai, the latter a major Khmer center in northeast Thailand in the vicinity of Nakhon Ratchasima (Khorat). This again suggests the continuity of an axis of communications over time, as well as the persistence of a cultural milieu, strongly Buddhist in character, that reached well into the interior regions inhabited by the Tai prior to the rise of the Angkorian empire and during its long period of dominance over central Southeast Asia.

The Dvaravati period of the sixth through ninth centuries remains problematic because of unanswered questions concerning its political constitution and ethnic composition. We do not know what areas were included within its sway at any particular period, nor can we by any means be certain who its people were. We do not even know if it had a single capital or where that might have been. There is a high degree of probability that the Tai were moving into the northern portions of the region with which Dvaravati civilization is associated, but of this we cannot be certain until the eleventh century, when Tai began to appear in the epigraphy of the lowland monarchies.

Angkor and the Tai

It would be temptingly easy to depict the Angkorian period primarily in terms of contrasts with the earlier Dvaravati period. In the eleventh and twelfth centuries, Angkor, after all, had a clearly defined capital and left numerous inscriptions; its political history appears as clear as Dvaravati's is dim. We know that, following the establishment of the capital in the Angkor region by Jayavarman II in the early ninth century, the empire quickly expanded westward and northward. It is reasonable to assume that, either by capturing the Dvaravati capital or by conquering its territories piecemeal, Angkor succeeded in replacing Dvaravati's hegemony over central Southeast Asia by the end of the ninth century; and there is ample evidence to conclude that Angkor had become the single most important power in most of the region by that time.

In assessing the significance to the Tai of the Angkorian Empire, it is useful to make a distinction, however arbitrary, between the core Khmer provinces of the empire and the surrounding fringe provinces that probably were inhabited by a substantial non-Khmer majority population. Working backward in time from the situation at the end of this period—the beginning of the thirteenth century—we can hazard the supposition that during the eleventh and twelfth centuries the Khmer formed a majority of the population within the limits of present-day Cambodia, in the lower Mekong valley as far north as about Savannakhet, in the Chi River valley north to about Roi Et, throughout the Mun River valley west to the Khorat region, and in the region immediately to the north and east of present-day Bangkok. Such Mon-Buddhist-Dvaravati populations as remained probably were concentrated for the most part in the west, in the lower Central Plain and in the upper Ping River basin of the Lamphun-Chiang Mai region. Their brethren further to the east, in what is now northeastern Thailand, would during this period have been absorbed either into the Khmer population or into the ranks of the Tai who were beginning to move into their midst.

On the basis of major monumental remains and of Khmer inscriptions, it would appear that the Angkorian rulers employed a variety of means to control the fringe areas of their empire. Establishing their supremacy by force of arms or by the threat of force coupled with diplomacy, they placed governors in the most important provinces, sometimes even princes with claims to the Angkorian royal succession. These were accompanied by what could have been an extensive retinue of officials—inspectors, tax collectors, quartermasters, scribes, judges, legal scholars, assessors, and a military garrison—as well as by a party of religious men to maintain the established religion, whether brahmanical or Buddhist. Outside the core of the Angkorian kingdom, the main provincial centers of the empire seem to have been at That Phanom, Sakon Nakhon, and Sai Fong in the central Mekong valley; Phimai in the Khorat region; Lopburi, Suphanburi, Nakhon Chaisi, and Ratburi (and perhaps also Phetburi) in the lower Chaophraya valley; and Phitsanulok, Sawankhalok, and Sukhothai/Satchanalai in the northern sector of Thailand's Central Plain.

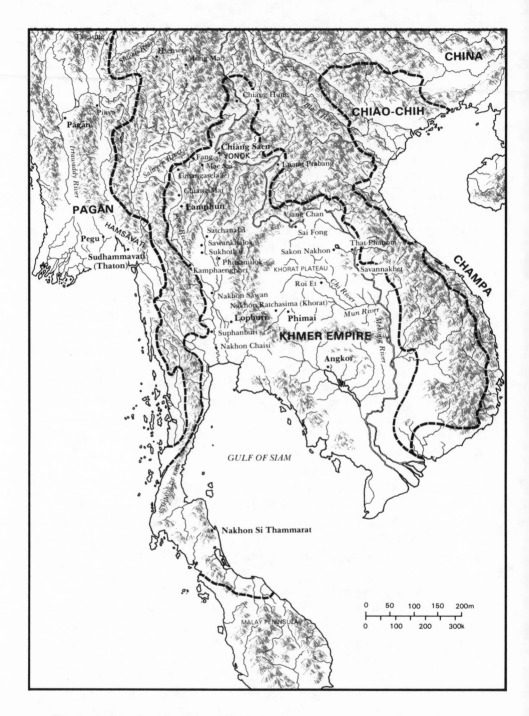

The classical empires: Angkor and Pagân by 1200.

Particularly from the reign of King Jayavarman VII (r. 1181–?1219), but certainly dating back much further, the Angkorian empire was held together by a network of communications and institutions that must have affected the regions they reached. A system of highways, raised some meters above the plain and provided with bridges over watercourses, certainly linked together the core of the empire. Traces of it are found both between Phimai and Angkor and between That Phanom and Sai Fong. We should assume that similar roads were built at least to Lopburi, from whence water transport both north and west would have been available. Under patronage extended by the king in distant Angkor and by the local governor or ruler, major religious institutions were founded in the fringe provinces. The most important of these are Mahayana Buddhist in inspiration, dating from a time when that form of Buddhism was in fashion at the court; but a considerable number also were devoted to Saivite or Vaisnavite cults served by brahmanical priests and preceptors. In either case, the foundation of a religious institution meant more to the surrounding population than simply the undeniable architectural splendor erected in their midst. Their resources, both in labor and in kind, were called upon to construct these enormous monuments. Many families were assigned to the support of these institutions in perpetuity as temple slaves, gaining exemption from taxation and conscription in return for work on the upkeep of the buildings or in the service of the religion. These institutions were intended as pious homage to the god and religion and as religio-political devices to bind the society to the king who was both ruler and god—Siva, Visnu, or Buddha. Thus, participation in the religious ceremonies that revolved around the temple was a political and a religious act.

During the eleventh and twelfth centuries, the ethnic composition of the population of the fringe areas of the Angkorian Empire became substantially Tai, both in the Lao areas of the central Mekong and the Siamese areas of central Thailand. The reasons for believing so have partly to do with their own historical records and partly to do with the direction in which their culture, and particularly their religious beliefs, evolved. It is noteworthy that, in both these areas, indigenous religious practices and beliefs, although increasingly influenced by Theravada Buddhism, still bear some slight imprint of an earlier Mahayana Buddhist exposure (expressed, for example, in the persistence of some Buddhist terminology in Sanskrit form rather than in the Pali-language forms of the Theravada) and, especially, are characterized by a lively admixture of brahmanical religion. In numerous ceremonies performed to ensure a good harvest, to restore health, or to celebrate rites of passage (puberty, marriage, death), non-Buddhist formulae are used and beliefs are expressed that stem from the popular forms of brahmanical religion known to have been practiced in Angkorian days. Moreover, there is ample evidence that the Siva-linga, the phallic representation of the god Siva, enjoyed a place of respect in most villages and many towns until comparatively recent times. We must assume that the Siamese and central Lao underwent a fairly early and lengthy exposure to and involvement in these religious traditions in order for them to have proved so durable. We might imagine that this occurred when, gradually absorbed into provincial Angkorian society as part-time laborers on great public works or as soldiers or temple slaves, they were not yet its ruling class.

But who were the ruling classes of provincial Angkorian society? Most must have been Khmer, the representatives of a distant capital sent out to the provinces for the glory of god and king. Take, for example, Lopburi, during this period undoubtedly the most important of the fringe provinces. Earlier a major center of Dvaravati civilization and presumably with its own ruling house, Lopburi maintained a tenuous independence as late as the first years of the eleventh century. At that time it was attacked by an army from Haripuñjaya. The Angkorian monarch, Udayadityavarman (r. 1001–02), came to the aid of Lopburi and undertook a massive campaign against Haripuñjaya. Thereupon a Cambodian prince, Jayaviravarman, coming from the ancient state of Tambralinga (at Nakhon Si Thammarat on the Malay Peninsula), seized Lopburi and moved on to take control of Angkor. He thereby provoked a counterreaction in the eastern and northern provinces of the empire, where another claimant to the Angkorian throne, Suryavarman I (r. 1007?–50), based a major military campaign that succeeded in taking the capital region and incorporating Lopburi into the empire.

As a province of Angkor, Lopburi apparently was ruled by governors and at least once by a son of King Jayavarman VII. Repeatedly, however, Lopburi appears to have attempted to assert an independent role in the affairs of the region, which it signaled by sending diplomatic missions requesting recognition from China, first in 1001, then in the wake of internal conflict in Cambodia in 1115, and yet again in 1155 following the death of Suryavarman II (r. 1113–50). It may have been a king of independent Lopburi who left an inscription at Nakhon Sawan in 1167. Jayavarman VII, however, reestablished Angkor's authority in central Siam before 1180 and even pushed southward some distance down the Malay Peninsula.

It would appear that Lopburi's repeated attempts at independence reflect more than political factionalism or regionalism within the Angkorian Empire. Lopburi, after all, maintained a cultural and religious tradition as heir to Dvaravati and seems also to have expressed a non-Khmer ethnic identity based on an earlier Mon-consciousness now tempered by an increasingly self-

The troops of Syam Kuk and their chief in procession before King Suryavarman II. Their chief carries a bow and rides an elephant (upper left), while they walk (rather than march!) and carry a sort of pike.

conscious Buddhist and Tai population. As far as Angkor was concerned, Lopburi seems to have represented *Syam* (i.e., "Siam") whether as the center of, or more likely as the administration responsible for, that population. This is strikingly conveyed by a scene sculpted in the bas-reliefs of Angkor Vat around the middle of the twelfth century. There, on an extensive series of panels depicting Suryavarman II reviewing a long procession of troops, there is a certain Jayasinghavarman leading the troops of Lopburi and a group of *Syam Kuk* mercenaries under their own commander. In contrast to the orderly,

disciplined, and even severe Lopburi soldiers, those of Syam Kuk who immediately precede them are more relaxed, undisciplined, and fierce. In the
Angkorian Empire they were becoming a force to be reckoned with.

How did the Syam and the Lao view the imperial society with which they
were coming into contact? Neither contemporary Tai inscriptions nor chronicles have much to say on this question. There are indications, from the way in
which early Tai kingdoms seemed almost perversely to devise public institutions that contrasted sharply with Angkorian institutions, that Tai chafed
under the heavy exactions of Angkorian rule, the impersonality and arbitrariness of Angkorian law, and the rigid hierarchy of Angkorian society, all of
which were directly opposed by the simpler and more personalized qualities of
their own society. The chief memory of Angkor that is preserved in the early
portions of Tai chronicles, however, is simply an impression of warfare, conflict
unwillingly entered into in order to preserve Tai independence.

The Tai of the Yonok Country

Of all the early Tai chronicles, only a few seem to preserve some folk memory
of contact with the Angkorian Empire. Most of these come from and are concerned with the Yonok country in the Chiang Saen region where north
Thailand today borders on the Mekong River (and including territory to the
north of the river). There, sometime after the seventh century (the chaos of
chronicle chronology permits no precision), a state arose that was in contact
with the Vietnamese in the east, with Nan-chao, and with the Angkorian
Empire or its predecessors. One chronicle relates that a state in this region was
attacked and subjugated by a "Khom" (Khmer?) army coming from
Umangasela (in the headwaters of the Ping River). The Khom ruler "was anti-
Buddhist and foolish. He observed none of the ten royal precepts, and oppressed
the people with taxes. He sought pretexts to inflict fines or punishments upon
foreign merchants who came into the country. Thenceforth there was great
confusion in Suvanna Khom Kham.... that city was plunged into the shadows
of ignorance."[1]

Another chronicle twice repeats a similar story concerning a Tai chief who
entered the same region, perhaps from the Sipsong Pan Na, with a large retinue
of Tai and convened the chiefs of the indigenous hill peoples to recognize his
authority. When the Khom ruler of Umangasela refused to accept his power,
the Tai prince defeated him in battle and went on to the conquest of all Lan
Na—the traditional name for northern Thailand. The kingdom thus formed
bordered on Vietnam in the east, Nan-chao to the north, and Lavarattha
(apparently Haripuñjaya, though the name is a form of Lopburi) to the south

and extended into the Shan regions of the upper Salween to the west. In the second retelling of this story, the image is strong of Tai suffering at the hands of the Khom ruler of Umangasela. The Tai prince, Phang, was defeated by the Khom and sent to serve as a village chief over (apparently) a village of Lawa people near Mae Sai, northwest of Chiang Saen. Prince Phang was required to render an annual tribute of four measures of gold to the Khom; and, as the chronicler reports, "We Thai suffered, whether prince or commoner, for all had to wash for gold to pay tribute to the Khom." [2] Prince Phang's first son, born a year later (in A.D. 918?), was named Suffering Prince. After nearly two decades of suffering, another of Phang's sons, Prince Phrom (Brahmakumara), led a massive attack which expelled the Khom from the Yonok city of Chiang Saen. They fled to the south and were chased for a month through all the hill-tribe villages of the north, "as far as the frontiers of old Lavarattha," where the god Indra, taking pity on the fleeing Khom, erected a wall of stone to stop Prince Phrom and allow the Khom to return to Angkor (Indapathanagara). Having reinstalled his father as ruler of Chiang Saen and his elder brother as heir-apparent, Prince Phrom then retired to found a new city, Wiang Chaiprakan, on the site of present-day Fang.

Around the end of the tenth century or the beginning of the eleventh, in a time of peace and prosperity, a religious revival swept over the Yonok country, probably brought through trading connections that seem to have gone via Haripuñjaya to the Mon cities of Thaton (Sudhammavati) and Pegu (Hamsavati) in coastal Burma. This was a development of immense cultural significance, for it transformed a weak and localized folk Buddhism, characterized more by isolated hermits than by major monasteries, into a universal, institutionalized religious tradition, linked with the Theravada Buddhist civilization of the Mons and Ceylon. It integrated the Tai into a wider "community of the faithful," in which Tai could feel they belonged. It supplanted local animistic spirits with more universal values and encouraged an ethic with social dimensions that transcended the village and müang.

The Buddhization of the northern Tai must at the same time have been associated with changes in their style of life. For the first time in their history, they were moving onto extensive, lowland plains suitable for the irrigated cultivation of rice. This made possible the development of Tai urban centers and the proportional growth of an urban ruling class freed from direct involvement in agriculture. These were still, however, societies of ruling families (chao) and freemen (phrai) bound together by personal, reciprocal bonds of obligation and responsibility. States were formed on the basis of social organization more than on the basis of simple territorial control. When Prince Phrom moved to the Fang region and founded Wiang Chaiprakan, for example, he presumably took with him his personal retainers and their families and on the basis of his control over them established a new müang. There he erected dwellings and fortifications, and the whole community saw to its moral security by providing support for a community of Buddhist monks.

The Rise of Pagân

Around the middle of the eleventh century, a great new empire arose in Burma, now to parallel the role of Angkor in influencing the life of the Tai in the uplands. Probably owing to Angkorian pressure from the east, the political and cultural (and perhaps also demographic) center of gravity for the Mon people had slipped westward from Dvaravati from the ninth century onward, and important Mon states centered on Pegu and Thaton gradually rose from obscurity to importance. Thaton in particular became a major center for the diffusion throughout mainland Southeast Asia of the new, institutionalized, rigorous, and scholarly Buddhism then flourishing in Ceylon. Thaton too was in regular and frequent contact both with Ceylon and with its hinterland in Burma, as well as with such states to the east and north as Haripuñjaya, Chiang Saen, Lopburi, and Angkor.

Meanwhile, in the middle valley of the Irrawaddy River, the Burmans were moving into the irrigated rice plains earlier established by the Mon and Pyu, centering by the middle of the eleventh century on Pagân. Pagân was still a small regional capital when Anorahta became king around 1044, but under his leadership and generalship it rapidly expanded. His conquests may have begun in the north, at the expense first of the hill peoples and then against Nan-chao in the upper Irrawaddy valley. Then, around 1050, he moved south. There the Mons were divided among themselves and still in disarray owing to Angkorian pressure. Local traditions assert that the king of Pegu invited Anorahta to help him stem an Angkorian invasion, while the king of Thaton stood aside. At the end of a successful campaign, the Burmese king assumed hegemony over the Mons, allowing the king of Pegu to remain a subordinate vassal but extinguishing the kingdom of Thaton. This episode traditionally is thought to have occurred in 1056–57.

The expansion of Pagân's rule over coastal Burma and the Mons had profound consequences. It marked the beginning of an increasingly intense relationship between Burmese and Mon characterized by the ascendancy of Mon culture and literary traditions, and Theravada Buddhism. Pagân Burma changed from a relatively isolated, parochial, inward-looking state, concerned only with its immediate hinterland in upper Burma, into an empire with what for its age were worldwide horizons. Pagân entered into a close relationship with the kingdom and Buddhist monkhood of Ceylon and became involved in the maritime trade of the Bay of Bengal.

Little is known about the Tai relationship to the rise of Pagân. The Burmese chronicles and inscriptions of the period are nearly silent on the subject. They do mention Syam (or Shan) among slaves dedicated to Buddhist temples in the vicinity of Pagân and refer to an area inhabited by Shans, with irrigation canals and rice fields, in Minbu district on the west bank of the Irrawaddy, eighty miles downstream from Pagân. For the eleventh and twelfth centuries, hardly any evidence is available on the possible expansion of Pagân into the northeastern and northern uplands later known as the Shan states. The Burmese records contain only an indication that the empire extended on the east "as far as the bank of the Salween River." [3] They intimate that kings from the twelfth century campaigned on the Malay Peninsula as far south as the Isthmus of Kra, so it is possible that the first Tai reached that region as Shan levies in Pagân's armies.

From the Tai side, the records are suggestive, if not conclusive on the subject. One northern Tai chronicle alleges that in A.D. 1017 a Mon king of Thaton invaded the Yonok country, forcing the abandonment of Wiang Chaiprakan, whose ruler, Chaiyasiri, emigrated with all his people to found a new city far to the south, around Kamphaengphet. Other chronicles report that, owing to a cholera epidemic, Haripuñjaya was temporarily evacuated to Thaton at some time in the first half of the eleventh century. The Pegu chronicles state that Anorahta, king of Pagân, conquered all the Shan country up to Yunnan and reached Angkor and Lopburi. Yet another set of Siamese chronicles allege that Anorahta besieged Lopburi in 1032. Together, these references indicate only some dim memory of an early connection with Burma that cannot be tied to specific historical circumstances. A tentative conjecture might lead one to suppose that, owing to the long-standing connections between Haipuñjaya and Lopburi, on the one hand, and Pegu and Thaton, on the other, the repercussions of Anorahta's conquests must have been felt further to the east.

The Shans

Traditions embodied in the Shan chronicles of northeastern Burma are especially vivid in this respect, asserting that major changes and important efforts of empire building were occurring among these Tai in the tenth and eleventh centuries. The Shan chronicles, still but poorly studied, are represented almost exclusively by texts from Hsenwi west of the Salween, to whose rulers they attribute stupendous feats of arms from the sixth century onward. Widely scattered through much of northern Burma by the eleventh century but apparently best organized and most densely settled in the Shweli valley, the Shans apparently were temporarily held in check by Anorahta. He is said to have accepted a daughter of the ruler of Möng Mao, thereby implying recognition of Pagân's suzerainty (at a date the chronicles give as equivalent to A.D. 1057). Through the succeeding century and a half, the chronicles give an impression of extreme confusion, with many dozens of petty Shan states attempting repeatedly to join in larger units under one müang or another. From the Burmese records, we know that this was a time when successive monarchs of Pagân were involved almost continuously in warfare to the north. They apparently succeeded by 1200 in separating the Shans east of the Irrawaddy from other Tai groups now moving farther west toward Assam in northeastern India.

The account given in the Hsenwi chronicle of this period pulls the whole Tai world together. The reign of *Sao* (= chao) Hsö Hkan Hpa (r. 1152–1205) is particularly striking. Assuming the leadership of the Shans of the Shweli (Mao) valley, he first subdued all the neighboring Shan principalities and then, in 1158, attacked China (presumably Nan-chao is meant). He marched all the way to Kun-ming and defeated the "Chinese." The following year he invaded the Lao states (Lan Sang), Chiang Saen, and the Yonok country, gaining their vassalage, and continued on to the Sipsong Pan Na. Next he sent his brother, Hkun Sam Lông (or Sam Lung Pha) to attack and subdue Assam. Finally, in 1200 he sent an expedition to raid the Pagân empire, which succeeded in taking Tagaung and Pyinnya. He died in 1205 at the age of seventy-three.

Like many other chronicles, the Hsenwi chronicle here treats the Tai world as a single entity, dotted with innumerable müang in communication with one another, stretching from the Black River valley of northern Vietnam to the Brahmaputra valley of Assam. There is little if any evidence that the Mao Shans of the Shweli valley in upper Burma attained anywhere near the expanse of territory that is claimed for Hsö Hkan Hpa; and there might well be legitimate doubt that he succeeded even in pulling together a single Shan confederacy in northern Burma. It is important, however, that the chronicle preserves a tradition of an open world—an environment in the eleventh and twelfth centuries when the political organization of the world was not fixed but was susceptible to the ambitions of any group of men who dared to challenge the old empires. By the end of the eleventh century, the Shans had become the dominant element in the population of northern Burma and extreme southwestern China. Those like the Mao shans, who were most closely exposed to the power of the great lowland monarchies but had at the same time a secure base among their own people, were in the best position to challenge a state like Pagân when it fell upon difficult times.

Nan-chao and the Sipsong Pan Na

Of the history of Yunnan in the eleventh and twelfth centuries little is known that bears directly upon the Tai, who then were living along the southern fringe of Nan-chao's territory. Nan-chao still was holding out against Sung dynasty China, and its rulers in this period seem to have been occupied more with the internal order of their kingdom than with external affairs. In the face of more or less constant rebellion in the heartland of the kingdom and of plotting at court, one king after another abdicated and entered the Buddhist monkhood. With such instability in the capital, the southern fringes of Nan-chao soon began to fall away.

That by the late twelfth century Nan-chao had acquiesced in the rise of independent Tai states in southern Yunnan is suggested by two chronicles and a genealogy of the ruler of Chiang Hung (Ch'e-li), in the Sipsong Pan Na. They record in detail how the dynasty that ruled that principality was installed in 1180 by the ruler of Nan-chao. This prince of Chiang Hung, Pa Chên or Chao Phaya Choeng, had four sons who "enjoyed the revenues" of Lan Na (the Yonok country), Meng Chiao (Chiao-chih, northern Vietnam), Viang Chan (Vientiane), and Chiang Hung. The last-named of these sons, K'ai Lêng (Khai Loeng), succeeded to his father's throne in 1192.[4]

The unstated implication of the Chiang Hung records is that the three older sons of Chao Phaya Choeng were sent out to rule over the principalities whose revenues they enjoyed. Again, there is no conclusive evidence that anything like this happened and certainly not on the geographic scale suggested by the chronicles. In this respect, the Chiang Hung accounts are very like those of the Mao Shans, already mentioned. However, it should be noted that there are references that seem to point to the king of Nan-chao in other chronicles of the period as well. They, like the Chiang Hung accounts, suggest that, by recognizing Tai rulers in the northern marchlands, Nan-chao somehow legitimized new Tai states.

On balance, it would seem reasonable to interpret such references as signs of Nan-chao's weakness in the face of rising Tai power, rather than as Tai meek submission to the benevolent power of Nan-chao. It was in the best interests of all concerned, both Tai and non-Tai alike, that a stable international order (even on this regional scale) be promoted by recognizing the more powerful müang and laying upon them the obligation to maintain order in their neighborhood. Nan-chao was promoting the creation of a buffer zone of Tai (or Shan or Lü) müang to shield it from a powerful Pagân, while the Tai were organizing to claim a share in the prosperity of the fertile plains to the south.

The Tai World in 1200

In the eleventh and twelfth centuries, throughout northern Southeast Asia the Tai were organizing new states; both their own chronicles and the records of the lowland empires convey this point. The grandiose claims of empires and conquests made by, or on behalf of, various Tai kings and princes mean less than the testimony such claims give concerning the horizons of the Tai in this chaotic period. Of warfare and battles there was a great deal, but we must avoid interpreting these in twentieth-century terms. Angkor, Pagân, and Vietnam conquered territory and then laid down civil administration, supported by military garrisons and fortifications, in the lands they captured. The Tai groups for the most part staged raids, moving quickly through the countryside on their ponies and elephants, looting and plundering and taking captives, but then moving on or returning home. The threat of their return might induce a defeated chief to send regular tribute to the prince who had conquered him; and an exchange of daughters between suzerain and vassal might work to form a personal and political bond between them. Whatever "empires" were formed by such means, however, were fragile and short-lived.

Especially in these centuries, when no Tai ruler developed a centralized administration by which to incorporate distant territory into his state, the individual principalities were much more important than the larger units into which they sometimes temporarily coalesced. As late as the end of the twelfth century, no regional Tai states had yet emerged to dominate their neighbors. Though now spread quite widely over the region, none of the Tai müang had yet descended to the great plains that alone would support the expansion and enrichment of a population to the point where it could form the basis of a major kingdom on the scale of Angkor or Pagân. That day, however, was rapidly approaching, as Tai began to settle in the rural provinces of the Angkorian and Pagân empires and on the plains of upper Laos.

What local Tai chieftains and princes had in these areas was control over manpower, which was always in short supply throughout Southeast Asia. Their ability to mobilize a population was both a danger to the major empires and a source of potential strength to them. It was natural that Tai chiefs were recognized as local rulers or district chiefs and given a place in the imperial society, perhaps (as in more than one case) even receiving an "emperor's" daughter in marriage. They retained, however, a separate ethnic identity, especially vis-à-vis the Khmer, that was reinforced by a separate language, a separate social organization, and a distinctive religious tradition, Theravada Buddhism. In their relationship with the indigenous population into which they had moved, it would appear that Buddhism may have played a critically important role in the process by which indigenous groups were assimilated to the Tai population, and not vice versa. Slowly, the countryside of the lowlands became increasingly Tai and Buddhist, and it was only a matter of time before they would challenge the old empires on equal terms.

3

A Tai Century, 1200–1351

The thirteenth century must have seemed a period of cataclysmic change to those who lived through it in continental Southeast Asia. Through the early decades of the century, the great classical Indianized empires of Pagân and Angkor had held firm, their glories still undiminished. Great architectural monuments were being constructed; works of art were being produced; stone inscriptions lauding meritorious acts of the great monarchs were being incised. Then, suddenly in the second quarter of the century, the imperial momentum and dynamic collapsed in Angkor and soon thereafter in Pagân. By the end of the century, both those great empires were but golden memories, no matter how potent, of a past that would never be recaptured.

That transformation of mainland Southeast Asia between the middle of the thirteenth century and the middle of the fourteenth was associated with three significant developments. The most important was the movement of the Tai down from the upland valleys onto the plains formerly dominated by the major empires and their founding both there and in upland regional centers of powerful new states, in an attempt (self-consciously or not) to imitate and supplant their rivals. These new states stretched all the way from the plains of Assam in northeastern India to northern Laos in the east and to Nakhon Si Thammarat on the Malay Peninsula in the south. Their early vigor itself suffices to make of this period "a Tai century." A second major development, closely associated with the rise of the Tai, was the revivification of the Buddhism already professed by the Tai through contacts with Singhalese Buddhism and the foundation of strong, well-supported Buddhist monastic institutions throughout the region. Finally, particularly in the last quarter of the thirteenth century, the political transformation of continental Southeast Asia was paralleled by the rise to power of the Mongols in China and the extension of that power into Southeast Asia by diplomatic and military means.

By the end of the thirteenth century, perhaps the most striking quality of the new world of mainland Southeast Asia was the diffusion of power that had taken place. Where the region had been dominated a century earlier by two major empires, Pagân and Angkor, its political landscape now was fractured into numerous, much smaller states, relatively more equal in their political and military power. This diffusion of power, moreover, involved cultural and religious power as well. Many smaller communities now regained autonomy in their religious and cultural decision making. These new communities lived according to Theravada Buddhism, of the Singhalese variety, adopting it as their own religion and way of life. In the plastic and performing arts, they expressed their own styles and, in the literary arts, their own idioms and languages. Through a century and a half of rapid and fundamental change, the political and cultural maps of continental Southeast Asia thus were transformed; and many qualities of the patterns so established were to endure into early modern times. This was no temporary break in the grand earlier traditions of the region, but rather a fundamental transformation. Elements of earlier traditions persisted, but they were recast in a new mold shaped partly by the circumstances of the era and partly by the character of Tai tradition.

In assessing this critical era in Tai history, it goes almost without saying that not all the Tai groups underwent these changes to the same degree or with the same intensity of involvement, nor did everything occur simultaneously throughout the Tai world. Virtually nothing is known at present about the history of the Chuang and other Tai peoples in southeastern China during this period, nor can much be said concerning the Tai groups of northern Vietnam until more research has been done. In terms of the major developments already outlined as critical to the history of this period—the collapse of the classical empires, the formation of new Tai states, the spread of the Singhalese form of Theravada Buddhism, and the repercussions of the Mongol conquest of China—the Tai peoples most closely affected by such changes were those already in contact with, or in a position to profit from the decline of, Pagân and Angkor. For those who lived beyond the fringes of the classical Indianized empires, the thirteenth century probably did not mark a break in the continuity of their history. Henceforth then we must be concerned only with those for whom that era was particularly significant.

For the Ahom of Assam, for the Shans, for the northern Thai and Siamese, and for the Lao, real history must in some sense have begun in the thirteenth century, for at that point nearly every chronicle from this region changes in character. Whereas most of their chronicles up to that time are simply lists of kings or collections of legends, usually undated, they become in the thirteenth and fourteenth centuries the annals of states, replete with detailed accounts of

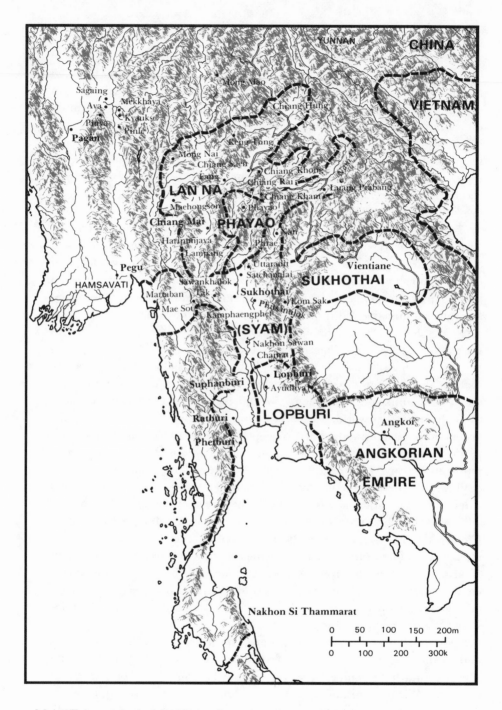

Major Tai states in the late thirteenth century.

religious events and wars, of dynastic conflicts and popular movements. While far from being completely reliable, the Tai chronicles, now supplemented by stone inscriptions, begin to paint in human colors a picture of a Tai world.

The Ahom, the Shans, and the Mongols

By the early thirteenth century, recently arrived Tai groups had begun to change the map of the northwestern uplands of mainland Southeast Asia. Countless müang were founded, first in the narrow river valleys of northern Burma and then even farther to the west, in what is now northeastern India. While their appearance now may have owed something to the weakness of older states and chiefdoms in this region, it must also have reflected the experience and power of small bands of Tai chiefs and their followers, who were self-confident and by now well accustomed to organizing and ruling over non-Tai populations they considered inferior to themselves.

The most enigmatic of these Tai were the Ahom, who by the late twelfth century had begun to carve out political dominion for themselves in the upper Brahmaputra River valley of Assam. As the Ahom were not Buddhists, but practiced an animistic religion, it is likely that they had left their Shan brethren to the east before Pagân promoted the spread of Buddhism among the Shans in the twelfth century. The Ahom chronicles date the Ahom incursion into Assam in the first decade of the thirteenth century and attribute the leadership of their campaigns to Shukapha, the elder brother of the great Mao Shan king Hsö Hkan Hpa whose exploits were narrated in the previous chapter. By 1227, Shukapha had established a small principality in eastern Assam, a base from which, over the next century, his successors were to expand their control over most of Assam. In the process, however, by moving accross the mountains that divide Burma from India the Ahom rapidly became separated from the cultural and political world from whence they had come. By intermarrying with the Assam elite, they maintained their power and a good measure of their social and political position, but their cultural traditions gradually were supplanted by the Indic culture of the region into which they had moved, and most of them ultimately were to lose even their identity as Tai. Their fate is one extreme outcome of the general phenomenon of the Tai encounter with the established civilizations of the region, a fate apparently shared by no other Tai group.

The Shans of Burma had in some ways a similar experience during this period, but in a very different context. They were in a position, poised on the fringes of the upland plains of northern Burma, to take advantage both of the decline of the Burmese Empire of Pagân and of the abrupt assertion of Chinese power in the region under the aegis of the Mongols. Like the Ahom, the Shan were to be drawn down into the lowland valleys; and also like the Ahom they were to be at least partially submerged by their alien host. Unlike the Ahom case, however, the core of a Shan culture and political identity was to remain intact in the hills from where they had come.

Pagân Burma had seemed strong in the early decades of the thirteenth century, but as the century progressed the dynasty was caught between reviving Mon separatism in the coastal region and Shan restiveness and Mongol aggression in the north.

Early in 1253, the Mongol armies of Qubilai Khan captured Ta-li, the capital of old Nan-chao, and moved eastward to subdue that kingdom and then supplant the Sung dynasty to rule the Chinese Empire. The newly aggressive and assertive China of the Mongols was to prove almost immediately to be a very different neighbor to Pagân and the Shans than Nan-chao had been.

Mongol China's immediate concern in Yunnan and the southwest was first to secure its own frontiers and then to reopen the main lines of communication leading across the mountains to Burma and India. Behind its dealings with states in the region lay the demand that all the world should acknowledge the primacy of the Great Khan. These concerns led the Mongols to become involved with the various Shan groups and other peoples who inhabited the mountainous territory between Yunnan and Burma. "Pacification" campaigns against the Shans and "other southern barbarians" (the Chinese terms are used) were sent through this region in the late 1250s, and around 1260 the chiefs of many of these groups sent tribute to the court. The Mongols established an administration for dealing with non-Chinese peoples and came quickly to see the use to which the Shans and other Tai groups could be put in furthering Mongol interests. For their own part, the Shans must have been just as eager to use the Mongols against Pagân.

The conflict between Mongol China and Pagân escalated rapidly from diplomatic misadventures in the early 1270s, to frontier raids contesting suzerainty over various Shan principalities, and finally to full-scale Chinese invasions of Burma in 1283–84 and 1286–88, the last of which reached all the way to Pagân itself. Caught between the Chinese and spreading Mon rebellion in the south, the Pagân court disintegrated in internecine strife. By the time the new Burmese king Kyawswa returned from the south to be crowned king in Pagân in 1289, the real power in upper Burma had passed to the Shans. Much of Pagân's territory had fallen away during the years of conflict with the Mongols. Some of the critical areas that remained were in Shan hands, most notably the Kyaukse district, the fertile, well-irrigated, rice-growing region upon which the economy of Pagân depended, especially with the loss of the Mon provinces in the south.

The key figures in this new situation were three Shan brothers, who controlled three of the chief towns and districts in the Kyaukse valley. It is said that their father had migrated into the district and that the three brothers had been brought up at the royal court in Pagân, implying that their father must have been a powerful Shan chief of that region. For some years the brothers played the role of faithful courtier, while their power at court and in their rural base grew. When King Kyawswa sent his son to Peking to stand in for him at his investiture in 1297, the three Shan brothers also were invested by the Mongols as "princes" of Myinsaing, Mekkhaya, and Pinle, towns in the Kyaukse district. The next year, they supported a rebellion that took Pagân, executed King Kyawswa, and installed on the throne his sixteen-year-old son Saw Hnit. Soon they revived warfare with China that successfully regained the northern regions lost fifteen years earlier. A combination of careful bribery and adroit diplomacy brought an end to warfare and the withdrawal of the Chinese frontier approximately to its present lines by 1303.

The legitimate line of the Pagân dynasty continued at Pagân through most of the next century, but Burmese kings reigned there more as governors than as kings. The Shan brothers now were the kings of upper Burma. The youngest, Thihathu, had himself crowned king in 1309 and after the deaths of his two elder brothers moved his capital to Pinya, in the vicinity of Ava, in 1312; his sons reigned there until 1364. Meanwhile, another of his sons established a new ruling line at Sagaing in 1315 to rule more or less independently the north and west of the kingdom.

The upper Irrawaddy valley was rapidly breaking up into small units. The Shan dominion over Pagân seems to have dissolved into the mere acceptance of tribute from the hereditary governors of outlying provinces, some of whom were developing their own royal style and semi-independence. The Shan brothers and their successors at Pinya/Sagaing/Ava became rapidly more and more Burman, leaving inscriptions in Burmese and relying for the most part on Burman officers in their administration. They were becoming part of the culture and society over which they ruled, as reflected by their intermarriage with the old house of Pagân and by the behavior of their descendants, which differed little from that expected of a Burman king.

Perhaps the Shan brothers had brought their troubles upon themselves. They had encouraged widespread popular resistance to the Chinese armies, increasing the spirit of self-reliance and rebellion in the countryside, and they had called in neighboring Shans to assist in their defense. Moreover, by diplomacy they seem to have encouraged the formation of what approached a united front against the Mongols, enlisting on their side the kingdom of Lan Na in northern Siam.

This particular connection opens wide the question of the relationships among the Tai groups of the region during this period, but fails to settle it. Certainly the Shans, the three brothers in Pinya and Kyaukse, and the various northern Tai, Lü, and Lao groups of north Siam, the Sipsong Pan Na, and northern Laos faced an enemy in common in the suddenly strong thrust of the Mongols south- and southwestward from Yunnan. Luce suggests that an alliance between the three Shan brothers and Lan Na was one Tai response to that threat. He holds that troops from the Chiang Mai region assisted in establishing the three brothers in the Kyaukse valley, probably early in the 1290s, gaining them four of the eleven districts of Kyaukse. And when the last major Chinese invasion of Burma was being planned in 1300, the emperor increased the number of troops to be sent because "Burma was strong and could rely on help from Pa-pai-hsi-fu [Chiang Mai, Lan Na]." [1]

The Pinya/Ava–Chiang Mai connection thus established may have had little direct military consequences after the 1290s, though over the years it was to have some cultural and religious content with the movement of artists and Buddhist monks back and forth between Ava and Chiang Mai. Its political significance must derive from a recognition on the part of the two rulers concerned in the 1290s—the Shan brothers and King Mangrai—of their own primacy and respective spheres of influence in the Tai/Shan upland world, and of their status as equal overlords over a scattered array of remote Shan principalities that dotted the mountainous uplands between their capitals. Neither of them could successfully enjoy that status while the Mongols still threatened the Shan uplands. At the same time, both of them seem to have recognized the opportunities created for them by the Mongol challenge to the older, established powers of the region—Vietnam and Pagân, Champa and Angkorian Cambodia—and the importance of avoiding intra-Tai conflict. The Shan brothers successfully kept the Mongols at bay, while using their military threat to end the rule of Burman Pagân, but they failed to establish any durable hegemony over the Shan upland world. Like the Ahom, they ultimately were assimilated by the culture and population over whom they ruled, while their Shan kinsmen in the hills went their separate ways.

The Kingdom of Lan Na

The chronicles of Chiang Mai trace the ruling house of Lan Na back to Chiang Saen in the Yonok region at the great bend in the Mekong. According to legend, around the middle of the twelfth century there ruled a certain Khun Chüang, heir perhaps to the King Phang mentioned above. He was invaded by a large army from the Kaeo ruler of Ho Müang Phrakan (or Phakan), a region apparently located in the Sipsong Pan Na or the upper valley of the Black River. Assembling troops from a wide region of north Siam and the Shan states, he defeated the Kaeo, and so impressed the rulers of Videha (apparently to the west or northwest) and Vietnam that they came to pay homage to him. Cautiously looking to his state's future relations with the Kaeo, he exempted them from paying tribute to him and raised a Kaeo to be the ruler of Müang Wong; he erected an inscription to that effect in Yunnan in 1140. Just before his death in 1172, he appointed each of his five sons to rule over a portion of his kingdom—the eldest at Chiang Saen, the second over the chief Kaeo müang, a third at Luang Prabang over all the Lao, the fourth at müang Chainarai (Siang Khwang?) over all the müang to the southeast, and the fifth to Chiang Hung in the Sipsong Pan Na.

It is difficult to assess the historicity of this tale, even shorn of its wilder exaggerations, nor is it necessary to do so. This tale, widely reproduced in the local chronicles of north Siam and Laos, conveys an image of another geograph- ically defined world, analogous to but distinct from those already met in the Ahom and Shan chronicles. This is the world of the upper Mekong River, peopled by folk who called themselves Lao and whose lives were threatened by Vietnam and by Yunnan, that is, Nan-chao. The chronicle establishes close relationships among the chief Tai centers of that world: Chiang Saen (or an older city by the same name on the opposite bank of the Mekong); Chiang Hung, the Lü capital in southern Yunnan; Luang Prabang, the early center of the Lao world; and apparently a Black Tai center in the valley of the Black River. Numerous later principalities were to trace their origins back to one of these capitals. Whether or not these quasi-genealogical connections among states reflect actual blood or even cultural and linguistic relationships, they do suggest continuities in political traditions. Here, Chiang Saen is important, not only as the progenitor of Lan Na and of numerous müang included within that kingdom, but also as the source, some claimed, of the line that was to rule in the greatest Tai capital of them all, Ayudhya.

The founder of the Lan Na kingdom of Chiang Mai, Mangrai, was born on October 23, 1239, at Chiang Saen. His mother was the daughter of the ruler of Chiang Hung, an important detail, as we shall see. When he succeeded his father as ruler of Chiang Saen in 1259, he is said to have observed that all the Tai principalities of this region were fighting among themselves to the distress of their people, and that, alone among his neighbors, he stemmed from a legi- timate royal house, graced with the full Indic rites of coronation and in possession of royal regalia. He determined to impose his own authority over them, and in quick succession he conquered his neighbors and placed his own officers over them, beginning with Müang Lai, Chiang Kham, and Chiang

Chang. He then began extending his power to the south, first by founding a new city at Chiang Rai in 1262 and moving his capital there and then by taking control of the Chiang Khong region and operating for some time around Fang (a town abandoned two centuries earlier by Prince Phrom).

While living in Fang in 1274, Mangrai was visited by a party of merchants from Haripuñjaya, who described their home to him in such extravagant terms that he determined to seize that ancient principality. His officers advised him that Haripuñjaya was too strong to capture and was protected by potent relics of the Buddha. But a Mon officer at his court, employed as a scribe and accountant, argued that Haripuñjaya could be conquered by guile. Mangrai then sent the scribe, Ai Fa, to take service under King Yi Ba of Haripuñjaya and secretly work to open the way for Mangrai's capture of the kingdom.

Mangrai spent the next decade in preparations. Unexpectedly, in the next year the Kaeo ruler of Müang Phrakan arrived at Chiang Saen, explaining that he had come to assist in the coronation of Mangrai, who like him was a descendant of Khun Chüang. Overjoyed, Mangrai went to meet him and was brought up to date on the family news: "Of your paternal uncles, there is one named Kham Hao who went to become ruler of Lan Sang [Luang Prabang]. Another, named *Thao* Chum Saeng, has become ruler of Nandapuri [Nan]. I myself am the son of *Thao* Pha Rüang Maen Kham Kha of Müang Kaeo Phrakan. When he died, I succeeded him, and the Ho ruler, lord of all under heaven [the Chinese emperor? or ruler of Nan-chao?] assembled all the [neighboring] rulers to crown me at Mount Hüt, just as his predecessor did to *Khun* Chüang. I am thus of your family, and wish today to crown you, that you may reign happily." [2] Then, having done so, he returned to Müang Phrakan in the Kaeo country.

Still awaiting word from Ai Fa, his agent in Haripuñjaya, Mangrai decided next to secure the land to the southeast ruled by Ngam Müang, the king of Phayao. Ngam Müang, by some accounts, was also a descendant of Chüang and was Mangrai's contemporary, born in 1238. As a youth of sixteen years, he had gone to Lopburi to study with a learned man and there made the acquaintance of another prince, who later was to become King Ramkhamhaeng of Sukhothai. Returning home, Ngam Müang succeeded his father as ruler of Phayao in 1258 and was still on the throne in 1276 when Mangrai brought an army to Ban Dai on the frontier between their states. Ngam Müang came up to meet him, but instead of fighting, they concluded an alliance of friendship and mutuality—notwithstanding which, Ngam Müang transferred to Mangrai a frontier district inhabited by five hundred families.

The network of relationships linking Mangrai to neighboring Tai princes was further strengthened a few years later when he was called upon to settle a dispute between Ngam Müang and Ramkhamhaeng of Sukhothai. Ngam Müang would have been within his rights to execute Ramkhamhaeng for seducing his wife. But Mangrai saw that little would be gained by doing so, and Ngam Müang might further incur the rancor of the rulers of [Nakhon] Si Thammarat and Ayudhya, "relatives of *Phraya* Rüang [Ramkhamhaeng]." Mangrai therefore had Ramkhamhaeng apologize to Ngam Müang and pay him an indemnity of 990,000 cowrie shells. Ngam Müang and Ramkhamhaeng were reconciled, and the three rulers meeting together swore a pact of eternal friendship. Why the legends' emphasis on harmony? At the least, the rulers of Chiang Saen/Chiang Rai and Sukhothai were engaged in ambitious schemes for expansion and could not afford local dissension among rulers who had mutually distinct interests and objectives. Even more important, there were far greater dangers and opportunities raised by Mongol incursions into Burma and Vietnam and threats against Angkorian Cambodia. In this climate of uncertainty, the three rulers laid stress upon their mutual ties, even their common descent—in short, their common identity as Tai.

Soon, Mangrai's plot to undermine Haripuñjaya was brought to fruition. Ai Fa had gained the king's confidence, isolated him from his people and court, and then in his name issued orders that outraged the populace. When they whispered their discontent with their ruler, Ai Fa encouraged them to look to Mangrai as an alternative. Finally he sent word to Mangrai that the time had come for him to act; he should send his army at once.

Mangrai immediately raised an enormous army and marched on Haripuñjaya. With Ai Fa sowing confusion in the city, Mangrai was able to conquer it easily. On April 23, 1281, Mangrai took his place on the throne of the ancient kingdom of Haripuñjaya in Lamphun, now master of all the north country. He spent several of the following years touring the countryside of the north, building new cities and fortifications, Buddhist monuments and monasteries, and establishing his administration. Around 1289 he decided to extend his empire farther by conquering Pegu, capital of the Mon region of lower Burma that just then was rebelling against Pagân. Leading his army to the vicinity of Maehongson on the Salween River, he met there with Suddhasoma, the king of Pegu, whose daughter he accepted in marriage. The two monarchs concluded an alliance, and "from that time, the Yuan [northern Tai], Thai, and Mons, of great and small villages, formed a single people," says one chronicler of the period.[3]

It was perhaps in the following year that Mangrai became involved with the three Shan brothers of Pagân. The chronicles state that Mangrai undertook a hasty expedition to Pagân-Ava in 1290. Arriving on its southern frontier, he was met by a dignitary (one of the Shan brothers?) sent out by the king to determine his intentions. Mangrai assured him that he came not to plunder but rather to obtain for his kingdom some of Ava's famous craftsmen in metal; and he was given five hundred families of goldsmiths, silversmiths, and copper-smiths whom he settled in various parts of his kingdom, including Keng Tung. If, as Luce believes, the Lan Na ruler at this time assisted the Shan brothers in conquering at least four districts of the Kyaukse region, it may have been from that region that these craftsmen came.

At about this time, a group of Buddhist monks arrived with two relics of the Buddha which they presented to Mangrai. The king enshrined them in lavish fashion and dedicated to their upkeep vast amounts of rice and land, including five hundred Mon families who had come from Pegu.

Finally, on March 27, 1292, Mangrai established his residence on the spot he had carefully selected as the new site for his capital, the "new city" Chiang Mai, which remains the center of the northern Thai to the present day. Mangrai consulted at length with his brother rulers, Ngam Müang and Ramkhamhaeng, concerning the plan of the city and its layout and defenses, but its actual construction began only on April 18, 1296.

Why the four-year delay in undertaking the construction of Chiang Mai? For the next decade, King Mangrai was almost constantly preoccupied with the threat the Mongols posed to the Tai world. He, indeed, was a major military target for them. The Chinese were aware of his support of the Shan brothers of Pagân, which may have had its origins in Mangrai's alliance with the Mons of Pegu and reflected his desire to maintain some scope for his activities among the Shans east of the Salween. The Chinese authorities in Yunnan seem to have regarded Mangrai as the most important Tai chief through the wide region that included the Keng Tung plain and the Shan states east of the Salween, as well as the Tai Lü and Lao regions of the Mekong. Mangrai's mother, after all, was the daughter of the ruler of Chiang Hung, and he seems to have had some continuing influence in that state. Given the manner in which he dealt with Phayao, Sukhothai, Pegu, and Pagân—if not with poor Haripuñjaya, which he conquered!—Mangrai seems to have pursued a policy that minimized conflict among the Tai states and their immediate neighbors, and facilitated cooper-ation among them in meeting the common threat the Mongols posed.

The Mongol campaigns against Burma, Vietnam, Champa, and even Java in this period are well known to historians of Southeast Asia. Less well known are the Mongol campaigns against Mangrai and his allies. We can only guess how this warfare originated, probably when the Mongols gained the submission of Chiang Hung in 1290. Its ruler then, Thao Ai, Mangrai's second cousin, was but a young man of twenty-three years and must have appealed for help to Mangrai. When Chiang Hung subsequently rebelled, the Chinese emperor in 1292 ordered an expedition be sent against Mangrai and Chiang Hung. The Chinese managed to take Chiang Hung in 1296, but Mangrai immediately sent a force to retake the city. The Chinese response was delayed, and it was not until 1301 that preparations were undertaken for a major invasion of this Tai region, with the assembling of a force of twenty thousand men and ten thousand horses, reinforced by Mongol archers. This campaign was a disaster for the Chinese. Their failures seem only to have emboldened the Tai, for by 1309 Chiang Mai and Chiang Hung were acting in concert to raid as far north as Wei-yüan and continued as late as 1311. Tiring of warfare, the Chinese turned to diplomacy and received tribute of tame elephants and local products from Chiang Hung and Chiang Mai in 1312. Chiang Mai sent subsequent missions to the Chinese court in 1315, 1326 (when the mission was led by the king's son), 1327, 1328, 1329, and 1347. Chiang Hung was slower to give up its raids into Chinese territory, which ceased only in 1325.

It is all too easy to overlook the likelihood that Mangrai's power was based on a highly diverse population. A substantial proportion, perhaps a majority especially in the southern portions of his kingdom, was Mon; and there were significant communities of Lawa and other tribal peoples as well as a variety of Tai. The core of the ruling elite was Tai, though leavened by some intermarriage with women of older indigenous ruling families and by the recruitment of specialists for royal service, like the Mon Ai Fa, the scribe and accountant. Mangrai was particularly conciliatory toward the Mon, even to the point of allowing the defeated King Yi Ba of Haripuñjaya to live on in Lampang for more than a decade, until Yi Ba rebelled (1296) and was forced to flee to exile further south. Mangrai was particularly respectful of Mon culture and Buddhism and early demonstrated his royal patronage of the religion. By encouraging the propagation of a new, more scholarly, and ostensibly authentic Singhalese Buddhism toward the end of the century, however, Mangrai could begin to build a new common social and political identity on a religious ground that was not so readily identifiable with either Mon or Tai. Soon, in piety no less than through military and political successes, the population of Lan Na could express a common identity that only gradually became what is now thought of as Tai Yuan, "northern Thai."

Late in his reign, Mangrai, now past seventy years of age, began to consider the problem of the succession to the throne of his powerful and prosperous state. His eldest son had been killed many years earlier for attempting to seize the throne, and his third and youngest son was a ne'er-do-well. In 1311, Mangrai sent Khun Khrüa, the third, off to govern the eastern Shans from a new capital at Möng Nai, while Khun Kham, his second and favorite son, governed Chiang Rai. Finally the end approached. Khun Kham was

summoned to Chiang Mai, arriving in time to attend his father on his death in
1317.

In sixty years as king, Mangrai had constructed an extensive and powerful
kingdom out of a congeries of isolated müang and came to dominate the
heartland of interior, upland Southeast Asia. He had won influence among the
Shans to the west, the Tai Lü to the north, and the Lao to the north and
northeast; and he had held his ground against two decades of Mongol expeditions. He had hardly begun the work of building administrative and
political institutions, having gone barely beyond the strategy of sending his sons
and grandsons and trusted officers out to govern new principalities created in the
upland valleys. There was still little, by 1317, of a tradition of central control
from Chiang Mai, nor were firm rules yet established that could ensure the
peaceful transition from a ruler to his heir. But he did begin a legal tradition,
perhaps of Mon inspiration, of humane, reasonable laws, still known by his
name—"The Judgments of King Mangrai." Their spirit is nicely represented
in the assertion that "according to the ancients, the King can maintain his
kingdom only with the help of freemen. Freemen are rare and should not be
wasted [by allowing them to become slaves]."[4]

Mangrai's immediate successors lived in a world in some respects less
dangerous than Mangrai's had been. The threat of Mongol invasions from the
north had eased, and the powerful state of Sukhothai to the south began to
crumble. There was neither the incentive for unity nor the mantle of past
military and diplomatic successes to sustain Chiang Mai's primacy at the apex
to which Mangrai had brought it. A dynastic power struggle erupted among
Mangrai's descendants, each using his own local or regional power base to
contest the throne in the capital. Six kings reigned in eleven years, and it was
only with the accession of Mangrai's great-grandson Kham Fu in 1328 that a
degree of stability returned to a Lan Na whose influence and extent by then had
ebbed.

The Siamese, Sukhothai, and the South

When Mangrai, Ngam Müang of Phayao, and Ramkhamhaeng of Sukhothai
met and concluded their alliance against the Mongols in 1287, Sukhothai had
attained in the lands to the south and east a preeminence at least the equal of
Mangrai's Lan Na in the north. The conditions that encouraged this to happen
and the series of events by which it took place, however, are poorly known and
can only be guessed. The two elements critical to the history of the Tai in central
Siam during the thirteenth century appear to be, first, that substantial populations of Tai by that time already were established throughout the Central
Plain in the old core lands of Dvaravati and Lopburi, and, second, that they

had experienced substantial exposure to the society, the culture, and the politics of the old Angkorian Empire.

We have seen how a Yonok ruler, Prince Phrom, had been pushed out of his small principality at Fang by an invading army coming from the west in 1017. According to legend, he had fled to found a new principality in the region of Kamphaengphet, establishing a dynasty that was to rule there, on the fringes of the Angkorian Empire, for several generations. There clearly were other such principalities founded or gradually taken over by ambitious Tai princes with the assistance of their followers and slaves captured in warfare. Judging from the legends and tales related in the chronicles, intermarriage with the indigenous ruling elite must have been a particularly important means by which such Tai princes rose gradually to power. If one such chronicle tradition is to be credited, the most important of these dynastic connections were formed between the indigenous rulers (Khmers? or perhaps old Mon families threatened by rising Khmer power?) of the towns of the western fringe of the Chaophraya valley and the house founded by Prince Phrom. Out of that web of political and kinship relations, centered on the old towns of Suphanburi and Phetburi, came a series of chiefs and princes who founded new communities as far south as Nakhon Si Thammarat on the Malay Peninsula and ruled over established towns and provinces such as Chainat, Phitsanulok, and Nakhon Sawan.

The most puzzling early Tai appearance to account for is that of the ruling house of Nakhon Si Thammarat, which in the thirteenth century must have been a thriving local power on the peninsula. For two centuries it had been the focus of heated international rivalries as Khmer, Malay, Burmese, Mon, and south Indian rulers had sought to control international maritime trade by establishing their power there. Its chaotic local chronicle tradition gives no hint of any Tai arrival; but it would appear that at least a Tai ruling house was established there by no later than the middle of the thirteenth century. Ruling over a population as mixed as the principality's history and certainly including substantial numbers of Khmer, Mon, and Malays, the rulers of Nakhon had accommodated the state's traditional international interests by attempting to interfere in the politics of Ceylon. They reestablished old suzerain-vassal relations with Nakhon's neighbors, including the Malay principalities to the south and west, as well as Pahang and Kedah. In addition, by the middle of the thirteenth century, Nakhon Si Thammarat had become a major center for the diffusion of a new school of Theravada Buddhism based on the teachings of the Mahavihara monastery of Ceylon. It was from Nakhon that monks carried the new Buddhism to the Angkorian empire, to Lopburi, and to Sukhothai and Lan Na. Though in hardly so striking a fashion, similar effusions of Tai power seem to have been occurring widely through this region at about the same time.

This movement of political development must have gained particular strength as the power of the Angkorian Empire waned after the death of King Jayavarman VII around 1220. It might be reflected in the sending of diplomatic missions to China between 1200 and 1205, seeking political recognition and trade, by the state the Chinese called "Chen-li-fu," located perhaps in the Phetburi region. In the first third of the thirteenth century, however, such states as these seem clearly to have been merely local ones, constructed from a single town and its hinterland with only the loosest of relationships to neighboring towns. During this period, such principalities may periodically have been engaged in warfare with their neighbors or with Angkor; but in the intervals of peace they seem to have been occupied with settling immigrant or captive populations over the countryside and establishing administrative networks. Their experience in the relatively more developed, complex, sophisticated environment shaped by centuries of Angkorian Khmer rule and influence gave this Tai elite of the Chaophraya valley and the upper peninsula a distinctive culture, different in some critical respects from that of their cousins to the north who ultimately became known as Lao or Shans. They seem to have been accustomed to relatively more complex, hierarchical social and political organization than the Tai Yuan or Lao. To their native animistic religion, they added a considerable body of Indian brahmanical beliefs and practices, particularly associated with the rituals of rites of passage and domestic crises. These Tai—who may have had Mon or Khmer origins—historically have been referred to as *Siamese*, a local variant on the word *Syam* of the Cham, Khmer, and Pagân inscriptions. The term takes on political significance when one of their states, Sukhothai, is referred to in Chinese sources toward the end of the thirteenth century as *Siem*, that is, Siam.

In periods of Khmer strength, the Tai princes and local chiefs of the Chaophraya valley were subdued by Angkor and given official titles and perhaps even brides to bind them to the empire. The most prominent such example was Pha Müang, the lord of the small principality of müang Rat, near Uttaradit (?), on whom the Angkorian king conferred the title of Śri Indraditya. With the title went a Khmer rank equivalent to king or viceroy, a sacred sword, and a "daughter" of the Angkorian ruler. Pha Müang probably took a solemn oath of loyalty to Angkor and promised to remit tribute regularly to the capital, in return for which he would have been allowed to rule undisturbed.

At some time, perhaps in the 1240s, Pha Müang gathered together a body of troops and joined with those of a neighboring Siamese ruler, Bang Klang Hao of müang Bang Yang (located perhaps near Sukhothai), who had not submitted to the Khmer. After reducing nearby Bang Khlang and Satchanalai, they marched on the main Khmer outpost in the region at Sukhothai, which had been established perhaps a century earlier. The Khmer gave battle but were defeated, and Pha Müang entered the city. Perhaps because he had violated his sacred oath of allegiance to Angkor, or perhaps because he recognized Bang Klang Hao's superior power or seniority, Pha Müang then presented his conquest to his ally, Bang Klang Hao, together with his own title and sword, and he presided over the new Śri Indraditya's coronation as king of Sukhothai.

Who were these men, and where did they come from? Because they believed that certain spirits—dwelling in caves or on mountains located to the north up the Nan River valley and the Nam U valley of north Laos—would protect them, it is thought that their ancestors came from those regions. The language of their earliest inscriptions similarly suggests an affinity with the White Tai. They themselves, however, left no record of their background or early careers.

In the reigns of Śri Indraditya and his son Ban Müang (r. ?–1279?), Sukhothai remained only a local power on the fringes of the old imperial plain where the flatlands turn hilly then quickly mountainous. These kings seem not to have been concerned with any continuing threat from Angkor, but rather with the ambitions of other neighboring Tai princes, such as the ruler of Sot (near Mae Sot) who invaded Sukhothai's western outpost at Tak. When Indraditya's troops fled the battlefield in confusion, the king's nineteen-year-old son Rama held his ground, pushed through to the commander of the attacking forces, and defeated him, earning the epithet "the bold," thus, Ramkhamhaeng—Rama the Bold.

When Ramkhamhaeng succeeded his elder brother as king of Sukhothai around 1279, his kingdom still was quite small, confined probably to the region around present-day Sukhothai, Sawankhalok, Uttaradit, Kamphaengphet, and Tak. His ancestry, his firm grip on power in Sukhothai, and his reputation in battle would have given him some standing among the Tai of his own neighborhood and to the north. He apparently also had some standing farther to the south either through his mother or by his marriage into the ruling families of the south (perhaps into the line of Prince Phrom of the Kamphaengphet region). Most of all, the time was right, the opportunities ample, for a young man with ambitions and connections. Angkor clearly was on its last legs as a major power, and the political status of the Chaophraya valley was in doubt. Mangrai was in the process of forming a major empire to the north and northwest, and the Mons were gaining their independence from Pagân. Whether by design or of necessity, Ramkhamhaeng concentrated his efforts on the zone of greatest opportunity, giving major established powers a wide berth and avoiding conflict both with his Tai neighbors to the north and northwest, Mangrai and Ngam Müang, and with Lopburi to the southeast.

In what we take to be his own words, in an inscription of 1292, Ramkhamhaeng described his style and principles of rule and outlined the methods by which he carefully but quickly constructed an enormous empire.

In the time of King Ramkhamhaeng this land of Sukhothai is thriving. There is fish in the water and rice in the fields. The lord of the realm does not levy toll on his subjects for travelling the roads; they lead their cattle to trade or ride their horses to sell; whoever wants to trade in elephants, does so; whoever wants to trade in horses, does so; whoever wants to trade in silver and gold, does so. When any commoner or man of rank dies, his estate—his elephants, wives, children, granaries, rice, retainers and groves of areca and betel—is left in its entirety to his son. When commoners or men of rank differ and disagree, [the King] examines the case to get at the truth and then settles it justly for them. He does not connive with thieves or favor concealers [of stolen goods]. When he sees someone's rice he does not covet it, when he sees someone's wealth he does not get angry. . . . He has hung a bell in the opening of the gate over there: if any commoner in the land has a grievance which sickens his belly and gripes his heart, and which he wants to make known to his ruler and lord, it is easy; he goes and strikes the bell which the King has hung there; King Ramkhamhaeng, the ruler of the kingdom, hears the call; he goes and questions the man, examines the case, and decides it justly for him. So the people of this *müang* of Sukhothai praise him.[5]

In this self-advertisement, Ramkhamhaeng paints a picture of an idyllic kingdom free of constraints, presided over by a just, benevolent, and thoroughly accessible monarch beloved by his people. He is generally referred to as what we might translate as "Lord Father," and the social relationships described in the inscription invariably connote a familial style. Through the passage quoted, and elsewhere in the inscription, there is an implicit contrast drawn between the king's apparent paternal benevolence and accessibility and the opposite qualities—rigid social hierarchy, arbitrary administration of justice, heavy taxation, and so on—of some other unspecified rule, presumably the style of Angkor. Ramkhamhaeng seems to have been anxious to present, to people in general but especially to Siamese, an alternative form of government, one that was Siamese or Tai. The king presents himself as one who respected the animistic spirits that populated the supernatural world of the Tai, but also as one who, as a devout Buddhist, vigorously promoted the cause of the religion and supported the monkhood. By offering his subjects justice and prosperity he assured their lives and property, but he also showed his concern for their souls.

Above all else, Sukhothai was a Buddhist state, lavishly supporting a monastic community newly reinforced and invigorated by a celebrated patriarch who had come from Nakhon Si Thammarat. The people of Sukhothai observed the Buddhist precepts and celebrated with exuberance the ceremonies of the religious calendar. The king shared the very throne from which he heard his subjects' plaints and petitions, weekly giving it up that learned monks there might preach the Dhamma of the Buddha. With king and monks sharing the same throne, Buddhism and the state were very closely identified. The state was Buddhist, but the religion was also political, certainly to the extent that political unity and identity were founded upon a religious basis.

King Ramkhamhaeng built an extensive kingdom by a judicious combination of force and diplomacy. He refers to having raided towns and villages, capturing elephants, precious metals, and prisoners whom he did not kill. But at the same time he encouraged, by his moral as well as his military repute, numerous petty rulers and local chiefs to make their submission to him.

> If anyone riding an elephant comes to see him to put his own country under his protection, he helps him, treats him generously, and takes care of him; if [someone comes to him] with no elephants, no horses, no young men or women of rank, no silver or gold, he gives him some, and helps him until he can establish a state of his own.[6]

Ramkhamhaeng's inscription includes a passage, added posthumously, that lists "the places whose submission he received," extending outward from Sukhothai in the four cardinal directions. To the east, these included Phitsanulok, the Lom Sak region, and Vientiane. To the south, the string of dependencies extended through Nakhon Sawan and Chainat to Suphanburi, Ratburi, Phetburi, and Nakhon Si Thammarat. To the west were even Pegu and Martaban, where a Mon adventurer who had married Ramkhamhaeng's daughter ruled from 1287 to 1306. To the north, the inscription named Phrae, Nan, and Luang Prabang.

The geographical extension of Sukhothai's power, which was matched only rarely in later centuries by the Kingdom of Siam, should not be understood in modern political terms. Ramkhamhaeng certainly did not raise a massive army and march over these several thousands of miles, conquering all the principalities his inscription names. From the epigraphic evidence, we are certain only that he took his armies to Tak when still a prince. The Chinese records suggest that he campaigned in the Ratburi-Phetburi area in 1294. Although the Nakhon Si Thammarat chronicles claim that Ramkhamhaeng came there and ruled over the state from 1274 to 1276, it is best to regard this legend as a late insertion. It is much more likely that Ramkhamhaeng's claim to the Malay Peninsula derived from his conquest of, or the submission to him of, the ruler of Phetburi or the house of Suphanburi. We might speculate that

Nakhon Si Thammarat in turn brought into the Sukhothai orbit its own vassals and dependencies on the Malay Peninsula, which may have extended as far to the south as Pahang.

Such a pattern, by which political relationships could pyramid from vassals to overlords and their overlords, and so on, seems typical not only of Tai states during this period but indeed of much of the political structure of East and Southeast Asia, best exemplified in the tributary system of China. Unlike the highly formalized Chinese system, however, political loyalties in the Tai world tended to be personal. Thus, for example, the ruler of Nakhon Si Thammarat might have owed personal allegiance to the ruler of Phetburi, who in turn might have owed it to the powerful prince of Suphanburi, who himself had submitted to Ramkhamhaeng. This meant that all but the core of the kingdom remained separated into small müang units, each with its own ruler; and the relationships between local rulers and the king were defined by the relative power of the individuals concerned and confied to the duration of their lifetimes. It is particularly tempting to regard Ramkhamhaeng's southern empire as a product of marriage or kin relations with the ruling houses long established in the region between Suphanburi and Nakhon Si Thammarat.

The northward extension of Ramkhamhaeng's empire similarly might be interpreted in terms of his kin relationships if, as it seems, his ancestors came from the northeast. One passage in his inscription asserts:

> All the Ma, the Kao [Kaeo?], the Lao, the Thai of the lands under the vault of heaven [southernmost Yunnan?] and the Thai who live along the Nam U and the Mekong come to do obeisance to King Śri Indraditya's son King Ramkhamhaeng.[7]

The passage suggests voluntary submission, rather than conquest. Ramkhamhaeng's power, compounded of military strength and moral prestige, simply radiated outward from his capital, and those who recognized his superiority and leadership submitted to him.

The notable omissions in the list of Ramkhamhaeng's vassals are those neighboring states that would have been the equals of Sukhothai: King Mangrai's Lan Na, the Phayao of King Ngam Müang, and old Lopburi. With the first two rulers, Ramkhamhaeng had concluded an alliance in 1287, leaving his northern flank protected while Mangrai (presumably assisted by Ngam Müang) bore the brunt of Mongol invasions that continued for several decades. Might Ramkhamhaeng have come to some similar accommodation with the rulers of Lopburi? Lopburi had shaken free of Angkor around the middle of the thirteenth century and began sending diplomatic missions to the Mongol court around 1280 that continued with some regularity until 1299. Griswold and

Image of the Buddha, bronze; height 2.2 m; Sukhothai period, fourteenth century. Wat Benchamabophit, Bangkok.

Prasert suppose that the ruler of Lopburi must have been friendly with the Sukhothai court, for a Chinese visitor to Angkor in 1295 reported that Hsien, which we take to be Sukhothai, recently had been laying waste large portions of the Angkorian kingdom and had forced the Khmer kings to introduce universal military conscription. It is difficult to imagine how Ramkhamhaeng's forces could even have approached the frontiers of Angkor without moving through Lopburi's territory. Perhaps Lopburi surrendered any claims it may have had to influence in the western half of the Chaophraya valley in return for Sukhothai's assistance against Angkor. Lopburi, however, retained its independence and was firmly in control of the eastern half of the Chaophraya valley and regions to the east and southeast.

Ramkhamhaeng's Sukhothai is remembered as much for its art and ideas as for its political achievements. Although little of the sculpture known to have been executed in the king's lifetime has survived, the few pieces that remain indicate that the characteristic features of the classic Sukhothai style developed before the end of the thirteenth century. Images of the Buddha, for example, bear the distinctive stamp of Tai physiognomy; and the images in the walking posture are cast with such a flowing grace that they seem to move before the observer's eyes. In describing his own capital, Ramkhamhaeng refers to several major monuments constructed during his reign, the ruins of many of which remain to the present day, silent testimony to the grandeur of his capital. In fashioning works of art, just as in creating a patriarchal government and in making for Theravada Buddhism the place it had in the life of the community, the people of Sukhothai were uniquely creative. Remaining true to their own Tai traditions, they were nonetheless alive to the best that a wider world could offer them. Their art was strongly influenced by that of Ceylon and Nakhon Si Thammarat, and they imported potters from China who created brilliant works in celadon and the famous Sankhalok ceramics. Whatever its origins and influences, however, Sukhothai art, like Sukhothai life, was a thing of its own, more than eclectic and distinctively Siamese.

The general picture that emerges is one of a powerful and prosperous capital, calmly self-assured and self-confident, very much in contact with the outside world but on its own terms. The framework of values that underlay the kingdom's culture remained essentially Tai, and especially so in its political culture. Sukhothai had transplanted, from the upland valleys to the edge of the great Chaophraya plain, the social and political organization of the upland müang. There was relatively little social and political differentiation, the essential division being between chao and commoners, and the kingship was based firmly on personal, kinlike relations, rather than on impersonal, formal relations. The environment in which Sukhothai was set, however, was a new one. There were considerable non-Tai populations, long-standing Mon and

Khmer communities ruled by their own leaders, and cultural and religious traditions that were foreign to the Tai.

All these new elements posed political problems to the rulers of Sukhothai, which they seem to have attempted to solve as upland valley rulers might have done. Socially and administratively, the preexisting populations were fitted into Sukhothai society either as slaves or as men and women of rank owing a vassal's service, as subject or dependent ruler, to the court. Siamese Tai was becoming the language of administration and prestige, and Ramkhamhaeng himself claims to have invented in 1283 a script that deliberately made the written, tonal Tai language comprehensible to the speakers of nontonal languages. The brahmanical religion long practiced in the region was given court patronage, and court sculptors even fashioned bronze images of Viṣṇu and Siva in a style similar to that expressed in Sukhothai's Buddha images. Most of all, Ramkhamhaeng responded to the new possibility of extending his power over vast distances by creating a sort of "super-müang," held together by pyramided personal loyalties, just as the upland müang had been integrated on a much smaller scale. He did not centralize all power, whether political or economic or cultural, in a single capital, and the disparity in strength between Sukhothai and its major outlying vassals was not considerable. Even in his inscription, Ramkhamhaeng suggests that his power rested primarily upon his moral authority and leadership. Because he was virtuous and ruled with justice, all should recognize his goodness.

On the death of King Ramkhamhaeng in 1298, his son Lö Thai (r. 1298–1346 or 1347) succeeded him, and the vast empire rapidly disintegrated. Sukhothai's dominion to the north of Uttaradit collapsed almost immediately, and various petty principalities both struggled among themselves and attempted to maintain their independence vis-à-vis Lan Na. Luang Prabang, Vientiane, and the middle Mekong similarly slipped quickly into independence and a state of some disorder. To the west, the Mon state centered on Pegu no longer recognized Sukhothai's suzerainty after 1319, and by 1321 even Tak, one of the oldest dependencies of the kingdom, had fallen under the sway of Lan Na. In the south, the key city was Suphanburi, which probably broke with Lö Thai early in his reign. By doing so, it blocked Sukhothai's access to its vassals farther south and set in motion a series of developments that by mid-century would lead to the creation at Ayudhya of the state that ultimately would absorb Sukhothai. Thus, by about 1320 at the latest, Sukhothai again had become a relatively small kingdom of local, rather than regional, significance.

By the 1340s, then, the Tai had become major participants in the cultural and political life of mainland Southeast Asia; but despite attempts to the contrary they had not succeeded in re-creating major empires on the model of the classical empires of the past. The Shan brothers had not taken over intact the empire of Pagân, nor had Ramkhamhaeng supplanted the Khmers of Angkor. Perhaps such imperial ambitions were not their intention. It is possible that, for reasons peculiar to each region, the more ambitious attempts at empire building were either opportunistic scrambles for vacated power or defensive confederations formed in times of danger. Lan Na was the major state of durable power formed during this period, but even it was of considerably smaller extent in 1350 than it had been in Mangrai's lifetime.

By the middle of the fourteenth century, small local Tai states were sprinkled across the map from eastern Assam in the west to Nakhon Si Thammarat in the south and Sukhothai in the east. Farther to the north and east, there remained innumerable petty Lao and upland Tai principalities, as there had been for centuries. These states may from time to time have been caught up in the affairs of the larger states or have been inspired by their successes. They were not, however, in the same position as their cousins to the south and west to capitalize on the breakdown of the old classical empires, nor did they have the same potential base in rice land and manpower to begin to act as kingdoms. Perhaps, too, the spirit of the age was slower in reaching them— the combination of political opportunity, an exciting expectancy of change, and a flow of new ideas and techniques that included Theravada Buddhism. Where this spirit caught hold, it moved countless Tai to dramatic action, but by the middle of the fourteenth century it had worked more to the destruction of the old order of mainland Southeast Asia than to the construction of a new order.

4

Ayudhya and Its Neighbors, 1351–1569

As late as the middle of the fourteenth century, though innumerable Tai principalities now filled the map across the central and northern reaches of mainland Southeast Asia, only a few—notably Lan Na at Chiang Mai—might properly have been dignified with the title "kingdom." Moreover, none had attained enough regional strength to act as a powerful empire in the ways that Angkorian Cambodia and Burmese Pagân had done in earlier centuries. In the succeeding two centuries, one major Tai empire emerged, the Kingdom of Ayudhya, and it became a regional power of the first importance. Two Tai competitors, however, challenged its ambitions to lead the Tai world—a revived Kingdom of Lan Na, and the new Lao Kingdom of Lan Sang centered on Luang Prabang—and newly powerful Burman and Cambodian states attempted to check its international aspirations. The stakes were high. For the first time in Tai history, kings and their officers aspired to more than simply holding together the small müang of upland states against the ambitious chao who ruled them and defending them against non-Tai empires. There were now several major Tai kingdoms, each of which considered itself to be a legitimate political and cultural unit in an international framework of states that transcended the world of the Tai.

The magnitude and importance of this change in the international outlook of the Tai were considerable. The traditional Tai states of the preceding centuries had operated within limited horizons, over restricted territories, and with a relatively narrow range of political and military skills. Their rulers, with few exceptions, were little concerned with the affairs of the non-Tai world beyond the territories of their immediate neighbors. Their states, consisting of only a few müang, each with its few dozens of villages scattered among the hills and valleys of upland Southeast Asia, could be ruled on a small, personal scale, seldom troubled by incursions of the major empires—China, Vietnam, Champa, Angkor, Pagân, and Nan-chao.

When a handful of Tai states—preeminently Ayudhya—assumed imperial pretensions and ambitions, their rulers had to make radical shifts in their
ways of looking at and organizing their world, internally and externally. In the
international community of states of which they were rapidly becoming aware,
they strove to gain recognition as great powers, both from their erstwhile
"superiors" among the classical empires of the region and from their former
equals, who now became their vassals.

To accomplish this transition, the new Tai "empires" had to create new
identities for themselves, for the sake of internal cohesion and of external
recognition. They were confronted by accepted international standards of
behavior and values that the outside world employed to distinguish between
civilized and barbarian people, between states and tribes, between kings or
emperors and chieftains. The pressures on the new Tai rulers were not unlike
those encouraging modernization and Westernization many centuries later, and
similarly, the new standards could have been viewed as foreign and inimical to
Tai values and traditions. Bureaucratic administration, codified, impersonal
law, the state-organized and -taxed economy—all could be seen and rejected as
alien, as indeed they had been by Ramkhamhaeng of Sukhothai in the closing
decades of the thirteenth century. They could also, however, be welcomed as
useful ideas, particularly to the extent that they could be viewed as being no
more than new and "improved" political or administrative "technology."

Although much that went with the contemporary definition of *civilization*
was ultimately Indian in origin, so too was the Theravada Buddhism that now
was becoming so popular in the region. And like Buddhism, the new standards
of civilization were hardly new to the region, having over several centuries been
upheld by the classical empires and integrated into the lives of the first immigrant Tai communities. Now, after several generations of assimilation into this
civilized world, Tai groups expressed their heightened ambitions in the strongest manner possible, by staking a claim to leadership within the new system.

This was an auspicious moment to do so. The major empires were in some
disarray; they were in no position to concern themselves with the long, north-
south interior strip of the Indochinese peninsula where the heaviest concentration of Tai had come to live. Mongol China was slipping into the decline that
in 1368 would bring the Ming dynasty to power. Vietnam, now recovering from
the Mongol invasions of the end of the thirteenth century, was almost constantly involved in warfare with Champa, which itself had been sufficiently
weak to suffer a Tai invasion in 1313—perhaps from Sukhothai? The vast
confederation of Ramkhamhaeng's Sukhothai had disintegrated on his death,
Lan Na (Chiang Mai) was in a state of confusion, and the constituents of what
had been Pagân were squabbling among themselves.

In the middle of the fourteenth century, a stable new order rapidly began to emerge out of this chaos. In seeking the conditions that may have underlain this process of development, we have little firm information to guide us, but two international developments may be of some importance. First, there began around the middle of the century an upswing in the movement of international trade on the long routes between India and China. This was to lead to economic opportunities for Southeast Asian rulers and to Chinese diplomatic initiatives in support of the creation of a stable political and economic order in Southeast Asia. Second, this was a period of major religious and cultural change, the most prominent feature of which in mainland Southeast Asia was the spread of a new, more vigorous form of Theravada Buddhism of the Singhalese persuasion. This particular form of organized religion was eminently amenable to royal patronage and manipulation, and was intimately associated with the new empires that now arose in the region. To the extent that the future development of the region was based upon international trade and communication, the international currents favored the Tai region most exposed to them— Ayudhya, at the mouth of the Chaophraya River and the head of the Gulf of Siam.

The Rise of Ayudhya

The core of what was to become the Kingdom of Ayudhya had in the thirteenth century been the western provinces of the Angkorian Empire in the region centered on Lopburi. By about the middle of that century, Angkor's control of the region had faded, owing perhaps to dynastic difficulties in Angkor, to the separatist ambitions of a ruling line established in Lopburi and to the new assertive mood of the growing Tai population of the lower Chaophraya valley, who recently had been inspired by the example of Sukhothai's successful bid for independence. Around 1290, Sukhothai's leadership and military force had succeeded in wresting from Angkor the principalities on the western edge of the Chaophraya valley, while Lopburi seems to have maintained its sway over the eastern side of the valley. Lopburi signified its own attempt at state building by sending diplomatic missions to China between 1289 and 1299. That Angkor's knell was sounded in the west is strongly suggested by the report of Chou Ta-kuan, a Chinese envoy who visited Angkor in 1296. He reported that "in the war with the Siamese, all the population was called upon to fight" and elsewhere recorded that "recently, in the course of the war with Siam, [the villages] were completely destroyed."[1] Other evidence of a more peaceful intrusion also is mentioned: Buddhist monks were given a Tai appellation, and a curious reference is made to superior Tai textile technology:

Recently much attention has been given by Siamese settlers in this country to raising silkworms and cultivating mulberries; their mulberry seed and silkworm stock all come from Siam. ... The Siamese women can sew and mend, and when the fabrics worn by the Cambodians become worn, Siamese are called in to repair the damage.[2]

The "Siamese" of these references is almost certainly the Sukhothai of the 1290s, the power of which, extending down the western side of the Chaophraya valley, must have come into conflict and competition with Angkor and Lopburi.

After the death of King Ramkhamhaeng of Sukhothai at the turn of the century, however, the political status of the vast Chaophraya plain must have been thrown into confusion. Lopburi, the old Angkorian cultural and administrative center of the eastern portion of the plain, seems to have maintained its independence of both Sukhothai and Angkor. Its culture represented an amorphous amalgam of Mahayana and an older Burmese Hinayana Buddhism with Angkorian brahmanical religion and the Indian arts and sciences. Its population may have been predominantly Khmer in the long-established towns dependent on Lopburi—Inburi, Singburi, Chainat, Nakhon Nayok, and Prachinburi, for example—but it must also have included a substantial Mon element in addition to growing numbers of Tai. The Tai of this region must have been linguistically distinct from the Sukhothai Tai, for their language suggests movement into this region from the north and northeast via the Pa Sak River valley of present-day Phetchabun province and from the Khorat Plateau. Whatever the proportions of these three linguistic groups, we may at least assume some cultural heterogeneity among them.

The western side of the Chaophraya plain was dominated in this period by the principality of Suphanburi, the earlier history of which can only be surmised. Suphanburi may be regarded as the heir to a political tradition of rule over a region stretching from (about) Chainat in the north to the region of Chumphon in the south, a region the center of which many centuries earlier may have been at Nakhon Pathom and later at Phetburi. At least as early as the beginning of the thirteenth century, this region was closely connected with Nakhon Si Thammarat on the peninsula; and this entire strip of territory was at least nominally subject to Ramkhamhaeng in the 1290s. When Ramkhamhaeng's hand was removed, around 1300, Suphanburi quickly established its own independence and probably maintained influence, if not control, over the dependent regions stretching to the south. Suphanburi was preeminently a Siamese, Theravada Buddhist state, the strength of which lay in its rulers' ability to call upon the loyalties of the burgeoning Tai population of the western side of the Chaophraya plain, the men of Ratburi, Phetburi, Kanchanaburi, and Nakhon Pathom who had a strong interest in preserving their independence of Angkorian rule.

As late as the 1340s, however, the Chaophraya plain still lacked political focus and leadership of the quality that Ramkhamhaeng and, earlier, Angkor had provided. Although Lopburi and Suphanburi enjoyed some eminence as centers of power and influence, there was then still a multiplicity of small towns and principalities in the region, each uncertain of its own future and all insufficiently organized to grasp such political and economic opportunities as the times now offered, with its upsurge in international trade and the collapse of Angkorian power. Inward-looking and preoccupied with their local concerns and the preservation of their own prerogatives, such alliances and confederations of states as may have occurred during this period were fragile affairs, the products of relationships among individuals and families, cemented by political marriages or forced by temporary military imbalances.

The leadership that transformed the region in the middle of the fourteenth century was provided by an obscure adventurer known as U Thong, "Prince Golden Cradle." U Thong was born in 1314, perhaps (according to the hypothesis of Charnvit Kasetsiri) to a powerful Chinese merchant family who may have been located in Phetburi. We know that he was married to a daughter of the ruler of Suphanburi; and he may also have married a princess connected to the ruling line of Lopburi. This combination of relationships—to two powerful principalities and to a growing commercial community—represents at least in symbolic form the fundamental strength upon which U Thong was to base and develop his political ambitions.

One version of the Royal Chronicles of Ayudhya makes U Thong the successor of a king of "Kamphucha," perhaps best understood as Lopburi, and narrates his foundation of the city of Ayudhya.

> The king passed away and no member of the royal family could be found to succeed him. So all the people raised Prince U Thong, who was the son of Chodüksethi [the leader of the Chinese merchant community], to be anointed as king and govern the kingdom. At that time there was a severe outbreak of smallpox and much of the population succumbed to it. So the King left troops in charge of his capital and, moving the population out of the city at nighttime, went to the south in order to flee the pestilence. And his [wife's?] older brother took up temporary residence with his forces in the country of the city of Suphanburi. King U Thong, however, marched his troops on a journey of several days until they came to a large river and saw a circular island, smooth, level, and apparently clean, standing in the center of the area. So he had his troops cross over and establish themselves on Dong Sano Island. . . .
>
> In 712, a Year of the Tiger, second of the decade, on Friday, the sixth day of the waxing moon of the fifth month, at three *nalika* and nine *bat* after the break of dawn, the Capital City of Ayudhya was first established [i.e., Friday, March 4, 1351, shortly after nine o'clock in the morning].[3]

The foundation of Ayudhya, from a nineteenth-century Siamese painting.
National Museum, Bangkok.

Taking the name of Ramathibodi, U Thong sent his queen's elder brother
Pha-ngua to take charge of Suphanburi, his family's traditional seat of power,
and his own eldest son Ramesuan "to mount the royal throne in Lopburi."
With his own capital located at Ayudhya, some distance from but within easy
reach of both major cities by water, and being in a port city of some antiquity
with a thriving international trade, Ramathibodi was in a position with strong
natural advantages. Capitalizing upon them and upon his political and kin
connections with the leading peoples and principalities of the region, he rapidly
constructed a kingdom that soon overwhelmed his nearby rivals.

The mixture of forces and interests that combined to Ayudhya's strength
through the first centuries of its existence is revealed in the vicissitudes of its
internal politics, the fluctuations of its foreign policy, and the form taken by its
institutions. In each of these areas are revealed tensions and a potential for
conflict that can have been eased and directed only by creative and forceful
leadership.

The Ayudhya of Ramathibodi I and his immediate successors politically was based upon an uneasy alliance between Tai manpower from the western portion of the state, Khmer prestige and statecraft from Lopburi and the eastern provinces, and Chinese (and other Asian) commercial power concentrated at the center in the port-capital. As a resident alien community, the Chinese may be said to have had political influence rather than power, and it is possible that they attempted to exercise that influence by assisting various court factions to expand their wealth or to make diplomatic connections abroad. The Tai chiefs of the western plains built their strength mainly upon their claim to the manpower of the regions under their control, a claim founded at least at first upon personal allegiance, transmitted hereditarily from one generation to the next, and exercised especially in raising troops for war. The Lopburi people, and those like them in the eastern regions, may be seen as being most at home in formal government. Here was skilled manpower, functionaries, and specialists for a new and expanding kingdom. The three sources of strength represented by these elements—economic, military, and administrative—were not always in concert, and it may have been some generations before a workable accommodation among them was reached.

The main arena of political conflict in Ayudhya centered on the succession to the throne, which passed back and forth between the Suphanburi and Lopburi houses for several generations. The first major succession crisis occurred in 1369 on the death of Ramathibodi I. Prince Ramesuan, his son, came down from Lopburi to assume the throne. He held it, however, only briefly. The next year the young king's uncle, Borommaracha, his mother's (or stepmother's) elder brother who had been governing Suphanburi, arrived before the capital, presumably in force. Probably on the advice of his ministers, Ramesuan abdicated and returned to govern Lopburi as he had in his father's reign. Where the thirty-year-old Ramesuan may have been inexperienced, inattentive to public affairs, and unmilitary, his sixty-three-year-old uncle is said to have been "a war-minded ruler, a lover of weapons, [who] took great care of his soldiers and the community."[4] Their confrontation may not have been quite so peaceful as the chronicles suggest. One source states that "the land was blackened with civil war under [Borommaracha's] rule, but he settled everything with little bloodshed, bringing everyone under submission and under one head."[5]

Eighteen years later, the tables were turned. When Borommaracha died in 1388, his seventeen-year-old son, Prince Thong Chan, was placed upon the throne. Assembling followers secretly in Lopburi and its vicinity, ex-King Ramesuan stormed the palace in Ayudhya, had the young prince executed, and assumed the throne, thereby restoring the Lopburi faction to power.

King Ramesuan's second reign lasted for only seven years, until 1395. He was succeeded then by his twenty-one-year-old son Rama (or Ramaracha), who seems to have made a concerted attempt to conciliate the Suphanburi faction. He appointed Nakhon In, the younger brother of Prince Thong Chan (from whom his father had usurped the throne) to govern Suphanburi and apparently even allowed him to conduct direct diplomatic relations with the Chinese court (who recognized him as heir-apparent to the Ayudhya throne). This policy worked well until 1409 when, for reasons unexplained, Ramaracha suffered a falling-out with the chief of his ministers, who fled the capital and invited Nakhon In to join him in deposing the king. Their forces sent Ramaracha into exile, Nakhon In ascended the throne as King Intharacha, and the minister was rewarded with the daughter of a royal concubine.

The dynastic crisis of 1409 seems to have marked the end of the Lopburi-Suphanburi rivalry, for thereafter Lopburi rarely appears in the chronicles. The chronicles, however, may have obscured the demise of Ramesuan's line, for one source says, "During this king's [Intharacha's] reign the land was bur-dened with internal wars, but he conciliated the two parties." He must have asserted direct administrative control over Lopburi, for he posted his three mature sons to the government of northern and western provinces: Suphanburi, San (Sankhaburi), and Phitsanulok. And subsequent challenges to the throne were to come, not from Lopburi, but from farther to the north.

By this point in its history, less than sixty years after the foundation of the kingdom, Ayudhya already was on the verge of becoming a major power in the interstate relations of mainland Southeast Asia. King Ramathibodi I (r. 1351–69) had been preoccupied with the heartland of his kingdom and with securing its eastern frontier against the Angkorian Khmer. In this warfare, in the course of which Angkor itself may temporarily have been occupied, con-siderable numbers of people were rounded up and resettled in Ayudhya's domains. The security of Ramathibodi's northern flank during this period may have been assured by some sort of personal pact or alliance with King Mahathammaracha I (Lüthai, 1347–68/74?) of Sukhothai that allowed each the opportunity to consolidate his kingdom.

When Borommaracha I (1370–88) came from Suphanburi to assume the throne of Ayudhya, his attention turned to the north. This monarch, whom one imagines as a crusty old warrior in his sixties, seems to have viewed Sukhothai as Ayudhya's chief rival for paramountcy in the Thai world. Sukhothai indeed had recovered its strength under Mahathammaracha and had regained many of the dependencies that had fallen away since the death of King Ramkhamhaeng. Borommaracha spent nearly all his reign at war in the Sukhothai region, perhaps hoping to profit from political uncertainties in Sukhothai following the death of Mahathammaracha I between 1368 and

1374. By 1378 he had captured Nakhon Sawan, Phitsanulok, and Kamphaengphet, and forced King Mahathammaracha II (1368–98?) to swear his allegiance and submit to Ayudhya's suzerainty. He was subsequently drawn first into warfare against the Kingdom of Lan Na, which brought the submission of Lampang in 1386, and then, in alliance with Lan Na, into renewed warfare against Sukhothai. He was thwarted, however, by the rebellion of Kamphaengphet, and died while returning home from a campaign against that city in 1388.

King Ramesuan's return to the throne (1388–95) marks what some have seen as a return to a policy of benevolence toward Sukhothai. If the chronicles can be trusted, Ramesuan was at war with Lan Na and Angkor. By their account, Ramesuan attacked and gained the submission of Chiang Mai in 1390 and took large numbers of people captive whom he resettled in Phatthalung, Songkhla, Nakhon Si Thammarat, and Chanthaburi. (This campaign, however, is not mentioned in the Lan Na chronicles.) Shortly thereafter, when the Cambodian king raided Chonburi and Chanthaburi for manpower, Ramesuan sent an army into Cambodia that again took Angkor. Neither of these wars, however, is attested with any certainty by reliable sources; and all that can be concluded about the foreign policy of Ramesuan's reign is that it seems to have shied from confrontation with Sukhothai.

Ramesuan's son Ramaracha (1395–1409) attempted more vigorously to assert his authority in the north. In 1396, an Ayudhya envoy assassinated the ruler of the principality of Nan, and in the following year Ayudhya imposed its own legal system upon Sukhothai and its dependencies. Sukhothai soon struck back. In what has been called his "declaration of independence," King Mahathammaracha III (Sai Lüthai, 1398–1419) of Sukhothai seized Nakhon Sawan from Ayudhya in 1400, thus blocking riverine communications at a critical junction, extended his authority in the principalities of Nan and Phrae, and even attempted to intervene in the succession to the throne in Lan Na. It has been argued that this setback to Ayudhya's prestige in the north contributed to the decline of Ramaracha and the Lopburi line.[6]

When Intharacha (1409–24) came from Suphanburi to mount the throne of Ayudhya, he acted to establish the kingdom's authority in the Sukhothai domains. As early as 1412, following a series of unrecorded events, an Ayudhyan chief resident was installed in Sukhothai, and Mahathammaracha III was reduced to the status of a vassal ruler. Intharacha himself even visited Sukhothai for a period in 1417. When Mahathammaracha III died in 1419, Intharacha again traveled to Nakhon Sawan to adjudicate the succession to the Sukhothai throne and install Mahathammaracha IV (1419–38). The latter moved his seat to Phitsanulok around 1430, and on his death in 1438 Sukhothai was incorporated as a province into the Kingdom of Ayudhya. Just as King Ramathibodi of Ayudhya had sent his son Ramesuan to govern Lopburi, now King Borommaracha II (1424–48) sent his son Ramesuan (later King Borommatrailokanat) to govern Phitsanulok.

Borommaracha II could not have expected to succeed his father (Intharacha) on the throne of Ayudhya, for he had two elder brothers with superior claims to the throne. On their father's death in 1424, however, his brothers contested for the throne in a duel on elephant-back, as a consequence of which both died. By now a mature man of thirty-five years, Borommaracha proved himself an effective and powerful king. He inherited an already extensive kingdom with armies tested against the Khmer, Sukhothai, and Lan Na. His subjects, their numbers swelled by war captives, are remembered by the chroniclers as having been rich and prosperous. It was left to Borommaracha II and his son to complete the process of consolidating the kingdom and making of it a power of international stature.

Borommaracha II resumed the struggle against Angkor that had been pursued, but not concluded, by Ramathibodi and Ramesuan. The late Angkorian kings, about whom little is known, seem to have maintained up to this period a frontier running perhaps from Chanthaburi to Chonburi and Nakhon Ratchasima, along which there may have been intermittent raiding for manpower and plunder. By the 1420s, Angkor was clearly in decline. Caught between the Chams in the east, who frequently raided into the Khmer heartland, and Ayudhya to the west, Angkor's resources were taxed to the point where upkeep of the intricate irrigation system upon which the state's prosperity was based began to suffer. Finally, in 1431–32, Borommaracha II sent a major expedition against Angkor which succeeded in taking the city. The capital was looted—the palace of the royal regalia—and Borommaracha's son was briefly installed as the vassal ruler of the state, comparable in status to Mahathammaracha IV of Sukhothai. Soon the city was abandoned, and the heir of the last Angkorian king fled to found a new kingdom in the region of Phnom Penh far to the east. Now, after nearly a century of conflict, Ayudhya was at least for a time to feel secure on its eastern flank.

Sukhothai and the northern expanse of the Central Plain was next. On the death of Mahathammaracha IV in 1438, Borommaracha was sufficiently confident of his power to install there his seven-year-old son Ramesuan as its viceroy, presumably with a corps of administrators and a military garrison.

Finally, in 1442, Borommaracha turned his attention to Lan Na, beginning what was to become a century of nearly continuous warfare. The weight of this burden fell most heavily upon his son Ramesuan, who succeeded him as King Borommatrailokanat (or Trailok) when in the course of a campaign against Chiang Mai Borommaracha died in 1448. With the kingdom now incorporating larger territories and many more people than his father had inherited in 1424, and engaged in ambitious full-scale warfare far afield, King Trailok must have been under some pressure to systematize and strengthen the administration of his state, all the more because he found it necessary temporarily to move his capital to Phitsanulok, the better to conduct his military campaigns in the north.

From the very beginning of the Kingdom of Ayudhya, its core provinces, at least, had been very tightly organized and controlled. Economically and politically the state was constructed on the claim of the ruling class to the manpower that resided in its territory. All freemen were obligated to render six months' labor each year to the crown and could be employed on public works or in military service. Their labor was organized and coordinated by *mun nai*, territorial officers appointed by the government who were responsible for keeping track of the freemen assigned to them and producing them when they might be required. Such territorial, bureaucratic control over manpower stood in sharp contrast to the traditional Tai patterns of freemen customarily rendering service to personal patrons, with no regard for territorial jurisdictions or bureaucratic controls, a system characteristic of Sukhothai and other Tai states to the north. The extending of bureaucratic control over manpower in Ayudhya and the surrounding territories immediately dependent on the capital from the last half of the fourteenth century was an important new source of strength that gave Ayudhya an advantage over its neighbors. It was an innovation, however, that was neither easily nor completely accomplished. Freemen naturally preferred the flexibility and personal quality of the traditional patron-client relationship to the impersonality and arbitrariness of the new bureaucratic system, and they constantly sought means to evade it. Some did so by successfully attaching themselves as personal clients to powerful officials, whereas others fled to other territories or the uninhabited wilds, or even sold themselves into debt slavery. The natural tension between personal and bureaucratic control over manpower was to prove a persistent dynamic in Ayudhya's history.

The officials of the early Ayudhya state were in the process of being transformed into a bureaucracy, probably on the Angkorian model earlier established in Lopburi and the Central Plain. Ramathibodi must have recruited his specialized personnel—scribes, court brahmans, jurists, chamberlains, accountants, physicians, astrologers, and the like—from the Khmerized urban elite of Lopburi, Ayudhya, Phromburi, Inburi, Sankhaburi, and Nakhon Nayok. Such men spoke Khmer and from the beginning buttressed the majesty of the throne with a special court vocabulary based on Khmer and

Sanskrit. For them, a truly royal king should be raised far above the level of his subjects, insulated by layers of officials from direct contact with them, and wrapped in a cloak of mystery and sanctity compounded out of brahmanical religion from the cults of Siva and Viṣṇu.

Ramathibodi and his successors were distant in quite another way from the general and provincial officials who administered the kingdom's numerous provinces. Some of these officials probably originated as personal retainers, trusted friends, and clients of the king into whose charge various territories were entrusted. Such officers may originally have come from the ruling elite of one town or another, being drawn into the king's service as the kingdom expanded. Now part of the capital and the various ministries of government, they were separated from the personal clients they once had. Their impersonal, bureaucratic command over manpower was held only at the king's pleasure. They might be sent off to serve as governor, or registrar of manpower, or inspector, or tax collector, in a particular locality for a year or two. Then they could be transferred elsewhere, with or without a promotion or rise in their emoluments. All their actions were carefully prescribed and circumscribed by written documents, codes of law, and royal decrees.

Ramathibodi and his successors went beyond their contemporaries in their role as legislator. With Burmese, Cambodian, and Javanese kings they shared a common belief in Dharma, the immutable natural law concerning the universe that was known to generations of Southeast Asians through versions of the *Dharmaśastra*, the Indian law text attributed to the sage Manu. While other kings simply rendered judicial decisions in accord with their knowledge of Dharma, the kings of Ayudhya issued real legislation, formal codes of civil and criminal law—law that by definition was mutable, temporal, and changeable. To Ramathibodi I are attributed various titles of Ayudhya's law, including the Law on Evidence, the Law on Offenses against the Government, the Law on Receiving Plaints, the Law on Abduction, the Law on Offenses against the People, the Law concerning Robbery, and the Law of Husband and Wife. Although the dates of most old Siamese laws are in dispute, we can be certain that portions of the Law on Abduction were in use at least by 1397, for portions of it were included in an inscription erected in Sukhothai in that year.

That the administration of the kingdom, and especially of the provinces, was not completely smooth in Ayudhya's first century is suggested by the fact that the early kings customarily appointed blood relatives to superintend the government of the most important provinces. As Ramathibodi's line usually sent young princes to rule Lopburi and Borommaracha's line sent them to Suphanburi, we may assume the persistence of some locally or regionally based power, represented in personal relationships with local elites and with freeman manpower. In this way, both political and economic power could be brought to bear on such critical events as the royal succession. Thus, while institutionalized, bureaucratic administration provided the kingdom with an enduring, effective strength at the center, the succession to the throne repeatedly went to the claimant who could best muster manpower and allies from the major provincial centers.

King Borommatrailokanat (1448–88) undertook a major attempt to strengthen the administrative institutions of the kingdom. He issued two important pieces of legislation, the Law of the Civil Hierarchy and the Law of the Military and Provincial Hierarchies, that took as their chief concerns hierarchy and functional differentiation. Building upon principles and practices long established in the kingdom, these laws in effect delineated an enormously complex hierarchical society in which the place and position of every individual was carefully specified. The laws assigned to everyone a number of units of *sakdi na*, literally "field power." Although at first this may have at least symbolically represented actual measured rice fields, expressed in terms of *rai* ($2\frac{1}{2}$ rai $= 1$ acre), by the fifteenth century it did not carry this meaning, for even Buddhist monks, housewives, slaves, and Chinese merchants were assigned sakdi na. Ordinary peasant freemen were given a sakdi na of 25, slaves were ranked 5, craftsmen employed in government service, 50, and petty officials, from 50 to 400. At the sakdi na rank of 400 began the bureaucratic nobility, the *khunnang*, whose members ranged from the heads of minor departments at a na of 400 to the highest ministers of state, who enjoyed a rank of 10,000. The upper levels of the nobility ranked with the junior members of the royal family, and most princes ranked above them, up to the heir-apparent, whose rank was 100,000. In the exhaustive laws of Trailok's reign, which read like a directory of the entire society, every possible position and status is ranked and assigned a designation of sakdi na, thus specifying everyone's relative position. Furthermore, sakdi na status was reinforced by the civil and criminal law. Fines and punishments were proportional to the status of the individual involved. If a peasant committed assault on a powerful official, it was much more serious than an assault on a slave, for the crime was an affront to the social order and to the king from whom the official derived his status. The paramount concern of royal authority, as expressed in the law, was to regulate natural human inequality for the sake of the proper functioning of the social order.

The other critical feature of King Trailok's hierarchy laws was the provision they made for the effective conduct of government administration. The laws divided the bureaucracy into two grand divisions, with the military under the minister of the Kalahom and the civilian under the minister of the Mahatthai. Each division was then broken down into numerous departments, sections, subsections, and the like, each with specified functional duties. On the civilian side, for example, there were four ministries under the Mahatthai—the capital, the palace, agriculture and the treasury. Each ministry was then subdivided into departments (*krom*) and smaller units, and it is important to note that separate sections responsible for foreign trade, foreign affairs, and the regulation of immigrant trading communities lay within the Phrakhlang, the Ministry of the Treasury. The effectiveness of this administration was to be severely tested in the last half of the fifteenth century, when Ayudhya became involved in almost constant warfare. The bureaucracy regularly provided the troops, supplies, and leadership that enabled the kingdom to endure.

The warfare that was to be so characteristic of King Trailok's forty-year reign was not the product of royal megalomania. Rather, it was the outcome of a process of development that had been maturing within the Tai world for more than a century. By the 1450s, major new Tai states had arisen in three separate regions, Ayudhya now being joined by a revived Kingdom of Lan Na and the new Kingdom of Lan Sang. In the course of their development, the rulers of each found it necessary and desirable to break out of the parochial, local focus of their predecessors and neighbors and redefine their state's existence on a new, broader, more international plane. Ayudhya now had two powerful rivals for the leadership of the Tai world.

The Renewal of Lan Na

The Chiang Mai chronicles of the fourteenth and fifteenth centuries are filled with warfare; it seems to have occurred almost as a feature of everyday life. The Kingdom of Lan Na was in conflict with nearly all its neighbors at one time or another, and all too often was even at war with itself. This makes Lan Na's success against Ayudhya's armies all the more surprising and raises the question of the sources of its enduring strength.

One aspect of Lan Na's strength is suggested by a chronicle's account of the foundation of a new city at Chiang Saen in 1328. The chronicle first relates how Chiang Saen's administrative boundaries set it apart from major principalities in all directions—Chiang Rai, Fang, Sat, Keng Tung, Chiang Hung, and Chiang Khong. It then enumerates the guard posts some distance from the city in every direction and goes on to discuss the müang's internal administration. The principality or, perhaps, province of which Chiang Saen was the capital was composed of ten districts, some of which are referred to as müang; each district comprised a certain number of thousands of na, or rice fields. Chiang Saen as a whole, including all its districts, had 32,000 rice fields (the name of the Kingdom of Lan Na translates as "One Million Rice Fields"). It is probable that, like the sakdi na of Ayudhya, the enumerated rice fields of Lan Na were notional rather than actual measures; but they do seem to have functioned as a useful device for apportioning revenue collections and measuring the relative strengths of components of the principalities and the kingdom.

The chronicle goes on to survey the central administration of the principality of Chiang Saen. It explains that there were twelve chiefs (*khun*) for administration, plus one for justice, one for the rice granaries, one for implements of war, two for the ruler's household, and one for service outside the city. There is nothing here to suggest that the governor of Chiang Saen (or his counterparts elsewhere) directly involved himself in the administration of the districts and towns of his principality. They seem to have retained their own leaders and rulers, though under the overall control of the rulers or governors of the major principalities. Probably in proportion to their rice-field assessment— their na—they had to provide men for labor and military service and render taxes on the produce of the land and water, the right to which was claimed by the ruler. Lan Na's strength lay in its ability to command the produce, the loyalty, and the manpower of hundreds of such semiautonomous districts through the agency of the principalities at the intermediate level. And because these principalities were of such critical importance to the fortunes of the kingdom, the kings in Chiang Mai laid great emphasis upon controlling them by means of personal relationships. They often sent their sons, brothers, close retainers, or at times an abdicated father to rule over the major principalities: Chiang Rai, Chiang Saen, Chiang Khong, Keng Tung, Sat, Fang, Lampang, and others captured in the course of warfare.

From the 1320s to the 1350s, King Mangrai's immediate successors appear to have had difficulty in pulling the principalities of the kingdom into a coherent whole. King Saen Phu (r. 1318–19, 1324–28) abdicated and went to govern Chiang Saen, leaving his son Kham Fu (1328–37) to reign in Chiang Mai. After his father's death in 1334, Kham Fu seems never to have been at rest. He ruled for a time in Chiang Saen and unsuccessfully attempted to get the ruler of the independent principality of Nan to eliminate the rival state of Phayao; his own attempt to capture independent Phrae failed.

Like his father, King Pha Yu (r. 1337–55) spent some years in charge of the government of Chiang Mai while Kham Fu was in Chiang Saen. Unlike his father, he devoted his reign to pious works.

It was only in the reign of King Kü Na (1355–85) that Lan Na's development as a kingdom seems to have regained some momentum, both politically and culturally. Kü Na is remembered as an accomplished and effective ruler who was remarkably well educated for a man of his day. He was thoroughly familiar with the classical Indic arts and sciences, including especially astrology and elephantry (for application in warfare), and took a strong interest in the establishment in Lan Na of a new, ascetic, scholarly sect of forest-dwelling Buddhist monks. In 1369, he invited the Venerable Sumana, a Sukhothai monk who had studied at Martaban in the Mon country, to establish his Singhalese Order in Lamphun. Kü Na built a new monastery for him in Chiang Mai, of which the monk became abbot in 1371 and where he remained until his death in 1389. The cultural importance of this act, and of the continuing patronage of Kü Na and his successors, cannot be underestimated. The Buddhist sect established in Lan Na by Sumana became the leading intellectual and cultural force in the kingdom over the next two or three centuries. Its members were responsible for many of the written texts that have survived from this period, and the monasteries they founded served culturally and religiously to influence generations of northern Tai. Coupled with the slowly increasing political preponderance of Chiang Mai, the cultural leadership exerted by the Singhalese sect encouraged the centralization of the kingdom and the development of a regional sense of identity as Tai Yuan among its population.

In the next two generations of Lan Na rulers, Chiang Mai's international involvements again became more intense, as also did its internal politics as the stakes of power grew. On the death of King Kü Na, his son Saen Müang Ma (r. 1385–1401) was elevated to the throne. Kü Na's younger brother, Maha Phrom, plotted with the governor of Lampang to seize the throne, but failed and fled to Ayudhya. He then managed to get King Borommaracha I of Ayudhya to send an expedition against Lan Na, which was repulsed. When later Maha Phrom disgraced himself at court, he returned to Lan Na and was sent to rule Chiang Rai, as he had before 1385. He apparently had a local following of clients and supporters that could not be ignored. Saen Müang Ma's reign also was marked by an unsuccessful campaign against Sukhothai in 1387 or 1388; and the king may have campaigned in the Tai Lü region, for it was there that his son and successor, Sam Fang Kaen (r. 1401–41) was born in 1389.

The young Sam Fang Kaen was raised to the throne despite the claims of an older (13-year-old) brother, who was sent to govern Chiang Rai. Perhaps taking over Maha Phrom's old supporters and calling on a now briefly independent Sukhothai for assistance, this older brother mounted an attempt to seize the throne. The conflict involved armies on both sides from all over the region, and in the end he was defeated and fled to Sukhothai. Next, in 1404, Lan Na had to meet a major challenge from Chinese Yunnan, whose governor sent armies against Chiang Saen in 1404 and 1405. By raising 300,000 (?) men from Chiang Mai, Chiang Saen, Fang, Chiang Khong, Thoeng, and Phayao, Lan Na repelled the invaders. Sam Fang Kaen seems to have spent most of the rest of his reign in peace, and he slowly strengthened his hold on the kingdom by posting his sons to the governments of the major principalities, including Chiang Saen, Phayao, Chiang Rai, and Fang.

The crisis that ended Sam Fang Kaen's reign in 1441 reveals something of the continuing institutional fragility of Lan Na. The king was overthrown by a minor palace official, Sam Dek Yoi, who surreptitiously brought the king's sixth son in from the provinces and forced the old king to abdicate and remove to exile in Sat. This son then was crowned King Tilokaracha (r. 1441–87), recalled subsequently as the greatest of the kings of Lan Na. It took nearly a decade for Tilok to establish his authority against other claimants to the throne, including the ambitious Sam Dek Yoi, who ultimately was advised by those whose aid he sought that he was not of princely blood and thus could not become king. (Lacking a rule of primogeniture, this was as close as the Lan Na people could get to establishing royal stability by blood!) Perhaps encouraged by this early success, Tilok now moved to seize Sat from his father; but this attack only provoked near civil war when the governor of Fang joined Sam Fang Kaen in resistance. Seeing an opportunity for intervention, Ayudhya then sent an expedition against Lan Na. After quickly subduing his enemies at home, King Tilok mounted a stout defense at Lamphun, only a few hours away from Chiang Mai, and repelled the Ayudhya armies. Finally, in 1443, the ruler of still independent Nan decided to challenge Tilok and inaugurated a period of warfare between the two states that came also to involve Phrae and Luang Prabang, at the conclusion of which Lan Na suzerainty over Nan was established by 1449.

By 1450, Tilok of Lan Na had secured his home territory and began to undertake military and political ventures farther afield. In that year he conducted a campaign against the Lü of Möng Yawng. In this campaign, as in those that were to follow against Luang Prabang (1454) and Chiang Hung (1455 and 1456), Tilok may have been trying to strengthen his reserves of manpower and draft animals for the major war against Ayudhya that clearly was coming. This war had been signaled earlier by Ayudhya's absorption of the old Kingdom of Sukhothai in 1438 and its attack as far as Lamphun in 1442. At issue were the small principalities on the northern fringe of the great Central Plain, as well as hegemony in the Tai world.

In 1451, Tilok had received at his court a prince of the Sukhothai line who had been sent by Ayudhya to govern Phitsanulok and subsequently considered himself betrayed by his overlords. The Lan Na army sent to regain the Sukhothai region for him in that year was defeated. After a long period of preparations, warfare was renewed in 1456 or 1457 when Trailok of Ayudhya sent an army to seize Phrae and Lampang; it was to continue for nearly three decades. Briefly, Ayudhya's initial thrusts in 1456 and/or 1457 were repulsed.

In 1459, Tilok swung to the offensive, besieging Phitsanulok. The Ayudhya forces apparently withstood this siege, for the northerners again attacked the same region the following year, this time with the assistance of the governor of Satchanalai. Tilok's attacks on both Phitsanulok and Kamphaengphet in 1460 failed, and he again returned to Chiang Mai empty-handed. The war continued, year by year. In 1462, old Sukhothai itself rebelled against Ayudhya and had to be suppressed by the main force of the Siamese army. Recognizing the need to maintain a strong military and political presence in the region at the northern end of the Central Plain, King Trailok of Ayudhya transferred his capital to Phitsanulok in 1463 and appointed his son Intharacha to act as regent in Ayudhya.

A touching and curious episode followed in 1464. In that year, Trailok constructed a new monastery just to the south of Phitsanulok. Having requested and been refused an alliance or truce with Tilok of Chiang Mai, he formally abdicated in favor of his son and underwent ordination there as a Buddhist monk. Tilok, as well as the kings of Luang Prabang and Mon Pegu, sent him the requisites of monkhood, but refused a subsequent request that the province of Satchanalai be restored to him in order to provide alms for his sustenance. For all his public piety, Trailok by no means had given up his designs against Lan Na. He sent a sorcerer-monk to Chiang Mai to act as a spy and attempt to undermine and weaken the northern state from within.

Neither was Tilok of Lan Na inactive. He, too, sent spies against Phitsanulok and Ayudhya, and he undertook further military campaigns against such Shan states as Lai Hka, Hsipaw, Pun, and Möng Nai— presumably in order to gain additional manpower for his armies. Meanwhile, the damages wrought by Trailok's sorcerer-spy began to have their effect. Among other things, Tilok's only son Bun Rüang was falsely accused of plotting rebellion and was executed.

Early in 1466, Ayudhya's ministers of state prevailed upon Trailok to leave the monkhood, resume his throne, and return to Ayudhya. Soon thereafter, Trailok sent a group of emissaries to Chiang Mai ostensibly to sue for peace but also to discover how his spy's projects were proceeding. In the course of this mission, one of the Ayudhya envoys tried to steal a gold vase from Tilok's palace, and Tilok also learned of the treachery of Ayudhya's sorcerer-spy. He had the sorcerer beaten to death and the envoys killed on their way back to Ayudhya. The wars, curiously, seem to have fallen into abatement. There were but two further engagements, the first in 1474, when Sukhothai attempted to seize Satchanalai and was repulsed, and again in 1486, when Ayudhya sent an army against Nan but failed to take the city. For the time being, the struggle between these major Tai powers was at an impasse.

Maha Chedi Luang, Chiang Mai.

For his part, King Tilokaracha of Chiang Mai seems to have spent the last decade of his reign preoccupied with more local concerns. Between 1475 and 1478, he had constructed the enormous Maha Chedi Luang, the great Buddhist spire that rose in the center of Chiang Mai. Soon thereafter, while Tilok was campaigning against the Shans, word arrived of a threat from a new source. A major Vietnamese invasion of Luang Prabang in 1478–79 now threatened Lan

Na's eastern outpost at Nan. Only with difficulty was the threat contained. Captives taken by the Lan Na forces were sent to the Chinese authorities in Yunnan, perhaps with the aim of eliciting Chinese assistance, military or diplomatic, against a renewal of Vietnamese activity in this area. Within the next year, the Chinese court sent two missions to Chiang Mai to request submission to China's tributary system, to which Tilok apparently yielded. Finally, in the mid-1480s, Lan Na became involved in warfare to the north when a group of Lawa people seized Möng Yawng and then fled to Chiang Hung. Tilok sent an army after them, which eventually succeeded in taking Chiang Hung, at least for a time. Not long thereafter, having overcome a conspiracy of some provincial dignitaries to seize the Lan Na throne for the governor of Lampang, King Tilokaracha died on May 24, 1487, after a reign of forty-six years. For all the inconclusiveness of his warfare against Ayudhya, the Kingdom of Lan Na now was stronger than ever before. More than any of his predecessors, Tilok had made it a power to reckon with, a state whose influence extended hundreds of miles in every direction.

Tilok's arch-rival Trailok of Ayudhya outlived him by only a year, dying at Phitsanulok in the course of 1488. The institutional strength that his legislation had given Ayudhya was in the long run to give his kingdom an advantage over Lan Na, but it was to be several generations before this would become apparent.

His only son having been executed for treason seventeen years earlier, Tilok was succeeded by his grandson, Yot Chiang Rai (r. 1487–95). This ruler proved so unpopular that his ministers deposed him and elevated to the throne his thirteen-year-old son, King Müang Kaeo (r. 1495–1526). There is little in the chronicles of this period to suggest that either of these kings was able to uphold the traditions of military and political strength of the best of their forebears. Müang Kaeo's state in particular was almost constantly involved in warfare with Ayudhya in the Sukhothai region from 1507 onwards, in which the Lan Na forces invariably were defeated. In 1515 Ayudhya even captured Lampang, but only carried away war booty and captives and failed for some years to follow up its advantage—perhaps because major efforts were made in the next two years to strengthen Chiang Mai's fortifications. That the chronicles here record substantial movements of Shan populations into the Lan Na region at this time may indicate that Lan Na was suffering from a manpower shortage caused by wartimes losses. The young king underwent full coronation only in 1520 at the age of thirty-eight; and it might appear that such political centralization as Lan Na may have achieved by this time was precarious at best. Yet Lan Na does seem to have been institutionally strong. The high-ranking officers of the court maintained a certain vitality in political and military affairs.

Military campaigns normally were conducted by such officers, who were rewarded with governorships or court posts when successful. It is surely significant that the chronicles record the construction of buildings for the conduct of official business in 1520–21, particularly the Khao Sanam Luang from whence the central administration was conducted.

Only at the end of his reign did King Müang Kaeo become actively involved in a major external adventure in Keng Tung, probably the most important of the Shan states. There the throne was disputed by two princes who called upon Hsenwi and Lan Na for assistance. In 1523, Müang Kaeo sent two armies, both of more than twenty thousand men, against Keng Tung, one by way of Chiang Saen and the other by way of Sat. Owing to what Müang Kaeo considered poor generalship the expedition was a disaster, and he had the culpable general executed.

In other ways, however, the reign of Müang Kaeo was a glorious time in the history of Lan Na. Of this period, the Pali-language chronicle, *Jinakalamali*, written at Chiang Mai shortly before his death, provides an eloquent witness. The chronicle expounds at great length upon the numerous works of Buddhist merit performed by King Müang Kaeo—the foundation of new monasteries, the copying of the Tipitaka, the casting of images of the Buddha, his lavish bestowal of alms—but stresses particularly his strong patronage of the strict Singhalese order of Buddhism, the same order introduced into the kingdom in the reign of Kü Na more than a century earlier. This was a policy of considerable religious and cultural importance, for with the backing of royal prestige it reaffirmed the dominance of a scholarly, textually oriented school of Buddhism whose informed, educated monks would long provide the society of Lan Na with vigorous intellectual leadership.

Upon his death early in 1526, King Müang Kaeo was succeeded by his younger brother, known as King Ket Chettharat (r. 1526–38, 1543–45). His accession marked the beginning of a rapid decline in the fortunes of Lan Na. After an undistinguished reign and an attempt on the part of some officials to depose him in 1535, King Ket antagonized his officials with his appointment of a new governor of Chiang Saen and was dethroned in 1538. His son, Chai (r. 1538–43) "did not reign in conformity with the ten royal precepts,"[7] and the leading officials had him executed and recalled his father to the throne. King Ket's assassination in 1545 may have been due to his religious policies, for it seems he attempted to require the reordination of one order of monks by the rituals of another order. Whatever its cause, his death marked the beginning of the end of independent Lan Na.

First, some leading Lan Na officials invited the ruler of Keng Tung to assume the throne of Lan Na; and when he proved reluctant, the Shan ruler of

Möng Nai was invited. Before he arrived, however, another group of officials from all the principalities met in Chiang Saen and decided to invite the ruler of Luang Prabang to reign. Amidst the confusion, the neglected Shan ruler of Hsenwi invaded and attacked Chiang Mai. Checked by a stout defense of the city, he retired to Lamphun and sent a delegation to the ruler of Ayudhya requesting assistance. Meanwhile, the leading officials converged on Chiang Mai from Chiang Saen and enthroned Queen Chiraprapha (r. 1545–46).

The ensuing events wrought much confusion and destruction. First, an army from Ayudhya marched into Chiang Mai and, having ostentatiously and perhaps pointedly carried out full funeral obsequies for the late King Ket, returned to Ayudhya, now considering Chiang Mai a vassal state. A few months later, the Shan ruler of Möng Nai besieged the city but failed to take it. Next, two high-ranking officials came from Luang Prabang "to protect Chiang Mai"; and a few days later an Ayudhya force arrived at nearby Lamphun to negotiate Chiang Mai's capitulation. Soon the city was closely besieged, but the seige was raised after heavy fighting and the Siamese force retreated, early in 1456.

For but a few months in that year, 1546, the people of Lan Na may have thought that the period of confusion was ending. Amidst impressive pomp and pageantry, the young son of the king of Luang Prabang was conducted through the kingdom from Chiang Saen to Chiang Mai and then was enthroned as King Setthathirat (r. 1546–51). But thirteen months later, on the death of his father, Setthathirat returned to rule in Luang Prabang. Though now part of a greater Lao kingdom, Lan Sang, and still ruled by the same king, Chiang Mai and all of Lan Na fell quickly into a state of civil war. Officials and principalities fought each other for the spoils of power. For four years chaos reigned. Unable to restore order, Setthathirat handed over the throne of Lan Na to his Chiang Mai queen, Thao Mae Ku (r. 1551); but she was no match for the querulous dignitaries of the kingdom, who deposed her and placed Prince Mekuti (r. 1551–64) of the Shan state of Nai on the throne.

By the mid-sixteenth century, Lan Na again had lost its focus and was the helpless prey of contending factions based in the principalities of the northern upland valleys.

The Rise of Lan Sang–Luang Prabang

The Kingdom of Lan Sang, with its capital at Luang Prabang, was briefly— with the inclusion of Lan Na in its dominions in the middle of the sixteenth century—a major power of the Indochinese peninsula. Two centuries earlier, the central valley of the Mekong had been politically as fragmented as the

Chaophraya valley or the Tai Yuan and Shan uplands had been in the thirteenth century. In the course of several centuries of exposure to Dvaravati and Angkorian civilization, a few small principalities had arisen in the area— Savā (Luang Prabang), Phuan (Siang Khwang), Viang Chan (Vientiane) or Sai Fong, Kham Koet, and a few others. Their growth was stimulated by an overland trade in metals and exotic forest produce as well as by the civilizing power of Buddhism and all that accompanied it. By the end of the thirteenth century, King Ramkhamhaeng briefly claimed hegemony over both Luang Prabang and Vientiane, but both regions soon went their own ways.

Lao legends tell of a son of the ruler of Luang Prabang who fled to exile in Cambodia, where his wife bore a son. This prince, Fa Ngum, later was provided with an army by the Khmer monarch and, beginning in 1351, fought his way up the Mekong valley, subduing first the Khammouane-Kham Keut region in central Laos, then Siang Khwang on the Plain of Jars, and finally Luang Prabang itself, where he was invited to ascend the throne of the Kingdom of Lan Sang in 1353. In the course of the ensuing decades, he expanded the state far afield— northwest to the frontiers of Chiang Hung, northeast into the Black Tai region west of the Black River, south through the Vientiane Plain to the Thakhek-Nakhon Phanom region, Savannakhet, and Tchepone, and apparently even west of the Mekong on the Khorat Plateau, perhaps as far south as Roi Et.

The internal constitution of the early Lan Sang state seems to have been highly decentralized. The local rulers of the various müang remained in place, enjoying a high degree of autonomy. Fa Ngum and his successors could demand some share of their revenues and claimed the use of their resources and manpower in time of war. In the short run, Luang Prabang maintained its control by exercise of its superior reserves of manpower and material, and of its leadership and prestige. The internal balance of power, however, was delicate, and even Fa Ngum himself was deposed by his own ministers in 1373 and sent into exile because of what they considered his excessive demands on the population through warfare and his disposition to requisition the wives and daughters of his subjects no less readily than he conscripted their men as soldiers.

Fa Ngum's only son, Un Hüan, is remembered as the "King of Three Hundred Thousand Tai" (Sam Saen Thai, r. 1373–1416), to recall the grand census taken at his direction in 1376, which enumerated 300,000 male Lao eligible for compulsory labor (and military) service each year, in addition to 400,000 non-Tai. That his long reign was relatively peaceful may be attributed in part to sound military organization that equitably shared the burdens of fighting and provisioning wars and in part to a wise policy that allied him through marriage to the ruling houses of Ayudhya, Chiang Hung, and Lan Na.

This policy forwarded the peaceful settlement of such disputes as arose with his more powerful neighbors.

After the death of Un Hüan, Lan Sang went into a long period of decline, with eight kings in twenty-two years and endemic political infighting in the capital. Finally, in 1442, the leading ministers invited the ruler of Vientiane, who was the son of Un Hüan by a queen from the Ayudhya ruling house, to ascend the throne as King Sainyachakkaphat Phaen Phaeo (r. 1442–79). Sainyachakkaphat was a worthy but undistinguished contemporary of kings Tilok of Ian Na and Trailok of Ayudhya, with whose reigns his almost exactly coincided. He appointed his six sons to administer some of the chief provinces of the kingdom, as Ayudhya had done in the fourteenth century and Lan Na continued to do. Such strength as he was able to build in his administration was sorely tested when Vietnam captured the Plain of Jars and then Luang Prabang itself in 1478. Humiliated, the king abdicated and fled. His younger brother, King Suvanna Banlang (r. 1479–86) was an energetic military leader who regrouped the confused and scattered Lao troops and went at their head to lead the recapture of Luang Prabang and the reconquest of the kingdom. The Vietnamese were sufficiently chastised to determine upon a course of good relations with Lan Sang that was to last for more than two centuries.

The reigns of Suvanna Banlang's three successors—La Saen Thai (r. 1486–96), Somphu (r. 1496–1501), and Visun (r. 1501–20)—were peaceful and constructive. They were noteworthy for their reestablishment of close relations with Ayudhya, including commercial relations across the Khorat Plateau. In Visun's reign, the image of the Buddha that gave Luang Prabang its name was brought to the capital from Vientiane in 1512. With the Prabang image seems to have been associated an attempt on the part of Lao rulers and Buddhist monks to define Lao identity in terms that distinguished the Lao from their Tai cousins to the west and southwest. This phenomenon attested as much to growing Ayudhya influence in the middle Mekong valley as to increasing Lao determination to maintain their independence.

The florescence of Lan Sang in the sixteenth century is associated mainly with the reigns of kings Phothisarat (r. 1520–47) and Setthathirat (r. 1547–71), the son and grandson of King Visun. Where Visun and his predecessors had ruled in peace, avoiding conflict with the kingdom's (admittedly distracted) neighbors and quietly amassing strength and wealth which they expended in public works and the adornment of their capital, Phothisarat and his son saw themselves as the equals of their neighbors and their rivals in might, splendor, and Buddhist piety. In 1527, Phothisarat signaled his determination to break with local traditions and adhere instead to the more universalistic values of Buddhism. He proscribed animistic and brahmanical observances and ordered the destruction of the religious buildings around which they centered. In the same spirit, he chose to reside at Vientiane for much of his reign rather than at Luang Prabang. In Vientiane, better served by routes of communication, he had not only more convenient access to routes linking Laos to Vietnam, Cambodia, Ayudhya, and Lan Na but also a more central location within the expanding Lao world. The center of population gravity had been moving slowly southward into the more level and fertile regions of the central Mekong valley over the preceding several centuries. With the collapse of the Angkorian monarchy in the previous century, the Lao had no rivals in extending their sway over the Khorat Plateau and down the Mekong valley.

Tradition credits King Phothisarat with raising the Great Reliquary of That Phanom to a central position in the religious life of the Mekong region south of Vientiane, and his bestowal of land and slave endowments to that shrine in 1539 reflects his power and interests in the region. Centered on Nakhon Phanom and That Phanom were trade routes directed eastward across the mountain chain to the coast of central Vietnam and southward to the new capital of a reviving Cambodian kingdom at Phnom Penh.

Affirming his major-state aspirations for Lan Sang, Phothisarat established a wide network of diplomatic relations extending both into the traditional Tai world of interior mainland Southeast Asia and outward to the coastal powers that for several centuries had dominated the region. Early in his reign he accepted a daughter of King Müang Kaeo of Lan Na as his chief queen; he may also have received consorts from Ayudhya and Phnom Penh. He intervened in the internal politics of semi-independent Siang Khwang and was the recipient of gifts or tribute from Keng Tung, Hsenwi, and Chiang Hung. Farther afield, he established diplomatic contact with the Vietnamese court at Hanoi, the Chinese authorities in Yunnan, and even the shadowy court of Champa in southern Vietnam.

But the main focus of Lan Sang's interest and ambitions now lay in the west and southwest, where Phothisan and Setthathirat saw Lan Na and Ayudhya as Lan Sang's chief rivals for influence in the Tai world. Lan Sang may have been involved in skirmishes with Ayudhya troops in the 1530s and 1540s, but it was to Chiang Mai that Phothisan's attention suddenly was directed by events in 1546, already related above. An invitation ensued— probably organized by Phothisan himself—for his son to assume the throne of Lan Na. Scarcely had Setthathirat been installed there when his father died. Leaving his Chiang Mai queen behind to cope as best she could with numerous challenges to the throne of Lan Na, Setthathirat hurried back to Luang Prabang, where groups of officials were backing one or another of his brothers for succession to the Lan Sang throne. Setthathirat, born in 1534, was still a boy when in 1548 he subdued his brothers' challenges and took the throne of Lan Sang in Luang Prabang. Still nominally the king of Lan Na, his royal authority now was threatened not only by usurpations in Chiang Mai but also by international warfare that soon engulfed the entire region.

Universal Monarchs, Universal Warfare

From the death of King Trailok in 1488, the Kingdom of Ayudhya had continued its steady development as a power in the Tai world. Under Trailok's sons Intharacha (r. 1488–91) and Ramathibodi II (r. 1491–1529), Ayudhya prospered. By the 1460s, the kingdom already had established a commanding presence on the Malay Peninsula and on the coast of the Bay of Bengal, and so was in a position to profit from a major upsurge in international trade that followed the foundation of Malay Malacca as an important international entrepôt at the beginning of the century. Through much of the century, the rulers of Malacca acknowledged the suzerainty of the kings of Ayudhya, and Trailok included Malacca in a list of his major dependencies in mid-century. Whatever the actual content of their relationship, which may have been conducted through Nakhon Si Thammarat, it served primarily to structure commercial, economic contact. Ayudhya was a major supplier of rice to Malacca and from Malacca imported both luxury goods and Indian cotton cloth. Ayudhya's seizure of control of Tenasserim (by the 1460s) and Tavoy (1488) seems to have been intended primarily to secure direct access, rather than indirect access through Malacca, to the international trade of the Bay of Bengal and the Indian Ocean.

It was customary throughout Asia at this time for kings to have monopolistic controls over international trade. No visiting trader might sell goods until the king had bought what he required at his own price, and none might buy staple trade commodities until the king's supply, usually collected from his subjects in kind in lieu of taxes, was exhausted at the king's asking price. This arrangement worked naturally to strengthen the crown vis-à-vis the ruling elite, the capital at the expense of the rural producers, and states with easy access to the sea more than landlocked states like Lan Na and Lan Sang.

The effects of economic development, spurred by dramatic increases in international trade in the fifteenth and sixteenth centuries, on the rise of Ayudhya cannot be understated. They worked at times in an almost circular fashion. The more the king gained wealth through trade, the better able he was to overawe or overcome both domestic and neighboring rivals and join their territory to his, thereby further improving his ability to trade. There are obvious signs of such royal wealth in King Ramathibodi's program of public

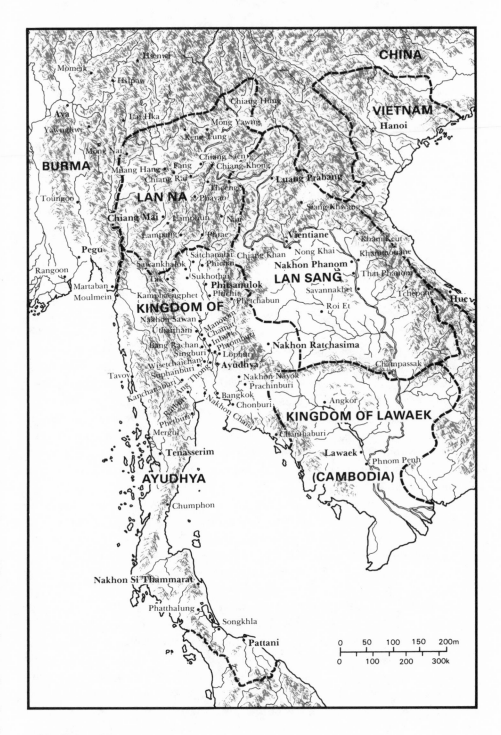

The Tai world, ca. 1540.

and pious works. Through the 1490s, he constructed several important religious monuments in his capital, and between 1500 and 1503, be ordered to be cast the largest standing metal image of the Buddha ever known, sixteen meters high and covered with nearly 173 kilograms of gold. At the same time, aided by his increasing wealth, the king took steps to strengthen his army, undertaking a grand registration and enrollment of adult males for compulsory military service and reorganizing the procedures and institutions for controlling military manpower. Finally, for the guidance of his armies, a "Treatise on Victorious Warfare" was compiled, outlining the causes of war, military strategy, and martial arts and tactics. The versified text is written in such a manner as to suggest that military accomplishments had become accepted as worthy of a man of culture.

When the Portuguese captured Malacca in 1511, they immediately sent a mission to Ayudhya, in part out of political concern, as they believed Malacca to be a Siamese vassal, and in part to assure the continuation of Malacca's immense maritime commerce, a significant part of which consisted of Siamese rice. Duarte Fernandes, the first Portuguese envoy to visit Siam, arrived rather modestly on a Chinese junk, but was well received and sent back with lavish presents for the king of Portugal. Later in the same year, another Portuguese mission arrived in Ayudhya, this time with a commissioner charged to gather commercial intelligence; and in 1518 a third mission confirmed the peace pact concluded in 1511. In return for granting the Portuguese the rights of residence and religious liberty in Siam and special commercial privileges, the Siamese were assured of Portuguese supplies of guns and ammunition (and soon recruited Portuguese mercenaries to assist in their use and ultimately their manufacture).

At least in the short run, the arrival of the Portuguese does not appear to have had much material affect upon Ayudhya. The commercial relationship simply replaced Ayudhya's earlier dealings with Malay Malacca; and though Siamese international commerce must have kept up with the rapid growth in seaborne trade that followed, doubling between about 1500 and 1560, their success owed as much to new trading connections with the Muslim states (like Patani, Acheh, and Bantam) organized in competition with Portuguese Malacca as it did to the treaty relationship with the Portuguese. The tarnishing barrels of hundreds of old cannon in Bangkok and Nakhon Si Thammarat perhaps attest to a significant innovation introduced by the Portuguese that worked to "modernize" warfare. However, the Portuguese also traded in guns and ammunition with Ayudhya's major rivals, thus somewhat neutralizing this innovation. In any case, it has been argued that firearms already were in the process of development in the region at this time, owing to imports through the Arab and Chinese trade.

It would be more productive to see the changing scene of sixteenth-century mainland Southeast Asia as evolving out of a number of interrelated developments, in which the Portuguese played one, but not the only, part. The critical elements of this situation were the interrelated economic and political developments, sketched above, that worked generally to the advantage of the region's coastal kingdoms and hastened their centralization. These developments in turn were paralleled by the slow growth of social and cultural cohesion as what we might call "capital cultures" assumed their unique expression in language, literature, and the public rituals of sacral life. Here again, the wealth of the coastal kingdoms accelerated the leadership of the port-city capital as the kingdom's elite were exposed to cosmopolitan cultures and more self-consciously identified with their own culture. As communications developed further, spurred by increasing commerce, the culture of the urban elite could begin to seep out over the countryside. In Ayudhya's case, the style, tastes, and values of the capital, which had been distinctively defined out of that region's culturally mixed Mon, Khmer, and Tai background, began to take their characteristically "Siamese" form, distinct from the cultures of the Lan Na "Tai Yuan" or the Lan Sang "Lao.."

King Ramathibodi had direct political concerns that challenged him much more than the Portuguese ever were to do. The Kingdom of Lan Na renewed the previous century's wars by invading the Sukhothai region in 1507. Ayudhya responded by moving back to the offensive, capturing Phrae in 1508 and even Lampang, only eighty kilometers from Chiang Mai, in 1515. Ayudhya did not press its advantage after its successes in the north in that campaign. For the remainder of his reign, Ramathibodi adopted a defensive policy in the north, appointing his eldest son, his heir-apparent or viceroy (uparat), to govern Phitsanulok in 1526. That same viceroy, No Phutthangkun, succeeded to the throne in Ayudhya as King Borommaracha IV in 1529. He was king only long enough to reaffirm his father's policies by sending ambassadors to negotiate a peace treaty with Lan Na before dying of smallpox in 1533.

Borommaracha's five-year-old son Prince Ratsada held the throne for only five months before his father's half-brother Chairacha had him put to death and ascended the throne early in 1534.

King Chairacha (r. 1534–47), for all his questionable usurpation of the throne, was long remembered as a good and wise king. He began his reign with public works intended to facilitate seaborne trade, as his father had done, by improving the Chaophraya River channel in the area of present-day Bangkok. Also like his father, he engaged 120 Portuguese mercenaries to act as his bodyguard and instruct his army in the use of firearms. With his improved army, he soon came into conflict with both Burma and Lan Na, both of which episodes became part of the long prologue to the warfare that soon devastated all the Tai world.

As we have seen, old Burma had fallen apart on the collapse of Pagân at the end of the thirteenth century. The kingdom erected in the Ava region by the three Shan brothers in the 1290s rapidly lost whatever Shan or Tai character it had and, with it, its sway over the Shan principalities to the east. Meanwhile, the Mon kingdom centered on Pegu on the seacoast gained independence and the prosperity that can come with international trade. Gradually a new and aggressively Burman state arose at Toungoo, some distance up the Sittang River from the sea, sufficiently distant from both Ava and Pegu to be secure. For some centuries, the Shans of the eastern uplands went their own way, and for much of this period Hsipaw, Mohnyin, Yawnghwe, Momeik, and Mogaung, to list but a few states, were fully independent. In G. E. Harvey's memorable phrase, "Upper Burma was a bedlam of snarling Shan states" by the early sixteenth century.[8] In the 1540s, Shan power in Ava revived with the accession to the throne of the ruler of Hsipaw and the active participation of other Shan chiefs. But this coalition of Shans rapidly dissolved into warfare, and Ava was left inviting prey for Burman armies by 1555.

Through this period, Toungoo survived and modestly prospered mainly because it was out of the way of the major warfare that embroiled Pegu and Ava; it quietly received group after group of Burman immigrants from the north. As late as the 1490s the ruler of Toungoo was recognized, even confirmed in office, by both Ava and Pegu, as well as by Lan Na and by the Karen peoples who bordered him to the east. His armed strength was sufficient to elicit bids for alliance from all his neighbors, and he deftly manipulated this situation to his advantage. King Tabinshwehti (r. 1531–50) of Toungoo began early in his career to capitalize on his strengths and his rivals' weakness. He turned his attention first to the south, extinguishing the ancient Mon kingdom of Pegu in the late 1530s and acquiring both its wealth and its abundant manpower.

In the course of his campaigns against Pegu, Tabinshwehti occupied a müang, Chiang Krai, in the Moulmein district that was tributary to Siam, whereupon King Chairacha of Ayudhya assembled an army and drove the Burmese force from the region in late 1538. There was no significant immediate reaction from the Burmese, and Chairacha may have thought that his expedition had served its purpose, to warn both potential rivals and restive friends and provinces that he would not fail to deal quickly and effectively with any challenge to his authority.

But perhaps Chairacha also was concerned by the ominous rise of major powers on both his flanks. Quite apart from the union of Pegu and Toungoo under Tabinshwehti, Lan Na was disintegrating and threatening to fall under the control either of Shans loosely allied with Ava or of Lan Sang. Thus, in mid-1545, the king led an army all the way north to Chiang Mai, where they invested the city but failed to take it and, suffering heavy losses, had to retreat back to Ayudhya. Barely had he returned to the capital when, responding either to news of Lan Sang reinforcements for Setthathirat or to an invitation from one party or another, Chairacha immediately assembled another army and headed back to Chiang Mai. Early in 1547, they took Lamphun and then advanced on Chiang Mai; but again the army had to withdraw without taking the city. Almost immediately upon his return to Ayudhya, the king died.

In the months that followed, Ayudhya seemed to be heading for the identical crisis through which both Lan Na and Lan Sang were passing at that same moment, an internecine succession conflict embroiling most of the political elite in the capital. Chairacha had left two sons, both born of a royal concubine, Lady Si Sudachan, and also a younger half-brother, Prince Thianracha. The elder of the two sons, Prince Yot Fa (r. 1547–48), then eleven years old, was placed on the throne with his mother as regent, while his uncle, Prince Thianracha, sought refuge from the political storms by being ordained a Buddhist monk. The queen regent, meanwhile, pursued an infatuation with a minor palace official by whom she had a daughter, and she resolved to raise him to the throne. Nobles who dared voice their disapproval of these proceedings were executed. The queen regent finally had young King Yot Fa poisoned in June 1548, and her lover, now titled Khun Worawongsa, was placed on the throne. He lasted only six weeks. A conspiracy of the leading nobles assassinated the new king and recalled from a monastery Prince Thianracha, who became king of Ayudhya in late July 1548, taking the title *Chakkraphat* from the Pali-Sanskrit designation of the wheel-turning, universal monarch, a king whose righteousness and might makes all the world revolve around him.

Within months the Burmese had resolved upon warfare with an Ayudhya they saw engulfed in turmoil. Gathering an enormous army that may have numbered several hundred thousand troops, King Tabinshwehti led them south to Martaban and then, crossing the mountain chain through the Three Pagodas Pass, swept through Kanchanaburi and Suphanburi to invest the capital. As if this were not enough, the Khmer king of Lawaek (near Phnom Penh in Cambodia) took advantage of the confusion to attack Siam on its eastern flank in Prachinburi province, raiding for pillage and prisoners while Ayudhya was distracted. King Chakkraphat successfully withstood this brief war, which lasted only for the first few months of 1549. Forays sent out from the besieged city, led on one occasion by Queen Suriyothai and her daughter, shook the Burmese will, which further sagged on news that Ayudhya's northern army was about to arrive from Phitsanulok. Though early in his retreat

Tabinshwehti's forces managed to capture the Siamese king's eldest son, Prince Ramesuan, and his son-in-law, Maha Thammaracha, the viceroy of Phitsanulok, the prisoners were restored on condition that the Burmese forces be allowed to continue their withdrawal unmolested.

Chakkraphat gained no false security from this easy success and in the next few years set about to prepare for the warfare the Burmese soon would resume. First, early in 1550, the old earthen walls of the capital were demolished and replaced with stout brick ramparts. In succeeding years, he improved his naval fleet, fortified a number of strategically located provincial towns, reorganized military commands, scrutinized the registers of men eligible for military service, and undertook a campaign to add to the army's reserves of elephants, which served as the armored tanks of premodern Southeast Asian armies. In 1555–56, a strong land and naval expedition was sent against Lawaek to ensure Khmer submission on Ayudhya's vulnerable eastern flank.

A long Burmese delay in following up their 1549 attack on Ayudhya was caused, not by growing Siamese strength, but by internal confusion. On his return from Ayudhya, Tabinshwehti, given over to drink and dissipation, grew more arbitrary and erratic in his rule and finally was killed by his Mon courtiers. His brother-in-law, Bayinnaung (r. 1551–81), succeeded him only with difficulty, having first to put down numerous rebellions among his kinsmen and Mon partisans. Bayinnaung proved a better organized and more aggressive general than Tabinshwehti had been, and the disciplined mass army he sent against Ava in 1555 had little difficulty in subduing upper Burma. He followed that campaign with one against the Shan states in the late 1550s and even received Hsenwi and Keng Tung as vassals. These conquests added more than glory to his throne. In addition to valuable tribute and forced levies of manpower, he also gained a strategic position across the northern flank of the Tai world that tightened his pressure against Ayudhya.

Once Setthathirat left Chiang Mai to assume the throne of Lan Sang in 1548, Lan Sang, caught in the throes of civil turmoil, was highly vulnerable. Rival claimants contested the throne, and a Lan Sang expedition sent to restore order and reassert Setthathirat's claims in 1550 failed. When Setthathirat had reluctantly decided to hand over Lan Na to his Chiang Mai queen in 1551, the notables of the kingdom instead installed Prince Mekuti (r. 1551–64), a prince of the Shan state of Möng Nai and a direct descendant of King Mangrai. The new king's brothers, ruling in Nai, attempted with the aid of the principality of Fang to seize Lan Na's Mekong region and by 1555 had taken Chiang Rai and Chiang Saen, though opposed by both Mekuti and Lan Sang. When Nai was invaded by Bayinnaung's Burmese armies in 1557, Mekuti was not at first inclined to listen to his brothers' cry for help. Bayinnaung, however, could not resist the opportunity presented him by Chiang Mai's helplessness. Taking Nai, he quickly advanced on Chiang Mai and took the city without fighting on April 2, 1558. Mekuti was retained on the Lan Na throne as a Burmese vassal, watched by a military garrison.

An attempt by Setthathirat to restore his position in 1558–59 was cut short on the king's realization that Lan Sang now faced not a weak Lan Na but a powerful Burmese presence on its western frontier. Such autonomy as Lan Na retained eroded rapidly, first when Mekuti failed in a plot to displace the Burmese and was deposed in 1564, and then when Lan Na became simply a military base for the forward operations of the Burmese army against Ayudhya and Lan Sang. With the end of King Mangrai's dynasty in 1558–64, an era in northern Tai history was concluded. From this Lan Na would never recover.

Given a solid position now to the north of Ayudhya, Bayinnaung could return to the unconcluded war with King Chakkraphat. Both Ayudhya and Lan Sang could recognize the increased danger posed by the Burmese capture of Lan Na. Their reactions, however, were more defensive than offensive. Realizing his capital in Luang Prabang was in an exposed position, distant from the greater resources and more convenient communications of the central Mekong region, King Setthathirat transferred his capital to Vientiane in 1563 and quickly set about fortifying it with brick walls. He also proposed a marriage alliance with Ayudhya by requesting the hand of Princess Thepkasatri, the daughter of King Chakkraphat by Queen Suriyothai who had donned soldier's garb to ride out against Burmese forces encircling Ayudhya in 1549. Setthathirat deserved better treatment than Chakkraphat gave him. On the pretext that Thepkasatri was ill, the Siamese attempted to fob off on Setthathirat her younger sister, Princess Kaeo Fa.

In the midst of these delicate interchanges, the Burmese suddenly invaded Siam again, this time crossing the mountains to enter the kingdom in the vicinity of Tak, gaining a position easily reinforced down the Ping River from Chiang Mai. Bayinnaung's troops quickly captured the northern cities of the kingdom with little effort and, more important, seem to have gained an influential supporter in the Siamese camp in the person of Maha Thammaracha, the viceroy or governor of Phitsanulok. Thammaracha was high born and well connected. His mother was a relative of King Chairacha and his father a descendant of the kings of Sukhothai. As an officer of the palace guard, he had led the conspiracy that had placed Chakkraphat on the throne in 1548 and had been rewarded by being given the new king's eldest daughter in marriage and a semiroyal title as virtual viceroy of the northern provinces, based in Phitsanulok. Given his Sukhothai heritage and perhaps still unfulfilled ambitions, one wonders at his remarkable propensity for falling into Burmese hands—first in the 1549 attack and now in 1564. Having suddenly lost his northern provinces to the Burmese and faced with a vastly superior force, King Chakkraphat had meekly to capitulate to Bayinnaung's demands that he swear royal friendship and deliver up his son Ramesuan as a hostage.

However much he may have disdained King Setthathirat's request for Princess Thepkasatri the previous year, Chakkraphat now yielded and prepared to send her off to Vientiane with a large and opulent retinue. Maha Thammaracha of Phitsanulok moved quickly to sabotage what could develop into a close alliance. He sent word to the Burmese of the princess's route, and a small Burmese force ambushed her party in Phetchabun province and spirited her away to Burma. Setthathirat, humiliated and furious, sent an expedition against Phitsanulok, encouraged by Chakkraphat's growing impatience with his son-in-law and by a promise of assistance against Thammaracha. Maha Thammaracha, however, outsmarted them both, calling upon Burmese forces and bluffing both his rivals into withdrawing. The Burmese then sent an army against Vientiane. They besieged and then entered the city, only to find that Setthathirat had escaped to launch harrying sallies against Burmese patrols and supply lines in the following months until, in mid-1565, they gave up and withdrew to Burma.

The Tai world was now in disarray. King Chakkraphat of Ayudhya had been humiliated. He had been forced to capitulate to the Burmese, he had bungled a possible alliance with Lan Sang, and he had demonstrated his inability to control Maha Thammaracha of Phitsanulok. A party of Malay rebels from Patani even had managed to seize his palace for a short while in the aftermath of his defeat in 1564. At Chiang Mai, King Mekuti and the governor of Chiang Saen were implicated in a plot against the Burmese in the same year, and both were sent away to Burma. The new ruler, Queen Wisutthithewi (r. 1564–78), was a helpless tool in the hands of the Burmese, incapable even of defending her capital against the raids of Shan rebels in 1566 that threw the north into chaos and inaugurated a three-year famine. King Setthathirat of Lan Sang so far had lost least at the hands of the Burmese, but then he had much less to lose. Having at least survived the first Burmese capture of Vientiane without major damage, he now set about building up popular morale and political identity by sponsoring the construction or renovation of Buddhist shrines—in particular erecting the massive That Luang spire in Vientiane and renovating the ancient That Phanom monument south of Nakhon Phanom.

In an effort to try to pull his kingdom together in the face of the Burmese threat, King Chakkraphat in 1568 took advantage of Maha Thammaracha's absence in Burma to attempt to regain his northern provinces. He took

Phitsanulok, but failed to gain Kamphaengphet and fell back on his capital. Finally, at the end of 1568, the Burmese mounted their final assault on Ayudhya. With an enormous army swelled by numerous Mon, Shan, Lü, Lao, and Lan Na levies, King Bayinnaung swept down upon Ayudhya via Tak and Kamphaengphet, joined now by Maha Thammaracha's forces from the northern provinces. The king's efforts to rally the capital's defense were met with a certain lack of enthusiasm for, or confidence in, the royal leadership. The king

> had the troops of all the outer cities driven into the Capital, but they only received into the Capital about a fraction of those in the four districts close to the Capital. Those who did not come in to the Capital went out to live in the forests in exceedingly great numbers. In addition, none of the troops of the minor cities entered the Capital, but instead went out to live in the forests for the most part; only the rulers of the cities and their personal troops entered the Capital.[9]

King Chakkraphat, now old and disheartened, fell ill and died late in January 1569 and was succeeded by his son Mahin. As the Burmese drew a tight siege ring around the city, King Mahin showed himself an ineffective leader who passively left the city's defense to his ministers. The months of the dry season passed slowly as the two sides shelled each other. The Burmese first dug trenches to approach the river moat around the city and then started to construct causeways across the river itself. With effective leadership and determined resistance, the Siamese might have held out for another year. In the end, a party of Burmese gained entrance to the city by a ruse, helped by treachery within the Siamese ranks, and the city fell on August 8, 1569. Bayinnaung then installed the obsequious Maha Thammaracha as vassal king of Ayudhya and set off for Pegu with the hapless Mahin, who died on route.

Of Bayinnaung's major Tai rivals, now only Setthathirat remained in power. On an appeal from King Mahin in February 1569, Lan Sang had sent an army to relieve Ayudhya, but these troops were defeated in the Pa Sak valley of Phetchabun before they ever reached Ayudhya. Bayinnaung then sent an expedition against Vientiane late that year, but, again, though they briefly occupied the city, Setthathirat escaped and directed a guerrilla warfare against them that provoked their retreat in April 1570. Setthathirat's active role in the international politics of the Tai world, from his involvement with Chiang Mai at the beginning of his reign to his intervention in the warfare between Burma and Ayudhya, had placed heavy demands on the resources and energies of the Lao kingdom. Moreover, the move of the capital of Lan Sang from Luang Prabang to Vientiane may have provoked some resentment on the part of local and regional leaders in the central Mekong valley. One of these, the ruler of

Nakhon Phanom, in 1570 lured Setthathirat into a military campaign against the mountain peoples of extreme southern Laos, in the course of which the king simply disappeared. Virtual civil war ensued over the succession to the throne, which was concluded by yet another Burmese invasion of Vientiane. This time, the Burmese captured both the city and its rulers in 1574; and both the self-crowned king and Setthathirat's infant heir were led off to captivity in Burma. Bayinnaung of Pegu now held sway from Arakan and Manipur to the frontiers of Vietnam. Where there had been three kings all styling themselves "Universal Monarch" in 1548 (both Chakkraphat in Ayudhya and Setthathirat in Lan Na and Lan Sang included such titulature in their regnal names), only one now remained. Bayinnaung had succeeded where they had failed in giving reality to the unity of the Tai world.

Bayinnaung's imperial unity was not one that the Siamese, Lao, Tai Yuan, or Shans could readily accept, for it ran counter to the sense of distinctive identity that had been developing in the Tai kingdoms through the previous two centuries. Where Chakkraphat and Setthathirat had striven for moral leadership over their peoples, expressed through the civic rituals of Buddhism, and had sought to create orderly institutions for the regulation of the peaceful life, Bayinnaung instituted only the rough and ready order of command and obedience, brought by men the Tai saw as uncouth foreign soldiers. Through decades of warfare they had wrought enormous distress and destruction. The Ayudhya chronicles contain many vivid descriptions of the bitter glory of war:

> The King of Pegu moved his companies of brave soldiers out to take up positions in the rice-fields about four kilometers away from, and directly in front of, the army of King Chakkraphat, and halted his royal elephant to wait for an auspicious moment. Then he ordered the cavalrymen to shake their tasselled lances up and down enticingly and the footsoldiers to caper in front of the enemy. The soldiers ... danced and shouted in a great tumult, while those carrying sword and shield, or a sword in each hand, wheeled back and forth with mocking gesticulations. At that moment the King of Pegu looked up into the sky and saw that the sun was unobscured by cloud or mist. Then a king of vultures flew out in front of the army. When the King [of Pegu] saw such a royally auspicious omen, he had the victory gongs, the conch shell trumpets, and the drums of Indra sounded together and he commanded that the soldiers be driven in to attack the army of King Chakkraphat. King Chakkraphat ordered that his army be divided into two flanks. The companies of soldiers of both sides, some shouting excitedly, advanced and met in battle, striking, slashing, stabbing, fighting, and shooting their guns in volleys so that smoke filled the air. Soldiers of both sides, some dead, some wounded, were rolled and scattered across the rice-fields in great numbers.[10]

Great were the casualties and the loss of property and livelihood, and burdensome were the exactions of desperate defenders and assertive conquerors alike. Many—like those who fled to the mountains and forests when they knew war was coming or like Maha Thammaracha who bent with the winds—set for themselves the minimal strategy of doing whatever was necessary in order to survive.

Why the relatively easy success of Bayinnaung's arms? Why the swift collapse of Tai institutions and states that had been developing over two centuries and more?

For all the institution building of generations of Tai rulers, the kings of the mid-sixteenth century still founded—and lost—their power on the pyramiding of personal relationships. At every critical juncture in the history of this period, there were divisions within the ruling elite of the Tai state that sapped its strength. Neither Ayudhya nor Lan Na nor Lan Sang had managed yet to encourage the secure formation of overarching loyalties to monarch and state that could transcend the personal ties around which cliques and factions formed—the bonds of physical proximity or association in common endeavors cemented by marriage or kinship or mutual obligation. Kings ruled through the cohorts of friends and allies who had assisted their rise to the throne and on whom they had come to rely in the awful, exposed vulnerability of close-quarters warfare. Such, for example, was the relationship between Chakkraphat and Maha Thammaracha before 1564, or the relationship between Setthathirat and the general Phanya Saen Surin, who succeeded him as regent for his infant heir in 1571. Only their solidarity and successful leadership could long keep at bay alternative factions at the court and in provincial towns and cities.

What especially worked to the instability of court and dynastic politics in these early centuries of the great kingdoms was the perennial problem of the control of manpower. The predominant approach to this problem in Lan Na and Lan Sang still was the forging of personal relations between rulers and ruled. This structure of administration, however, meant that the Tai Yuan and Lao rulers were heavily dependent on local lords and rulers for the manpower that alone could defend their states against the Burmese. The Shans never resolved this problem; and the efforts of Mekuti and Setthathirat to subdue the local and regional lords as often as not were met with failure. The Ayudhya kings had begun, a century earlier under King Trailok, to institutionalize the control of manpower through the appointment of officials from the capital to take charge of the labor and military service owed by all freemen. This bureaucratic approach to the problem could work, however, only if the monarch could be absolutely sure of the loyalties of his chief officers. At the beginning of a dynasty's rule, this group would be composed of the new king's closest friends and allies. Over the course of several reigns, however, the close personal relations between a powerful, prosperous nobility and successive monarchs would naturally lose some of the personal quality with which they had begun, until finally one or more factions within the nobility would amass the manpower and resources necessary to depose the king and begin the cycle again with a new dynasty. This process of disintegration of the institutional ties within the Ayudhya state already had reached an advanced stage by the 1560s. Maha Thammaracha was virtually independent in Phitsanulok, and "only the rulers of the cities and their *personal* troops" or retainers came within Ayudhya's walls for the final defense of the city against the Burmese in 1569.[11]

5

The Empire of Ayudhya, 1569–1767

When Burmese armies captured and sacked all the major Tai capitals between 1558 and 1569, they left more than death and destruction in their wake as they withdrew westward to Pegu. Enormous areas were literally depopulated and quickly overgrown with vines and weeds. The engulfing of once bustling thoroughfares by vegetation mirrored a similar choking off of social and cultural institutions. The social will and self-confidence of Tai communities suffered, too, when the order and regularity of several centuries of common life suddenly came to an end and they were faced with an uncertain future. Within a few decades, however, the damage had been repaired through much of the Tai world, and the foundations were laid not only for a new golden age of power and prosperity but also for the social and cultural identities that would assume national form in the late nineteenth and twentieth centuries. The Tai world as a whole shared unequally in this development, however; especially in the seventeenth century, the institutional differences between the cosmopolitan polity centered on Ayudhya and the more parochial kingdoms and principalities of the interior of mainland Southeast Asia widened most rapidly.

Of all the institutions that needed to be fashioned out of the chaos of the late sixteenth century, an effective military organization was especially important in order to defeat the Burmese. The challenge Burma posed to Tai survival was sufficiently strong to spur quick action, yet also sufficiently distant and intermittent to allow Ayudhya and Lan Sang time to mobilize their scattered resources and develop new leadership. Two hundred years later, in the 1760s, the Tai world again was laid waste by Burmese armies, but it was not because Ayudhya and Lan Sang had stagnated in the interim. On the contrary, both states had developed and matured, and had experienced golden ages that subsequent generations would remember with pride. They did, however, develop differently. Uniquely in the Tai world, Ayudhya now underwent important social change that made its governing elite much more cosmopolitan than their Lao and Tai Yuan counterparts, that made of them, indeed, the nucleus for what ultimately would become a national elite.

Ayudhya, the Burmese, and the West

It is difficult to imagine that the history of Ayudhya would have been the same without King Naresuan, for he is one of those rare figures in Siamese history who, by virtue of dynamic leadership, personal courage, and decisive character, succeed in herculean tasks that have daunted others before them. The difference Naresuan made emerges all the more sharply because it was so long before he burst suddenly upon the scene of a discouraged Ayudhya that by then had suffered more than a decade of defeat and humiliation.

On the fall of Ayudhya in 1569, the Burmese installed Maha Thammaracha (r. 1569–90) on the throne, thoroughly looted the city, and led thousands of prisoners, both commoners and nobles, away to captivity in Burma. To control their new vassal state, they relied both on Thammaracha's obligation to them and on a small military garrison and the promise of swift retaliation should the Siamese prove truculent. Virtually defenseless now, Ayudhya was at the mercy of its neighbors. The Cambodians repeatedly took advantage of this situation and invaded Siam six times in the next two decades (1570, 1575, 1578, 1582 twice, and 1587), each time sweeping up war captives from the prosperous eastern and gulf provinces from Chanthaburi to Phetburi in order to populate their own territory. The Siamese dealt with these raids only with great difficulty, given their own scarce resources of manpower, arms, and draft animals. In addition, the Burmese had razed many of their fortifications. The depredations they suffered at the hands of the Khmer, however, did assist the Siamese in making a case to the Burmese for being allowed to improve their army and fortifications. In 1580 the walls of Ayudhya were dismantled yet again and rebuilt stronger than before.

From the flow of events, one senses that the Siamese passed a turning point around 1580. The rebuilding of the city walls hints at some change in their relationship with Burma. It demonstrated both a new determination to take effective charge of their own security and the ability to mobilize the enormous amounts of manpower and supplies that the task required. In the following year, the court was unnerved by an enigmatic popular rebellion led by a self-proclaimed holy man in the countryside between Ayudhya and Lopburi, in which the minister of civil affairs (the Mahatthai) was slain. The rebellion was quelled almost by chance when a "foreigner"—perhaps an Indian or Portuguese—shot its leader and his followers dispersed. A few months later, the Siamese were disgraced by the loss of Phetburi to yet another Cambodian invasion. In the midst of the confusion, Naresuan began to assert the leadership the kingdom had lacked for two decades.

Naresuan, born in 1555, was the son of King Maha Thammaracha by his chief queen, who was the daughter of King Chakkraphat. He had been taken off to Burma as a hostage for his father's good behavior in 1564; he returned home in 1571 only when his sister was presented to King Bayinnaung. Though Naresuan was then only sixteen years old, his father sent him north to take charge of the Phitsanulok region, thereby maintaining the Sukhothai line's traditional claim on the manpower of that region. At the same time, Naresuan was officially designated *uparat*, heir-presumptive to the throne of Ayudhya. Over the next decade, he matured to power and demonstrated his great military capabilities in several actions against Cambodia. In the midst of Ayudhya's difficulties in 1581–82, the young prince was sent to Pegu to represent his father (now sixty-six years old) in paying homage to King Nandabayin, who had succeeded Bayinnaung at the end of 1581. There he must have seen at first hand the factionalism and jockeying for power that soon threatened to shake the powerful Burmese Empire apart. Legend has it that, in the course of that visit, Naresuan participated with his troops in a Burmese expedition against a Shan state and succeeded in taking a city after the Burmese crown prince and another prince had failed to do so. He thereby gained the jealous enmity of the crown prince, and the Ayudhya chronicles' accounts of the Thai-Burmese conflict that followed are enlivened by the personal rivalry and animosity between the two men.

Soon, relations between Pegu and Ayudhya worsened. In 1583, reports reached Naresuan that the Burmese were constructing a road toward Ayudhya; and in the following year, Naresuan was summoned to assist Nandabayin in a campaign against a rival prince in Ava. Naresuan complied and marched with his troops from Phitsanulok to the Mon region of the lower Salween River. There he was informed that the Burmese planned to ambush and kill him. After rounding up captives in the region, he marched back to Phitsanulok and then moved down river to Ayudhya, bringing with him considerable numbers of men to bolster the defenses of the capital. Naresuan now clearly was in defiance of the Burmese court. When a small force sent to punish him early in 1585 was easily repulsed, the Burmese sent vast expeditions against Ayudhya in 1585–86 and 1586–87, but on both occasions Naresuan was able to withstand them. In the latter case, he also dealt successfully with a small Cambodian attack. Following the death of Maha Thammaracha in June 1590, Naresuan formally became king of Ayudhya, perhaps appointing his younger brother Ekathotsarot as his junior coruler; soon thereafter the Burmese resumed their attacks.

Annual expeditions culminated in a major Burmese offensive at the end of

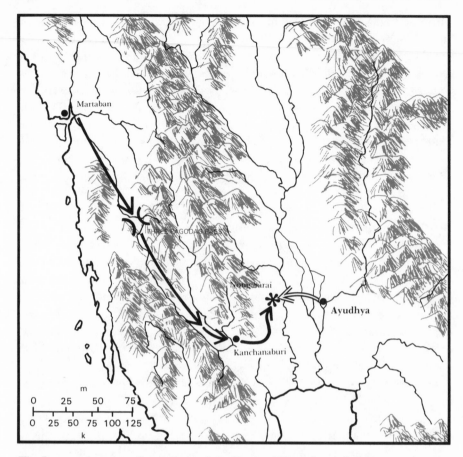

The Burmese invasion of 1592–93 and the Battle of Nong Sarai. Solid arrows denote movement of Burmese troops; open arrows, the movement of Siamese troops.

1592. Led by the crown prince, Naresuan's old rival, Burmese troops marched over the Three Pagodas Pass to Kanchanaburi and from there northward toward Suphanburi, aiming to approach Ayudhya from the west. Informed of their approach, Naresuan led a force from the city and encountered the Burmese at Nong Sarai, twenty-three kilometers northwest of present-day Suphanburi. A massive battle between the two forces ensued on January 18, 1593. The Burmese won the initial skirmishes and pressed down hard on Naresuan's main force. Rather than reinforce his vanguard, Naresuan stood his ground while the Burmese rushed forward, breading ranks in pursuit of the crumbling vanguard. Naresuan and his brother, Ekathotsarot, then plunged into the fray mounted atop war elephants and, on seeing the elephant of the Burmese crown prince, advanced toward it. To the crown prince, Naresuan shouted out, "Come forth and let us fight an elephant duel for the honor of our kingdoms."[1] In a few moments it was all over. As the two elephants closed, the crown prince slashed a glancing blow at Naresuan with his war scythe, where-upon his body lay exposed to a sudden slash of Naresuan's sword. The crown prince was slain, and the Burmese army fell into disarray and retreated toward Kanchanaburi. The Ayudhya army followed, inflicting heavy casualties upon them. Ayudhya's independence now was secured, and for the next generation, the Burmese kings would be on the defensive against Ayudhya, the tables of war thus turning for the first time in thirty years.

In the years that followed the Battle of Nong Sarai, Naresuan and Ekathotsarot may not have been as successful on the offensive as they had been in defending their kingdom. Their actions and policies, however, displayed a confidence and sense of purpose that were to carry through much of the following century as Ayudhya began to assert itself in a wider world. If it had done nothing else, the preceding half-century of warfare had underlined the dangers and opportunities presented by Ayudhya's location and position in the world. The Burmans had united Pegu, Toungoo, and Ava and had extended their power to Lan Na and even Lan Sang. The Cambodians frequently had taken advantage of Ayudhya's helplessness to raid the kingdom from the east.

The Battle of Nong Sarai, 1593, from a nineteenth-century Siamese painting.

Thus surrounded by hostile, aggressive neighbors, the rulers of Ayudhya were ever watchful of developments in the interior that might affect their security and sought opportunities to divide their rivals. In addition, Ayudhya had developed in the preceding century strengths and resources that might potentially give the kingdom advantages over its neighbors. Ayudhya long had been and remained an important international trading center, and the commodities and profits of trade strengthened the state. Ayudhya imported firearms from the Portuguese and other weaponry from Japan. The kingdom also had a powerful navy in the sixteenth and early seventeenth centuries—recruited perhaps from Chams after the fall of Champa to the Vietnamese in 1471—and Ayudhya fleets ranged widely in east Asian waters, to the Philippines, Taiwan, and the Ryukyu Islands, for example. With international trade came diplomacy and the flow of political intelligence and new ideas. All these sources of strength, however, might have remained only potentialities without the wisdom and statecraft to maximize the advantages that might be gained from them. Naresuan and his successors made the most of them.

As early as 1575, Ayudhya had sent a diplomatic mission to China to request a new royal seal of office to replace that destroyed by the Burmese, in a sense thereby gaining Chinese recognition of Siam's independence. There followed in 1592 an extraordinary episode that says much about Naresuan's view of Siam's place in the world. Japan under Toyotomi Hideyoshi had embarked upon an expansionist policy, threatening trade (including that of Siam) throughout East Asia, and invading Korea in mid–1592. Naresuan promptly learned of these developments, probably through commercial channels. Despite his preoccupation with Burma and with Cambodia, which had invaded Siam in 1587, Naresuan at once sent a mission to China in October 1592, offering to send the Siamese navy against Japan. This was no empty gesture. Naresuan understood the interconnectedness of international relations, and he wanted to maintain a balance of power favorable to open international commerce and to China's dominance in an orderly Asian state system. In the end, the Chinese rejected his offer in February 1593, but by then Naresuan had defeated the Burmese at Nong Sarai and embarked upon successful campaigns against Cambodia and the Burmese coastal provinces of Tenasserim and Tavoy. Through the remainder of the decade his campaigns against Burma continued. These included expeditions to the Pegu region in mid-decade and against Toungoo in 1599–1600, and a campaign that placed Lan Na under Ayudhya's suzerainty in 1598. Following the death of King Nandabayin in 1599, Burmese unity collapsed. When the new king of Ava determined to restore the Burmese position in the Shan states, Naresuan moved to forestall him by heading an expedition into the region. But on reaching

Müang Hang, thirty kilometers northwest of Fang in the Shan states, Naresuan fell ill and died on April 25, 1605, at the age of fifty.

Naresuan's loyal brother Ekathotsarot, who had reigned virtually jointly with him, inherited a vigorous and extensive kingdom. The core of the state was secure, its population augmented by thousands of refugees and war captives taken from the Mon country and Cambodia. Its international trade flourished, thanks to continuing good relations with the Portuguese, the Spanish Philippines (with whom Naresuan had concluded a treaty in 1598), China, Japan, and the Ryukyu kingdom. It now had an important opening to the trade of the Bay of Bengal again with the reacquisition of Tenasserim and Tavoy. Burma was engrossed in internal problems and posed no immediate threat, and the Cambodian state was in disarray. In short, Ayudhya had been restored as a major political and economic power in the region. The Ayudhya chronicles of this period, filled as they are with epic tales of military campaigns, lead naturally to the conclusion that Naresuan almost single-handedly revived Ayudhya on the battlefield. Surely his leadership was built upon broader foundations. Naresuan was a scion of the ancient Sukhothai ruling house, yet he appears consistently to have conceived of the unity of Siam within a broader ethnic, cultural, and political framework, maintaining the preeminence of Ayudhya over provincial identities, just as he also saw Siam as part of a much larger international order. He appears actively to have encouraged Ayudhya's trade and to have taken steps to organize more securely the manpower of the kingdom to support both the state service and the Buddhist religion. That his vision, statecraft, and statesmanship were balanced by military genius and bravery meant that he could create the security upon which the success of his policies depended. The blend of these qualities in an exceptional individual earned him the sobriquet "the Great," shared by only five other monarchs of Siam.

Following Naresuan's death, the history of Ayudhya in the seventeenth century seems to be marked by two notable qualities: uneven institutional development exacerbated by increasing relations with Western European powers. As these two developments ran their course, culminating in the so-called Glorious Revolution of 1688, we can see more clearly the relationship between politics and economics in early-modern Siam.

It is not a little remarkable that virtually all successions to the throne of Ayudhya in the seventeenth and eighteenth centuries were, at the least, irregular, and in many cases either disguised or real usurpations. Why should this have been the case? And what does this phenomenon signify? Let us for the moment consider only the seventeenth-century cases. Ekathotsarot's succession to Naresuan posed no problems, for he and his brother had ruled jointly for fifteen years in perfect harmony for all we know; and though the two were 650 kilometers from the capital on the king's death, there is no suggestion that anyone else attempted to seize the throne on this occasion. Thereafter, however, the story was different.

Ekathotsarot's reign was brief. We know of at least four of his sons. Two were born of a queen, Suthat and Si Saowaphak, and thus had stronger claims on the throne than Thong and Si Sin, who had been born of concubines. Ekathotsarot named Suthat heir-apparent, but an official in league with a powerful group of Japanese mercenaries and traders at court denounced Suthat for plotting rebellion. His father ordered him executed shortly before his own death, which occurred sometime between October 1610, and November 1611. Most Ayudhya chronicles maintain that Ekathotsarot then was succeeded by Si Saowaphak, who a year and two months later was executed by the monk Phra Phimontham, who reigned (ca. 1611–28) as King Intharacha or Song Tham ("the Just King"). Foreign visitors present in Ayudhya shortly after these events, however, assert that Song Tham was the son of Ekathotsarot by a concubine and directly succeeded his father; they do not mention Si Saowaphak. Given the textual vicissitudes to which the chronicles were subject, we are obliged to accept independent foreign evidence and regard the succession as regular. Remember, however, the untimely demise of Prince Suthat.

The next succession crisis came at the end of Song Tham's long reign. He apparently never appointed an heir-apparent, but his younger brother Si Sin was generally regarded as his successor. Song Tham's cousin, Phraya Si Worawong, however, promoted the candidacy of Song Tham's eldest son, Chettha; and as the king lay dying late in 1628 he nominated the fifteen-year-old Chettha to succeed him. The machinations of Si Worawong brought Chettha to the throne on December 13; Si Sin and other potential claimants to the throne were eliminated by Si Worawong (or Suriyawong), who took over the Kalahom (military) ministry. Soon, Si Worawong disposed of both Prince Chettha (in August 1629) and (in September) Chettha's younger brother Athittayawong who had succeeded him; at last he took the crown for himself. Known as King Prasat Thong, the "King of the Golden Palace," he reigned for twenty-seven years. He must be regarded as a usurper, for he had little blood claim to the throne, though one story claims that his mother and Song Tham's were sisters and another dubiously says that he was an unacknowledged son of Ekathotsarot. The power that enabled him to undertake such a ruthless and extended struggle for the throne was founded on his bureaucratic position as Kalahom, the minister of military affairs, and the patronage and control of manpower that this post gave him. The strongest resistance he encountered along the way came from a strong body of Japanese mercenaries at court, headed by Yamada Nagamasa. Si Worawong got Yamada out of the way, apparently with little difficulty, by sending him to quell rebellion in Nakhon Si Thammarat. Note again, however, the role of foreigners in the succession struggle.

Yet another struggle followed the death of Prasat Thong in August 1656. Again, as in 1628–29, three kings ascended the throne of Ayudhya in little more than two months. First Prasat Thong's eldest son, Prince Chai, "with armed men seized the court, and ascended the throne." [2] Then his younger brother, Prince Narai, deposed him and placed Prasat Thong's brother, Suthammaracha, on the throne. Finally, scarcely ten weeks later, Narai seized the throne for himself on October 26, 1656. The circumstances of his coup are difficult to unravel. George Vinal Smith notes that Narai had asked the Dutch for assistance as early as August and then states that "in October Narai made his move with the aid of his supporters and of the Japanese-Thais, Pattani Malays and perhaps Persian Muslims." [3] A Persian writing thirty years later claims a primary role for his compatriots and mentions that one of Narai's first acts as king was to appoint a Persian as his prime minister. [4] Once again, the hint of foreign involvement is very strong.

Finally, there is the famous Ayudhya "Revolution" of 1688, which accompanied the death of King Narai. Without going into details at this point, we need only note that the major thrust of the conspiracy that placed King Phetracha on the throne was directed against a Greek adventurer who had become prime minister and was based in that sector of the bureaucracy least directly concerned with foreigners, foreign trade, and the outside world.

Taken together, these four succession crises between 1610 and 1688 lead to some general observations on the politics of succession, the kingship, and the changing bases of political power in seventeenth-century Ayudhya. First, as absolute as royal power was during this period—and there are ample instances of its exercise and abuse—it was still more personal than institutional. Kings lacked the power to name their own successors, and blood was less effective a claim to the throne than strength. The crown was more worth fighting for than ever before. Naresuan had strengthened the capital at the expense of the provinces, and Ekathotsarot had begun a dramatic expansion of foreign trade that enhanced the crown's wealth and power. These developments brought with them a new degree of instability. By diminishing the power of provincial authorities and virtually eliminating some provincial ruling houses, and by taking direct control over much provincial manpower, Naresuan and Ekathotsarot did much to repair the military weakness that had brought about the fall of the kingdom a generation or two earlier. However, the chief ministries controlling manpower, the Kalahom and Mahatthai, profited much more from these developments than the other departments of the central administration. That the Kalahom was especially powerful is suggested by Si Worawong's seizure of that ministry in 1628 preparatory to capturing the throne itself.

Kings seem to have had continuing difficulty in controlling the provinces and manpower and in maintaining a ready military force. Early in the period, the recruitment of royal bodyguards from foreigners outside the Ayudhya manpower-control system—from among Japanese, Chams, and Malays, for example—seems to have constituted one such attempt. This, of course, could backfire, as it did with Japanese involvement in the deposition of Suthat around 1610 and in their opposition to Prasat Thong. Prasat Thong attempted to curb the power of the nobles by dividing control of the provinces between the Kalahom and the Mahatthai, the former taking the southern provinces and the latter the northern. This at least divided the responsibilities for manpower control between two ministries, while a third department maintained central-ized registers of all freemen liable for labor service. Throughout the period, kings seem to have tried also to strengthen their position vis-à-vis those whose power was based on control over manpower by building up a new kind of wealth through control over commodities and trade. Here, from early in the century, Ayudhya rulers embarked upon a particularly novel policy. Perhaps realizing that their control over the bureaucracy was only as strong as their hold on the men who staffed it, they repeatedly hired foreigners to conduct their foreign trade, men who no doubt also possessed commercial skills otherwise in short supply. As their so-called prime ministers, these men did much to hasten Siam's involvement in the wider world. Their employment, however, like the engagement of foreign mercenaries, also complicated the politics of the period.

Some of the most important of these foreigners were members of a single Persian family founded by a pair of brothers who arrived from the Persian Gulf in 1602 and soon took Siamese wives. The elder, Sheik Ahmad, was appointed to head that division of the Phrakhlang (the ministry of finance and foreign affairs) that dealt with Muslim traders from the Archipelago, India, and the Near East. Early in the reign of Song Tham he was made Phrakhlang, and by the end of the reign he was *samuhanaiyok* (prime minister), the head of the Mahatthai, with the rank of chaophraya. Around 1630, he was succeeded in that office by his eldest son, Chaophraya Aphairacha (personal name, Chün), who served in that position until about 1670, when he was succeeded by his eldest son, Chaophraya Chamnanphakdi (Sombun). Family control of the Mahatthai was interrupted only in 1685, when Narai appointed the Greek adventurer, Constantine Phaulkon, to the office. Sheik Ahmad's younger brother, Muhammad Said, similarly founded a powerful official family; and his son Aga Muhammad Astarabadi was particularly powerful in the early years of Narai's reign. We note here, then, whether it was a deliberate policy or not, a balancing of foreigners in the Mahatthai and Phrakhlang, with their resources in commodities and international trade, against the traditional elite's control of manpower in the Kalahom ministry. Outsiders thus were enabled not only to rise rapidly to high official positions but also to found veritable dynasties of royal officers who, generation after generation, monopolized certain state offices and played prominent political roles. Their descendants—members of the Bunnag, Siphen, and Singhaseni families, for example—continued in such positions into the twentieth century.

King Ekathotsarot is said to have been "greatly inclined toward strangers and foreign nations" and to have taken a special interest in "enriching his treasury" by introducing new taxes.[5] Under the circumstances, neither policy was unusual. The kingdom had been impoverished by decades of warfare, and its population could not easily bear the high financial costs of rapid reconstruction. At peace and confident of his power, the king could cultivate relations with foreign powers and hope to improve his kingdom's international commerce.

It was economic considerations, rather than political ones, that primarily governed Siam's foreign relations over the next quarter-century. It was Ekathotsarot who received the first Dutch ships to call at Ayudhya and sent the first Siamese diplomatic mission to Europe, to the Netherlands in 1608 (and one to Portuguese Goa in 1606). Through the decade that followed, the Siamese were concerned about Portuguese influence in the Bay of Bengal in general, and on the Burma coast in particular, because it threatened their own trade from ports on the Tenasserim coast. For a time, Song Tham even urged the Dutch to fortify Mergui and thus ally themselves with Ayudhya against the Portuguese; but the Dutch were more interested in using Ayudhya and Pattani as entries into the trade with China and Japan. Ships of the English East India Company first came to Ayudhya in 1612, and soon, like the Dutch company, it established trading stations ("factories") at Ayudhya and Pattani. The English, however, generally were unable to compete with the Dutch and completely withdrew from Siam by 1623, not to return until the 1660s. Even the Dutch were disappointed in their returns on the Siam trade and for a time in the 1620s considered pulling out altogether. Asian trade, conducted by Chinese and by foreign Muslims, had developed considerably, and was on a scale that rendered it susceptible to management and manipulation by the Ayudhya bureaucracy for its public and private interests (most officials did not distinguish between the two).

By early in the reign of King Prasat Thong, both economic and political conditions had changed, producing a new relationship between Ayudhya and the Dutch. There appears to have been a general rise in the international demand for Ayudhya's exports. The most important of these was hides, especially deer hides, which were in high demand in Japan. Dutch and other Asian traders needed hides to sell in Japan to generate profits to purchase Japanese commodities. When, after a number of years, the Japanese reopened their country to international trade in 1633, the value of Ayudhya's hide exports naturally increased. In addition, there was stong international demand for Siam's rice, spices, and various forest products, such as sappanwood, eagle-wood, lac, and benzoin. In its turn, Siam imported Indian cloth, luxury goods, firearms, metals, and, especially, silver. For much of the century the Siamese could, on their own initiative, have managed this complex international trade on their own, making use of Asian traders—Chinese and Sino-Siamese, plus Muslims from India and farther west. There was, however, some additional economic advantage to be gained by commissioning royal ships—manned by Chinese or Sino-Siamese crews—for trading voyages to China and Japan and by inviting European participation in the trade. This at least might stimulate competition to drive up the prices of Siam's exports and further stimulate demand.

But by the 1630s, King Prasat Thong was moved also by political considerations to encourage the Dutch. These had mainly to do with Ayudhya's relations with states on the Malay Peninsula, particularly Pattani and Nakhon Si Thammarat. Nakhon had become a Siamese province a century or so earlier, ruled by governors sent out from the capital, and it had been an important source of manpower for the wars with Burma in the late sixteenth century. It had, however, considerable economic wealth that encouraged it to play an independent role in international commerce, and its distance from the capital made firm control difficult for the kings of Ayudhya. When Prasat Thong sent Yamada Nagamasa to quell a rebellion in Nakhon in 1629, the populace soon revolted against Yamada and then against Prasat Thong's usurpation.

For its own reasons, Pattani, a strongly Malay kingdom that long had prospered as a nebulously defined tributary of Ayudhya, also rebelled and allied itself with the Portuguese; it attacked Phatthalung and Nakhon Si Thammarat in 1630. Soon, Songkhla similarly was at war with Pattani. To make matters worse, Japanese whom Prasat Thong had run out of Ayudhya had gone to assist Cambodia in attacking Siam, and the Burmese were threatening his western frontiers. Beleaguered, the king was anxious to secure Dutch military aid in return for trading privileges, notably a monopoly on hide exports and a contract for sappanwood purchases. By the time these negotiations were concluded in 1634, the Siamese themselves had managed to bring Nakhon under control and were worried mainly about Pattani and Cambodia. A small Dutch fleet sent to assist an Ayudhya army against Pattani in mid-1634 arrived too late to save the Siamese from defeat, but the king appreciated their aid and continued to value Dutch friendship as one crisis or another erupted in his foreign relations over the next few decades.

The relationship with the Dutch, too, had its ups and downs, as when the Dutch in 1636 opened a factory in Cambodia and antagonized the Siamese, or in 1644 proposed an alliance with Siam against Cambodia, or between 1647 and 1655 aided the kingdom against rebellious Songkhla. In general, the whole of the reign of Prasat Thong was marked by considerable Dutch involvement in Ayudhya, both economic and political. Prasat Thong shared several interests with the Dutch. Their trade was valuable and growing, and both sides viewed Ayudhya as a natural focus for the stability of the Gulf of Siam region. Prasat Thong felt isolated and threatened by neighboring kingdoms and vassals and by the Portuguese, and needed more naval power than he could usually muster. He appears to have felt that because Dutch cooperation was so heavily motivated by economic considerations, he could keep the Dutch under control by carefully rationing their commercial privileges.

Conditions changed considerably during the reign of King Narai (1656–88), when what had been a somewhat uncomfortable but workable Dutch-Ayudhya relationship broadened to include many other powers. The developments of the period were complex, involving as they did many parties and a variety of interests. Though to many historians the dominant quality of Narai's reign has come to be his involvement with foreign powers, notably the French, it is not unreasonable to argue that internal considerations were of at least equal importance. Ultimately, Siamese individuals and groups undertook policies and actions in defense or pursuit of their own interests.

Consider the way in which the reign began and the alliances that were formed at the time. Following the death of Prasat Thong, Narai, it will be recalled, asked unsuccessfully for Dutch aid in making his bid for the throne. A few months later he came to the throne with the aid of "Japanese-Thais, Pattani Malays, and perhaps Persian Muslims." [6] He spent much of the next decade at war with Lan Na and Burma, in 1662 even conquering Martaban, Rangoon, Pegu, and the surrounding area. This warfare necessarily drew heavily upon manpower and financial resources and probably involved different noble and provincial elements than those employed against the south in the previous reign. In order to finance these wars, the king's Persian Phrakhlang instituted a number of changes in the ways Siam's international trade was conducted. Late in 1662, the crown imposed a royal monopoly on all trade, which meant that goods destined for export had first to be sold to the crown, despite the Dutch monopoly on hides. In addition, the king began again to send his own trading vessels to Japan.

The Dutch position deteriorated to the point where they closed their trading operation in Ayudhya early in 1663. Narai then realized that he had gone too far. It was dangerous to alienate the Dutch, and the kingdom stood to lose a very valuable trade; so he sent a mission to Dutch Java to seek a renegotiation of their relations. By a treaty of 1664, the Dutch returned to Ayudhya under more or less the same terms as previously, with a limited monopoly on hide exports and a new concession of extraterritoriality under which Dutch accused of offenses in Siam were entitled to trial by their own laws and courts. For their part, the Siamese gained Dutch good will, on which Siamese ships in trouble in the Bay of Bengal trade would come to rely, and were assured supplies of European goods and the services of European crafts-men. Neither Narai nor the Dutch desired Dutch political involvement in Siam, and none occurred for the rest of the century.

As Narai's court and his government stabilized over the next few decades, the kingdom's economy flourished. The benefits of development, however, were not evenly shared within the elite. Competition became more severe as royal Siamese ships became steadily more active in the trade of the South China Sea and the Bay of Bengal; as the English (1661), Danish (1620), and French East India companies entered Ayudhya's trade; and as increasing numbers of private traders—Europeans as well as Asians—began regularly to call at Ayudhya and other Siamese ports, including Tenasserim and Mergui as well as Nakhon and Pattani. This was an economic situation in which the large European trading companies, with their heavy overhead expenses and need for large profit margins, could not successfully compete on equal terms with either royal monopolies or private traders. Moreover, resident foreign communities in Siam—or, more accurately, domesticated or assimilated foreign communities, for these had existed for some generations—were far better able to profit from their international connections and knowledge in this new commercial environment. Under these circumstances, none of the European companies was flourishing by the 1680s.

Between 1680 and 1688, there occurred a dramatic development in relations between Ayudhya and the France of Louis XIV. Its origins owed much to the Greek adventurer, Constantine Phaulkon (1647–88). Phaulkon had spent a wanderlust youth in the English merchant fleet, including a spell in London, and came to Ayudhya with the English East India Company in 1678. Within two years, having learned to speak Siamese fluently, Phaulkon ingratiated himself into the service of the Phrakhlang as interpreter and accountant, and may even have conducted a Siamese diplomatic and trading mission to Persia in 1680. He rose rapidly in the royal service at the expense of many others. He antagonized the Dutch and English companies by favoring private traders and failing to promote company interests, and he threatened the Muslim trading communities who had long had influence in the Phrakhlang. These, presumably the Persians, Malays, and Indians already mentioned, he showed to have falsified financial accounts and accused of trying to promote the conversion of the kingdom to Islam. Narai took a great liking to him and increasingly came to rely on his advice.

Narai's first initiatives toward the French antedate Phaulkon and appear to have stemmed from nothing more than a desire to make his kingdom known and recognized abroad. To this end he regularly had sent missions to Persia, Golconda in India, and China, as well as to many neighboring states. French Jesuit missionaries, established in Ayudhya since 1662, had made themselves useful to the court by rendering technical assistance in such matters as the design and construction of fortifications and palaces. Narai had favored them, as he did many foreign communities, by allowing them to preach Christianity and operate a seminary in the capital. In 1673, a French ecclesiastical mission brought Narai letters from Pope Clement IX and King Louis XIV of France, and it must have been the latter that Narai was reciprocating at the end of 1680 when he sent a mission to France.

Though Narai's first mission to France was lost at sea, the French returned the compliment by sending a small commercial mission to Ayudhya in 1682. This party, headed by Mgr. Pallu, found a receptive court at which Phaulkon had continued to rise, by now to the position of acting Phrakhlang and soon thereafter to the highest position in the civil bureaucracy, the Mahatthai. Phaulkon, who recently had been converted to Catholicism by the Jesuits, acted as Pallu's interpreter and quickly identified himself with the French and Jesuit interests. Most agree that Phaulkon was excited by the idea of converting Narai, and Siam, to Christianity. Such an aim was enormously difficult of accomplishment, especially given the close identification of the king and kingdom with Buddhism; and Phaulkon, of course, could not have pursued such an aim openly. Instead, by extended philosophical discussions with Narai, he provoked the king toward a rational examination of his beliefs and encouraged him to debate points of Buddhist doctrine with leading monks and scholars at court. Phaulkon persuaded at least the Jesuits, and perhaps himself, that there was a real possibility of converting Narai. Realizing that the political consequences of such an action might be severe—that Narai might be deposed and that other foreign powers might be invited to assist in the effort—Phaulkon pushed for a closer relationship with France, even an alliance.

Accordingly, a second Siamese mission was sent to France in 1684 to request that French envoys be sent to Ayudhya for the purpose of concluding an alliance. This French mission of 1685–86, headed by the Chevalier de

French Jesuits join King Narai and his court in observing a lunar eclipse, 1685; from an engraving by C. Vermeulen in Guy Tachard, *Voyage de Siam des Pères Jésuites envoyez par le Roy aux Indes et à la Chine* ... (Paris, 1686).

request that French envoys be sent to Ayudhya for the purpose of concluding an alliance. This French mission of 1685–86, headed by the Chevalier de Chaumont, had as its primary purpose the conversion of Narai. (It had some competition: a mission from Shah Sulaiman the Safavid (1666–94) of Persia was in Ayudhya at the same time, trying to gain the king's conversion to Islam!) The outcome of their extended negotiations was a draft treaty that granted the French commercial concessions comparable to those long enjoyed by the Dutch and others, plus the right to station troops at Songkhla—which chronically was in rebellion against Ayudhya. For his part, Narai at this point seems mainly to have been concerned to bolster his peninsular defenses, which had become strained by repeated rebellions and war scares involving the Dutch. But perhaps most of all, Narai must have been flattered by the attentions of a "real," powerful king, not just a company governor-general, whose diplomatic equal the exchange of missions and conclusion of treaties made him.

While another Siamese mission was in France in 1686–87, two crises occurred in Siam. First, in July 1686, while the king and Phaulkon were at Narai's summer palace at Lopburi, a plot to overthrow the king was fomented by a community of Makassarese, or Bugis, in the capital. This group, numbering only a few hundred families, had become established in Ayudhya only within the previous decade, after the Dutch had displaced them from their commanding position in the trade of the Java Sea. Not surprisingly, they were vigorously anti-Dutch. According to contemporaries, their conspiracy was organized by a Bugis prince with, perhaps, the complicity of several Cham princes; and they planned to burn Ayudhya and place one of Narai's younger brothers on the throne, providing that he become a Muslim. Word of their plans was leaked to Phaulkon, who organized a strong military expedition which, with the assistance of numerous Europeans, surrounded and virtually decimated the Makassarese quarter of Ayudhya in September 1686. In the course of these events, Phaulkon further ingratiated himself with the king, while Phaulkon's chief rival in the Siamese bureaucracy, Phra Phetracha, then head of the Elephant Department, used the opportunity to discredit Narai's younger brothers and diminish their chances to succeed to the throne.

Second, in July 1687, there occurred the Mergui Massacre, in which some sixty Englishmen were killed at Mergui, a port on the Tenasserim coast. The origins of this episode have to do with the relations among the English East India Company, private English traders especially on the Bay of Bengal, Phaulkon, and the Siamese government. Relations between the company and Phaulkon and the Siamese for some years had been bad. The company's affairs in Ayudhya had been ill-managed and ran consistent deficits. Phaulkon, on the other hand, had been making extensive use of private Englishmen in the Siamese service, even to the point of arming them for service against the Makassarese and commissioning private English ships for privateering expeditions against ships of the Kingdom of Golconda in south India. As the company was endeavoring to maintain good relations with Golconda, it regarded such privateers as pirates, and by 1686 it had determined on war against Siam. Word of English intentions soon reached Siam, and the government grew cautious and suspicious. Phaulkon had appointed two old English friends, Richard Burnaby and Samuel White, to govern Mergui, from where they ran privateering expeditions and amassed a considerable fortune.

Matters finally came to a head when the company in April 1687 demanded £65,000 in damages from Narai and threatened to take reprisals against Siamese ships and subjects and to blockade Mergui. In June, two company frigates appeared at Mergui to enforce the claim. Burnaby and White, fearing being charged as pirates in English courts, temporized and by lavish entertainment tried to win over the commander of the company expedition. Suspicious that the English might join forces and take over the town, local Siamese authorities on July 14 suddenly opened fire on the warships and massacred every Englishman they could find. The next month Narai declared war on the English East India Company and handed Mergui over to a French governor and a small party of French troops.

In September 1687, an imposing French mission arrived in Ayudhya, headed by Claude Cébéret du Boullay, a director of the French East India Company, and Simon de la Loubère, borne by six large warships and accompanied by nearly five hundred troops and an assortment of Jesuits, diplomats, and artisans. The French already had determined to station their troops at Bangkok, rather than Songkhla, where they would be in a better position to control the kingdom's trade. They welcomed the opportunity to send some to Mergui, which might serve them as a vantage point on the Bay of Bengal. Their negotiations with Phaulkon were difficult and protracted, and they were shocked to discover that Phaulkon now gave no encouragement to their hopes for the conversion of Narai to Christianity. The new treaty they concluded, on December 11, 1687, differed little from the commercial treaty of 1685, nor did it regulate the status of French troops at Bangkok and Mergui. The French envoys soon left, la Loubère to write probably the best account of seventeenth-century Siam. Franco-Siamese relations rapidly deteriorated.

Within months Siam underwent a major upheaval foreign contemporaries termed a "revolution." At issue certainly was power and its exercise. Those who took the lead in forcing the issue included, most prominently, Phra Phetracha and his son, Luang Sorasak. Phetracha was of rural origins, from Phlu Luang village in Suphanburi province, and of some undefined blood relationship to previous kings. He owed his rise to power, however, to the fact that his mother had been wet-nurse to Narai and he and the king had been raised as foster brothers. As head of the elephant corps, he had demonstrated military leadership and valor in campaigns earlier in the reign, and he enjoyed a continuing close relationship with the king. By the 1680s he had emerged as the leading official in the opposition to Phaulkon, and was more successful than other officials at court in furthering his own interests without running afoul of Phaulkon's close relationship with the king, which had destroyed many other officials. Phetracha's son, Sorasak, may have been a great deal more ambitious and ruthless than his father, though their motives and actions cannot be discerned with complete certainty. At any rate, by early 1688, they had embarked upon a course to unseat Phaulkon and seize power on Narai's impending death.

Antiforeign and anti-French sentiment had been growing. As people saw it, the king's most powerful minister was a Greek, who had married a Japanese Christian and lived in European style, surrounded by French priests and

English merchants. Phaulkon seemed more solicitous of foreign, Christian interests than those of his king. The arrogant and licentious behavior of the French troops antagonized many. Buddhist monks and laypersons were suspicious of the growing prominence of Christian priests; and many foreign trading communities had been hurt by Phaulkon's policies which favored private English traders and, they thought, the companies. All such considerations might have fueled a xenophobic outburst, but what in fact occurred is much more complicated.

In March 1688, King Narai fell seriously ill with what all knew to be a terminal illness. Among the claimants to the throne were two of Narai's brothers, Prince Aphaithot and Prince Noi, and an adoptive son, Mom Pi. Phetracha and Sorasak had compromised all three. They had implicated the princes in the Makassarese uprising and then made it appear that Pi had blamed them in order to improve his own fortunes. Once the leading officials had prevailed upon Narai to make Phetracha regent during the king's illness, Phetracha quickly had Mom Pi murdered. Next, he had Phaulkon arrested on charges of treason and promptly executed on June 5, 1688. The next month, immediately after Narai died on the eleventh, Luang Sorasak had Aphaithot and Noi killed. Even if Phetracha had hoped to stop short of usurping the throne, he now had no choice and became king. The French garrison at Bangkok, now besieged by Siamese troops, finally agreed to quit the country, pending which French missionaries were imprisoned and Catholics persecuted. The new court, however, was by no means blindly antiforeign or anti-Christian. Englishmen remained at liberty, and Phetracha concluded a new treaty with the Dutch in July. Soon the missionaries were released, and they resumed proselytizing as before.

The Ayudhya revolution of 1688 certainly was fueled by xenophobic sentiments, particularly to the extent that Phetracha mobilized some sectors of popular support—as from Buddhist monks and low-ranking officers—on the basis of such appeals. The active leaders of the conspiracy, however, were moved by more sophisticated arguments or, at times, simpler considerations of power. They were less frightened of Christianity, which in a century had succeeded in converting no more than a handful of Siamese, than they were of its use by a few individuals unduly to influence the culture and civilization of their society. They were upset by the abuse of power, whether by king or by powerful minister, to favor individuals and groups who lacked durable commitments to Siam. And some may have believed that Ayudhya had stepped too far into the deep, murky, dangerous waters of great-power politics. They may have felt more comfortable in a world in which commerce and international relations were conducted on a simpler, smaller scale. They did not want to reject the outside world, but they did want to deal with it on a more manageable and perhaps traditional level.

Lan Na and Lan Sang in a Time of Tumult

A strong case for the growing divergence within the Tai world can be made from a comparison of Ayudhya's history in the 1569–1688 period with the histories of Lan Na and Lan Sang in the comparable period. The two up-country "Lao" states remained similar in their social and economic organiza-tion, but differed in their policital conditions, owing in large part to different geopolitical situations. Lan Na became a weak subordinate of a more powerful Burmese state, whereas Lan Sang recovered its independence and enjoyed a golden age of prosperity and cultural growth.

As we have seen, the dynasty of King Mangrai was snuffed out after the fall of Chiang Mai to the Burmese in 1558 and the exile of the helpless King Mekuti in 1564. Thereafter, Chiang Mai long was ruled by a succession of hapless puppets of the Burmese, and Burmese generals and collaborators were posted to control the other major towns of the region. Lan Na then regularly suffered levies of troops and supplies for the wars against Ayudhya. Only toward the end of the century did this vicious cycle begin to break, as resistance against the Burmese began to stir. In 1595, the king of Lan Sang joined with Nan in attempting to expel the Burmese, but failed. The time for action, however, had come. Naresuan in the mid-1590s was raiding the Pegu region almost annually, and King Nandabayin of Burma also faced internal rebellion and challenges from neighboring Arakan and some Portuguese adventurers by 1599. On the death of Nandabayin in that year, Burma virtually fell apart. The Burmese Tharrawaddy prince was ruling in Chiang Mai, but had no chance of help from home. Thus, when Lan Sang invaded his dominions and seized Chiang Saen, he had no choice but to appeal to Siam for assistance, offering to place Lan Na under the suzerainty of King Naresuan. Naresuan was only too happy to respond and sent north an army which recaptured Chiang Saen and installed a Lao noble as a sort of Siamese commissioner there. He did not attempt to impose any stronger influence over Chiang Mai, however. Even when the commissioner quarreled with the Tharrawaddy prince a few years later, Naresuan sent Ekathotsarot to Chiang Mai to adjudicate the dispute in Chiang Mai's favor.

This anomalous situation—a Burmese prince ruling in Lan Na under Siam's suzerainty—lasted for more than a decade, until the Burmese under King Anaukpetlun (r. 1605–28) determined to reassert their direct control in the region. They had a relatively easy time of it, probably because of the serious damage done to the fabric and leadership of Lan Na society by decades of conflict. The north was divided into numerous small, competing, and mutually suspicious müang, over which Chiang Mai under an isolated Burmese prince hardly could have exerted leadership. As it was, the Tharrawaddy prince had died in 1607 and rapidly was succeeded by three of his sons, the youngest of whom, Thadogyaw, was ruling by 1613. First Anaukpetlun neatly detached Chiang Saen by installing his own man as governor there and then, in 1614, invaded Chiang Mai. Thadogyaw fled to Lampang, fortified the city, and there made his stand. The Burmese siege of the city was faltering when they received timely aid from Prince Si Song Müang, a descendant of the ruling house of Nan whom the Burmese had installed as ruler in 1603. When Lampang fell and Thadogyaw died, the Burmese made Si Song Müang the ruler of Chiang Mai— but not ruler of Lan Na, which now was divided among many.

This arrangement held until the mid-1620s when, faced with revolts in Nan, Chiang Khong, and Chiang Hung, the Burmese sent a military expedition into the region, led by a prince who for a time superintended Burmese rule in the north. Then, in 1631, Si Song Müang declared his independence of Burma and seized Chiang Saen. The Burmese retaliated by capturing Si Song Müang, whom they sent into exile in Pegu, and installing, not a new vassal ruler, but a governor, a Phraya Thipphanet. A new regime began in the region, and for decades the chronicles record only the transfers of governors from one müang to another, each backed by Burmese military force, or the exile to Ava of the more recalcitrant or less successful.

Later, in 1660, there occurred another period of upheaval after Chinese troops invaded northern Burma in search of the exiled Yung-li emperor, the last of the Ming dynasty. Just as at the beginning of the century, the governor of Chiang Mai, fearing a Chinese invasion and despairing of help from a prostrate Burma, asked for Ayudhya's protection. King Narai sent an army north at the end of 1660, but as it approached, Chiang Mai learned of the Chinese retreat from Burma and pulled its men out of the Siamese armies. Narai's force continued on to take Lampang, but failed to capture Chiang Mai and withdrew early in 1661. Later that year, Narai sent a much larger army, led by the best of his generals, against Chiang Mai. This force succeeded in taking Lampang and Chiang Mai and seizing much valuable booty including the famed Buddha Sihinga image; it soon was driven from the city by a Burmese army. From this point forward, the Burmese followed a hard line in imposing their will on Lan Na. Burmese princes regularly were installed in Chiang Mai as viceroys for the region, and for a half century, the Tai Yuan—and Lü, and Shans, and mountain peoples—silently suffered an onerous regime that taxed them heavily and often levied on them conscription for Burmese armies far from their homes.

If for Ayudhya the century or so following the first major Burmese invasions of the 1560s was a period of recovery, economic development, and political diversification, for Lan Na the period was one of suffering. Caught in frequent wars, towns and villages frequently were depopulated, their families deported across the mountains to one principality or another or even off to Burma. The surviving chronicles of some of the principalities suggest a rapid turnover and disruption of local ruling houses, a situation in which only the most opportunistic survived in power. By the early eighteenth century, the region hardly deserved a single name, for its leadership was less integrated than in many centuries before, and its rich cultural heritage, especially the glories of the sixteenth century, was neglected.

The history of Lan Sang in this period is more complicated than that of Lan Na and even less coherent, for we cannot even be sure of the names of some of the kings who flitted across the throne in Vientiane. Unlike Lan Na, however, Lan Sang at least had a long period of independence, stability, and prosperity in the seventeenth century, though by the eighteenth century it, too, had disintegrated.

As we have seen, King Setthathirat disappeared in the course of a military campaign against the mountain peoples of extreme southern Laos in the early 1570s and was succeeded by his leading general, Phanya Saen Surin, who became regent for the king's infant son. Saen Surin was a commoner, a man of peasant origins from Nong Khai whose strong rule was disliked by the aristocrats of the capital, some of whom blamed him for Setthathirat's death. Some accounts state that he crowned himself king in 1572, provoking the flight of population from the Vientiane Plain to the regions of Roi Et and Champassak in the south. In 1574–75, the Burmese sent an expedition to Lan Sang to place their own nominee on the throne, the crown prince whom they had taken hostage from Vientiane in 1565; but this new king, Voravongsa, lasted only four years. In 1579, a rebellion broke out among the mountain peoples of the extreme south, led by a holy man who claimed to be a reincarnation of Setthathirat, who marched on Vientiane with a considerable following and forced Voravongsa to flee. The Burmese returned in 1580 and placed the aged Saen Surin on the throne. On his death two years later, he was succeeded by his son, who had been governor of Nakhon Phanom. In 1583, he, too, was deposed by a popular rebellion, and then the kingdom simply fell apart. There were no more kings for eight years, and the instability continued for half a century.

The strong king who restored stability to Lan Sang was Surinyavongsa, one of the greatest and longest reigning kings of Laos. He came to the throne around 1637 as a young man aged about twenty-four, already the victor of a violent struggle for the throne among his brothers and cousins. Once he put his rivals out of the way, he settled on the throne for fifty-seven years. But did the king rule or merely reign?

Surinyavongsa received a number of foreign visitors in the mid-seventeenth century, among them a mission from the Dutch East India Company in 1641 and a party of Jesuits who remained from 1642 to 1647. They describe the internal constitution of the kingdom, noting that three chief dignitaries divided among themselves the main powers of the state. One, the minister of the palace, ran the royal secretariat and conducted foreign relations. A second headed the army and governed Vientiane and its vicinity. The third was "the governor of Nakhon [Phanom] or viceroy, who commanded all the southern part of the kingdom." [7] These three had audience with the king only once every two or three months. We might conclude that the internal peace of Surinyavongsa's long reign was achieved by accommodation among several regional interests within the kingdom, whose representatives, assured of some degree of autonomy in their home regions, found it useful to agree on a single, royal focus of auhtority. Only through such an arrangement, apparently, were the ruling families of the central Mekong region willing to accept a ruling line whose roots still were in the north in Luang Prabang.

Surinyavongsa, however, was no cipher. Though he rarely showed himself in public, he was popular, known mainly for his firm administration of justice. Crime was rare, and European visitors depicted a peaceful and prosperous state. As the Genoese, Gian Filippo de Marini, put it:

> Because it is so fertile, and because the necessities of life grow there in such abundance, the Kingdom is so populated that not long since, when they made a census of those who were considered capable of serving the King in time of war and of bearing arms, they counted five hundred thousand, without taking into account the old men who are so numerous and so robust that if necessary an army of considerable size could be formed for the defense of the Kingdom out of those alone who have reached the age of a hundred. I must nevertheless admit that the population is a peaceable one and very little versed in the art of war and the exercise of arms, probably as a result of the favourable situation of the Kingdom and of the mountains and inaccessible precipices that surround it on every side like so many ramparts that none can force their way through, and which thus serve as a protection against the insults of their enemies. [8]

The Buddhist religion, the traditional arts and letters, and grand monumental architecture flourished. What these had required was stability, and this

Surinyavongsa and his court provided for more than half a century.

Within the Lao world, Surinyavongsa consolidated his influence by entering into marriage alliances with regional rulers. When around 1650 the ruler of Siang Khwang refused his request for the hand of his daughter, he invaded the principality, seized the daughter and hundreds of captives, and required that Siang Khwang pay regular tribute to Vientiane. Around the same time, he received at his court the ruling family of Chiang Hung, who had been evicted from their state by Chinese forces. The king's only son took in marriage the sister of the Chiang Hung ruler, and by her had two sons, the princes Kingkitsarat and Inthasom. The king himself took as a concubine a daughter of the emperor of Vietnam and delimited his frontiers with that state along ethnographic lines: those living in houses raised on piles above the ground were in Lan Sang, and those living in houses at ground level were in Vietnam. As for Ayudhya, a frontier delimitation concluded a century earlier between Setthathirat and King Chakkraphat of Ayudhya still held on the watershed line between the Chaophraya and Mekong basins. Lan Sang continued to hold sway in the northern and eastern quarters of the Khorat Plateau, and there seem to have been only minimal contact between the two kingdoms through most of the seventeenth century.

Having executed his only son for adultery, Surinyavongsa left the kingdom without a clear heir to his throne when he died around 1694. The three separate regions of the state soon went their own ways.

The Vientiane region was the most troublesome, as dignitaries based in various towns of the middle Mekong, especially Vientiane and Nakhon Phanom, were too finely balanced in power for any one faction to gain a clear preponderance. Their squabbling was tenuously quelled by a Lan Sang prince who came from exile in Vietnam with a considerable army and took Vientiane in 1700, establishing a new Lan Sang kingdom there. The price of his Vietnamese support was heavy triennial tribute to the Vietnamese rulers in Hue—four hundred bars of silver, ten elephants, ten rhinoceros horns, and so on.

Surinyavongsa's grandsons, the princes Kingkitsarat and Inthasom, had fled to Luang Prabang in 1694 and then northward to the Lü principalities of the Sipsong Pan Na to seek assistance from their mother's relatives in Chiang Hung. With Lü and northern Lao aid, they recaptured Luang Prabang in 1706 and then attacked Vientiane. The Vientiane ruler appealed for assistance, not from Vietnam, but from Ayudhya. A Siamese army soon arrived and effected a peaceful settlement under the terms of which Lan Sang was divided into two kingdoms, Vientiane and Luang Prabang, the frontier being at Chiang Khan near the elbow in the Mekong west of Vientiane (1707).

But division did not stop there. There had long been tension between the Vientiane Plain region and the towns of the Mekong valley farther south; and in 1709 the governor of Nakhon Phanom rebelled against Vientiane and sent troops against the capital. Only with difficulty was the rebellion put down, and the Vientiane ruler did not fully regain control until the governor of Nakhon Phanom died in 1715 and the king was able to appoint the late governor's son-in-law to rule Nakhon Phanom. The late governor's sons fled farther south, to Champassak, where yet a third principality had arisen.

Of the early history of Champassak, little is known. Local traditions maintain that in the late seventeenth century the state was ruled by a queen, who late in her reign turned the state over to an eminent holy man. He in turn sought out a young prince, reputed to be a posthumous son of King Surinyavongsa, and in 1713 installed him as King Soi Sisamut, founder of the new ruling house of Champassak.

By the early eighteenth century, then, Laos was divided into three kingdoms, each connected to the ancient ruling line of Lan Sang by tenuous—perhaps even fictive—blood lines and each dominating one of the three historic regions of the kingdom. Through the remainder of the century they were to remain mutually antagonistic, frequently at war with one another. They were easy prey to hostile or ambitious neighbors, and the longer their disunity prevailed, the more difficult their reunification became. It was as if the Lao had contracted in upon themselves, into the small, poor, and relatively isolated communities of the constricted river valleys of the interior uplands.

Much the same might be said of Chiang Mai and the old Lan Na region, at the turn of the century still ruled by Burmese-appointed governors. That Chiang Mai managed to regain some independence during this period says less about the strengths of Lan Na society than it does about the waning of Burmese strength in the region and about the ability of exceptional rulers to make their own opportunities.

In 1727, a rural Lao living outside Chiang Mai, a certain Thep Sing, gained a large following in the countryside as a *phu mi bun*, a "holy man," one with access to supernatural power. He first defied the Burmese governor of the city and then entered it and assassinated him. But Thep Sing ruled the city only a month or so before remaining Burmese in the region gained the assistance of Khamon Noi, a Lü prince of Chiang Hung who already had a long political career in the Lao world and had briefly been king of Luang Prabang. The Burmans and Khamon Noi deposed Thep Sing, and Khamon Noi was placed on the Chiang Mai throne as King Ong Kham (r. 1727–59).

Ong Kham contended with numerous attempts to unseat him, first by the Nan ruler, then, the following year, by a Burmese expedition. These he repelled, with growing local support as the nobles and people saw in him an effective leader against Burmese domination. The Chiang Mai he ruled, however, was but a shadow of Mangrai's Lan Na. The Burmese maintained a strong force at Chiang Saen, to which Phrae, Nan, Phayao, Lampang, Fang, Sat, Chiang Khong, and Thoen were subject. In effect, he controlled only the Ping valley around Chiang Mai, a small base from which to support resistance against Burmese invasions until Burma itself began to fall apart in the 1740s. The rhythm of events came to be dictated by events in Burma. As the Mons of Pegu gained independence in the 1740s and went to war against Burmese Ava, Ong Kham bid for their support by sending his daughter to the ruler of Pegu. And when Ava itself succumbed in 1751, a variety of ethnic groups in the Chiang Saen area revolted the next year, including Lü, Khün, and some hill peoples. When Ong Kham died at the end of 1759, there were ominous signs that not only Chiang Mai and the north, but all the Tai world, was darkly threatened; and soon not even Ayudhya would be able to withstand "the thunder out of Burma."

By the middle of the eighteenth century, neither in Lan Na nor in Lan Sang was there a kingdom fully comparable with Ayudhya in strength. What Ayudhya now had that its Tai Yuan and Lao cousins lacked was a kingdom-wide elite, a court nobility of well-established families who were committed, both by their culture and values and by their possession of vested political and economic interests, to the integrity and independence of the kingdom as a whole. By "nobility" is meant not a group defined by descent from royalty but rather a social group defined by continuing service to the state, whoever the monarch. Ayudhya's bureaucracy was more elaborate than those of the Lao kingdoms and more highly differentiated and specialized. The court could maintain them at a high standard of living, in part off the exertions of peasant labor and their taxes and contributions in kind and in part off the substantial revenues the Siamese court gained from international trade. In these respects, Ayudhya was more highly developed and stronger, and with its international contacts, more cosmopolitan. Ayudhya thus was far better able than its upcountry neighbors to recover quickly from the next onslaught of Burmese armies after the middle of the eighteenth century, and ready subsequently to expand its territory substantially at the expense of Lan Na and Lan Sang.

Ayudhya: Sources of Strength and Instability

Superficially, the Kingdom of Ayudhya in the period marked by the ascendance of the dynasty founded by Phra Phetracha seems to have been much like its northern neighbors. The chronicles of the period, which are virtually our only source, are similar to those of Lan Na and Lan Sang in the same period. They are filled with stories of dynastic squabbles, disputes over the succession to the throne, and glorious military expeditions. We encounter persons with colorful names—"King tiger," for example—and are meant to be awed by reports of the capture of white elephants or of a king's pious donations and constructions. Recent scholarship on the period, however, has begun to outline more profound developments that were taking place below the surface of the chronicles, developments that had a great deal to do with the growing differences between Siam and its northern neighbors.

As we have seen, Phetracha ascended the throne of Ayudhya in 1688 as a usurper. Throughout the nearly eighty years of his dynasty's rule, he and his successors were haunted by this fact, especially early in the period when they suffered numerous challenges to their authority. Phetracha himself felt sufficiently insecure to take—seize would be a better word—as wives King Narai's sister and daughter, thus intimately surrounding himself with some of Narai's royal power and ensuring that any children he had by them would have royal blood from at least one side of the family. Moreover, Phetracha took the extreme step of raising to the rank of royal prince those who had played important roles in placing him on the throne. His son, Luang Sorasak, was made uparat, to reside in the so-called Front Palace usually reserved for the heir-apparent, and two others in effect were placed in the Rear Palace with royal rank. Phetracha's strategy here appears to have been to create a royal establishment, with its own reserves of and control over manpower, in order to counter the power of the nobles of the central and provincial administrations. Luang Sorasak, however, was uncomfortable with this situation and jealous of his royal rivals, and within a year plotted to have them both killed. His actions reduced the centers of royal power to two: the king and Luang Sorasak, which left the crown somewhat exposed.

The next few years were dangerous for them. A major rebellion led by a certain Thammathian, a retainer of Narai's brother, Prince Aphaithot, whom Sorasak had killed the year before, nearly succeeded in toppling the throne early in 1690. Furthermore, the next three years were spent subduing the governors of Nakhon Ratchasima and Nakhon Si Thammarat, both of whom had refused to acknowledge Phetracha as king. In the course of supervising numerous expeditions against these two principalities, the king and Sorasak treated the nobles harshly: when commanders failed to take a city, they were executed. Even their successes were short-lived, for Nakhon Ratchasima again was the center of rebellion between 1698 and 1700, when a holy man, Bun Khwang, held out for more than a year, claiming to be Narai's brother. Taken together,

the popular risings and provincial rebellions kept at least part of the administration mobilized on a war footing for much of Phetracha's reign. Phetracha
may have used the opportunity to weed out officials loyal to Narai, and by
conscripting men from the most rebellious provinces, he managed to keep the
lid on insurrection.

In addition to Sorasak, Phetracha had two other sons born to queens:
Prince Phra Khwan (b. 1691) and Trat Noi (b. 1694), whose mothers were the
sister and daughter of Narai, respectively. As they grew older, Sorasak increas-
ingly feared they might displace him from the succession, and so, when
Phetracha fell seriously ill early in 1703, Sorasak unceremoniously had Phra
Khwan killed. Furious, Phetracha on his deathbed named his nephew, Prince
Phichaisurin, as his successor; but the hapless prince dared not press his claim
and stepped aside for Sorasak, who was crowned as King Suriyentharathibodi.
That he is better known as King Süa—"King Tiger"—surely reflects the
ruthlessness, even bloodthirstiness, with which he had pursued power in the
previous two decades. If his reign was more peaceful than his father's, it is no
doubt because he had cowed all challengers when ruling as the power behind
the throne in Phetracha's reign; by 1703, he was, if grudgingly, accepted as king.
He named his own two sons uparaja, but never fully trusted them and often had
them flogged. Surely few wept upon his demise in 1709, when he was succeeded
by his eldest son, the uparat, Prince Phet, whose claim to the throne was not
disputed.

Prince Phet was crowned as King Phumintharacha, but he was popularly
referred to as King Thai Sa (literally, "end of the lake," referring to the pond
that surrounded his palace). He had a relatively long and peaceful reign, a fact
that suggests that by now a certain stability had been attained in the political
arrangements of the kingdom. Two important developments occurred, however, both of which were to have important long-range repercussions.

First, King Thai Sa became increasingly involved in Cambodia, now
clearly acting the suzerain to Cambodia's vassal. Siamese involvement was
elicited by Cambodian princes and an exiled king who had been evicted from
their kingdom by rivals with Vietnamese backing in 1710, marking the real
beginnings of Vietnamese involvement in Cambodia proper. In 1720, a major
Siamese expedition, led on sea by the Phrakhlang and on land by the
Mahatthai (Phraya Chakri), attempted to reinstall King Thommoreachea on
the Cambodian throne. They failed to do so, but King Ang Em did agree to pay
the regular tribute of vassalage to Ayudhya. Over the next century, this sort of
thing was to recur with distressing frequency.

Second, the reign of Thai Sa was marked by major increases in the volume of trade with China, particularly involving the exportation of Siamese rice. In some ways, of course, such trade had gone on since the foundation of Ayudhya and before, though it was conducted under severe government restrictions in China for periods in the seventeenth and early eighteenth centuries. By the latter time, much of the Siamese trade with China and Japan that earlier had been conducted by the Dutch now fell into the hands of private Chinese merchants, who also came to conduct trade on behalf of the Ayudhya government and entered the official service of the state. In particular, Thai Sa's Phrakhlang, who had been prominent at court since King Süa's reign, was a Chinese especially important for the role he played in integrating the local Chinese community into the economic and social life of the capital, to the point where the Phrakhlang ministry virtually was dominated by Chinese at all levels. When in 1727 the Chinese government almost completely opened South China ports to shipments of rice from Siam, the trade began to boom, and all those involved with it prospered, including the Siamese court and the Phrakhlang.

The turning point in the history of Ayudhya during this period came upon the death of King Thai Sa in January 1733. A hotly disputed succession had profound effects on the political and economic structure of the kingdom. Throughout his reign, King Thai Sa had been loyally served by his younger full brother, the uparat, Prince Phon. Thai Sa himself had three sons born to his only queen, the princes Naren, Aphai, and Paramet. On his deathbed, the king expressed his choice for Aphai to succeed him. Naren was at the time serving briefly in the Buddhist monkhood and chose not to dispute the succession; but all the other parties prepared militarily to contest it. On the death of Thai Sa, Aphai and Paramet were based in the royal palace and backed by most of the leading officials, prominently by the Chinese Phrakhlang. A mile or so to the east in the Front Palace, the uparat, supported by his own officials, could muster only about four thousand troops against the twenty to thirty thousand of the Royal Palace. When the forces were engaged in battle, the uparat's out-numbered forces were on the verge of defeat when a leading Front Palace official, a certain Khun Chamnan Channarong (U), volunteered to take charge. In a swift attack he wiped out the leadership of the royal troops, who thereupon fled. The uparat and Khun Chamnan then took the royal palace and Prince Phon ascended the throne, to be styled King Song Tham or Borommathammikarat. He is best known, however, as King Borommakot, literally "the king in the urn [awaiting cremation]," because he was the last Ayudhya king to enjoy that ceremonial end.

Out of his own experience as uparat and contender for the throne, and probably also reflecting on the earlier reigns of the dynasty, Borommakot made a number of changes in the political arrangements of the state. His first had to do with the problem of balancing kingly and princely power against the power of the nobles of the central administration. When, as in 1733 and on numerous prior occasions, the kingdom came to its ultimate political contest in struggles for the throne, the outcome invariably turned on the access of the contenders to the manpower of the state. Because the fundamental task of the central administration was to control manpower, the heads of the key ministries naturally had ready access to large numbers of armed or armable men, particularly the Mahatthai and Kalahom, who since the reign of King Prasat Thong had divided the provinces between them. Therefore, at least from the reign of Phetracha, the kings of his dynasty had sought to create independent, princely departments (*krom*), the primary function of which was to give a few royal princes in the line of royal succession their own access to manpower, outside the bureaucratic establishment. Borommakot varied earlier practice in this respect, however. Where his predecessors had allowed only a handful of such departments—usually on the average three during each reign, each with control over some thousands of men—Borommakot instead created thirteen smaller departments, so that no single prince could by himself seize the throne, while the princes together could counterbalance noble departments. The effect of this change perhaps was to render the succession smoother, but it also further fragmented state control over the limited amounts of manpower available to it.

A second major change instituted by King Borommakot stemmed from the particular circumstances of the succession dispute of 1733. As we have seen, many leading officials including the Phrakhlang had sided with the princes against the uparat. One Kalahom official, Phraya Ratchasongkhram, remained neutral, though he was long a personal rival of the uparat. When the uparat came to the throne, he purged all the supporters of the princes and rewarded those who had assisted his successful campaign. Most importantly, Khun Chamnan was raised to the title of Chaophraya Chamnanborirak and given the Phrakhlang department, while Luang Chasaenyakon was made Chaophraya Aphaimontri and given the Mahatthai. Phraya Ratchasongkhram was given the Kalahom. However, King Borommakot clearly readjusted the relative positions of these three powerful ministries by changing the system of provincial control. He shifted the southern provinces from the control of the Kalahom to the Phrakhlang. Perhaps this was simply a matter of politics. The former Phrakhlang had, after all, sided with the princes and had to be replaced. Ratchasongkhram's neutrality had at least grudgingly to be rewarded, but at the same time the king might have preferred that Chamnan have control over the vital manpower of the southern provinces. In any event, the net effect was further diffusion of central power. The Kalahom, though shorn of its southern provinces, remained powerful, in control of a number of military units. The strong resident Chinese community lost its chief spokesman at the highest level of the government in the Phrakhlang.

The appointment of Chaophraya Chamnanborirak (U) (1686–1753) confirmed the rise to power of another of the important official families of Siam, one of which, the Persian family, we noted in connection with the reign of King Song Tham. The son of the governor of Phitsanulok, Chamnan was the descendant of a line of Indian Brahmans who had come to Siam in the reign of King Prasat Thong and served in ceremonial capacities at court in the seventeenth century. The title of his father's brother, Chaophraya Mahasombat (Phon) suggests that he may have served as Phrakhlang, either prior to the unnamed Chinese encountered earlier or, more likely, after Chaophraya Chamnan. Both of Chamnan's brothers attained the rank of chaophraya as did two of his first cousins and three of his sons; and one of his daughters was to marry the Phrakhlang of the last reign of the Ayudhya period. Most surprisingly, when the Mahatthai died in 1742, Chaophraya Chamnan's son Sawang was given that office and styled Chaophraya Ratchaphakdi (and Sawang himself was succeeded in that office by his younger brother Arun in 1757). Thus, in the latter years of Borommakot's reign, we find the exceptional spectacle of two of the three most powerful ministries held within the same family. We shall encounter members of this family again and, for convenience's sake, shall refer to it as the Brahman family.

To a generation that, in the 1780s and 1790s, was looking back at Ayudhya, the reign of Borommakot must have seemed a sort of golden age, an ideal to be recaptured. There was much about Borommakot's reign that accorded with traditional ideas of the virtues of good kings and so won him acclaim. He was, first of all, a strong supporter of Buddhism. His reign is perhaps best remembered for an exchange of missions with the Kingdom of Kandy in Ceylon. In 1751, a mission arrived from Ceylon requesting aid in restoring Singhalese Buddhism, which had declined under Portuguese and Dutch rule. Accordingly, a party of eighteen Siamese monks was dispatched to Kandy to reordain Singhalese monks and establish what was to become a Siam order of monks on Ceylon. A second mission also was sent to Kandy in 1755. The implications of these events were not lost on Siamese who for centuries had regarded Ceylon as the preeminent center of Buddhism. Did not this exchange imply that Siam now had won that position?

Second, in Borommakot's reign Ayudhya could be seen as again acting the role of a great kingdom in its relations with neighboring states. In 1737, the three Cambodian princes (including ex-king Thommoreachea) who had taken refuge in Ayudhya finally were allowed to raise an army in the Nakhon Ratchasima region, with which they toppled the reigning king and placed Thommoreachea on the throne (for the third time!) in 1738. Also in 1749, the Siamese intervened in Cambodia to assist in deposing a king backed by the Vietnamese, again successfully.

During the same period, Ayudhya resumed relations with Burma, after a century of virtually none. This had primarily to do with events consequent upon the later Toungoo dynasty's gradual collapse. As the kings of Ava failed to deal with military raids from Manipur that gained in intensity through the 1730s, the Mon region on the coast drifted into rebellion, creating finally an independent Mon state at Pegu in 1740. Some Burmese refugees from the area fled to Ayudhya, and it was ostensibly to thank Borommakot for his hospitality toward them that the king of Ava sent a mission to Ayudhya in 1744. His real purpose probably had to do with heading off any possible alliance of Ayudhya with Mon Pegu. Of this there was little likelihood. As over the previous century Ayudhya's scarce manpower had been supplemented by the substantial numbers of Burmese refugees, the Siamese kings did not wish to encourage the formation of an independent Mon state that might serve as an alternative focus for their loyalty. Borommakot sent a polite return mission to Ava in 1745 and thereafter carefully watched events across the border. When King Sming Htaw Buddhaketi (r. 1740–47) of Pegu was deposed and fled to Ayudhya in 1750, he was imprisoned and eventually sent off to China.

To the end of the reign, Ayudhya faced no serious external threats, and there was no military *levée en masse*. There were, however, some tense episodes in the internal politics of the kingdom that boded ill for its future stability.

These began mildly early in the reign and mounted in intensity as time wore on, becoming urgent whenever the king fell ill. First, in 1734, while the king was out of the capital on a hunting expedition, a force of three hundred Chinese stormed the palace in Ayudhya, probably reacting to their loss of influence in the Phrakhlang. They were routed, and many were executed. The following year, one of the king's sons was implicated in an abortive attempt to assassinate Borommakot's nephew, Prince Naren, who had remained in the Buddhist monkhood since 1733. Then, in 1746, another holy man began a rising in the Lopburi region. But internal squabbles became serious only from 1753, by which time the king had reigned twenty years and was seventy-three years old. In the short space of two years, considerable shifts of power occurred in the top levels of Ayudhya society. The uparat, Prince Senaphithak, the eldest of Borommakot's sons, joined with two of his half-brothers also born to queens to curb what they perceived as the pretensions and ambitions of three of their half-brothers, sons of royal concubines. The junior three, in fact, had quietly been expanding their departments, promoting their officials, and recruiting additional retainers. When Senaphithak went so far as to have some of those officials arrested and flogged, the junior party in return revealed that Senaphithak had been carrying on a love affair with one of his father's three queens. Senaphithak pleaded guilty to the charge, and he and the woman were flogged to death. As of 1755, with the death of the uparat, the question of succession to the throne was left unsettled.

During the same period there was substantial turnover in the ranks of the leading ministers. On the death of Chaophraya Chamnan (U) in 1753, the Phrakhlang was handed over to an official of Chinese descent, Chaophraya Phrakhlang (Chim) who was married to Chamnan's daughter. In 1755, both the Kalahom and the Mahatthai died. The records are not clear, but it appears that the Kalahom now went to a descendant of the Persian Family, Chaophraya Phetphichai (Chai), and the Mahatthai passed from the Brahman family to an outsider. Judging from the number of titles associated with the chief ministers of the last decade of the Ayudhya period (1758–67), there must have been a great deal of competition and jockeying for power among a small group of large extended families well entrenched in the central administration. Though several of these factions—notably the Chinese group represented by Chaophraya Phrakhlang (Chim) and the Persian family, which continued to dominate that part of the Phrakhlang department that dealt with Muslim traders—had an important base in overseas trading activities, the critical counter in all power struggles as always was the control of manpower. In this contest, all were involved, princes and nobles alike.

That there were difficulties in this respect was signaled early in Borommakot's reign. When Chaophraya Ratchaphakdi (Sawang) first assumed office as Mahatthai in 1742, he soon discovered that the manpower registers for his provinces to the north of the capital were severely deficient. His people undertook the registration of men in Wisetchaichan, Suphanburi, Nakhon Chaisi, Phromburi, Inburi, Singburi, Chainat, Manorom, Uthaithani, and Nakhon Sawan, and "tens of thousands of *phrai* were then registered for government service."[9] Evidently, however, this signaled rather than solved the problem. Through much of the century, repeated royal laws and edicts had called attention to shortages of manpower available to the government. It is clear that many freemen subject to annual compulsory labor service were evading their obligations. Some managed simply to avoid registration; others placed themselves under the protection of individual princes or officials. Furthermore, it seems plausible that, with the government's increasing interest in promoting Siamese exports, many freemen were allowed to commute their labor service by promising annual payments in commodities, either by formal arrangement with the government or by informal agreement with various officials. Whatever the precise dimensions of this problem—and Akin Rabibhadana has written extensively on it—it seems clear that by the end of Borommakot's reign there was a serious manpower shortage in Ayudhya. Moreover, control over such manpower as existed was fragmented among numerous small departments; and the important reserves of the southern provinces were under the control of the Phrakhlang, a department perhaps more heavily involved in trade than in provincial administration.

After the death of the uparat, Prince Senaphithak, in 1755, the Front Palace of the heir-apparent was left vacant until the three leading ministers urged the king to appoint Prince Uthumphon to the office in 1757. On his deathbed, King Borommakot again confirmed his preference for Prince Uthumphon as his successor, despite the slightly better claims of his elder brother, Prince Anurakmontri. But not unlike many previous occasions, the succession did not go as the king wished. On Borommakot's death on April 13, 1758, three leading princes gathered up their retainers and armed themselves from the royal arsenal to oppose Prince Uthumphon's accession to the throne. Uthumphon gained the support of the leading officials and dignitaries of the Buddhist monkhood and first forestalled and then executed the princes. He was crowned king at the end of the month, but his elder brother resided in the royal palace. Uthumphon lost the will to oppose him, and after a reign of only ten days, he abdicated in favor of his brother, who reigned as King Borommaracha (1758–67), but is popularly remembered as the Suriyamarin Palace King, after his residence.

This inauspicious beginning to the reign was but the first wave in what was to be a sea of troubles. Suriyamarin distrusted the leading nobles, who, he rightly judged, preferred his younger brother. Indeed, a group of officials led by the Kalahom plotted in 1759 to depose him and restore Uthumphon to the throne. It is not surprising, then, that the king should have had difficulty gaining the effective cooperation of his officials when, the following year, the kingdom again was thrown into calamitous warfare with the Burmese. Within seven years, this conflict would overturn the entire Tai world and bring to an end the ancient Kingdom of Ayudhya.

The Burmese and the Tai World

If the Burmese Kingdom of Ava was at the mercy of Manipuris and Mons in the 1740s, the opposite became true in the 1750s after a cataclysmic collapse of the old kingdom. As had happened before in the sixteenth century, Burmese recovery included a strong measure of imperial aggression that threatened all its neighbors.

In the late 1740s, the revived Mon Kingdom of Pegu took advantage of Ava's seeming helplessness in the face of Manipuri and Shan raids, and in April 1752, they succeeded in taking the capital and ending the later Toungoo dynasty. Almost immediately, however, Burman resistance in a rural district northwest of Ava coalesced around a magnetic and powerful personality, who quickly rallied the people against the Mons. By the middle of the year, he had gained wide recognition throughout the region as King Alaunghpaya. He first restored the Kingdom of Ava and then recaptured the south, taking Pegu in 1757. Soon thereafter, his attention turned to Siam. A variety of explanations have been put forward for his doing so. Most immediately, Siam had received large numbers of Mon refugees from the warfare that ravaged the Burma coast from 1754, and Alaunghpaya could fear Ayudhya's backing for the revival of the Kingdom of Pegu. It is also argued that much of Burma was depopulated by the warfare of the period, and Alaunghpaya waged war in order to replenish his state's manpower. Others might argue that successful expeditions against major states in the region would validate Ava's statehood, indicating to Ava's hundreds of vassal states that they could not hope to challenge Ava's suzerainty. Finally, one might simply guess that Alaunghpaya, apparently a rather rude country fellow with scant experience of statecraft, was simply continuing to do what he early demonstrated he could do best: lead armies into warfare. He may also have aspired to the legendary greatness that had characterized the great Burmese warrior-kings of the sixteenth century who, among other things, had reduced Ayudhya, Lan Na, and Lan Sang to vassalage.

Early in 1760, Alaunghpaya personally led an expedition that reduced Martaban, Tavoy, and Tenasserim and then crossed the peninsula to take Kui, Phetburi, and Ratburi. By April 1760, the Burmese forces besieged Ayudhya. The Siamese had been unprepared; they had raised forces too small for defense and had dispersed them too widely. The siege might have been successful had not one of the Burmese siege guns burst, injuring Alaunghpaya and sparking a Burmese retreat. Alaunghpaya died on the way back to Burma.

Alaunghpaya's immediate successor, Naungdawgyi (r. 1760–63), after first suppressing internal challenges to his rule, undertook the subjection of Chiang Mai. There, Prince Chan had succeeded his father, Ong Kham, in 1759 and soon was embroiled in troubles. Profiting from Burmese distractions elsewhere, Burmese garrisons in Chiang Saen were challenged, and insurrection seemed everywhere. Chan himself, perhaps because he was an outsider, finally was overthrown by Lan Na princes in 1761. Then, early in 1763, an enormous Burmese army besieged Chiang Mai and, after six months, seized the city, as well as Lamphun. A Burmese general now ruled in Chiang Mai until he was overthrown by a local rebellion a year or so later. The Burmese response came with overwhelming force early in the reign of King Hsinbyushin (r. 1763–76) of Ava. An army of thirty thousand men, mostly Shans led by their own rulers and commanded by the general Thihapatei, invaded Lan Na by two routes, one army advancing on Chiang Rai and the upper Mekong and the other pressing down on Chiang Mai. Within a few months, Thihapatei's forces had subdued all of old Lan Na. As the Burmese chroniclers put it, "Then, having mopped up all the people in the towns of the 57 districts of Chiang Mai who insolently were unsubmissive, there was no trouble and everything was as smooth as the surface of water."[10]

Luang Prabang was next, probably at the instigation of King Siribunyasan of Vientiane who had sent a letter to Hsinbyushin apparently offering aid against his rival. At the end of 1764, Thihapatei set out from his base at Nan where he had spent the previous rainy season. By March 1765, he had reduced Luang Prabang and taken hostages for King Sotikakuman's future good behavior and assistance. Vientiane troops are said to have assisted in the capture of Luang Prabang, thus further fueling the rivalry between the two kingdoms.

Finally, the Burmese troops began to mass for the final assault on Ayudhya. The northern forces, led by Thihapatei, began from Lampang where they had spent the rainy season of 1765. Their original ranks of Shan contingents now were swelled by troops from Lan Na and Lan Sang, each led by local governors and rulers. These advanced southward through Tak, Kamphaengphet, Sawankhalok, Sukhothai, Phitsanulok, Phichai, Phichit, Nakhon Sawan, and Ang Thong, beginning in late July 1765. Meanwhile, a southern expedition, commanded by Mahanawrahta, set out from Tavoy in late September and, advancing by way of Chumphon and Phetburi, joined with a small contingent that had crossed into Siam via the Three Pagodas Pass to take Ratburi and Suphanburi. By February 1766, the two main Burmese forces had effected a junction on the outskirts of Ayudhya and besieged the city.

Against this massive invasion, the Siamese resistance was both belated and uncoordinated. King Suriyamarin appears to have allowed his forces to relax after the close call of 1760. He responded to a request for help from Chiang Mai in 1763 by sending a small expedition north, but it arrived too late and did not engage the Burmese. If there was a last chance for a successful response, it was in 1764–65 when the Burmese were winning the north and effectively outflanking

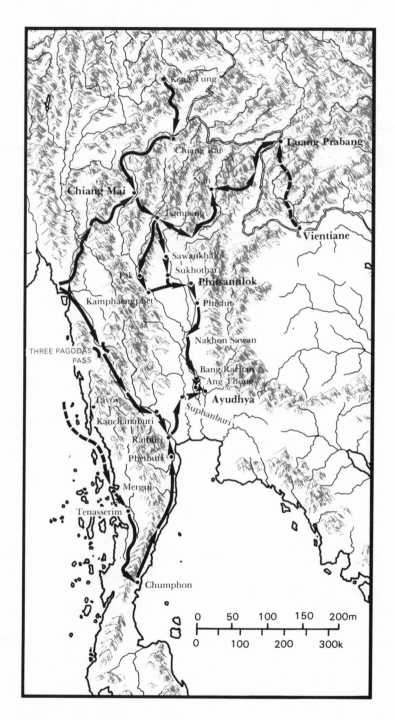

The Burmese invasion of 1763–67.

Ayudhya; but Suriyamarin let the opportunity pass without doing anything. As a result, when the final assault started in the last half of 1765, the Siamese were unprepared, cut off from potential assistance from the north, and forced to meet the Burmese on two fronts at once. The Burmese encountered only token resistance from many of the provincial governors and their troops. The most effective Siamese resistance early in this campaign came from the small village of Bang Rachan, northwest of Ayudhya, where Thihapatei's troops were stalled for five months. A few months later, a major force of sixty thousand men was sent out from the capital to meet Mahanawrahta's advance, but they were defeated by the much smaller Burmese force and had to retreat to the capital. Here and there across the countryside, a leader might gather troops and harass the Burmese for a few days, but these efforts were futile, and soon fighting was reduced to the siege around Ayudhya.

Suriyamarin must have hoped, as his predecessors had done, that the onset of the rains and the flooding of the great Central Plain would force a Burmese retreat. The Burmese, however, concentrated on and fortified high ground, commandeering boats to keep their forces in action. Toward the end of 1766, the governors of Phetburi and Tak led waterborne expeditions out from the capital to attack the Burmese, but the governor of Phetburi was killed and the attacks blunted. The governor of Tak, an able and ambitious commander, was unfairly blamed for the expedition's failure and hindered in his attempts to mount an effective counterattack. As the city's fate grew dimmer, he quietly escaped from the city with a few hundred followers and headed eastward. As if growing famine and raging epidemics were not enough, a fire broke out within the city early in 1767 which burned ten thousand houses. Seeing his cause lost, King Suriyamarin then offered to surrender and become a vassal of the king of Burma, but the Burmese would agree to nothing but unconditional surrender. At length, the Burmese intensified their efforts against the city and, on April 7, 1767, finally breached the walls and took the ancient capital.

The Burmese wrought awful desolation. They raped, pillaged, and plundered, and led tens of thousands of captives away to Burma. They put the torch to everything flammable and even hacked at images of the Buddha for the gold with which they were coated. King Suriyamarin is said to have fled the city in a small boat and starved to death ten days later. Ex-King Uthumphon and countless members of the royal family and nobility were led away to Burma. Those who survived suffered worst of all. As a contemporary described the scene some decades later,

> The populace was afflicted with a variety of ills by the enemy. Some wandered about, starving, searching for food. They were bereft of their

families, their children and wives, and stripped of their possessions and tools. . . . They had no rice, no fish, no clothing. They were thin, their bodies wasting away. They found only the leaves of trees and grass to eat. . . . In desperation many turned to dacoity. . . . They gathered in bands, and plundered for rice and paddy and salt. Some found food, and others could not. They grew thinner, and their flesh and blood wasted away. Afflicted with a thousand ills, some died and some lived on.[11]

Had the two centuries since the previous Burmese sack of Ayudhya brought no new strength to Ayudhya or its contemporary states in the Tai world? In many ways they were no better prepared to meet the Burmese onslaught now than they had been two hundred years earlier. In particular, their capacity to mobilize the manpower of the state had not improved. There, however, the similarity between Ayudhya and its northern neighbors ends. In the preceding two hundred years, Ayudhya had developed effective institutions for carrying on a broad range of specialized state functions and especially had developed economic institutions that were capable of supporting a highly differentiated metropolitan society that, on the whole, was responsive to a wider world. Ayudhya effectively managed a wide range of economic, cultural, religious, and legal activities and usually could govern effectively a large number of provinces spread over a considerable area. It regularly absorbed, and made the best use of the considerable talents of, a heterogeneous population of great cultural, ethnic, and linguistic variety.

It is easy to forget that for nearly two hundred years Ayudhya had maintained a high degree of unity. For a time in the seventeenth century, chronic rebellion had been the rule for the more distant reaches of the Malay Peninsula; but the core of the kingdom had been ruled remarkably effectively, in sharp contrast to both Lan Na and Lan Sang. Perhaps Ayudhya's inability readily to mobilize its manpower in the 1760s was less a failure of its administrative institutions than a symptom of a much more persistent problem inherent in a situation where manpower is more valuable than land. Controlling land is relatively simpler, if only because it is immobile and has no volition of its own. People, possessed of individual wills, naturally seek to act in their own best interests. They can respond to the common interest to the extent that they are well led; and it was here that Ayudhya's lack of strong, durable political institutions, and mechanisms for the transfer of political power from one generation to the next, threatened the kingdom's survival.

As in both Lan Na and Lan Sang, virtually every royal succession in these two centuries turned into a political crisis. These crises became increasingly dangerous as the stakes grew higher. The nobles of the central bureaucracy had well-established economic, social, and political interests to preserve, and any new king might radically alter the existing balance of power among them. If there was a real general crisis in the seventeenth and eighteenth centuries, it stemmed from the tension between royal and noble power, between the paramountcy of the throne and the competition among elite, noble factions and interest groups. Ayudhya at least, during these two centuries, nurtured the development of noble power and the growth of diversity from which could come further development and change. It remained for the successors to Ayudhya to find means of ensuring the stability that would allow the kingdom both to grow and to maintain its independence.

6

The Early Bangkok Empire, 1767–1851

Following the Burmese destruction of the Kingdom of Ayudhya in 1767, one might have expected a long period of slow recovery and reconstruction during which the Tai world would be fragmented into numerous weak principalities. Quite the opposite happened. Within a decade or so, a new Siam already had succeeded where Naresuan and his Ayudhya predecessors had failed in creating a vast new Siamese empire encompassing Lan Na and much of Lan Sang, as well as Cambodia and large portions of the Malay Peninsula. By the middle of the nineteenth century, the empire had further expanded and seemed stronger than ever before. There seems to have been a new energy, a dynamism, at work, pulsing outward from the core of old Siam. This was not, however, mere military momentum carried on the crest of battlefield successes, though this was an important part of the phenomenon. It was more than that. It involved what seems to have been a new Siamese vision of their place in the world and a new self-confidence in their ability to lead their neighbors in the face of the dangers and uncertainties around them. It began as a response to the calamities of 1767, but it soon was to become at least as much creative as reactive.

The Abortive Reconstruction of King Taksin

When the Burmese captured Ayudhya in April 1767, the countryside was in a state of great turmoil. No central government and little authority of any kind existed. However, because their homeland recently had gone to war with China in the extreme north, the Burmese soon withdrew from Siam, leaving only small garrisons behind, and a scramble for power began in the Chaophraya River basin. At the local level, this amounted to the spread of dacoity, the organization of bandit gangs who plundered and robbed for their livelihood while beginning slowly to enter into relations with remnants of local ruling families or members of the capital bureaucracy who might provide them with leadership, support, or an aura of respectability. The more ambitious established their own principalities, even "kingdoms," to contest for primacy in the region at large.

There were five main centers of power in 1767. Only one made claim to the legitimate royal succession to the kings of Ayudhya. This was a court located at Phimai, the ancient Khmer center near Nakhon Ratchasima (Khorat), under the leadership of Prince Thepphiphit, a son of King Borommakot. A very different sort of state was centered on Sawangkhaburi, or Fang, east of Uttaradit on the Nan River. There a group of Buddhist monks seized power, clad in reddish robes instead of saffron yellow and living as laymen. Surrounded by an aura of sanctity, they grew sufficiently powerful to be able in 1770 to subdue a third principality at Phitsanulok. There the local governor had formed a state and even had himself crowned as king. A similar situation arose at Nakhon Si Thammarat on the peninsula, but with a significant difference. The governor of Nakhon was descended from generations of rulers of that region and was able naturally to call upon the loyalties of provinces as far north as Chumphon, making his state relatively more formidable than Phimai, Sawangkhaburi, or Phitsanulok. For the most part, however, none of these four principalities attempted to contest for power in the heartland of old Ayudhya in the Central Plain.

The fifth, and most important, contender for power in 1767 was, on the face of things, a very unlikely personage. This was a young man named Sin, the son of a Chinese father and Siamese mother who had been adopted by a noble family and raised in the capital. By the time of the Burmese invasions, he was serving as governor of the province of Tak, and to distinguish him from previous governors, he was referred to as Phraya Tak (Sin)—or "Taksin." With his troops he had withdrawn from Tak to aid in the defense of the capital, but seeing the hopelessness of the situation, he fled the city when the Burmese encircled it and, with a following of troops, made his way to the southeast, to Chanthaburi, which he captured in June 1767.

The most important of Taksin's assets in those troubled times was a compelling personal charisma, an ability to convince others that he was indeed a "man of merit," one whose karma from previous existences and meritorious actions was so strong as to allow him to lead other men and vanquish all opponents. People needed his leadership and courage and vision. At the same time, Taksin was an excellent military tactician and strategist, and he was able very rapidly to expand his base of power across central Siam. In October, he took the small port of Thonburi on the west bank of the Chaophraya River across from present-day Bangkok. Making his headquarters there, the next month he defeated in the west the only sizeable Burmese force remaining in the region. In only six months from the fall of Ayudhya, Taksin had made himself a power to be reckoned with. A considerable contribution to his success came from the Teochiu Chinese trading community of the region, on whom Taksin was able to call by virtue of his paternal relations. In the short run, the Chinese trade provided the foodstuffs and goods needed for the warfare that enabled Taksin to build up his fledgling state. In the long run, it produced income that could be used "to defray the expenses of the state and for the upkeep of the individual royal, noble, and wealthy commercial families."[1] As one contemporary observed, under the famine conditions of 1767–68, Taksin

> showed his generous spirit. The needy were destitute no longer. The public treasury was opened for the relief. In return for cash, foreigners supplied them with the products that the soil of the country had refused. The Usurper [Taksin] justified his claims [to be king] by his benevolence. Abuses were reformed, the safety of property and persons was restored, but the greatest severity was shown to malefactors. Legal enactments at which no one complained were substituted for the arbitrary power that sooner or later is the cause of rebellions. By the assurance of public peace he was able to consolidate his position and no one who shared in the general prosperity could lay claim to the throne.[2]

Significantly, Taksin elected not to return to Ayudhya but instead to make his capital at Thonburi, which being only twenty kilometers from the sea was much better suited for seaborne commerce.

Having established his base, Taksin's immediate task was to reestablish central authority by subduing his rivals. His first such attempt, an expedition against Phitsanulok in May 1768, was unsuccessful. Toward the end of the year, however, he captured Phimai and early in 1769 sent an army into Cambodia and annexed Battambang and Siem Reap. Later in the year, his armies subdued Nakhon Si Thammarat and in mid-1770 took Phitsanulok and Fang. Within three years, he had reconstituted the territories of the Kingdom of Ayudhya and already, from December 1768, was reigning as a crowned monarch.

Taksin ultimately was to prove more successful as a warrior than as a ruler—and even his military duties he increasingly delegated to others. At stake in the warfare of the 1770s was the security of the state. The Burmese had been able to strangle Ayudhya by seizing the north and the south. Thonburi could not be safe unless these territories at least were denied the Burmese or preferably were brought within the Siamese orbit. To a certain extent, Taksin's task was rendered easier by the desire of the Malay and Lao principalities to gain Siamese aid against the Burmese. Early in 1769, for example, Lom Sak,

Trengganu (or Kedah?), and Pattani sent tribute to Thonburi. Soon Taksin was attempting to put a Siamese protegé on the throne of Cambodia, and at the beginning of 1771, King Siribunyasan of Vientiane sought his support against Luang Prabang.

The most important accession to the kingdom, however, was Lan Na. For many years Chiang Mai and the north had chafed under Burmese military rule, particularly when the area came to be used as the major forward base for Burmese military operations against Ayudhya and Thonburi and its Lao population repeatedly was called upon to provide manpower and supplies. Under the leadership of Phraya Chaban of Chiang Mai and Chao Kavila of Lampang, Lan Na forces sent by the Burmese to resist an invading Thonburi army in 1774 went over to the Siamese side and joined Taksin in capturing the main northern cities and expelling the Burmese. A Burmese counterattack the following year drove down from the north as far as Phitsanulok, and only after extended fighting did Siamese armies recapture Chiang Mai late in 1776. By now the north was exhausted and depopulated by years of almost continuous warfare. Chiang Mai itself was abandoned for twenty years, and following the death of Phraya Chaban, Chao Kavila of Lampang in effect ruled the north, tributary to the Siamese kings.

The heaviest fighting of the northern campaigns was directed by Chaophraya Chakri (Thong Duang) and his younger brother Chaophraya Surasi (Bunma). These two young men (born in 1737 and 1743) were the descendants of an old Ayudhya noble family that included a Phrakhlang in Narai's reign; they were the sons of a middle-level official in the Mahatthai, the ministry of the northern provinces, by his Chinese wife (who, to quote his grandson, was "a beautiful daughter of a Chinese richest family").[3] Their family connections deserve special emphasis. We have had occasion to note previously the leading noble families of the late Ayudhya period—the Persian Bunnags, the Brahman family, and the Chinese family. At least by 1775, and in some cases earlier, the Chakri and his younger brother were related to all three. The Chakri's chief wife was closely related to the Bunnags; through his elder sister's husband he was related to the Brahman line; and at least through one of his concubines, if not also through his mother and by the marriages of his siblings, he was well-connected to the Chinese line.

When Ayudhya fell in 1767, Thong Duang was serving as crown representative in Ratburi, where his wife's family was powerful; his father was in Phitsanulok and became the Chakri, the military commander, of the ambitious governor of that principality, which now was trying to assert its independence. That effort, which it is tempting to view as the chief hope of the old noble elite, was cut short by the premature deaths of the governor and of Thong Duang's father and by the fall of the city to the red-clad monks from Fang. Meanwhile, Bunma had joined Taksin's service and brought his elder brother to the king's attention. After notable successes in the campaigns of the early years of Taksin's reign, Thong Duang was appointed Yommarat by 1771; by 1775, he was the Chakri and was campaigning without the royal presence, his brother always at his side.

Soon after the conquest of Lan Na and the installation of Kavila as a Siamese vassal in the north, the Chakri and his brother undertook an ambitious campaign to the east. Apparently the Siamese leaders felt that the time had come to end the perpetual political turbulence along Siam's eastern frontiers— the petty squabbling among three or more Lao kingdoms and the endemic instability in Cambodia. In the early 1770s, Burmese troops had been drawn into the conflict between Vientiane and Luang Prabang. This fact may have encouraged the Siamese to take advantage of a peaceful lull in Burma's policies under King Singu (1776–82) and deny the Burmese access to the upper Mekong valley. Similarly, the Vietnamese states of this period increasingly were distracted by internal rebellion and were unlikely to act in the Lao states or in Cambodia. Thus, in the last months of 1778, Chaophraya Chakri set out with a force of twenty thousand men to march from Nakhon Ratchasima across the Khorat Plateau toward Vientiane, while Chaophraya Surasi took ten thousand men across Cambodia and, requisitioning additional men and supplies there, struck up the Mekong River. Having gained the submission of Champassak and Nakhon Phanom along the way, Surasi joined the Chakri and a small Luang Prabang force before the walls of Vientiane. The city quickly fell. Many hundreds of Lao families were rounded up and dragged back to settle in the region of Saraburi, while the two Buddha-image palladia of Lan Sang, the Emerald Buddha and the Phrabang, were brought back to be enshrined in Thonburi. The Siamese had firmly established their suzerainty over Champassak and Vientiane and had cowed Luang Prabang into unequal alliance with Siam.

By the time the armies returned to Thonburi in April 1779, it was clear that all was not well with the king and his court. French missionaries reported that Taksin increasingly devoted himself to religious excesses: "He passed all his time in prayer, fasting, and meditation, in order by these means to be able to fly through the air."[4] More seriously, he was provoking schism in Siamese Buddhism by requiring that the monkhood should recognize him as a *sotapanna* "or stream-winner, a type of deity who had embarked on the first of four stages to enlightenment: stream-winner, once-returner, never-returner, arahat."[5] Monks who refused to bow to Taksin, to worship him as a god, were demoted in status, and hundreds were flogged and sentenced to menial labor. Such de-

velopments in any age might have upset many orthodox Buddhists; but
Taksin's aberrant behavior must have seemed all the more threatening to
Siamese who believed that the calamities of 1767 had occurred because the
kings of Ayudhya had not been properly pious and the society was sinking in a
state of moral decay. Their current perception of Taksin's right, by merit, to
reign was shaken by the king's increasingly arbitrary and cruel actions. Again,
the missionaries describe the situation:

> For some years, the King of Siam has tremendously vexed his subjects and
> the foreigners who dwelt in or came to trade in his kingdom. Last year
> [1781] the Chinese, who were accustomed to trade, found themselves
> obliged almost to give it up entirely. This past year the vexations caused by
> this King, more than half-mad [plus qu'à demi-fou], have become more
> frequent and more cruel than previously. He has had imprisoned, tor-
> tured, and flogged, according to his caprice, his wife, his sons—even the
> heir-presumptive, and his high officials. He wanted to make them confess
> to crimes of which they were innocent.[6]

What might be described as paranoid behavior on Taksin's part may, of
course, have become self-fulfilling. He was, in a sense, an outsider, a parvenu,
one who, though he had risen from mixed birth on the fringe of society to the
very highest position in it, still felt somehow outside it. His roots in Siamese
society were shallow, only a generation deep. The old families who had run
Siam for generations under the umbrella of Ayudhyan and now Taksin's
kingship could, with peace and prosperity restored, continue to pursue their
own interests. Taksin must have heard them whispering about him and felt
their disapproval of his actions and activities. It was not long before he had
alienated all those who counted for anything in the power structure of the
capital: the monks, the old families, the officials, and the merchants.

Taksin was king of a Siam that extended farther afield than Ayudhya ever
had done; yet, below the surface, a great deal of power remained in the hands of
others. To cite only a few suggestive examples, Nakhon Si Thammarat in the
south and Lan Na in the north remained under the control of local ruling
families; the Bunnags shared control of the Phrakhlang department with the
Chinese and Brahman families; and the young heirs to the fortunes of the old
noble families used their names, connections, and expertise to maintain or
improve their positions. Because they were knitted together in numerous
cliques and factions, and often buttressed by their personal control over manpower in the towns and villages outside the capital (and within it), it is likely
that by the end of 1781 some consensus had begun to emerge within the elite
that Taksin had to be replaced—for the good of all, for the fate of Buddhism,
for the future of Siam.

That same year a rebellion in Cambodia had led to the death of the king and widespread unrest. Taksin was determined to place a pro-Siamese monarch on the Cambodian throne and again sent the Chakri and Surasi with twenty thousand men to accomplish the task. As these armies moved at a leisurely pace across the border, a crisis rapidly developed back at the capital. Organized local bands in Saraburi and Ayudhya provinces joined to attack the tax-farmer of Ayudhya, a Taksin appointee who was notoriously rapacious. The officer sent from the capital to put down the rebels instead joined with them and called for the overthrow of Taksin and the elevation of the Chakri to the throne. Meeting little resistance, the rebels marched on Thonburi, seized Taksin, and invited Chaophraya Chakri to accept the throne, which he did on April 6, 1782, having hastened back from Cambodia.

The fifteenth-century palatine law of King Trailok provided unusual methods by which royalty might be executed. Taksin is said to have met his end tied up in a velvet sack and struck on the back of the neck with a sandalwood club, later to be secretly buried in the outskirts of Thonburi. (A persistent folk tradition in Thailand insists that another unfortunate was substituted for Taksin in the velvet sack, while the ex-king was spirited off to a retreat hidden in the hills above Nakhon Si Thammarat where a luxurious palace was built for him. There he is said to have died only in 1825.) Taksin was not widely or publicly mourned, though his successor did sponsor a royal cremation for him in 1784. In their haste to correct Taksin's excesses, few spared the time to consider his monumental accomplishments. At the very least, Taksin had provided the energetic leadership that Siamese had needed to pull themselves out of the dire straits into which they had fallen in 1767. At best, he had constructed a framework of military and diplomatic security within which Siam might survive.

Rama I's New Siam

After undergoing an abbreviated victory coronation, the former Chakri reigned as King Ramathibodi. (He was posthumously given the title of Phra Phutthayotfa Chulalok, but is generally referred to as King Rama I, 1782–1809.) One of his first acts as king was to move the capital across the Chaophraya River to Bangkok on the east bank, where the government might be less vulnerable to a Burmese attack from the west. The city soon bustled with craftsmen constructing a new royal palace and imposing Buddhist monasteries, while princes and officials constructed homes along the network of canals radiating eastward from the palace and Chinese and Indian merchants built their shops and warehouses along the river to the south. Not unlike Ayudhya in

earlier centuries, groups of families bound to service in the different departments of government created their own neighborhoods immediately outside the
main walls of the city: here the Chams attached to the army; there a group of
Malays who manned naval vessels, clustered around an Islamic house of
worship; north of the city, a settlement of Roman Catholics descended from
Portuguese and Japanese Christians. The personal retainers of individual
princes and officials often lived near their patron and protector. The city had no
roads, and the canals that crisscrossed the city and its environs bustled with
traffic. The transition from Ayudhya to Bangkok was more than symbolic.
Thousands of boatloads of bricks were taken from the ruins of Ayudhya and
used in constructing the city's walls and public buildings.

King Rama I faced formidable problems, primary among these being
those that had brought about Taksin's end. One of his first actions was to
reestablish the Buddhist monkhood. The king and many of his comtemporaries
appear to have believed that Siamese Buddhism was in a state of crisis. Many
monks appeared ill-disciplined, poorly educated, and susceptible to immorality
and heresy. Substantial numbers had encouraged the more extreme pretensions
of Taksin, while their more learned and pious brethren were demoted or
punished for resisting them. Beginning within a month of his accession to the
throne, Rama I issued a series of ecclesiastical laws intended to restore discipline
to the monkhood; and he coupled these with a series of ecclesiastical appointments that restored the most learned and pious monks to positions of leadership
within the hierarchy. The king further encouraged the working harmony of the
monkhood by sponsoring ecclesiastical commissions to consider textual questions, which culminated in 1788–89 in the convening of a grand council to
establish a definitive text of the Pali-language Tipitaka, the scriptures of
Buddhism. The king's leadership and patronage, which included the building
of large numbers of monasteries in the capital and the maintenance and
education of thousands of monks, seems to have worked quickly to ally church
and state in the interests of the new dynasty.

In this and numerous other ways, the court seems to have been concerned
to restore the glories of Ayudhya, to return in some sense to an imagined golden
age of the past—often associated with the reign of King Borommakot. Early in
his reign, the king sponsored the revival of state ceremonies that had been in
abeyance since the fall of Ayudhya, thus ritually acting out the conceptions of
community, hierarchy, and identity upon which the state was based. Only
when the proper forms had been researched—and dynasty and state had been
consolidated—did Rama I undergo his full coronation in 1785. Ultimately the
king was to take a similar, systematic approach to his legislative functions. In
1805, he appointed a commission of judges and scholars to examine the entire

corpus of Siamese law. He directed its members to establish, revise, and edit a definitive text of all the laws, after which "His Majesty would himself strive to revise those laws that were irregular or defective so that they would be in accordance with justice." [7] The resulting code, the Three Seals Laws, served the state for the next century.

These religious, ceremonial, and legislative activities, as well as the literary and cultural activities we will examine below, were consonant with the traditional expectations Siamese had of their rulers. To a certain degree, even King Taksin had involved himself in them, though not to the same extent. Rama I himself frequently explicitly claimed that what he was doing was restoring traditional ways. However, his actions must not be taken at face value, for he was not simply reinstituting Ayudhyan ecclesiastical life, court ceremonial, or legislation. That he was, in a sense, doing something radically new is indicated in two ways. First, Rama I consistently applied to all his actions certain abstract standards rooted deeply in Siamese and Buddhist tradition. His ecclesiastical laws were intended to bring monks back, not to the way things were in late Ayudhya, but to the way Rama I and his associates thought they were in the time of the Buddha, according to the canonical texts. The court ceremonials were "carried out as in [the time of] King Borommakot," [8] but with their Buddhist elements and values enhanced and brahmanical and animistic elements diminished. Similarly, the old Ayudhya laws were reaffirmed, but they were systematically organized along the lines of traditional Indian law and purged of anything the king considered not to be "in accordance with justice." [9] At work here, of course, was an active, creative intelligence, a mind or minds (for we do not know to what extent the king's work depended on others) not merely content to transmit the past but wanting to shape the past and in so doing to shape the future.

A second way in which the reforms of Rama I can be seen to be radically new is suggested by the style in which they were accomplished. Unlike any previous royal legislator, Rama I seems to have been compelled to explain and justify himself. All his laws, decrees, and proclamations, as well as the prefaces attached to his literary and religious compilations, are extraordinarily candid. His laws characteristically begin by describing a situation to be corrected and explaining why the situation is immoral or dangerous. They often place themselves in historical context and elucidate the abstract principles that should be applied. They are, above all, rational arguments intended to persuade a public.

We know, of course, that in the absence of printing in Siam and in the dependence of the government on armies of scribes to hand copy all official communications, the public addressed by royal decrees must have been very small, limited no doubt to narrow official circles. In a rigidly hierarchical society like eighteenth-century Siam, however, these were the "people who mattered," the people who among other things had rebuilt the kingdom after Ayudhya's fall and had turned against Taksin and accepted Rama I. These were people not unlike the man the king had been a decade or so earlier, men with whom the Chakri had shared battlefield rations, men with whom he long had dealt as equals. Many of them were his kinsmen, and most of them came from backgrounds like his own. Many Ayudhya kings, like Prasat Thong or Phetracha, became distant, officious, royal on their accession to the throne. Rama I had seen Taksin do so and must have reckoned the cost to be too high. On the whole, it appears that Rama I worked with his officials as a first among equals. He had a good working relationship with them. He rewarded talent and punished inefficiency, but always he was perceived to be fair.

Modeled closely on that of late Ayudhya, the government of Rama I was based mainly on the six great ministries. Four of the six had direct territorial responsibilities within which their officers exercised all official functions. The most important, as it had been historically, was the Mahatthai, responsible for the provinces north and east of the capital; Rama I appointed Chaophraya Rattanaphiphit (Son Sonthirat) to head it. He was the son of an old Ayudhya noble family and during Taksin's reign had served the Chakri as his secretary (holding the same title Rama I's father held in Ayudhya times). The Kalahom ministry, governing the provinces from Phetburi south, was placed in the hands of Chaophraya Mahasena (Pli). Pli was the son and nephew of two late-Ayudhya Kalahom, was closely related to the Bunnag family, and had served Rama I's younger brother during the wars of the 1770s. The Phrakhlang was Chaophraya Phrakhlang (Son), a holdover (perhaps because of special expertise?) from the Thonburi period who soon was demoted and replaced by Chaophraya Phrakhlang (Hon). His office controlled the provinces around the head of the Gulf of Siam, south of Bangkok. The Krom Müang was responsible for the capital and its environs, and was placed under the control of Chaophraya Yommarat (Thong-in), who had fought beside the Chakri in the Thonburi period. He, too, was soon replaced, succeeded by the leading heir to the Bunnag family's fortunes, Bunnak, who served as Yommarat from 1785 to 1787 and then became Kalahom. The remaining two ministries were controlled by members of the old Brahman family. The Ministry of Lands (Krom Na) was put under Chaophraya Phonlathep (Pin Singhaseni), who in 1805 was to become Kalahom. The Ministry of the Palace (Krom Wang), responsible for the administration of the court, was under Chaophraya Thamma (Bunrot Bunyarattaphan), who had served under the Chakri in the Thonburi period and was the son of a court brahman.

Considered as a group, these ministers were broadly representative of the

leading families of the old order. At least initially, the most sensitive positions—
the Mahatthai, Kalahom, and Yommarat—were in the hands of men with
close personal ties to the monarch, while the Phrakhlang and Palace positions
went to men with special expertise. The Brahmans and the Bunnags were well
provided for; the Chinese family might be represented by the two Phrakhlang,
though this is by no means certain. It is both important and fascinating to note
that almost all of Rama I's early ministers came to be related to him by
marriage. Most provided him with concubines by whom the king had children,
and these royal children were to be further bonds, knitting Siamese elite society
together.

Rama I's state met its first great test in a massive Burmese invasion in 1785.
King Bodawhpaya of Burma (r. 1781–1819) sent more than a hundred
thousand troops in five armies against Siam. The first was sent against the
peninsular region, crossing overland from Mergui to Chumphon and Chaiya
and thence south. The second pushed off from Tavoy across the mountains to
Ratburi and Phetburi to meet up with the force at Chumphon. The main force,
under the command of Bodawhpaya himself, crossed the Three Pagodas Pass
from Martaban toward Kanchanaburi and was directed against Bangkok. The
fourth army was to proceed to Tak and Kamphaengphet and then close in on
the capital from the north; the fifth moved from its base in Chiang Saen to
Lampang and thence southeastward toward Phitsanulok. This was an exceptionally ambitious and, for the Siamese, dangerous attack.

The Siamese resisted the temptation to spread their forces any more than
absolutely necessary. Informed late in 1784 of Burmese preparations, the court
mobilized approximately seventy thousand men and divided them among four
key points. The main force, under the command of the uparat (Rama I's
younger brother, the former Chaophraya Surasi) went to Kanchanaburi to
block the Three Pagodas Pass invasion route. One smaller force, under the
king's nephew, Prince Anurakthewet, was positioned at Nakhon Sawan to
block the northern approach to the Central Plain; and another small force,
under the command of Chaophraya Thamma (Bunrot) and Chaophraya
Yommarat (Thong-in) was stationed at Ratburi to keep the supply lines to
Kanchanaburi open in case of an attack from the south. The king, with a force
of twenty thousand men, remained in Bangkok in reserve.

Early in 1785, the conflict began in the desolate hinterland upstream from
Kanchanaburi. The uparat's forces successfully contained the Burmese there,
while harassing their supply lines farther up the Khwae River. As the Burmese,
now famished and tired, became demoralized, the uparat attacked and sent
their advance guard fleeing in disarray. Bodawhpaya, farther up the river,
panicked and withdrew his main force back to Martaban. Meanwhile, the

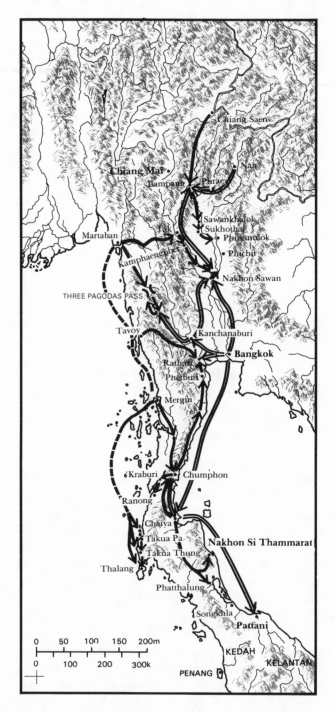

The Burmese invasion of 1785. Solid arrows denote the movement of Burmese troops;
open arrows, the movement of Siamese troops.

Thamma and Yommarat negligently had allowed the Burmese second force to swing in from the southwest and encamp in the Ratburi region. A detachment from the uparat's main army encountered and defeated them after heavy fighting. As punishment for their dereliction of duty, the Thamma and Yommarat had stripes shaven across their heads and were demoted from their offices.

In the north, Chao Kavila managed to hold up one of the Burmese armies for several months before the walls of Lampang, while the main Siamese northern army held the remainder of the fourth and fifth Burmese armies north of Nakhon Sawan. Once the main battle in the Kanchanaburi region was over, Rama I brought his forces north to join in the defense. When the armies had been drawn up, a major battle was fought near the juncture of the Yom and Nan rivers. The Burmese forces were decimated. A portion of the Siamese armies then moved north to relieve Lampang and expel the Burmese from Lan Na, joined now by provincial armies from Phrae and Nan and other principalities of the north.

While all this heavy fighting was going on during February and March of 1785, the Burmese southern army was having a field day in the peninsular south, taking most of the cities on both coasts of the peninsula from Chumphon south with little resistance until they were halted by vigorous defenses on Thalang, on the west coast, and were advancing on Phatthalung, on the east coast. It was at this point that forces from the Siamese western army, under the uparat, moved into the region. Fearful of being cut off, the Burmese began to pull back north, and after a brief engagement with the Siamese at Chaiya, fled across to the west coast and northward back to Burma.

Many of the southern principalities, and especially Nakhon Si Thammarat, had offered little resistance to the Burmese, believing that Bangkok had either fallen or was in grave danger and would be unable to assist them in repulsing superior Burmese forces. This situation was potentially dangerous to Siam, for Burmese control of the south would give them a strategic forward base and considerable supplies of foodstuffs and manpower. Rama I therefore took two major steps to strengthen the south. First, he directed the uparat to impose and enforce Bangkok's suzerainty over the Malay states of the mid-peninsula. Pattani at first resisted, so the uparat quickly invaded the state and imposed on it a new ruler. The neighboring states—Kedah, Kelantan, and Trengganu—quickly fell into line and sent the traditional ornamental gold and silver trees of tribute to Rama I. Second, the administrative lines of control in the south were readjusted. Songkhla was taken out from under the control of Nakhon Si Thammarat. Its ruler, a relative newcomer of Chinese origins, was given high status as a chaophraya and made to report directly to Bangkok; he assumed direct responsibility for Siam's relations with the Malay tributary states. Meanwhile, in the midst of the uparat's attempts to subdue the Malay states, the sultan of Kedah, having been bullied by both the Burmese and the Siamese in the preceding year, attempted to win a new ally by ceding to the English East India Company (August 27, 1785) the port and island of Penang off his west coast. Bangkok seems hardly to have noticed, and it was to be forty years before the full implications of this event would begin to be felt in Bangkok.

The far-flung warfare of 1785 and the careful, even brilliant, Siamese successes marked the beginning of the end of the Burmese threat to Siam's existence, though few if any Siamese were sure of the outcome for some years. The wars continued, but none was quite as threatening as that of 1785 had seemed at the outset. The Burmese tried another invasion, this time using only one invasion route via the Three Pagodas Pass, at the end of 1785 and first months of 1786. The Siamese were kept well informed of Burmese troop movements by dissident Mons and organized espionage units; the king quickly sent thirty thousand men up the Khwae Noi River to engage the Burmese in the jungled headwater districts. Within a few days the Burmese retreated in disarray.

Rama I now felt justified in staging his own invasion of Burma, but before he was able to set out, he received word that the Burmese were attacking Lan Na early in 1787. The king thereupon divided his forces, sending the uparat north to relieve Lampang and setting out himself to attack Tavoy. In concert with provincial armies, the Siamese troops quickly attained their objectives in the north. They began seriously now to resettle western Lan Na and revive Chiang Mai as a bulwark against Burma. Meanwhile, the king's armies marched by two difficult routes to attack Tavoy. After extended fighting, they besieged the city but had to withdraw after a few months when their supplies ran low.

Four years later, encouraged by dissident Mons in peninsular Burma who invited Rama I to assist them against Bodawhpaya, a Siamese force occupied Tavoy and its environs for some months; by early 1793, it was strongly reinforced to meet a Burmese attack. The Mon support on which the Siamese had counted proved chimerical, and the Siamese finally had to withdraw in the face of superior Burmese armies. At best, Rama I gained only some small additional influx of Mon refugees to add to the still depleted manpower rolls of his government.

The wars with Burma in the early part of Rama I's reign at least served to strengthen the young kingdom internally. By the mid-nineties, Siam had survived some formidable military challenges. The administration worked reasonably well. It was able to recruit manpower, and place and sustain it in the field. The chains of administrative and military command were clear, and ineffective and incompetent officers were quickly weeded out. The burdens of defense seem to have been equitably shared, and battlefield councils of war involved vigorous and lively debate among a socially wide range of officers ranging from high-ranking princes to the equivalent of majors and colonels. A good many people within the kingdom might increasingly have had some confidence that the government was capable of defending them. This is true not least of the rulers of the tributary states. We note particularly Chao Kavila in Lampang (and from 1796 reestablished in Chiang Mai). Twice, in 1797 and 1802, he found himself besieged by powerful Burmese armies. He had sufficient faith in the Bangkok regime to hold out for months in each case until a Siamese force, both times commanded by the uparat, came to his assistance. On both occasions, the Siamese were joined, albeit belatedly, by large contingents not only from the small northern principalities but also from Vientiane. Clearly, by the turn of the century, Siam was both willing and able to take the primary role in the leadership of the Siam/Lao world and make something meaningful of their empire—even if this was cast primarily in terms of their negative preoccupation with defense against the Burmese.

Rama I's court, indeed, felt comfortable in a world quite widely conceived. It had, to begin with, an indigenous social base of some considerable diversity. In addition to the powerful families we already have encountered whose origins lay overseas, there were countless people at court who spoke other languages, dressed differently, and professed religions other than mainstream Siamese Buddhism. Nowhere is this diversity more graphically represented than in the mural paintings of the early Bangkok period. These invariably feature crowds of people who, even though the scene painted might be intended to represent India in the time of the Buddha, are clearly Bangkok city dwellers. Complexions cover a wide range of colors, and hairstyles and dress represent different ethnic groups. Some people in the painted scenes are behaving properly in an upper-class Thai fashion, whereas others betray lower-class origins or different cultural patterns. This was no monolithic, homogeneous society, then, but one with a good deal of diversity and vitality.

The same cosmopolitanism is reflected in the literature of the First Reign of the Bangkok Period. Its chief monument is usually taken to be the enormous *Ramakian*, the complete Siamese version of the Indian epic *Ramayana* which Rama I and his courtiers set to verse in 1797. (The contemporary printed text runs to more than three thousand pages.) This is no blind translation of an Indian text, but rather a recasting of a classic central to Indian civilization in such a way that it was domesticated into Siamese tradition. The central figure in the *Ramayana* is, after all, a Rama (not completely alien to Rama I) who lives in a city called Ayodhya (or Ayudhya) and ascends his throne through virtue and bravery after a long dark period of dangerous warfare. The point is, however, that the characters and setting of the *Ramakian*, no less than the language, are clearly Siamese.

A somewhat different process was occurring in some of the other literary production of the First Reign. It was a period notable for its cosmopolitan literary taste, a period when a wide range of classics was translated from other Asian languages, and, in a sense, appropriated as part of the Siamese literary tradition. Among the works translated during the reign, the most important in the long run was to be the Chinese *Romance of the Three Kingdoms*, a historical novel set in the first and second centuries and filled with battles and court politics. The novel gradually became extremely popular in Siam and served, as it must have for some in the First Reign, as a model for the public behavior of rulers, counselors, and soldiers. Among the other translations of the period are the chronicle of the Mon kings of Pegu (*Rachathirat*), the *Dalang* and *Inao* from Java, the *Unarut* based on a section of the *Mahabharata* of India, the *Duodecagon* cycle of tales from Persia, and the *Mahavamsa* chronicle of Buddhism in Sri Lanka, translated from Pali. Moreover, not only was a great deal of this new literature in prose rather than in the more customary verse, but the considerable verse production of the First Reign was written in a language much less flowery and more like everyday speech than Ayudhyan literature. Even the meters were closer to the meters of ordinary folk. Implicitly, then, an increasingly cosmopolitan literary culture was at the same time becoming more vernacular, more popular.

By the turn of the century, then, we might conclude that Rama I's Siam was settling down as a stable, enduring empire, at least in the minds of those who lived within its compass. Economically, a profitable trade with China was developing, involving mainly the exchange of Siamese surplus rice production for Chinese luxury goods and crockery (and indeterminate amounts of copper and silver). Bangkok prospered on the growth of this trade. Not least among the beneficiaries of the trade was the Siamese court. An anecdote illustrates the point. In 1796, the uparat complained to Rama I that the eighty thousand baht per year he received to run his palace was insufficient. The king replied that the taxes collected were needed for public purposes; if the prince required more, he should invest in the China trade and use the profits to improve his establishment! Certainly many noble families had been doing so for generations.[10]

The long-term consequences of economic change occasioned by the growth of external commerce were not to become clear for a generation or two. For the time being, Rama I was more concerned to avoid a repetition of the deterioration of the manpower situation that had repeatedly weakened Ayudhya. As we have seen, the Ayudhyan kingdom cyclically suffered from the slippage of manpower out from under the control of the government and into the control of individuals and groups. Rama I took several steps to arrest this movement. First, he ordered that all freemen must be tattooed with the name of their masters and the name of the towns in which they resided, thus making it almost impossible to evade performing royal service. The practice gradually developed of carrying out mass registrations and "marking the people" at the beginning of each reign. Second, from 1785, Rama I required that all freemen, whether "king's men" (*phrai luang*) or "private retainers" (*phrai som*), perform corvée labor; by the end of the reign the period of service was reduced from four to three months annually. Third, in general the king followed a dual policy of making it increasingly difficult for kingsmen to evade their duties and at the same time extending them privileges (like exemptions from certain taxes) that made kingsman status less onerous. Finally, in order to prevent the amassing of large bodies of manpower by princes and officials, the manpower situation was carefully monitored. On the whole, princes in particular did not have the manpower necessary to challenge the king in the Bangkok Period. As we shall see, however, there were loopholes in this system, so that the nobles were not completely neutralized.

By the end of the eighteenth century, even Siam's tributary states seemed willing subordinates in a Bangkok-centered world, many aspects of which certainly worked to their advantage. The most important of these was security against the Burmese, for all save the Cambodians and southern Lao. Chao Kavila, in Chiang Mai, seems to have used his relationship with Rama I and the uparat, which dated back to 1775, to great advantage. (It should be noted that the uparat Surasi's chief wife was Kavila's sister.) The Siamese counted upon Kavila to defend the northern frontiers of Siam, to provide troops for Siam's defense in the south should this prove necessary, and annually to render tribute to Bangkok, usually in the form of the gold and silver trees. In return, Kavila was confirmed and maintained as ruler of Chiang Mai and could count on Siamese troops for his defense. Moreover, when Rama I determined he could trust Kavila, he in effect made Kavila de facto Siamese viceroy in the north (i.e., Lan Na), giving him supervisory responsibilities over Thoen, Tak, and Nan.

Kavila was determined to revive the north and, through the eighties and early nineties, began first to repopulate and resettle the Chiang Mai and Lamphun region (the upper Ping valley) and then more actively to raid into the northern and western Shan regions still controlled by the Burmese from their base at Chiang Saen. These raids yielded additional manpower for his resettlement efforts and provoked Burmese retaliation—which the Siamese assisted him in repelling. He was able to return to Chiang Mai from Lampang for good in 1796. By 1802, he raided Keng Tung and carried off many families of prisoners for resettlement farther south. Finally in 1804–05, he not only expelled the Burmese from Chiang Saen but also subjugated Möng Yawng, Müang Luang Phukha, and Chiang Hung, as well as numerous smaller müang in the upper Mekong highlands. With his brothers ruling in Lamphun and Lampang and set to succeed him in Chiang Mai, Kavila had come about as close as any could have done to reviving the ancient state of Lan Na by the time of his death in 1813.

The Cambodian state was in a very different situation. As we have noted, Cambodia was plunged into the chaos of rebellion and regicide late in 1781, and the army sent by Taksin to quell the disturbances was recalled before accomplishing its mission so that Rama I might ascend the Siamese throne. In 1783, the nine-year-old prince Eng, who had been named king in the interim, had to flee Cambodia and seek refuge in Bangkok where Rama I came to act as his "stepfather." [11]

Amidst endemic civil war within the country, exacerbated by the Tay-son rebellion in Vietnam and a semi-independent Chinese principality at Ha-tien, the main Siamese concern was to end the turbulence on the vulnerable eastern frontier. To do so, they followed a twofold policy. On the one hand, they cautiously supported Prince Nguyen Anh, heir to the Nguyen dominions of southern and central Vietnam who briefly had sought asylum in Bangkok in 1784–87, in his attempts to end the Vietnamese civil war and reunify the country. On the other hand, they also supported a powerful Cambodian officer, Chaophraya Aphaiphubet (Baen) from Battambang, having him function as a sort of viceroy for Siamese interests (and the absent Eng) within Cambodia itself. Finally, when Eng came of age in 1794 and Cambodia was at least temporarily at peace (thanks to Nguyen Anh's and Baen's successes), Rama I invested Eng as king of Cambodia in a grand ceremony in Bangkok and sent him back to the royal capital in Udong. Eng was carefully managed by a suite of pro-Thai officials at his court and was expected to send tribute to Rama I annually, to pay a personal visit to Bangkok in alternate years, and to supply the Siamese king with manpower for warfare or public works whenever called upon to do so. At this point, Baen, who was not on good personal terms with Eng's court, was given control over the large provinces of Battambang and Siem Reap and made directly responsible to Bangkok, an act that marks the beginning of the absorption of western Cambodia into Siam.

On Eng's premature death in 1797, the pro-Siamese officials at the Cambodian court ruled through Eng's infant son, Chan, until the latter was raised to the throne at the age of sixteen in 1806. It would appear that this premature coronation was the result of pressure from a newly reunited (1802) Vietnam. The young king, lacking the close ties with the Siamese court that his father had forged in a decade of exile in Bangkok, resented the sometimes overbearing paternalism of Rama I's court and tried to gain a measure of independence by playing the Siamese off against the Vietnamese. He began also to send tribute to Hue, though quadrennially as compared with the annual tribute he rendered to Bangkok. This numerical relationship is probably as good an indicator as any of the relative influence of Siam and Vietnam at the Cambodian court.

It should suffice for now simply to sketch in the remaining components of the empire of Rama I to the early years of the nineteenth century. The situation in Laos was little changed from what it had been in the late 1770s when the Chakri and Surasi campaigned there. The Siamese treated Champassak and Vientiane much as they treated Cambodia. In Champassak, which seems to have controlled both banks of the lower Mekong west to the Ubon region and eastward to Attopeu, Siamese forces intervened to investigate charges of misgovernment and to suppress rebellion. When King Sainyakuman died in 1791, the Siamese installed King Visainyarat.

The Vientiane court had been removed to Bangkok in 1778, and the leading members of the Lao royal family served the Siamese court during the warfare of the next decade. One by one, the princes returned to Vientiane as kings. Nanthasen was the first, sent back with the Phrabang image (which Rama I decided was bad luck for Bangkok) in 1782 to rule as vassal king. Soon he revived the old conflict with Luang Prabang, and attacked and took that city in 1792. He is said to have gained suzerainty over the Hua Phan (Black Tai) müang for his efforts. Like other ambitious vassal rulers before (and after) him, he may have dreamed of challenging his overlord. In 1794 he was accused of conspiring with the ruler of Nakhon Phanom (who presumably was directly tributary to Bangkok at this time) against Siam and was recalled to Bangkok where he died. Nanthasen was succeeded as ruler of Vientiane by his brother Inthavong, whose younger brother Anuvong (or Anu) was uparat. Over the next decade, Anu regularly brought Vientiane Lao armies to assist Siam in the wars with Burma, gaining a reputation as an able general. By the time of Inthavong's death in 1804, however, Vientiane already was regularly sending tribute to Vietnam; and Anu immediately notified Hue when he was chosen to succeed his brother as ruler of Vientiane.

Finally, during the same period, Luang Prabang also was brought slowly within the Siamese orbit. King Vongsa annually sent tribute to Bangkok, and when he died in 1791 (?), the notables of the kingdom sent a mission to Siam seeking recognition of his son, Anuruttha, as his successor. At the same time, Luang Prabang also was sending decennial tribute to China, and following its capture by Vientiane in 1792, the Luang Prabang royal family successfully used the good offices of the Chinese to secure the restoration of Anuruddha, who was to reign until 1815.

On the whole, then, Siam's policy in Laos during the First Reign amounted to one of divide and rule. Vientiane, Luang Prabang, and Champassak, together with Siang Khwang and (perhaps) Nakhon Phanom, were allowed considerable internal autonomy, and none was allowed substantially to improve its position at the expense of the others, lest any one of them gain sufficient strength to challenge Bangkok.

Much the same policy was pursued on the Malay Peninsula. Early in his reign in the course of subduing his rivals, Taksin had allowed the governor of Nakhon Si Thammarat, Chaophraya Nakhon (Nu), who had a strong following in the region, to continue in his position as a vassal ruler. Rama I, however, demoted his son and successor, Chaophraya Nakhon (Phat), to the status of governor of a first-class province in the wake of the Burmese war of 1785. At the same time, he detached Songkhla and the chief Malay tributary states from Nakhon's control and placed them under the Chinese who was governor of Songkhla. Among the Malay states of the middle peninsula, Pattani was consistently the most resistant to Siamese control, having been intermittently at war with Siamese kings for more than two hundred years. The new ruler whom the uparat installed in 1785 attempted to organize renewed resistance, as a result of which a new Siamese expedition was sent into the state in 1791 to install yet another ruler. The remaining Malay states were farther away and historically less important to the Siamese, nor did they figure prominently in Siamese history during the First Reign. Rama I sanctioned the division of Kelantan and Trengganu in 1800 or 1801, but apart from demanding and receiving regular tribute from the states, the Siamese were little involved there.

In looking at Rama I's empire as a whole, one of its remarkable features is the large number of power centers that existed. Working from the outer layers inward, we encounter first a circle of semi-independent rulers who did little more than pay tribute to Bangkok on a regular basis and who often paid tribute to other states as well. Included in this group are Kedah, Trengganu, Kelantan, Cambodia, and Luang Prabang. A second tier of states, or perhaps more properly principalities, was relatively more integrated into the Siamese system. In addition to paying tribute, they often were required to provide Siam with manpower for warfare or public works, paid relatively larger amounts in tribute, sometimes were married into the Siamese royal family, and occasionally suffered Siamese interference in their internal affairs. This group of states included Chiang Mai, Vientiane, Champassak, and Pattani. The next layer consisted of large regional centers around Siam's periphery, ruled by chaophraya and considered to be major, but quasi-independent, provinces. These

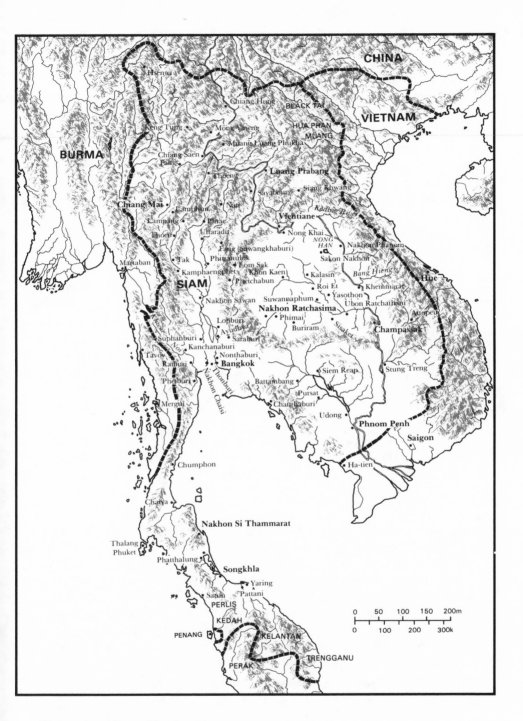

The empire of Rama I in 1809.

included Songkhla, Nakhon Si Thammarat, Battambang-Siem Reap, and, perhaps, Nakhon Ratchasima.

A fourth tier was a phenomenon mainly of the Khorat Plateau. Siamese power had begun dramatically to expand there in the last quarter of the eighteenth century, mainly by accepting the submission of petty rulers and their small müang, promising them protection in return for nominal tribute and manpower when necessary. The müang in this category numbered approximately twenty by the end of the First Reign and stretched from Nong Han and Nakhon Phanom in the north to Ubon and Buriram in the south. They included such centers as Khon Kaen, Kalasin, Roi Et, Suwannaphum, and Sisaket. Within the Siamese system, their rulers were styled phraya and ranked as governors, but their rule usually was hereditary. Finally, the inner core of the kingdom consisted of provinces properly speaking, ruled by officials appointed from the capital (though posts might pass down within a powerful local family from generation to generation) and subjected to the regulation of the central government through the chief ministries of state.

We have, thus, a hierarchy of degrees of control that in fact is neater in theory than it was in practice. Because the society, in the final analysis, was organized primarily upon the basis of personal relationships among individuals and small groups (such as families), there was always a good deal of tension within the system over the relative powers of the people involved. The system worked reasonably well because, in an environment in which wealth still was measured primarily in terms of control over manpower, the state was able to control the distribution of manpower among its constituent elements and reserve to the central authority a preponderant share of these resources. Any who would challenge the crown had first to find means of gaining control over a disproportionate share of manpower.

The court itself was not free from political disturbances, alarums and excursions, during the First Reign. For the most part these centered on the relationship between the king and his younger brother, the uparat. Relations between the two were often tense and were sparked by jealousy on both sides. In 1796, there were fears that an uprising of the uparat and his troops might occur, but the king surrounded the Front Palace, the uparat's establishment, and the princes' elder sisters managed to negotiate a reconciliation between the two. On the death of the uparat in 1803, two of his sons and Front Palace officials plotted to overthrow Rama I, but they were discovered and beheaded. The king thus was able to live out his life and pass his crown uneventfully to his eldest son Prince Itsarasunthon at his death on September 7, 1809.

Rama I's accomplishments were many, and they are all the harder to assess because of the extent to which he seems genuinely to have shared his power with his closest associates. Together, he and they constructed a new empire that was significantly more powerful, more flexible, and more complex than Ayudhya had previously been. The crisis through which he and his contemporaries had lived made them perhaps more aware of the necessity of working together for common ends, and their accomplishments in the face of enormous difficulties left them with a self-confidence that would stand their successors in good stead.

Interlude: Rama II, 1809–1824

It is tempting to pass over the reign of King Rama II as a relatively quiet interlude in Siamese history. True, the period was free of major crisis or warfare, and it is usually remembered chiefly for the literary production of the king and his courtiers. However, important developments were taking shape during the Second Reign that were to have a strong effect upon events through much of the century, and these deserve some brief attention.

First, the peaceful accession of Prince Itsarasunthon to the throne as Phra Phutthaloetla Naphalai (King Rama II) was itself a watershed, to the extent that it signaled the beginning of a dynasty of monarchs, as contrasted with the reign of an individual. Of necessity, it also implied the presence of an ongoing process of institutionalization of the governmental organs and modes of doing business that had been established in the First Reign. In political terms, the noble families that had been established, or confirmed, in the First Reign increasingly consolidated their power, but at the expense of royal power, it appears.

Rama II was born in 1768 and thus was forty-one years old on coming to the throne. On being given princely rank and his own household in 1785, he dwelt in the former palace of King Taksin on the Thonburi side of the river and was an active participant in his father's government. Rama II thus by 1809 was well-experienced in public affairs. But in order to rule effectively he needed a personal base of support, particularly as a source of recruits for positions demanding unquestioning loyalty to the monarch. It was both customary and natural for kings to turn to the families of their mothers and their queens. Rama II's mother, Queen Amarin, was closely related to the Bunnag branch of the Persian family. Her sister was the mother of Chaophraya Mahasena (Bunnak), Rama I's Kalahom, and Chaophraya Yommarat (Bunma), his minister of the capital. Rama II's queen, whom he took by 1790, offered an advantageous set of connections. She was the daughter of Rama I's elder sister by "her wealthy

Chinese hushand"[12] and also was closely related to the Singhaseni branch of the Brahman family, which included Chaophraya Mahasena (Pin), another First Reign Kalahom, among others.

Almost immediately upon Rama II's accession, the significance of these connections became apparent. Rama II shuffled almost all his father's ministers. He appointed Chaophraya Yommarat (Bunma) to be Kalahom, and Chaophraya Mahasena (Pin) to become the "prime minister" of the Uparat's Front Palace. His Mahatthai (Chakri) was Chaophraya Rattanathibet (Kun Rattanakun), a man of Chinese descent (from the same region as Queen Amarin) who had served as Phrakhlang late in Rama I's reign. The point here is not only that Rama II began his reign by distributing plums to the old leading families, but also that he selected his maternal and affinal relatives for special preferment. He thereby confirmed, and even accelerated, the growth of noble power that Rama I had accepted.

Rama II may have been somewhat uncomfortable with the growth of noble power. Early in his reign, he introduced a new practice of appointing princes to superintend the affairs of the ministries and departments of the central administration. Eight of these appointments are known, and there were probably more. Rama II had appointed Prince Senanurak, his only full brother by Queen Amarin, to be uparat, and he had him superintend the Mahatthai and Kalahom ministries. At the uparat's death in 1819, these responsibilities were divided between two brothers of the king's own queen; and another half-brother, whose mother was the daughter of Chaophraya Nakhon (Phat), shared responsibility for the Kalahom (in whose territory Nakhon Si Thammarat was included). Finally, Rama II's eldest surviving son by a concubine, Prince Chetsadabodin, was given superintendency of the Phrakhlang.

Prince Damrong suggests two reasons for these appointments.[13] First, a military campaign against Burma in 1810 was mismanaged, and the king may have wished to monitor more closely the activities of the ministers. Second, the royal family by now was growing rapidly. In addition to the nineteen princes and princesses of Rama I's generation, Rama I himself had forty-two children, his uparat had forty-three, and Rama II had seventy-three. There were a good many capable princes around, and the king may not have wanted to waste their talents. A third reason is suggested by the first. Rama II may not have fully trusted his officials and wished to place close relatives where they could keep an eye on things. In all events, the princes seem to have functioned as advisers to the ministries, and at least one of them gained valuable experience and connections that were to be of some help to him in the future.

Rama II's Siam still considered Burma to be the major enemy, but apart from minor warfare on the peninsula in 1810, the western frontier was quiet through most of the Second Reign. Rama II had, however, to be increasingly concerned about his eastern frontier.

Cambodia quickly was becoming the battleground for the clash of Siamese and Vietnamese interests, thanks now to the stable revival of both major powers. In the last years of Rama I's reign, King Chan was already at odds with the Siamese court; and apparently Chan was outraged when, almost immediately on coming to the throne, Rama II appointed Baen's nephew to rule Battambang–Siem Reap, thus perpetuating western Cambodia's separation from Chan's dominions. Chan made clear his feelings by refusing to attend the funeral obsequies for Rama I in 1810, sending instead his full brother, Prince Snguon, and two half-brothers, Im and Duong. The brothers returned to Udong with Siamese orders that Khmer troops be levied for an impending campaign against Burma. Chan refused and ordered the execution of two of his officials who attempted to comply with the Siamese orders. He wrote Vietnamese authorities in Saigon that he needed protection while telling the Siamese he had killed the officials for *refusing* to levy the troops. The Vietnamese sent a flotilla to anchor off Udong, while diplomatic correspondence passed between Bangkok and Vietnam. Matters came to a head early in 1812 when the Vietnamese warships withdrew. Snguon fled from the capital to Pursat and soon was marching back toward Udong with the assistance of Siamese troops. Chan fled to Saigon, while Im and Duong joined Snguon in Udong. Snguon remained there for nearly a year, but failed to rally much support from the countryside.

The Siamese, meanwhile, felt their military position to be weak and feared a major confrontation with the Vietnamese. In mid-1813, the Siamese finally withdrew, after razing the citadels of Udong and Phnom Penh, bringing with them the dissident princes and thousands of Khmer who were resettled in Battambang and Siam. Chan then returned to Cambodia with a large Vietnamese army and a small party of Siamese officials and moved his capital to Phnom Penh where the Vietnamese could more easily reach and aid him. The tables now had turned, and for some decades after 1813 Vietnam was the dominant influence in Cambodia, enforced with a ten-thousand-man garrison. The Siamese could console themselves with new control over large areas of the Cambodian provinces of Pursat, Stung Treng, and Kompong Svai. In the dissident princes Rama II held a legitimate alternative to Chan should the Cambodian king upset the precarious balance of power on Siam's eastern frontier.

Similarly ominous developments occurred during the Second Reign to the north of Cambodia in the principality of Champassak. When Chao Visainyarat

(r. 1791?–1811) died in 1811, it took two years to find a successor suitable to Siam; this prince, Chao Manoi, was neither strong nor effective. Siam had several times to intervene in Champassak's affairs in the next decade, first, to settle a dispute between Manoi and his uparat and then, in 1819, to quell serious internal disturbances. In that year, a revolt had broken out among the Montagnard population of the eastern uplands, led by a renegade monk named Sa who claimed magical powers. With popular support, he was able to take Champassak, and Manoi and his court fled to Ubon. Siamese troops moved in and restored order and were faced with the problem of replacing Manoi, who died in Bangkok.

The Siamese needed urgently to restore strong authority in Champassak. Chao Anu, the king of Vientiane, whose son Chao Yo had succeeded in capturing the elusive Sa, urged the Siamese to appoint Yo as ruler of Champassak. The elderly Prince Phithaksamontri, general adviser to the government, opposed doing so, arguing that Yo's appointment would extend Vientiane's influence to the south and make of Anu a dangerous vassal. Prince Chetsadabodin, on the other hand, reasoned that southern Laos must be strengthened, lest the Vietnamese encroach into the area as they had done in Cambodia, and supported the appointment of Yo. It seemed, perhaps, the lesser of two evils. Better a strong Vientiane and Champassak than a weak Champassak and a more serious Vietnamese threat.

As if these worries were not enough, it was in the last years of the Second Reign that Western pressures began to mount against Siam for the first time since Narai's reign more than a century earlier. The West had probably never been completely absent from the scene in Siam, but its presence was almost imperceptible. The Dutch had maintained a factory in Ayudhya until 1760 and thereafter sent occasional ships from their base in Batavia (Jakarta)— including a shipment of cannon to Taksin in 1770. The English East India Company long had relied on private, "country" traders and Asians to conduct its minimal trade with Siam. And Portuguese and French Roman Catholic missionaries, in very small numbers, ministered to the needs of the tiny Christian community in Siam. The situation began to change, though at first only faintly, when the British gained possession of the island of Penang in 1785, a foothold they were to enlarge with the acquisition of territory (Province Wellesley) opposite the island in 1800. For the time being, however, the European powers were preoccupied with the Napoleonic wars and the trade with China, and largely ignored Siam.

Two things then occurred that radically changed the situation. First, with the revival of international trade in the aftermath of the Napoleonic wars and the growth of new Anglo-Dutch rivalry for the trade of maritime Southeast

Asia, the English East India Company (EIC) founded Singapore as a free port in 1819. Singapore's commercial future was held, in part, to depend on the development of trade with the Malay Peninsula and Siam; and, in the eyes of Europeans, Siam's international trade was conducted in a monopolistic, anti-commercial, almost medieval fashion. Moreover, as Sir Thomas Stamford Raffles pointed out in 1819,

> When it is considered that Siam extends its influence over the whole of the Malay peninsula, with the exception of Johore, and that our settlement of Penang is but an islet recently subordinate to one of its dependencies, and that this influence prevails over states with which our unrestricted inter-course is indispensable, the advantage of a good understanding with that court is obvious.[14]

Second, in 1821, relations between Siam and Kedah broke down. Three years earlier, when the Burmese sent a raiding expedition down the west coast of the peninsula, Sultan Ahmad of Kedah had entered into some (unspecified) relations with them. When the Siamese, through the governor of Nakhon Si Thammarat, mounted their counterattack a few months later, they requisitioned supplies and manned boats from Kedah, but Sultan Ahmad rebuffed their orders. In 1820, Siamese officers captured at Phuket a Burmese letter instructing Sultan Ahmad to rebel against Siam as part of a major expedition the Burmese hoped soon to mount against Siam. Finally, later the same year one of the sultan's rivals went personally to Bangkok to accuse the sultan of misgovernment and disloyalty to Siam. Thereupon the Siamese in 1821 invaded Kedah. The sultan fled to Penang and attempted to invoke his treaties with the EIC to gain British assistance in restoring him to his throne.

With Penang's trade disrupted, Kedah in chaos, and Singapore officials urging the initiation of commercial and diplomatic relations with Siam, the governor-general of British India dispatched John Crawfurd to Bangkok at the end of 1821. The Siamese court was implacable. The princes and ministers felt justified in their conduct in Kedah, and not surprisingly given their personal interests in the existing trading system, they were not inclined to make commerce easier for British traders. Crawfurd left Bangkok having managed only to gain Siamese recognition of the British possession of Penang—forty years after the fact! The issues were left unresolved for a new king to deal with a few years later.

Viewing the Second Reign as a whole, one is left with the impression that the leadership of the state was hesitant and uncertain. This was a period neither of forceful royal leadership nor of dynamic ministerial drive. Is it the case that nobody was really in charge, that the partnership between princes and nobles

"View of the City of Bangkok," 1822; from John Crawfurd, *Journal of an Embassy from the Governor-General of India to the Courts of Siam and Cochin China* (London, 1828).

did not function effectively and decisively? It is probably significant that Rama II is remembered chiefly as one of the great Thai poets and that none of his ministers is counted among the great nobles of the kingdom. The reign, then, is justly considered as an interlude between the First and Third Reigns, a breathing spell between crises.

Rama III: Conservative or Reactionary?

On July 6, 1824, King Rama II assembled some members of the royal family together and told them that the time had come for his son Prince Mongkut to be ordained as a Buddhist monk. According to the court chronicler, he told them that "as this was an ill-omened time, owing to the death of the Royal White Elephant, the ordination should be arranged without losing any time."[15] With little of the ceremony that usually accompanied such ordinations, Prince Mongkut was ordained the next day. Exactly a week later, Rama II fell gravely ill, so seriously that he was speechless until his death on July 21 at the age of fifty-six. Within a few hours a grand assembly of the royal family, high officers of state, and members of the Buddhist monkhood led by the supreme patriarch was convened within the palace walls and quickly decided to invite Rama II's eldest surviving son, Prince Chetsadabodin, to ascend the throne. The prince was to reign as Phra Nangklao, but he is usually referred to as Rama III.

There has always been some controversy about the manner in which the Third Reign began, controversy that has centered on the relative claims of Chetsadabodin and Mongkut to the throne. Chetsadabodin was much the senior, having been born in 1788 to a royal concubine, daughter of the governor of Nonthaburi. He had long played a leading, responsible role in government. He chaired a commission to investigate a plot against his father in 1809 and through most of the reign superintended—or perhaps advised concerning— the business of the Phrakhlang, which involved close attention to provincial government, the royal and state treasuries, and relations with immigrant communities and foreign states. Mongkut, on the other hand, was born in 1804 not to a concubine but to a queen who was herself of royal blood—she was the daughter of Rama I's sister. Contemporary Westerners considered Rama III to be an illegitimate son of Rama II, even a usurper. It was not that simple. For hundreds of years, Siamese had accorded higher status to princes born of queens, particularly queens of royal blood, than to princes born of concubines. But in law and in practice all sons of a king had some claim to the throne, and it was up to the accession council that met on the death of a king to choose his successor.

When reading the account of Rama II's death given above, it is reasonable to interpret the mention of the death of the white elephant as symbolic: the elephant died on June 19, almost three weeks before Mongkut's ordination. What seems rather more likely is that Rama II knew he would die soon and, convinced that the accession council would choose Chetsadabodin, desired to protect Mongkut from political intrigues—and perhaps spare his kingdom the internecine conflict that might follow the elevation of a concubine's son to the throne. Had such a conflict occurred, Chetsadabodin would have won with the support of the powerful Bunnag family; its leading member, Dit Bunnag, had become Chaophraya Phrakhlang in 1822 and thus had worked closely with Chetsadabodin for the preceding two years. Thus, though technically underage for ordination and without the usual ceremonial preparations, Mongkut was figuratively bundled off to a Buddhist monastery where his saffron robes might shield him from the winds of intrigue.

Among Rama III's first tasks was the constitution of his government. For the post of uparat he curiously selected neither a younger brother nor a son, but rather his uncle, Prince Sakdiphonlasep (1785–1832), the son of Rama I by a daughter of Chaophraya Nakhon (Phat). Like his father, he also appointed senior princes to superintend the affairs of some of the departments of state. Among these, the most important were Prince Surin (1790–1830), a son of Rama I whose mother and wife both were Bunnags, over the Phrakhlang (which Dit Bunnag headed); Prince Rakronnaret (1791–1848), a full brother of Prince Surin, over the Kalahom and palace ministries; and Prince Itsaranurak (1773–1830), son of one of Rama I's sisters, over the Mahatthai. The latter, however, "upon the accession of ... [Rama III] retired from all public business on the plea of old age. He is said to have been dissatisfied with the succession to the throne."[16]

Rama III kept on nearly all his father's ministers and in effect appointed only one at the beginning of his reign. The Kalahom had recently died, so he promoted the Yommarat (Noi Sisuriyaphaha) to the Kalahom and appointed a man named Chim, who was the son of Chaophraya Phrakhlang (Hon) of the First Reign, as Yommarat. The Mahatthai, Phrakhlang, Phonlathep (lands department), and Thamma (place department) continued in office.

The most urgent business of the early years of the Third Reign concerned foreign and military affairs. In May 1824, Britain had gone to war with Burma over Burmese attacks across the frontiers of India. Within a year, the Siamese were alarmed by rumors that the British were preparing a great expedition to seize Kedah, after which they would proceed to attack Siam. The Siamese were sufficiently worried to strengthen the defenses at the mouth of the Chaophraya River, stretching a great iron chain across the river to which every blacksmith in the region had to contribute a certain number of links. Moreover, conflict on the Malay Peninsula was increasing, which also involved the British. The Siamese invasion of Kedah in 1821 had succeeded in extending Siamese suzerainty over the neighboring state of Perak. By 1824, Perak was requesting Siamese assistance against nearby Selangor, and soon the governor of Nakhon was preparing an expedition to move south from Kedah into these two states.

Late in 1825, the British Indian government appointed Captain Henry Burney as its emissary to Siam to deal with these and related issues. At the time, the war with Burma was not going well, and the British wished to secure at least provisions for its troops, as well as Siamese neutrality if not the active engagement of Siamese troops on the British side. By its seizure of territory in southeast Burma, the British had become the neighbor of Siam, and they were anxious that there be no conflicts or misunderstandings on this new frontier. Concerning the Malay Peninsula, the British sought at least a cessation of Siamese pressure against Perak and Selangor, and if possible the restoration of Sultan Ahmad of Kedah to his throne. Finally, the British wished to end a broad range of restrictive and discriminatory practices that severely limited

Western trade in Siam. Seeking to achieve these ambitious goals, Burney arrived in Bangkok in December 1825.

At first the Siamese court was seriously divided over the proper responses to make to Burney's propositions and demands. Those, like the Phrakhlang and his relatives, who were deeply interested in, and profiting from, the existing trading arrangements, did not wish to give them up. The Kalahom, Chaophraya Nakhon (Noi), and the uparat had interests in the expansion of Siam's power on the peninsula and were wary of becoming involved in the Burma war. Burney at first made no headway, particularly as news kept arriving of British reverses in Burma; but when in early February 1826 news arrived that the British had concluded the war by inflicting a serious defeat on the Burmese, the Siamese attitude immediately changed. The king initially was opposed to entering into any agreements, but the uparat, Prince Surin, the Phrakhlang, and Chaophraya Nakhon—those who had the most to lose— induced him to change his mind. They argued that the British had been rebuffed previously and this time might be provoked into hostility if turned down again; and that future conflicts might easily arise along the new Burma-Siam border if amicable relations could not be constructed now. Negotiations then began in earnest, and in June 1826, a treaty and a commercial agreement were signed by the two parties.

In the treaty, which was primarily political, the Siamese yielded little. Provisions were drafted for defining the boundaries between Siam and British Burma, for the general conduct of trade, and for the settlement of disputes. The Siamese position in Kedah, Kelantan, Trengganu, and Pattani was recognized, as was the independence of Perak and Selangor. The commercial agreement, on the other hand, entailed considerable sacrifices for the Siamese. Taxes on trade were reduced by substituting a new single duty, based on the measurement of a ship's beam (1,700 baht per fathom if it carried import cargo, 1,500 baht if not), for the myriad of fees, taxes, and gratuities that ships previously had paid; and royal monopolies on various commodities were eased. In the short run, the Siamese seem to have believed that they could bear economic sacrifices in order to win political security. In the long run, they must have felt that they could make up for the loss in customs duties by raising new taxes.

The conclusion of the Burney Treaty was important in a number of ways. First of all, it set a constructive pattern for the conduct of Siam's relations with the West. It was characterized by compromise and by the court's thoughtful discrimination between its primary and secondary interests. It can only have reinforced Siamese self-confidence in their ability to deal effectively and con-structively with an increasingly dangerous international environment. Finally, the treaty brought about a substantial increase in Siam's international trade. By the 1840s, more than fifty square-rigged Western vessels called at Bangkok each year; and the value of Siamese trade with Singapore alone increased roughly 50 percent within a few years. With increasing trade was to come increasing contact with the West, which in the end was to affect the kingdom profoundly.

For the time being, however, the king and court had to concern themselves with more conventional preoccupations, particularly the vassal states to the east.

The most serious immediate problem resulted from the ambitions of Chao Anu of Vientiane. As we have seen, Anu's power in Laos was greatly expanded with the appointment of his son, Chao Yo, as ruler of Champassak in 1819. The two began to fortify their territories, and Anu attempted to win an alliance with King Mangthaturat of Luang Prabang. Mangthaturat must have had an inkling of what was coming, for when he and Anu visited Bangkok for the obsequies for Rama II in 1825, Mangthaturat stayed on for a full year, returning home only late in 1826 when an epidemic broke out in Luang Prabang. Anu was more anxious to get home. He felt that Rama III had insulted him and that he was not being treated as the important vassal he thought he was. He was not shown the favors Mangthaturat enjoyed. Anu heard the rumors of a British attack on Siam and observed the Siamese pre-parations for defense. He returned to Vientiane and prepared for rebellion. He envisioned sweeping across the Khorat Plateau, taking Bangkok, and then withdrawing with numerous captives and material to further strength his state.

In January 1827, Lao troops began their invasion from Vientiane and Champassak. They took Nakhon Ratchasima by claiming to be rushing to defend Bangkok against a British attack and, by late February, had reached Saraburi, only three days' march from Bangkok. After flying into a brief panic, the Siamese court responded with vigor. Early in March, the uparat led a force to halt the Lao advance below Saraburi while the main armies were called up. By early April, three Siamese armies were on the march. A small force swept up the Pa Sak River valley to secure Phetchabun and Lom Sak. A second, larger army, under Phraya Ratchasuphawadi (later Chaophraya Bodindecha, Sing Singhaseni), recaptured the central and southern portions of the Northeast Plateau and Champassak itself, capturing Chao Yo in the process. Meanwhile, the main force, under the uparat, advanced on Vientiane. Fifty miles south of Vientiane, they engaged the main Lao army at Nong Bua Lamphu over the first four days of May and defeated them. Anu returned to his capital, packed his baggage, and fled to Vietnam. A few days later the Siamese occupied Vientiane.

After rounding up prisoners, looting the city, and destroying its defenses, the main Siamese army withdrew, leaving the newly promoted Chaophraya Ratchasuphawadi to complete the subjugation of the region. The general had been instructed to complete the devastation of Vientiane and teach the Lao and other vassals the price of rebellion. After a few months, however, he decided the Lao had suffered enough and, leaving a small government of Lao nobles and a Siamese garrison behind, withdrew in February 1828.

Rama III was not satisfied; he wanted Vientiane utterly destroyed. Moreover, he was worried that the Vietnamese might take the opportunity to move not only into Vientiane's territory but also into the Black Tai müang and Siang Khwang. Ratchasuphawadi regrouped his forces and headed back for Vientiane. By the time he approached the city in early August, Anu had returned from Vietnam with a small force of Vietnamese and Lao and had recaptured Vientiane. With only a small contingent under his command, Ratchasuphawadi fell back to Yasothon. Anu went after him, but was badly beaten in mid-October and again fled eastward. This time the general completed the tasks he had been assigned a year earlier. Anu was captured and sent to Bangkok, where after being placed on public display for a few days he died early in 1829. The Siamese destroyed all buildings in the environs of Vientiane save for Buddhist monasteries and removed all the population from the area for resettlement in Lopburi, Saraburi, Suphanburi, and Nakhon Chaisi provinces. Even forty years later, when a party of French explorers reached Vientiane, they found nothing but forest and decaying ruins.

Through the decades that followed the Anu Rebellion, the Siamese worked systematically to regroup and reorganize their eastern Lao provinces. Worried about trying to defend the more distant trans-Mekong provinces, they instead began the massive resettlement of Lao populations across the Mekong to the Khorat Plateau. In particularly, central Laos between the Bang Hian and the Kading rivers was systematically raided in the 1830s and 1840s and its population resettled in the east-central portion of the Northeast Plateau. When the Vietnamese moved into Siang Khwang in the early 1830s, Siam in cooperation with Luang Prabang recaptured the area in 1834 and then removed much of its population to the south and west. This military display encouraged the Black Tai müang to resume their allegiance to Siam, which had faltered under Vietnamese pressure, and thereafter this extreme northern region paid homage to the Siamese kings through Luang Prabang.

All this activity in the northeast during the Third Reign substantially increased Siam's influence there. Approximately forty new müang were created during this period, some tributary directly to Bangkok and others through the intermediary of another müang—Champassak, Kalasin, Khemmarat, Nong

Khai, Nakhon Phanom, or Sakon Nakhon, for example. Some of these were completely new creations, formed by the immigration of a whole community, with its chao müang and his family, from across the river. Others were older villages, whose population had been swelled by population transfers from Laos. What had been an extremely thinly populated region, densely forested, now began to be filled up, while the population of the east bank of the Mekong dramatically declined. The two major Lao principalities of the past, Vientiane and Champassak, were eliminated or reduced in size. Only Siam gained in the process.

While the Mahatthai ministry, the ministry of the northern provinces, had through the 1830s to be concerned with the northeast, the Kalahom as part of its responsibilities was concerned with the southern provinces of the Malay Peninsula, where warfare and military expeditions were fully as frequent as in the Lao country. Trouble with the southern dependencies was not new, as we have seen in the case of Kedah; nor was the new head of the Kalahom, appointed in 1830, a stranger to the region. This was the Phrakhlang, Dit Bunnag, who on concurrently taking over the Kalahom ministry became only the second man in premodern Siamese history to hold two of the major offices of state simultaneously.

Trouble for Siam erupted first in Kedah in 1831, when partisans of the exiled Sultan Ahmad launched a rebellion that managed to expel Siamese officials in Kedah. The governor of Nakhon Si Thammarat, Chaophraya Nakhon (Noi), began to levy an army and asked Songkhla and Pattani to do the same. Songkhla resisted, and Pattani again rebelled. Pattani had been divided into seven petty states under Songkhla's control since 1817, but these states now joined forces in what they thought was an opportunity to end Siam's overlordship. When they attacked Songkhla, the latter had to call upon Bangkok for aid; and even the four armies Siam sent were insufficient to repulse the Pattani Malays, who were supported by Kelantan and Trengganu. Additional forces were sent to the region and were reinforced early in 1832 by the Nakhon Si Thammarat armies, which had succeeded in recapturing Kedah and reinstalling Siamese government there. By mid-year, the seven states of Pattani were subdued, and new governors were appointed to most of the states, including Siamese in Pattani itself and in Yaring. The sultan of Kelantan also quickly fell into line, threatened with the large Siamese armies now to his north. He offered to pay a large indemnity and to hand over the fugitive ruler of Pattani in return for being allowed to continue as sultan. Only Trengganu remained. The proud sultan was unwilling to apologize, and so the Siamese forced his removal and replacement by a cousin. Their work completed, the Siamese armies returned home, accompanied by several thousand prisoners and considerable war booty.

Much the same scenario was played again less than a decade later. Again, rebels supporting Sultan Ahmad took Kedah and were advancing on Songkhla and Pattani, and again they had some support from the seven states. A few months later, early in 1839, the Siamese counterattacked from Nakhon and Songkhla, and by late March they had reconquered Kedah. Meanwhile, Kelantan had fallen into civil war, and only the threat of military intervention brought the contending parties to resolve their differences.

After decades of chronic unrest, the time had come to make a new approach to the government of the peninsular region. First, the territory of Kedah was somewhat reduced by the creation of several small new states from its territory, including Perlis and Satun. The Siamese abandoned their policy of attempting to rule the region with Siamese governors and allowed Malay rajas to rule these states. In 1841, they even permitted Sultan Ahmad to return to rule Kedah. The Kelantan disturbances were resolved by exiling the sultan's rivals in 1842. Finally, following the death of Chaophraya Nakhon (Noi) in 1839, though he was replaced by his son, his family's influence in the region was markedly reduced and the powers and responsibilities of Songkhla and Nakhon Si Thammarat were more equally balanced. On the whole, then, by the early 1840s, Siam's position in the mid-peninsula region had been substantially improved. After decades of struggle, they had managed to bring a modicum of order and stability to the region, which for most of the rest of the century was to cause Bangkok little concern.

As serious as was the warfare that occupied Siam in the northeast and the south during the Third Reign, it was as nothing compared to the Cambodian wars. These had their origins in the competition between Siam and Vietnam for influence over the Cambodian court at Phnom Penh and in the bitter rivalries between King Chan and his dissident brothers, Im and Duong (Snguon died in Bangkok in 1824). After nearly two decades of Vietnamese interference, the most resented aspect of which may have been the conscription of Cambodians for corvée labor, Chan appears to have been chafing under their yoke by 1829, but was kept in check by Le Van Duyet, the Vietnamese viceroy in Saigon. On Duyet's death in 1832, the government in Hue moved rapidly to impose more rigorous control over southern Vietnam, which Duyet had managed to keep somewhat autonomous, and by 1833 the region was in rebellion.

Having been kept well informed of Cambodian resentment of Vietnamese control, Rama III decided to intervene. Siamese and Lao armies advanced against Cambodia from Bangkok and Champassak, while a naval force rounded the coast to join the rebels in Saigon. After initial successes, the 1833–34 Siamese expedition turned into a disaster. The armies were defeated by superior Vietnamese forces west of Saigon, and as they began their retreat, slowed by masses of prisoners and loads of booty, they were harassed by Cambodian guerrillas. Chan, who had fled to Vietnam, returned to Phnom Penh even more under Vietnamese control. When Chan died in 1834, the Vietnamese took the unheard-of step of securing the elevation of his daughter, Mei, to the throne as queen of Cambodia (r. 1835–41). They then began a thoroughgoing program of Vietnamization, beginning by recostuming court officials and requiring them to speak Vietnamese, these policies being carried out by large numbers of Vietnamese mandarins. Cambodia's thirty-two provinces even received Vietnamese names.

Through the 1830s the tension built. The Vietnamese secretly flirted with both Im and Duong and tricked Im into returning to Phnom Penh, where he was arrested and shuffled away to house arrest in Hue. When in 1840 the Vietnamese began further to tighten their control, imposing regular, high taxation rates, undercutting the identity and status of the Cambodian ruling class, and demoting and taking away Queen Mei, a massive anti-Vietnamese rebellion broke out. As the Cambodian chronicle relates, "All the ministers, local officials and common people of Cambodia agreed to join forces to kill the Vietnamese."[17] Vietnamese troops had to be withdrawn to quell Cambodian rebels in southern Vietnam, and Rama III sent Chaophraya Bodindecha (Sing) back into Cambodia, in the king's view, to "save" Buddhism and Cambodian institutions the Vietnamese had threatened. After arduous campaigns, Bodin finally escorted Prince Duong to Udong by mid-1841, and sought to encourage Cambodian officials and common folk to rally to him as king of Cambodia. By the end of the year he was in Phnom Penh. The war dragged on for another three years and on the Siamese side involved contingents from many provinces of the empire who suffered heavy losses. Finally, in 1845–46, the Siamese and Vietnamese negotiated a settlement, under the terms of which Duong was crowned king of Cambodia by the Siamese in 1848; he then sent triennial tribute to Hue and annual tribute to Bangkok. Once again, as in the First Reign, the dominant influence in Cambodia was Siam.

Some aspects of the Cambodian wars may have been profoundly unsettling for the Siamese. After centuries of concern about their western frontiers with Burma, they now had to look to the east and a new, and in many ways formidably different, rival. Rama III and his court seem to have reacted to this conflict in ways that suggest that their identity was at stake. In their confrontation with non-Buddhist Vietnamese whose institutions were derived primarily from Chinese models, Siamese conceptions of the qualities of their own civilization were strengthened. Here, even more strongly than in their struggles with the Lao and Malay, they were confronted with limitations on their powers.

They had to assess the prospect of exerting their influence through indigenous rulers rather than their own officials and institutions.

Rama III, and the Third Reign in general, has gained the reputation of being extremely conservative, even reactionary. Some suggest that the king and court adopted a posture of blind resistance to change, of stubborn defense of traditional ways. Like most such generalizations, these are neither completely true nor fair. Rama III unquestionably was a vigorous defender of many traditional values and saw himself as acting in defense of Buddhism in his policy toward Cambodia, a sincere posture, certainly. At the same time, he was little interested in secular literature or the arts in general. In discouraging literature (his shabby treatment of the great poet of his reign, Sunthon Phu, is an example), he may have been reacting against his father, Rama II, whom he may have thought spent too much time and resources on poetry. Rama III nevertheless appreciated and valued the Siamese cultural heritage.

One of the most extraordinary acts of his reign was his renovation of Wat Phrachetuphon (Wat Pho) in Bangkok. He had hundreds of inscriptions and mural paintings placed on public view: writings on every conceivable subject, including poetry, treatises on medicine, warfare, massage, astrology, botany, history, and religion, and lists of ecclesiastical establishments, provinces of the kingdom, and foreign peoples. What was he doing, and why? Apparently Rama III was acutely aware that his country was undergoing rapid change and that traditional culture would disappear unless some measures were taken to preserve it. He does not seem to have liked or approved of the direction of this change, but at the same time he did nothing to stand in its way. There was much he could have done—people he could have punished or expelled, practices he could have curbed, changes he could have resisted—but instead he allowed others to do as they wished while he himself clung to the old ways. He was a conservative, not a reactionary; and by the moderation of his defense of the old values and virtues he did more to preserve them than a more extreme policy would have done.

Of all those experimenting with change in the Third Reign, none was more prominent than the king's young rival, Prince Mongkut, who had begun the reign as a newly shaved Buddhist monk at a monastery not far from the royal palace. Even had he been otherwise inclined, Mongkut had no alternative but to take Buddhism seriously, for to leave the monkhood would have thrust him into the dangerous maelstrom of dynastic politics. Mongkut had a restless, inquiring mind, and at first he was disquieted by the Buddhism he found in Bangkok's hundreds of monasteries. He studied meditation to enhance his mental powers and concentration, but this did not satisfy him. He then moved back to the scholarly monasteries of the inner city and began the serious study of the Pali language in order to read the Buddhist Scriptures in the "original" language. At Rama III's urging, he sat for the oral Pali examinations in 1826 that were the usual road to ecclesiastical office and royal patronage. Before a large audience that included officials and members of the royal family besides high-ranking monks, Mongkut performed astonishingly well for a monk who had been ordained only a few years; he demonstrated not only great linguistic facility but also considerable knowledge of the religious texts set for that year. Because some princely rivals whispered that Mongkut's examiners were too deferential to his royal status, he declined to continue after the third day of the examinations. He had sufficiently impressed the king, however, to be awarded an honorary fan signifying completion of the examinations to the highest degree.

The young monk, upset by the questioning of his motives, decided that the pursuit of high ecclesiastical office was not for him, though a few royal princes had risen in the hierarchy and many were to do so later. He plunged himself into his textual studies, and the more he learned of the core of Buddhist teachings and the original practices of the religion, the more dissatisfied he was with the current state of Buddhism in Siam. Monks and laypeople alike, he came to think, blindly followed the Buddhism of their fathers and grandfathers without thorough knowledge of the doctrines and teachings of the original texts. On careful study of the texts governing ordination of monks, Mongkut was upset to find that Siamese ordinations probably were invalid. By chance he encountered the chief monk of the Mon sect in Siam, and through discussions with him was convinced of the validity of the strict Mon discipline.

After a period of careful study and reflection, with a few monk-students he moved to Wat Samorai north of the city and around 1833 had the group reordained according to rigidly defined ritual prescriptions. They now wore their monks' robes in the Mon fashion, with both shoulders covered rather than one. By the late 1830s, having reformed the daily practice, the rituals, the preaching, and even the pronunciation of Pali by his group of monks, Mongkut was invited by the king to move with them to Wat Bowonniwet, where he became abbot and in effect the head of a separate order within the Siamese monkhood. Mongkut named it *Thammayutika*, the "Order Adhering to the Dhamma," the teachings of the Buddha, as contradistinguished from the older order, the *Mahanikai*, to whom Mongkut derogatively referred as the "Order of Long-Standing Habit."

Now in a city monastery less than a kilometer from the center of government, Mongkut became increasingly active in the religious life of the kingdom, taking a particular interest in Buddhist education and supervising the training of a generation of scholarly leaders for Siamese Buddhism. Wat Bowon also became a major center of Western learning, growing out of the contacts Mongkut had developed since the early 1830s with Western missionaries resident in Siam.

It needs to be stressed that the chief outlines of Mongkut's intellectual development were in place before he first established contact with the American and French missionaries. He had already adopted an inquiring, rationalist mode of discourse. He wished by his own mental powers to arrive at the truth, going back to first principles and accepting or rejecting them in the light of reason. Within his contemporary framework, his approach was "scientific": there were reasons for everything, rational explanations accessible to all. Given his acute intelligence and lively, wide-ranging interests, it is not surprising that he should have come to enjoy the company and conversation of the American Protestants and the French Catholic Bishop Pallegoix. He studied Latin and English, and Western science and mathematics, particularly astronomy. He also aggressively cultivated contacts with Buddhist monks in Ceylon in an argumentative correspondence in the 1840s.

Mongkut was not alone in expanding his mental horizons beyond those of his father's generation. He was but one of a small number of highly placed Siamese who took an interest in Western learning. Whereas Christian missionaries elsewhere in Asia during this period had access for the most part only to the lower classes or to ethnic minorities, in Siam they reached young men of the elite. These included sons and nephews of Chaophraya Phrakhlang (Dit Bunnag), who was also Kalahom; Mongkut's younger brother Chudamani and half-brother Wongsathirat; and a few young sons of the leading families. Each had his particular interests, which in some cases derived from his official responsibilities. Chuang Bunnag, who assisted his father the Phrakhlang, took a great interest in shipbuilding and started the construction in Siam of square-rigged sailing vessels, which by the end of the reign were replacing indigenous and Chinese ships in carrying overseas trade for the Phrakhlang. Prince Chudamani became proficient in English, and because he had military responsibilities, he began to equip and drill troops in the European fashion. Prince Wongsathirat superintended the affairs of the Department of the Royal Physicians and studied Western medicine seriously enough to earn a correspondence diploma from a medical school in Philadelphia.

These young men seem to have been no more self-conscious about their studies and the innovations that derived from them than Rama I had been about going back to Indic texts or translating works from Asian languages. They had confidence in the power of their own minds to deal with the changing world around them, using whatever tools and techniques fit their needs, no matter what the source. Approaching mid-century, these men, now in their forties and fifties, were the leading figures of their generation in Siam.

Rama III seems never to have been entirely comfortable with his accession to the throne. He acted as though he thought that Mongkut should have become king in 1824 and that he would have, had it not been for his youth and inexperience. There are some curious hints of this. First, Rama III's uparat and heir-presumptive died in 1832, and no one was named to replace him. Second, in 1836 as we have seen, Rama III urged Mongkut to move to, and become abbot of, a monastery much closer to the palace; he renamed it Wat Bowonniwet—the name being a play on the name of the palace customarily inhabited by the uparat. Finally, for furnishing his new quarters in Wat Bowon, Rama III invited Mongkut to choose objects from the vacant uparat's palace. These actions, Mongkut's son later argued, were intended to indicate that Rama III considered Mongkut's status to be equivalent to that of the uparat, the heir-presumptive.[18]

Among the court faction unhappy with Rama III's failure to appoint a new uparat was Prince Rakronnaret—the prince who had disparaged Mongkut's attainments during the Pali examinations in 1826. The king received a petition in late 1848 complaining of the prince's judicial conduct. An official investigation revealed not only that he was guilty of malfeasance in office, taking bribes for favorable verdicts and misappropriating funds, but that he preferred the company of male actors to that of his concubines. He was building a clientele, it was asserted, in order to gain the throne on the death of the king, which in the court's eyes amounted to treason. Because Rakronnaret was then the highest ranking prince, the king levied the ultimate penalty. He was beaten to death with sandalwood clubs in December 1848.

By 1850 it was clear that the reign had not long to run. Rama III was now sixty-two and in failing health. Many, like Rakronnaret earlier, were anticipating the coming succession to the throne with a great deal of uncertainty, and this was no time for any political action that might compromise any faction in the capital. Unfortunately, Western powers were beginning to urge on the Siamese court radical changes in its foreign and commercial policies. Western aggressiveness increased in the wake of the Opium War in China (1839–42), and the Western powers were less willing than they had been a decade or two earlier to deal with Asian states on Asian terms. The Burney Treaty and a similar one concluded with the United States in 1833 were no longer satisfactory. The West now demanded an end to all restrictions on trade, the establishment of conventional diplomatic relations, and consular legal jurisdiction over foreign nationals (i.e., extraterritoriality). Two missions came to Bangkok in 1850 to work toward these ends: Joseph Balestier on behalf of the United States in March and April and Sir James Brooke representing Britain in August and September. Both were turned away empty-handed, and both left Bangkok angry at what they took to be the arrogance and intransigence of the Siamese court, which was unyielding on every point at issue.

The reason the Siamese were so unwilling to come to terms with the Western powers in 1850 was the approaching succession struggle. The main officers charged with the negotiations with Balestier and Brooke were Chaophraya Phrakhlang (Dit) and his younger brother Phraya Siphiphat (That Bunnag), who from a power base in the Phrakhlang and Kalahom that gave them both manpower and wealth might have been expected to play a major role in determining who would be the next king. They were already closely identified with Mongkut, who was associated with unorthodox Buddhism and foreignism in the eyes of many traditional Siamese. Had the Bunnags supported the concluding of treaties with the West, they would have given their more conservative (and reactionary or xenophobic) rivals an issue to use against them. Therefore they obstructed the new treaties, while writing privately to friends abroad that they should bide their time. Similarly, during the same period, both Prince Mongkut and his brother Chudamani seemed to people in Bangkok to have stopped receiving Western visitors.

Rama III was taken seriously ill in September 1850 and by January was much worse. The protraction of his illness only heightened tension over the question of the succession to the throne. After some months of discussing possible successors and some fear that the contest might explode into civil war, the king, on March 10, 1851, called in his leading officials and told them he would not name his own successor. He urged them to convene soon a full meeting of officials and princes to decide the succession. His ministers hesitated to act while the king still breathed, so two days later he called them again to his bedside and spoke particularly with Phraya Si Suriyawong (Chuang Bunnag), the son of the Phrakhlang. With Suriyawong he discussed the alternatives and declared that Mongkut was the only prince with the wisdom to rule. However, Mongkut, he said, was widely distrusted. People feared that he might make all Buddhist monks wear their robes in the Mon fashion—perhaps by implication he was saying that Mongkut was perceived as being too proforeign. For this reason, he said, he hesitated to name Mongkut as his successor. Mongkut soon wrote to reassure him on the subject and ordered his followers to return to the conventional way of wearing robes. Then, on the night of March 15, all the leading princes and officials were assembled in the palace. Mongkut later provided an account of that meeting to the American missionary, Dan Beach Bradley, who passed it on to a Singapore newspaper. Chaophraya Phrakhlang (Dit Bunnag) had stood before the Assembly and had the boldness to declare firmly that he saw no man in the kingdom, who had equal claims with his Royal Highness T. Y. Chaufat [*sic*] Mongkut with his brother Chaufat Krommakhun Izaret [Prince Chudamani] as his colleague to become successor to the Throne; and that he had made up his mind to use what influence and power he had to defend the rights of those princes, because he regarded them as being the rightful heirs to the throne, since they were the sons of the highest possible birth of the previous king; since the present king has no sons by a regularly constituted Queen, and since the Throne was, as it were, loaned by the present king of those true princes, whose right to it had never been yielded up to him as the permanent possession of his family. His Excellency entreated all in council to be quiet while the present incumbent should live, saying that if upon his decease there must be fighting to settle the question of the succession he would request them to fight with himself and not with the princes whose cause he has espoused.[19]

The Phrakhlang thereupon threw a heavy guard around Wat Bowon and Prince Chudamani's palace. Three weeks later, when Rama III died early on April 3, Mongkut and Chudamani were formally invited to rule conjointly as first and second kings of Siam. The progressive party, as Western observers viewed the Bunnags, Mongkut, and Chudamani, had won the day.

Rama III bequeathed his successors a Siamese empire that was more powerful and extensive than at any previous time. It dwarfed all its mainland Southeast Asian neighbors in its sheer size and set an example for them by its ability to act constructively and forcefully in a dangerous world. Its dynamic energy, its capacity for change and reform, surely derived at least in part from the stamp that King Rama I had imposed upon the kingdom half a century earlier. As strong as Siam was, however, it faced formidable challenges from the Western powers, and even the conservative King Rama III knew that more difficult changes lay ahead. On his deathbed, he is reported to have remarked to Phraya Si Suriyawong (Chuang) that

> there will be no more wars with Vietnam and Burma. We will have them only with the West. Take care, and do not lose any opportunities to them. Anything that they propose should be held up to close scrutiny before accepting it: Do not blindly trust them.[20]

7

Mongkut and Chulalongkorn, 1851–1910

The last half of the nineteenth century was an extraordinarily dangerous time for the Tai peoples. In 1851, a large majority of them lived within the bounds of the Siamese empire and had begun the refashioning of their links with their distant cousins, which had been broken for a millennium. By the early twentieth century, many of them had fallen under the control of Western colonial powers—the Shans under the British in Burma and the Lao and upland Tai under the French in Indochina. The onset of Western colonial control for the most part put an end to any ambitions some may have had for Siamese leadership of the Tai peoples, though these ambitions were to surface again during World War II. At the same time, however, what might be called Siamese colonialism did succeed in integrating within Siam many peoples, Tai-speaking and others, who had little previous connection with the Kingdom of Siam. Siam itself successfully evaded the direct colonial control of the Western powers.

Thus we confront three issues here: internal integration, external territorial losses, and the survival of an independent Siam. The outcome of all three was, directly and materially, a product of political developments centering around the court in Bangkok. In a sense, everything depended on the two men who were kings of Siam during the fifty-nine-year period from 1851 to 1910, Mongkut and his son Chulalongkorn. Ultimately it was on their shoulders that the burdens fell; it was they who had to make the difficult decisions. Someone once said of Mongkut that he was the last Siamese monarch to enjoy being king. But it is difficult to imagine that either he or Chulalongkorn could have enjoyed the difficult times through which they lived.

King Mongkut's Cautious Reforms

On his elevation to the throne in 1851, King Mongkut (Rama IV) was forty-seven years old and had been a Buddhist monk for twenty-seven years. His religious life, however, by no means had been cloistered; indeed, it can be argued that he was better prepared for the throne by his monastic experience, having had the opportunity to study and read widely, as well as to travel through the country and speak with people with whom princes only rarely came into contact. Because of his long absence from secular life, however, he lacked a secure political following of clients and retainers, and thus he was especially vulnerable to the pressures and power of the friends who had brought him to the throne. Prince Chudamani's concurrent elevation to reign jointly with Mongkut as Phra Pin Klao, the "Second King," seems to have been Mongkut's idea, a strategem intended to neutralize his powerful brother (and his small army) by holding open the possibility of immediate power as well as an enhanced chance at the succession to the throne should he outlive Mongkut.

The king's immediate agenda was to reward his friends and consolidate his power, and this meant confirming the preeminence of the Bunnag family. Chaophraya Phrakhlang (Dit), who had controlled the Phrakhlang and Kalahom concurrently for more than twenty years, was gracefully promoted, retired to a sinecure, and replaced by two of his sons, Chaophraya Sir Suriyawong (Chuang) as Kalahom and Chaophraya Thiphakorawong (Kham) as Phrakhlang. The king's immediate personal staff was filled with younger Bunnags. These initial appointments gave a single family a preponderant place in the central administration and secured the regime from immediate domestic competition.

Mongkut still faced one local war, a leftover from the reign of his predecessor. This had originated in a civil war in the northern Lü state of Chiang Hung, in which Rama III's troops had briefly intervened in 1850 before being recalled on the king's death. By 1852, the new ruler of Chiang Hung had sent tribute to Bangkok and was requesting protection against the Burmese, who exercised suzerainty over that region through Keng Tung. Accordingly, in 1852–53 and again in 1854, Mongkut sent expeditions against Keng Tung, led both times by his younger brother Prince Wongsathirat but manned almost entirely with levies of troops from Lan Na. Neither expedition succeeded in taking Keng Tung, owing to problems with supplies and low troop morale, and this ended Siamese ambitions in this area for the rest of the reign.

Soon Mongkut's government was more concerned with relations with the West, the seriousness of which had been underlined by the belligerent attitude of Sir James Brooke on leaving Bangkok empty-handed late in 1850.

Suriyawong and Mongkut both had written to British authorities in Singapore imploring their patience, and Mongkut soon extended that correspondence to the new governor of Hong Kong, Sir John Bowring. It was some years before the Siamese felt sufficiently secure to risk direct dealings with Britain, and before London, reassured about their chances of success, considered sending another mission. When that moment came, early in 1855, it was significant that Bowring was chosen as the British envoy and that he represented the British Foreign Office, rather than the government of India or of the Straits Settlements. The latter two were generally anti-Siamese because of their local perspectives on territorial disputes and ambitions, whereas the Foreign Office took a more global view; it was concerned primarily with the conduct and security of British trade and traders. The British, no less than the Siamese, wished to avoid a repetition of the Second Anglo-Burmese War (1852), in which the immediate casus belli had involved the legal status of British traders and the conditions under which commerce was conducted.

Bowring came to Bangkok with both impressive pomp and the threat of force behind him. His correspondence with Mongkut had emphasized the lengths to which the British were prepared to go, by force of arms if necessary, to protect their trade and interests. Mongkut and Suriyawong therefore received and entertained the envoy and his party with unexpected warmth, candor, and informality. Mongkut received Bowring in his private apartments and offered him cigars and wine from his own hand; Suriyawong in discussions with Bowring railed against the inequities and inefficiencies of Siamese administration, carefully repeating arguments rehearsed beforehand with American missionaries.[1] Within two weeks, an agreement emerged that provided for the opening up of Siam to foreign trade and that met London's chief conditions. Import duties were restricted to 3 percent ad valorum, and export taxes, to an average of 5 percent. British subjects were allowed to reside and own land in Siam, enjoying rights of extraterritoriality under the protection of a resident representative of her majesty's government. Taxes on their land and activities were restricted to a low level. The government commodity and trading monopolies, long the mainstay of the Siamese financial system, were abolished except in the case of opium, which remained, as in Singapore and Hong Kong, an official monopoly. At the stroke of a pen, old Siam faced the thrust of a surging economic and political power with which they were unprepared to contend or compete.

They were willing, however, to make the best of a situation they could not change. Although the king and ministers enjoyed enormous authority, their power to govern rested on the cooperation of extended networks of clients and patrons, all with vested interests in their slices of the existing economic and political structure; the court had to handle carefully any changes in that system. The commercial concessions they had granted the British gravely threatened the power and livelihood of almost every prince and official to the extent they depended on the trading and commodity monopolies and the myriad internal taxes the treaty abolished. Those who stood to lose most by these changes were Suriyawong and Thiphakorawong and their faction, for most of the monopolies were under their control. They must have been able to promise the government compensatory revenues from other sources to make up for those sacrificed in the interest of national security. In the years immediately following the conclusion of the treaty, state revenues dipped slightly for only one year and then returned to their pretreaty level. The difference was made up mostly by strengthening excise monopolies in opium, gambling, alcoholic spirits, and the lottery, which lay beyond the scope of the treaty. Their impact was felt most heavily not by the Siamese but by the kingdom's Chinese minority. Although this financial transition was risky, it clearly was a risk worth taking. Mongkut and Suriyawong knew better than anyone else the nature of the power that threatened the kingdom and the means by which Siam's sovereignty might be subverted or suppressed—they read the Singapore and Hong Kong newspapers.

In addition to transforming the revenue system, the Siamese turned to another strategy to minimize the dangers of their new situation. Mongkut and Suriyawong quickly made it known that they would welcome diplomatic overtures from other Western nations, and within a decade, Bowring-like treaties were negotiated with the United States, France, and a score of other states. In setting out on this multilateral path, the Siamese hoped to avoid such suffocatingly close bilateral relationships as those between British India and Burma, or France and Vietnam, which by the 1860s rapidly were bringing about the partition of Southeast Asia among the colonial powers. It was no less important to Mongkut's statecraft than to his vanity that he be accepted as a brother monarch by the other ruling houses of the world and that as a king he be able to communicate directly with the metropolitan governments in Europe. Thus, he could avoid being fobbed off on neighboring colonial officers as other indigenous rulers in Burma and the Malay world were. The Siamese dexterously played upon rivalries among the imperial powers and even within the ranks of the powers themselves. In the case of England, for example, the Siamese balanced the British Foreign Office, the Indian government, and the Colonial Office government in the Malay Peninsula, each of which had different interests in Siam. In the case of France, they tried to use the influence of the Quai d'Orsay against the aggressive designs of the colonial government in Saigon (from 1858). Such diplomacy moved well beyond the passivity of which it has so often been accused. These multiple balancing acts required subtlety and caution because of the increasingly serious dangers Siam faced. The keystone of Siamese policy was the conciliation of Britain, since it was so much more powerful and active than other nations. It was hoped that London's benevolence would blunt the designs of other powers upon the kingdom.

This course was not always smooth, and early in the 1860s, two events occurred that made the Siamese uneasy. First, the king and Suriyawong, exercising what they understood to be their suzerain rights over Kelantan and Trengganu, got involved by complicated means in a succession dispute in Pahang, yet farther south. When Siamese warships landed a claimant to the Pahang throne at Trengganu in 1862, a British warship shelled Kuala Trengganu to persuade the Siamese to desist from further interference. Second, and much more serious, the situation in Cambodia changed with the death of King Duong in 1860 and the establishment of French colonial control in southern Vietnam at almost the same time. Duong's successor was the young King Norodom, who almost immediately was faced with internal rebellions, continuing Siamese paternalistic pressure, and overtures from the French. France coveted the apparent wealth of his state and viewed the Mekong River as a possible golden highway to the hidden wealth of the interior of Southeast Asia and China. In 1863 Norodom agreed to place his state under French protection, while almost simultaneously signing a secret agreement recognizing the suzerainty of the Siamese—who held the coronation regalia of his father. The next year, when he started off for Bangkok to be crowned, the French raised the tricolor over his palace and he beat a hasty retreat back to Phnom Penh. King Mongkut was mortified and not a little resentful at what he perceived as Norodom's ingratitude for past favors and disloyalty to Siam and the Buddhist traditions it represented.

These two episodes, occurring very close together, were all the more disturbing because each was to a large degree provoked by local authorities without reference to their home government. In both cases, however, the home authorities backed their officials after the fact. There was little else the Siamese could do save worry about where the next blow would fall and redouble their efforts to ensure that their vassal states were as closely supervised as possible.

Though one might have expected major internal changes commensurate with the drastic shifts in foreign and fiscal policy, very little fundamental reform was undertaken during Mongkut's reign. Certainly a great deal of change followed upon the sudden opening of Bangkok to large-scale foreign commerce. Trade diverted rapidly from junks to steam vessels. The number of modern ships visiting Bangkok from Singapore alone jumped from 146 in 1850 to 302 in 1862, and the total annual value of trade moved from about 5.6 million baht in

"A Siamese Nobleman dictating a dispatch"; from a photograph album in the John M. Echols Collection, Cornell University Libraries.

1850 to around 10 million baht by 1868, by far the largest portion of which came from the export of rice.[2] With the expansion of trade came a refashioning of the waterfront and commercial quarters of Bangkok, with new wharves and warehouses, steam-powered rice- and sawmills, and rows of brick shops vending imported goods, while upon newly paved roads horse-drawn carriages bore merchants about the bustling city.

But the administration did not change, beyond the shift from commodity and trading monopolies to the opium, gambling, lottery, and spirits monopolies. Government was carried on in the homes of officials as it had been for centuries, and it was characterized by Europeans as corrupt, inefficient, and inhumane. Justice remained highly personalized and heavily subject to the social and economic pressures that could be mobilized by the individuals involved. The civil administration was seen to be riddled with nepotism, its officers remunerated largely by percentages of the business they transacted. Each of the offices of government attempted to control manpower, since rights to labor services still provided basic revenues and were still a source of political and personal strength. The three main ministries of government—the Mahatthai, ruling the northern provinces; the Kalahom, the southern provinces; and the Phrakhlang, the coastal provinces near Bangkok—exercised multiple functions, governing provinces, collecting taxes, organizing public works, raising troops, and running courts of law. Throughout the government, from the great departments of state in Bangkok to the smallest and most remote province, families and local oligarchies tried their hardest to transmit their power and prerogatives from one generation to the next, jealously guarding these against outsiders.

Extraterritoriality was the European response to Siamese justice; limitations of import and export duties and other taxation was the response to what was perceived to be chaotic and capricious revenue administration. The military threat of the West remained real and, on some fronts, began to grow, yet there was no professional army to speak of. Reform was vitally necessary on grounds of self-interest alone; and Buddhist morality no less than conventional Western standards required fundamental changes in the Siamese administration, legal codes, systems of slavery and debt bondage, and social and economic services.

Why were not such fundamental reforms at least initiated in Mongkut's reign by a king who himself stated that his country was backward and in need of reforms? In the first place, Mongkut thought he had ample time to make changes slowly, so as not to disrupt too seriously and too quickly the existing order. He thought the worst of the imperialist pressure was past. But even stronger reasons for the postponement of domestic reform lay in the political and social conditions under which Mongkut labored.

The ministries and departments of government were probably less subject to royal authority than they had been a half-century earlier when Rama I had created a government almost from scratch. The Kalahom and Phrakhlang had been controlled by a single family for most of two generations and were staffed by clients and retainers with personal bonds of loyalty and mutual obligation to their chiefs and their immediate subordinates. There were similar bonds between patrons and clients suffusing the central administration, as well as the provinces, most of which were controlled by semihereditary governors whose appointments the king could only confirm. To attack any existing abuses must inevitably have led to a confrontation with one or another of the families, cliques, or factions that gave Siamese society much of its cohesion in the middle of the nineteenth century. For better or worse, patrons depended on the perquisites of office to protect and reward their clients. Clients in turn relied upon their patrons for protection and for the sense of place and position in society upon which their identities were founded. All social relationships were

King Mongkut being carried in royal procession to Wat Phrachetuphon (Wat Pho),
1865; in the collection of Wiliam L. Bradley.

vertically structured by bonds between individuals of differing status which
were expressed in language and formalized in administrative ranks and titles.
There was little if any sense of social solidarity on a horizontal plane, between
equals. The Siamese language itself hardly provided for the concept of equal
relationships. Mongkut certainly knew this and was well aware of the limits of
his power. He could lead, slowly and cautiously, but he could not aggressively
push. He needed, above all, the broadest possible cooperation in order to build
the stability on the basis of which reform might ultimately take place.

Mongkut thus proceeded slowly. He started the publication of a government gazette and allowed the laws of the kingdom to be printed, that people
might be better informed. He experimented with the election of judges (and
abandoned the practice soon thereafter). He broke with tradition to allow his
subjects to gaze upon his face when he paraded in public, and he permitted
petitioning for the redress of grievances. He tried, with but limited success, to
ameliorate the condition of slaves and allow women some choice in marriage.
He also employed a handful of foreign advisers (there were fourteen in 1870) for
specialized, technical work that did not infringe upon existing interests. Some
served as translators and secretaries for the conduct of foreign affairs; others

King Mongkut and Crown Prince Chulalongkorn, 1865; in the collection
of William L. Bradley.

were drillmasters in semiprivate armies (such as that of Phra Pin Klao, the
second king), printers, bandmasters, and technical officers in the port and
police administration, both of which directly served the growing European
community in Bangkok.

These were small steps, but Mongkut was looking ahead to the day when
he or his successor might build upon them and make Siam a truly "civilized"

Somdet Chaophraya Si Suriyawong (Chuang Bunnag),
1865; in the collection of William L. Bradley.

country, instead of one "half civilized, where [the people] are acquainted with
some Code of Laws and their manners and customs are good."[3]

A New King versus the "Ancients"

The sons born to Mongkut before his exile to the monkhood all died before
1868, and with the death of Phra Pin Klao in 1866, the king's advanced age
opened the question of the succession to the throne. Mongkut's eldest son by a
queen, Prince Chulalongkorn (born 1853), was a mere boy, but he soon came
popularly to be regarded as the logical heir to the throne. Mongkut clearly
hoped his son would succeed him, and to prepare him for the throne, he
afforded Chulalongkorn in the 1860s the beginnings of a superb education
that combined traditional Thai and modern Western elements. It was

Chulalongkorn who was the chief object of the academic attentions of Mrs. Anna Leonowens, while at the same time he had the benefit of both a classical Thai education and a period of practical apprenticeship with his father, sitting in on the audiences at which public business was transacted and carrying messages to and from the ministers. Mongkut hoped to be able to hand over the government to his son when the prince came of age in 1873, but both were stricken with malaria on a visit to the Malay Peninsula to witness a solar eclipse in 1868. Not long after their return to Bangkok, Mongkut died on October 1, 1868, leaving a fifteen-year-old heir-apparent whose health was extremely precarious.

In audience with Chaophraya Suriyawong (Chuang) in the days before his death, Mongkut inexplicably refused to state a preference as to his successor, though he did ask that, should Chulalongkorn be chosen by the accession council, Suriyawong agree to serve as regent until the boy came of age. When the council met, Suriyawong presented the case for Chulalongkorn's succession, laying considerable stress on the narrow notions Westerners had about legitimacy (reflected earlier in the case of Rama III) and on Western expectations that Chulalongkorn would succeed to the throne. From the perspective of Siam's foreign relations, the choice of Chulalongkorn was safer. No one challenged this argument, Chulalongkorn was named unanimously to succeed his father, and Suriyawong was chosen to serve as regent for the boy-king until 1873. Then Suriyawong took the unprecedented step of declaring that Prince Wichaichan (also named "George Washington" by his Americophile father), son of the late Second King Phra Pin Klao, should be named heir-presumptive, an act that always before had been the prerogative of the new king. One prince dared to rise and challenge this unprecedented move, but his action failed to elicit any support from an assembly fearful of Suriyawong's power, and Wichaichan's appointment was pushed through.

It is uncertain how deviously Suriyawong was maneuvering on this occasion; but his actions generally have been interpreted as an attempt to preserve his position and influence in the kingdom. He is thought to have believed that Chulalongkorn would not recover from his illness and that Wichaichan then would come to the throne beholden to Suriyawong. In the short run, at any rate, his family's position was still further enhanced by the new ministerial appointments that followed. With Suriyawong becoming regent with the rarely awarded princely title of Somdet Chaophraya Si Suriyawong, his son Chaophraya Surawong (Won) succeeded him as Kalahom; another son, Chaophraya Phanuwong (Thuam) took over the Phrakhlang; and his nephew took over the Ministry of Lands with its substantial income from the land tax (a considerable portion of which was kicked back to the regent). Suriyawong was the real master of the administration in the regency period, as he had been earlier and was to remain until his death in 1883.

Chulalongkorn was not immediately in a position to challenge the regent's power, though they occasionally quarreled over money. As a boy-king, with no political following of his own and no maternal relatives in high places or princes of independent authority to support him, he was at the mercy of the regent. One of the strongest checks on the situation was the logic of history, the common knowledge of another Suri(ya)wong who became regent for a boy-king in 1629 and usurped the throne as King Prasat Thong. Suriyawong conducted himself well. He responsibly fulfilled his duties to the young king and the kingdom by supervising Chulalongkorn's education, finally allowing him to tour Dutch and British colonial possessions in Java, Malaya, Burma, and India in 1871–72 that he might become familiar with modern administration.

It was only in 1873 that the character of the new ruler began to be evidenced publicly. In the months preceding and following his second coronation as king in his own right (November 1873), Chulalongkorn began a series of reforms that displayed his modern sentiments and intentions. Royal decrees creating a special court to clear the judicial backlog of the clogged ministerial courts in Bangkok and clarifying judicial procedures directly threatened the jurists of the old order. Decrees requiring centralized budgeting and the public auction of gambling and opium monopolies challenged the official peculation rampant in Bangkok. The creation of a Privy Council and Council of State (so termed in English) with advisory, investigatory, and legislative powers, in the membership of which young men predominated—the brothers and friends of the king and some rivals of the Bunnags—clearly foreshadowed a political contest of the first order. Finally, decrees announcing the gradual abolition of slavery and placing more stringent conditions on the status of debt-bondsmen and making easier their redemption undermined the manpower and hence the economic status of the bureaucratic elite.

The king's motivation in undertaking these reforms, all of which in some way struck fundamentally at the old order, was mixed. All directly or indirectly strengthened the king's political position, yet at the same time all were proclaimed on moral grounds with which few could argue. The old guard—the "Ancients" (*hua boran*), as the king called them—might attack the reforms as Western-inspired innovations, but publicly these were justified primarily in terms of Buddhist moral principles. In light of the sentiments expressed in Chulalongkorn's private correspondence during these years, there is no reason to suspect his sincerity. Perhaps its best public demonstration was his celebrated second-coronation decree announcing the abolition of the custom of prostrating oneself in the royal presence, which he viewed as demeaning to the dignity of men. In all these decrees, the young man began to reveal a view of the Siam of the future, a state that would express the highest ideals of Buddhist morality but at the same time measure up to the expectations and standards of the West. Only much later did the king begin to perceive the contradictions inherent in this vision.

It took only months for the reforms of 1873–74 to provoke resistance and definance. Late in 1874, some of the more radical of Chulalongkorn's supporters in the Privy Council began to attack Prince Wichaichan, demanding, in effect, that the king's right to choose his own heir be restored. Wichaichan, feeling threatened and seeing the young king's strength growing as a result of the reforms, began to call in his troops and drill them in the Front Palace grounds in the dead of night. When informed, Chulalongkorn strengthened his own palace guard. Then, on the night of December 28–29, 1874, a fire was set near the gunpowder storehouse and gasworks in Chulalongkorn's palace, and Wichaichan's troops arrived at the gates, fully armed, demanding admission to assist in putting out the fire. They were refused admission, the fire was quenched, and both parties stood tensely awaiting the next move.

When it began to appear that the king's party was going to use the incident to reduce his prerogatives, Wichaichan fled his palace on January 2 and took refuge in the British Consulate. The country seemed on the brink of civil war, and there was much support for Wichaichan among the Bangkok nobility, who had been offended by the king's radical friends. For a time, Wichaichan suggested that he might return to his palace under an agreement with Chulalongkorn guaranteed by the French and British consuls, but the court could not accept such an arrangement so demeaning to the king's sovereignty. Chulalongkorn bombarded Paris and London with appeals for European neutrality and worked hard to regain the support of his ministers and the older conservatives at court. The British Foreign Office chose to regard the affair as a purely domestic quarrel, a message conveyed personally to Chulalongkorn by the governor of Singapore. Stripped of possible foreign support, Wichaichan finally had no alternative but to come to terms, accept the limitations of his status, and return to his palace.

The Front Palace Crisis of 1875 was of much more than immediate significance, for it brought into sharp focus all the dangers and intractability of the political environment in which Chulalongkorn had to work. He quickly had learned that his young radical friends could provoke great trouble and that they had little real support to offer him. He had found too that the pillars of the state—the ministers and officials of his father's reign—still possessed authority and power without which he could withstand neither external threats nor domestic challenges. The crisis had come close to costing him his throne and

Siam its sovereignty. The price he had to pay to resolve the crisis was the abandonment of many of the reforms of the preceding eighteen months. The councils ceased to meet; many of the financial reforms were forgotten or not enforced; the judicial administration returned to much the same state it had been in 1868; and the king's young friends were instructed to show more respect to their elders and to close down their Young Siam Society and their newspaper that espoused reformist views. The old order now clearly had the upper hand. If Chulalongkorn were to persist in fundamental reform, he stood to lose much more than time. At this critical juncture, some modicum of national unity was vital to the survival of the state, and only on its survival could the ultimate hope of reform rest. Chulalongkorn now must bide his time, working gradually to build the support and the strength that eventually would make reform possible.

Chulalongkorn's relations with the West in the seventies were hardly happy, despite the success of his appeals to London and Paris in 1875. In particular, the long-standing issues of Anglo-Siamese relations, defined as early as the 1820s, were growing steadily in importance. As British teak-exploitation activities in lower Burma moved into north Siam in Mongkut's reign, British interests and involvement in that area began to worry the Siamese. Chulalongkorn was afraid that the mishandling of forest leases by the vassal ruler of Chiang Mai would get out of control. He was also anxious that the prince of Chiang Mai not become involved in military adventures or disputes with the British Burma government that might embarrass Bangkok or bring about a collision with the British. Thus new policies toward Chiang Mai and the north were initiated in the seventies that were to begin the more secure integration of that region into the kingdom.

Bangkok was given its opportunity in 1870, when Chao Kavilorot (r. 1856–70) died. The regent and ministers in Bangkok passed over the logical heir to the throne of Chiang Mai, choosing instead Chao Intanon (r. 1870–97), whom they rightly expected would be more sympathetic to Bangkok's policies. After an Anglo-Siamese agreement of 1874 establishing a new system of bi-national courts to handle disputes between subjects of the two states, the Siamese sent to Chiang Mai a royal commissioner who slowly began to limit the prerogatives of the Chiang Mai ruling house and to bring the administration of the northern provinces into conformity with, and under the control of, the central administration. The procedures and tactics developed there, especially in the 1880s during the commissionerships of the king's brothers, princes Phichit and Bidyalabh, were later to be extended successfully to the provinces of the northeast and south and, with less success, to the Lao vassal states of Luang Prabang and Champassak.

Matters were not so immediately pressing in the Malay provinces of south

Siam, where the Siamese continued in nominal suzerainty over Kedah, Perlis, Kelantan, and Trengganu. With the assumption of an active British role in the states of the west coast of the peninsula from 1873, however, pressure for a British forward policy in the Malay states under Siamese suzerainty markedly increased. For the time being, the only check the Siamese had against British Malayan and Colonial Office ambitions was the decision of the British Foreign Office to secure the objectives of London's interests in Siam through diplomacy and conciliation, so long as such a course promised effective results.

Chulalongkorn and his government had some difficulty with the personalities representing Britain and France in Bangkok in the 1870s. Sir Thomas George Knox, once a drillmaster of Phra Pin Klao's troops and British consul-general in Bangkok from 1864 to 1879, was an intimate of Chaophraya Suriyawong, a friend of Wichaichan, and an open opponent of the young king, whom he viewed as willful, radical, and impractical. He himself was involved in the politics of the period and reportedly hoped to marry one of his daughters to Wichaichan and another to one of Suriyawong's sons. He constantly argued with Chulalongkorn and took the conservative position of Suriyawong in the debates of the period. Nonetheless, like British consuls before and after him, he did accept the argument of the Siamese and the British Foreign Office that the continued independence of Siam was in the best interests—political and commercial—of Britain, contrary to the view so often put forward by British officials in Singapore and by the Colonial and India offices. He seems to have felt that the success of such a policy depended on the continued receptivity of Siamese officials to the civilized reason of Her Britannic Majesty's representative.

The French consul at this time was much less sympathetic to the Siamese government and labored, as the French so often did in this period, under the disability of French inferiority to Britain, particularly as the British Empire began to grow rapidly in the seventies and France was suffering under the ignominy of the Franco-Prussian War of 1870. The French protectorate over Cambodia was regularized by treaty with Siam in 1867; by the seventies French interest in the lands drained by the Mekong River, especially Laos, was growing, fed by dreams of finding a "back door" to the supposed riches of the interior of China. This thrust inland took the form of increasingly well-organized efforts at exploration up the Mekong, conducted with Bangkok's reluctant permission. The most notable of these was the Lagrée-Garnier Expedition of 1866–68 which followed the Mekong from Phnom Penh to Chiang Hung, almost entirely through Siamese territory. Shortly thereafter, the Siamese began having increasingly serious difficulties with Laos. Groups of Chinese bandits (Ho, or Haw), fugitives from the civil wars of south China, were marauding through much of Laos, even sacking Vientiane in 1872. Siamese armies were sent repeatedly as far as the Plain of Jars (Siang Khwang), but were unable to restore order to that area for any lengthy period of time. The disorder of Laos, coupled with increasingly explicit French intentions and involvement there, augured no good for Chulalongkorn, who without the power or funds to undertake aggressive programs of reform and consolidation, was hoping against hope that the situation would not deteriorate.

In the early 1880s, the king's prospects began to improve. First, the number of appointments at his disposal increased as the officials of the regency period died or retired. More important, perhaps, was the fact that the generation of Mongkut and Suriyawong, many members of which had continued to dominate public life into the eighties, rapidly lost its influence following the death of Suriyawong in 1883 and Wichaichan in 1886. As Chulalongkorn's health improved, the prospects of his rivals diminished rapidly, and people became more willing to identify themselves with him. Nonetheless, the monarch lacked a strong political following until at least the mid-eighties. For some time, he had tried to bring to prominence groups and families of the old nobility, particularly people who were long-standing rivals of the Bunnags. However, some of the most important of these individuals were disgraced in public scandals in the late seventies and early eighties, dampening the king's hopes of establishing new patterns of behavior in public office among those comfortably wedded to the old order. The king's choice of agents for future modernization was reduced still further by the limited response of Bangkok's bureaucratic elite to the opportunities for modern education he offered them. The only enthusiasm for the new school he established in the palace came from the junior branches of the royal family and from his own brothers, who soon came to constitute the best-educated group in Siamese society. Given the king's commitment to reform and his need for men with modern ideas whose loyalty to the crown was unquestioned, it was not surprising that he should turn to his brothers when given the opportunity to make new appointments in the departments and ministries in Bangkok and, increasingly, in the provincial administration.

Nor were the royal younger brothers unprepared by practical experience for the tasks they now began to assume. Not only had they all received the traditional Siamese education commonly given princes, but most of them also had attended at least briefly the special modern school established in the royal palace in the regency period. Moreover, in 1873–74, a few received considerable instruction from an English tutor. Although princes by custom and practice rarely had been able to enter administrative service—at least not without marriage into the bureaucratic noble families—and although royal patronage prior to the eighties had been confined almost totally to his own palace precincts, Chulalongkorn had created meaningful and functional new positions in the palace. His own secretariat became a much more active body than the old Department of the Royal Scribes had been. The princes were drawn into the work of dealing with both foreign and domestic correspondence and were consulted by the king on business. The creation of the Royal Audit Office to carry out the financial reforms of the immediate postregency period made available a number of positions as accountants, bookkeepers, and auditors. The king himself personally worked late into the night with his brothers to straighten out the chaotic royal finances. Most of the princes served as officers in the military unit of the Corps of Royal Pages, which under Chulalongkorn became the state's laboratory of military reform, as well as his counterbalance to the private army of Wichaichan. It became too the nucleus of a modern army.

The first ministerial position to fall vacant was the Ministry of the Capital, responsible for justice and public order in the Bangkok-Thonburi area. In 1876, this post was assigned to Prince Phuttharet (1855–97), who had served with distinction on the special law court created to clear the backlog of Bangkok litigation. In 1882, Prince Prachaksinlapakhom (1856–1914) was appointed Minister of the Palace. For some years, he had been in charge of the various subdepartments of royal craftsmen in the palace administration, and he had just returned from conducting a military expedition against the Ho in Laos. He was later to serve for many years as royal commissioner in charge of the administration of a large portion of the northeast. In 1885, the king made two major appointments that firmly shifted the balance of power in the adminis- tration in his favor. On the retirement of Chaophraya Phanuwong (Thuam Bunnag) in that year, the old Phrakhlang was firmly broken up into two new ministries, the Treasury and Foreign Affairs (informally their work had been diverging for some years).

To head the Ministry of Foreign Affairs, Chulalongkorn chose Prince Devawongse (1858–1923), the elder brother of three of the king's own queens (all of them, of course, being the children of King Mongkut). A brilliant appointee, Devawongse was to conduct Siam's foreign relations for thirty-eight years with great skill and finesse to the satisfaction of two kings. In the same year, Prince Chakkraphat (1856–1900), the king's brother, was chosen to act as Minister of Finance. During the same period, other royal brothers were spread through numerous state offices, from the Royal Secretariat and Royal Audit Office, the Palace Guard and Royal Pages' Bodyguard Regiment, to the Royal Press, the Post and Telegraph Department, and the law courts. They soon began to take over these organizations as a new Department of the Army, an

Education Department, and offices for public health, public works, land survey, hydrography, and the like were created.

The king's strategy during the period from 1875 to 1885 had been forced upon him by the political and administrative intractability of the old order. As long as the ministers of state were not of his own choosing, but rather owed their appointment or their ability to function to the support of others, Chulalongkorn could do little more than suggest the policies they might carry out. Passive resistance commonly greeted any attempt to interfere in the personal power empires of the old ministers. The ex-regent Suriyawong, for example, stubbornly resisted the building of a telegraph line overland to Burma through his stronghold in the western provinces, whose semihereditary governors were his relatives. On the day after Suriyawong's death, however, the king issued an order to begin the construction of the telegraph line. There were numerous similar cases in virtually every ministry. So long as the ministers could count on the political, or familial, or economic support of Suriyawong, or so long as they continued to fear or respect his power, they could resist the policies of the king. With Suriyawong, Wichaichan, and all the old ministers dying or retiring between 1882 and 1888, their bureaucratic subordinates were left without the protection of their erstwhile patrons. By appointing his well-prepared and loyal brothers to key positions in these ministries, Chulalongkorn could effect a real transfer of power into his own hands.

That transfer of power, however, was accomplished very slowly. Many of the minor departments dealing with technical matters first were created within the palace administration, to be moved beyond its walls only when a secure ministry could be trusted to continue its work. Thus began the new Department of the Army and the Education Department in the Royal Pages' Bodyguard Corps, the new Ministry of Foreign Affairs in the foreign section of the Royal Secretariat, the new Ministry of Finance in the Royal Audit Office, and the survey, hydrography, and hospitals departments in the Royal Pages' Corps. These shared some elementary reforms of previous practices—Western paper and filing systems, copybooks and ledgers; regular office hours in designated offices instead of the traditional practice of locating a ministry in the home of the minister; the neat office practices of clerks, with the drawing up of précis of incoming correspondence for the minister's consideration and the drafting of replies for his signature; and the interminable writing of quarterly and annual reports, the submission of detailed financial accounts, and, most of all, the required reference to the king of all consequential decisions on policy and practice. In principle, and increasingly in fact, this was a highly centralized system; but for the moment the main business involved was the extension of royal control over the work of departments and ministries. In order to change Siam, Chulalongkorn first had to control his own government.

Internal Power and External Challenge

It was only in the mid-eighties that the king and his brothers could feel the reality of power, and almost immediately they were faced with the problem of how it was to be exercised. A small group at the court returned, in a sense, to the radicalism of the late-regency period. In a strongly worded sixty-page petition addressed to the king early in 1885, eleven young men, almost all of them recently returned from abroad, including three of the king's half-brothers, strongly urged that the king quickly move toward a system of parliamentary democracy under a constitutional monarchy. They criticized the growing concentration and confusion of executive, legislative, and judicial powers in the hands of the king to the neglect of much essential work by an overworked monarch. In order that reform might be accomplished to strengthen Siam against the West and in order that the benefits of reform might more quickly reach the bulk of the population, they asked the king to share his power with a prime minister, cabinet, and representative parliament—though they could agree that the time had not yet come when the legislature could be fully elective.[4]

In replying to this petition some months later, Chulalongkorn expressed sympathy with the intentions and objects of his critics, and his agreement with their perception of the necessary connection between domestic reform and the maintenance of national independence. He dwelt in particular on the extreme shortage of educated, loyal, effective men to carry out the monumental tasks of reform that lay ahead. Undoubtedly speaking from his recent experience, he expressed doubt as to the altruism, the independence, the efficiency, and the ability to subordinate personal to national interest of the country's small elite. The older men, he explained, were incompetent and the younger not yet fully prepared to carry out the tasks expected of them. To introduce the competition and diversions of electoral and parliamentary politics would weaken the state at precisely the moment it was most in need of unity and direction. He pleaded guilty to his critics' charges that he had neglected his legislative functions, agreeing that he had overconcentrated on executive business. "I, too," he stated, "want political reforms, but at present there are other matters more pressing.... We must first of all see that we can get the right kind of people to be our future legislators, or we are better off without them."[5]

Though from today's perspective the king's reply is obviously conservative, it was a liberal response within the context of his own time and place. His kingdom was then almost totally lacking in modern education; the bulk of the population, overwhelmingly agricultural, had little or no political independence of mind, being naturally respectful of those they considered their "betters" and unable to begin to think in the terms that electoral politics presuppose. The total number of men in Siam with any exposure to modern education could not have numbered more than a few hundreds, and none save the alien Chinese commercial minority had independent wealth or any social or vocational position outside the civil bureaucracy. Foreign pressure on the kingdom was within a few years of reaching its height, and yet the work of modernization on which the country's leaders felt the fate of the kingdom depended barely had begun. Chulalongkorn's reluctance to embark on political experiments under such conditions is understandable, and events in the subsequent decade justified his hesitation.

Perhaps influenced by the petition of 1885, but certainly required also by the functional needs of reform at the time, Chulalongkorn in 1887 asked Prince Devawongse, who was attending the celebrations in England marking Queen Victoria's fiftieth anniversary on the throne, to study and report on the organization of European governments. Upon returning, Devawongse recommended the formation of a cabinet of twelve equal ministers, including the heads of the seven old ministries and five new ones, the responsibilities of each to be newly defined on functional lines. The old ministries of the northern provinces (Mahatthai), southern provinces (Kalahom), foreign affairs and treasury (Phrakhlang), lands, palace, and capital were to become, respectively, the new ministries of interior, war, foreign affairs, finance, agriculture, palace, and local administration (of the capital region); and new ministries were to be created for public works, public instruction, justice, army, and privy seal (a combination of the royal secretariat and a sort of civil service commission).

In inaugurating the transition to this system early in 1888, the king delivered a lengthy and scholarly speech examining the historical development of the traditional system of government and analyzing its weaknesses. He then outlined the procedure by which the new system gradually would be introduced. Ministers-designate were chosen, almost all of whom were the king's brothers, and they immediately began to meet as a cabinet, though still without executive authority, in preparation for the full transfer of their powers that was not to take place until 1892. Two glaring omissions in the 1888 changeover were the continued overlapping of military responsibilities between the Kalahom and the new Department of the Army and the continued division of responsibility for provincial administration between the Mahatthai and Kalahom, necessitated in both cases because of the persistence of the old ministers in office. Until such time as they died or chose to retire, the king did not think it wise to challenge them. Both, however, were elderly and could be expected to pass from the scene before long.

Ultimately, the formal constitution of these changes was not nearly so important as the patterns of decision making that developed in the four-year trial period leading up to the inauguration of cabinet government in 1892. The ministers regularly met together as a body as they had rarely done before, and national policy began to achieve some coherence. The centralization of revenue collection in the Ministry of Finance in particular worked to create some interdependence between ministries that formerly had enjoyed fiscal independence. Finally, a great deal of information was shared more widely than before, and the advice and criticism of the ministers and king could make itself felt upon the actions of each minister. Such exchange was vitally important to the successful conduct of the massive program of reorganization and reform that had to be accomplished.

In the years immediately prior to 1892, while the new ministries were beginning to take shape with the transfer of old departments from one ministry to another and with the slow beginnings of new enterprises in Bangkok, the central government finally was able to move effectively to strengthen its control over outlying provinces, particularly in the former vassal or tributary states. It was in the late eighties that the royal commissionerships in Chiang Mai and Phuket (the center of the tin-mining area on the west coast of peninsular Siam) began to take effective control with the ability to promulgate laws and organize revenue collection, and that the first commissioners were appointed in the northeast, residing at Luang Prabang, Nong Khai (opposite old Vientiane), and Ubon Ratchathani. For most of these posts, royal princes were selected. As members of the royal house, they could override both the old guard in the ministries nominally responsible for these provinces and the entrenched local authorities, governors who for the most part had succeeded their fathers and grandfathers in office. Chulalongkorn chose his new commissioners carefully, and as a group they were very effective. Within a few years, for example, Prince Bidyalabh instituted a system for the leasing of timber rights which drastically reduced the arbitrary authority of the ruler of Chiang Mai; and Prince Prachak in Nong Khai began to organize a territorial army to check the chaos of central Laos and defend against the rising military threat of France in the region. These steps might have been taken earlier, had it not been for the lack of suitable men to undertake them and the shortage of funds to support them. They came none too soon, for these places quickly became the danger spots of the kingdom.

Never fully disengaged from their belief in the economic value of the Mekong valley and increasingly determined to match the growth of the British Empire in Burma with one of their own in Indochina, the French watched the increase of Siamese activity in Laos with growing alarm. Though Vietnam and Siam for centuries had contested unevenly the control of Laos, the Siamese were gaining the upper hand in the nineteenth century. The Siamese position, however, was both assisted and endangered by the activities of the Ho raiders. As was their duty as suzerains of the kingdoms of Luang Prabang and Siang Khwang, they had responded to the Ho incursions of the seventies and eighties with military expeditions and thereby increased the dependence of their vassals upon Bangkok. In particular, in 1885—simultaneously with the British invasion of upper Burma and the completion of the French conquest in northern Vietnam—a major Siamese expedition in Laos that ranged as far as the Black River led to the appointment of two Siamese commissioners to superintend the civil adminstration of King Un Kham of Luang Prabang (r. 1872–87). The ensuing dispute with France over the frontier between Vietnam and Siamese Laos quickly exploded into a French challenge to Siamese suzerainty over all Laos. The challenge was made in spite of the fact that a Franco-Siamese agreement of 1886, sanctioning the creation of a French vice-consulate in Luang Prabang, explicitly recognized the validity of Siamese suzerainty, and even sovereignty, over that area.

The French claim to Laos was manufactured for the purpose of imperial aggrandizement. It was based on the contention that France, as the "protector" of the Vietnamese Empire, succeeded to Vietnam's supposed former suzerainty over the Lao states, despite the fact that a check of the Vietnamese archives in Hue failed to uncover documents in support of such claims. There had been periods in the past when the Vietnamese court had achieved real suzerainty over various Lao kingdoms, especially in the Siang Khwang region in the 1850s, and earlier, for limited periods, over Luang Prabang and over Vientiane before its abolition as a kingdom in 1828. The French claims, in defiance of historical reality, rapidly were stretched to cover the whole of the Mekong valley.

The chief figure in the events that escalated into the Franco-Siamese Crisis of 1893 was Auguste Pavie, who for some years had been active in leading a group of explorers and scientists in the investigation of the history and present resources and condition of Cambodia. His appointment as vice-consul in Luang Prabang in 1886 made him the chief exponent of French expansion in central Indochina. The role suited him well. He had great personal sympathies for the peoples of Laos and Cambodia and was utterly committed to the task of persuading the French government to "protect" the princes and peoples of Laos from the supposed imperialism of Siam. His task was made easier by a grievous error on the part of the Siamese general in charge of troops in Luang Prabang who, though informed by Pavie in 1887 of a threatened Ho attack, chose to ignore the warning and return to Bangkok, leaving the city unprotected. When the Ho arrived, Pavie saved the king and his Siamese adviser and fled, eventually making his way to Bangkok. From this point, his opinion of the effectiveness of Siamese suzerainty markedly reduced, Pavie worked actively to sever all of Laos from Siam. In 1888, he worked with a French military force from northern Vietnam to annex the Tai müang of the Black River valley, tried and failed to send a party into Siamese-administered central Laos to seek out evidence of Vietnamese "suzerainty" there, and then returned to France in 1889 to persuade the French government to work for the extension of the Indochina empire to the banks of the Mekong River. Returning to Laos in 1890 at the head of the Mission Pavie, a well-staffed scientific and commercial party, Pavie quickly spread his men and French influence through most of Laos.

The Siamese response to this—strengthening the powers of the royal commissioners at Nong Khai, Ubon, and Champassak and readying the region's military defenses—was interpreted by the French as somehow unlawful, and Pavie was named French resident minister in Bangkok to voice this contention to the Siamese court. The crisis finally exploded early in 1893, following the unexplained expulsion of two French "commercial" agents from the middle Mekong region and the death (from natural causes) of the French consul at Luang Prabang. Paris authorized the Indochina authorities to take measures to secure "reparation" for these acts and explicity laid claim to all of Laos east of the Mekong by virtue of France's succession to the "rights" of Vietnam. When Siamese forces resisted French troops sent into Laos to take control of the territory in April 1893, killing a French officer who led an attack on them, the French government had the casus belli they had long sought. When the French were refused permission to send gunboats up the Chaophraya River to Bangkok, the French commander sent them up anyway, forcing the defenses at the mouth of the river (Paknam) in a short engagement, notwithstanding orders from Paris that the gunboats were to remain outside the sandbar at the mouth of the river.

Prince Devawongse made a brilliant attempt to save the situation, going down to the waterfront in Bangkok to congratulate the French commander on his daring in passing the Paknam forts and agreeing at once to the evacuation of Siamese troops from east of the Mekong. Pavie, however, with much French public opinion soon behind him, delivered an ultimatum and demanded the cession to France of the whole of Laos east of the Mekong, the payment of an indemnity of three million francs, and the punishment of Siamese officers responsible for French casualties in the fighting in Laos. Further demands soon were added, including the occupation of Siamese seaboard provinces (Chanthaburi and Trat) bordering Cambodia until the conditions of the ultimatum were complied with, and the creation of a twenty-five-kilometer demilitarized zone on the west bank of the Mekong and in the whole of western (Siamese) Cambodia. In a real sense, Siam was being forced to agree to outrageous demands simply because the kingdom had defended its own territory against foreign invasion. It was as if a new government coming to power in Britain had revived eighteenth-century claims to the United States, and then punished the American government for resisting a British invasion sent to enforce those claims.

Siam was defenseless against the naval blockade the French threatened if Bangkok did not comply, and, in the course of the long dispute, the British repeatedly refused to involve themselves. Two assumptions seem to have underlain Siamese policy during this period. They apparently believed, first, that the French would never sustain their ridiculous claims in a supposedly civilized world ruled by the same international law Siam had learned to use to its advantage in disputes with Britain, and, second, that, if worse came to worst, Britain could be relied upon to exert some force, if only moral, on their behalf. The French, however, did the unthinkable, and the British response was far less than the Siamese anticipated. What was operating, whether explicitly or not, was the doctrine of compensatory advantage, which somehow gave the French the right to as much empire in mainland Southeast Asia as Britain had acquired, no matter the means or justification of expansion. Britain saw in the 1893 situation the opportunity to establish a balance of power between France and Britain in mainland Southeast Asia that would render their rivalry there less dangerous. Chulalongkorn had no choice but to accept the terms offered and to conclude a treaty with France in October 1893. Afterwards, broken in spirit and health, he withdrew for some months from participation in public affairs.

The 1893 crisis was by no means the end of Siam's struggle for national sovereignty, but it did mark the beginning of the final phase in the kingdom's attempt to salvage what it could from an impossible situation. It was the last occasion on which the kingdom had to give up territory without compensation, and it was the point at which Britain and France began to face up to the necessity of coming to terms in Southeast Asia. The French annexation of Laos brought Britain and France into territorial contiguity in the upper reaches of the Mekong River. It made necessary a quick resolution of their conflicting claims in the region if they were to avert future conflict over the status of Siam.

After testing and discarding the idea of creating a buffer state on the upper Mekong by recognizing Siamese claims in that region (claims considerably less valid than those to the remainder of Laos), Britain and France in 1896 agreed on the Mekong as the boundary between British Burma and French Laos. They jointly guaranteed the independence of all that portion of Siam drained by the Chaophraya River system, each party further agreeing not to seek exclusive advantages there. At the same time, of course, each party tacitly reserved its right to advantages in, and even claims over, portions of Siam outside the

The judicial system under extraterritoriality, ca. 1900. Note the presence of two judges, one foreign, for a case involving a foreign subject.

Chaophraya valley—Britain on the Malay Peninsula and France in areas drained by the Mekong in the northeast, in western Cambodia, and in the provinces on the Gulf of Siam southeast of Bangkok. To confirm these assumptions, Britain and Siam secretly reached an understanding in 1897 excluding third-power activities in peninsular Siam and forbidding Siam from constructing a canal across the Isthmus of Kra. Simultaneously, France made it clear that it regarded the northeast and Siamese Cambodia as clear fields for its own influence and activities.

In the first decade of the twentieth century, conditions were much improved for a final settlement with Britain and France and for the revision of the unequal treaties of Mongkut's reign. Anglo-French rivalry had abated with the exhaustion of new opportunities, the necessity of concentrating on possessions in hand, and the increasing dangers of the situation in Europe. A new era was inaugurated with the conclusion of their Entente Cordiale in 1904. For its part, Siam was ready to bargain with the powers for the removal of the treaty disabilities under which the kingdom labored, particularly extraterritoriality. The French had especially absued their privileges in this regard, enrolling as "French subjects" anyone born or claiming descent from one born in Laos or Cambodia, or even Chinese who claimed to come from French Shanghai. Because French and British subjects lay beyond the reach of Siamese courts, having the right to be tried in consular courts, they were a menace to justice. Treaty restrictions on the rate of the land tax and import and export duties prevented the Siamese from raising much-needed revenues and increased the kingdom's dependence on the opium and gambling monopolies. These were just as distasteful to the Siamese as they were to the British and French (notwithstanding the use of both such taxes in their colonies).

Negotiations with Britain and France went on intermittently for many years, and results were slow in coming. By agreement in 1904 with France, territories opposite Luang Prabang and the small remainder of Champassak in southern Laos were ceded by Bangkok, and French privileges in the northeast were specified in return for a promised French withdrawal—at long last—from Chanthaburi and for stricter regulations concerning the registration of French "protected persons" in Siam. But the French still did not quit Trat and evacuated Chanthaburi only in 1906! Complete withdrawal and French abandonment of all claims of jurisdiction over their Asian "subjects" was achieved only with the conclusion of a 1907 treaty, which ceded to France the provinces of Battambang, Siem Reap, and Sisophon in western Cambodia.

Britain was no less demanding. Long negotiations were brought to a successful conclusion only after considerable soul-searching on the part of Devawongse and Chulalongkorn. Under the terms of a treaty, with several secret annexes, concluded in March 1909, the Siamese government transferred to the British government its rights of suzerainty over the Malay states of Kelantan, Trengganu, Kedah, and Perlis, in return for British agreement to transfer their consular jurisdiction over all British subjects in Siam to the Siamese courts as soon as modernized law codes were promulgated. The limitation on the rate of the land tax in Siam was explicity removed. The British government further demanded and received the exclusive right to finance and supervise the construction of the peninsula railway which was to link Singapore and Bangkok as well as Devawongse's formal promise that Siam would not permit any third power to establish a military or naval presence in the Siamese portion of the Malay Peninsula. Siamese officialdom did not easily accept the necessity for such heavy sacrifices. Those who felt most aggrieved by the transfer of the four states were their sultans, one of whom (ironically the sultan of Kedah) complained that "my country and my people have been sold as one sells a bullock."[6]

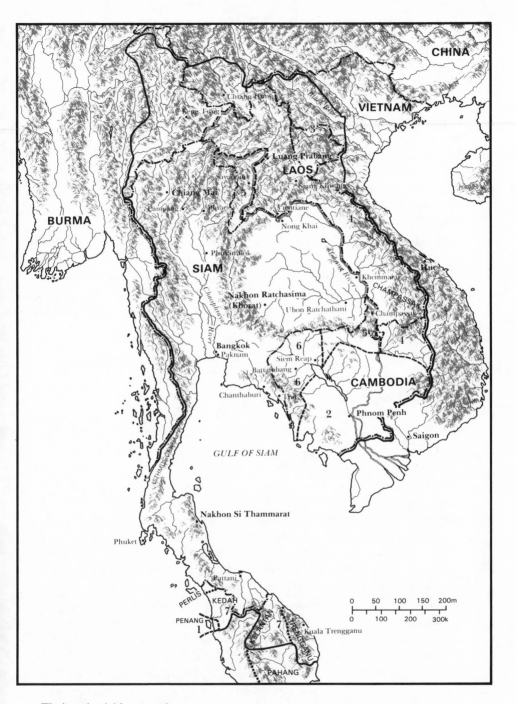

Thai territorial losses, 1785–1909.

1. Cessions to Britain by the Sultan of Kedah, 1785–1800.
2. Cambodian territory placed under French protection by Franco-Siamese Treaty, 1867.
3. Black Tai müang taken by France, 1888.
4. East bank of Mekong ceded to France by Franco-Siamese Treaty, 1893.
5. West bank territories ceded to France by Franco-Siamese Treaty, 1904.
6. Western Cambodian provinces ceded to France by Franco-Siamese Treaty, 1907.
7. Malay states ceded to Britain by Anglo-Siamese Treaty, 1909.

In the end, Siam yielded up 176,000 square miles (456,000 km²) of territory in order to preserve its independence—nearly half the area that had been under Bangkok's suzerainty at the end of the Third Reign. But territory was only part of the heavy price the kingdom paid. On the economic side, one must count foregone revenues from import and export duties and the land tax because of treaty limitations on their rates; the added costs of building railways between 1892 and 1906 out of current revenues instead of on borrowed money, a policy followed to avoid the political dangers of foreign loans; the cost of profitable concessions given to influential Europeans in order to gain their sympathy; the cost of conveniences provided for the European residents of Bangkok; and, especially, the heavy expenses of rapid military and naval modernization when revenues would have been much better spent on more productive schemes, like irrigation. Thus Siam did not purchase independence solely at the expense of the Lao, Cambodians, and Malays who found themselves transferred to European colonial control. Nor was the price the Siamese paid by any means wholly economic or the gains and returns wholly political.

From Reforms to Modernization

The basic accommodation reached with Britain and France in the nineties was possible only because both European powers by then had become convinced of the stability of the Siamese government, its ability to assure a modicum of security and public conveniences in the country, and its ability to protect the treaty rights of the European powers. That this assumption was so clearly established in both French and British policy by the turn of the century was directly attributable to the success of the reforms begun as recently as the mid-eighties and formally inaugurated only in 1892. Ironically, the most successful aspects of this modernization resulted from changes in policy that were unforeseen when innovation was begun in 1888.

It was the work of the new Ministry of Interior that by the turn of the century had begun effectively to make a nation out of the old Kingdom of Siam. As late as March 1892, Chaophraya Rattanabodin (Bunrot Kanlayannamit) had been designated to continue as the minister only of the northern provinces until such time as the southern and western provinces could be transferred to him from the Kalahom. Rattanabodin, however, suddenly took ill and had to be replaced. In what seemed a surprising decision at the time, the king appointed another of his half-brothers as minister, Prince Damrong Rajanubhab (1862–1943), who was then just thirty and had been minister-designate of the Ministry of Public Instruction. It soon became apparent that the king knew precisely what he was doing. Damrong set about his new responsibilities with a vigor and thoroughness that must have terrified his subordinates, numbers of whom soon found other positions. He toured the northern provinces, studied alternative methods of administration, and then embarked upon a program of centralization and wholesale reform which gathered momentum in 1894 when the southern and western provinces were transferred to his charge from the Kalahom.

In what he termed the *thesaphiban* system, introduced at Nakhon Ratchasima (Khorat) in 1893, Prince Damrong grouped a number of provinces into a single administrative unit (*monthon*, "circle") under the control of a resident commissioner in a manner similar to the royal commissionerships earlier established in Chiang Mai, the northeast, and Phuket. Given the power to override the semihereditary provincial governors, the commissioners began almost immediately to take control of local revenues and expenditures, overhaul the courts, introduce new police units, and curb corruption and injustice. Some older officials were retired, and others were incorporated into the new system. All were encouraged to send their sons to school in Bangkok, that they might carry on their families' noble profession (but in other provinces). Within a decade or so, young school-trained officers predominated in the provincial administration, especially at the district level. This dramatic and rapid centralization brought about a doubling of state revenues within a few years, the introduction of modern law, the extension of some social services, and a degree of security for persons and property previously unknown in the countryside.

Damrong was able to accomplish so much in the provinces partly by subverting the principle of functional differentiation that had been established in the administration by the reforms of 1888–92. Because his ministry was established in the provinces, with at least minimal staff (though he was very short-handed for two decades), and because the newer ministries were unable to cope with the work of the provinces without Interior's aid, Damrong rapidly took over functions formally assigned to other ministries, particularly with his creation of the Provincial Revenues Office to collect taxes in the provinces, a task that properly belonged to the Ministry of Finance. Quite a number of departments from other ministries were located in the Ministry of Interior during parts of this period—for example, the Survey Department, the Irrigation Department, and some public health services—simply because Damrong could be relied upon to make them work immediately. Damrong also took an important role in the introduction of modern education and the regulation of the Buddhist monkhood in the provinces. An indefatigable worker, incisive and direct, with an administrative genius unmatched in his generation, Damrong was given a free hand by the king and was frequently consulted on matters that lay outside his ministry's responsibilities.

There were not many as effective as Damrong, with whom all the ministers had to compete for funds and attention. The Ministry of Finance, advised by British officers who gave it a strongly conservative tone, effectively carried out its work of centralizing the budgeting process and for years avoided floating loans on the European money market. A heavy proportion of current revenues therefore went to capital expenditures, especially for railway construction which extended rapid communications to the northeast (the railroad reached Nakhon Ratchasima in 1900) and north, where security considerations were as important as economic or administrative concerns. The new Ministry of Justice languished for a time until taken in charge by Prince Rabi (1874–1920), the first of Chulalongkorn's sons to return from studies in Europe. Rabi set about energetically to revise Siam's law codes into conformity with Western law, in concert with French and Belgian jurists who followed their own Napoleonic model—a policy that at once both satisfied the government's desire for legal centralization and worked to counter French assertions about the "uncivilized" quality of Siamese law. Military reform was much slower in gaining coherence, but the core of a modern army had come into being by the turn of the century and universal military conscription was begun from 1902. The program of reform had proceeded by 1905 to the point where compulsory labor service— long the economic mainstay of the old order—could begin to be abolished, gradually to be replaced by a cash capitation tax and a more limited military conscription.

Conflicting pressures shaped reform into compromise. The strongest immediate pressure on Siam during this period was time itself. There was not time to proceed cautiously and deliberately with reform. Western demands for facilities and security had to be met quickly, so modern administration and the provision of minimal conveniences—transport, communications, contract law, and the like—had to be rushed through. At the same time, because Siam's modernization had been so long delayed by political difficulties, the agenda of reform had been allowed to pile up while the means of dealing with it had not yet been developed.

Easily the most serious need of the administration in the nineties was educated men for the civil service, men who had some understanding of the changes the government was trying to introduce. Yet the schools had started only in the mid-eighties, and the popular response to them was extremely slow until the mid-nineties. Thus a major argument for Prince Damrong's adoption of the thesaphiban system was that he had to staff only eighteen monthon offices, instead of more than a hundred provincial capitals. Similarly, the shortage of educated men prevented most of the ministries from developing their services rapidly, especially when these organs of state were new, poorly understood, and therefore unattractive to ambitious young men.

The backlog of reform was so enormous that the state budget, even when doubled and tripled by Interior's exertions in the provinces, could not begin to cope with all the claims upon its limited revenues. Money tended to go for the most pressing immediate needs—the provincial administration, the army, and the north-eastern railway, while the other ministries were short of funds. It did not help that much of the advice given government agencies by their foreign advisers—and each ministry had several, their nationalities carefully balanced—tended to be uninformed by local experience and impractical in terms of Siam's immediate requirements. The education and financial advisers, for example, were urging the creation of Etons and Harrows, and warning against the dangers of overeducation, while Damrong was desperately trying to find men to serve as deputy district officers, accountants, police officers, and typists.

Chulalongkorn was as acutely conscious as anyone of the contradictions of his nation's situation. By the nineties he knew well what the Europeans were demanding and the theory that lay behind their often contemptuous judgments of his kingdom. He knew how, according to European definitions of modernity, his country should develop, and he often despaired at the compromises that had to be made, the work left undone, and the imperfections in the system that was being developed. It took his first visit to Europe in 1897 to open his eyes to the unevenness of European modernity, the irrational persistence of local customs, and the extravagances and glaring inequities of European life. (He visited the East End of London, "where the poor people live," and went back for a second look, interrupting his itinerary.)

He returned to Bangkok refreshed, willing to accept the compromises that were necessary and convinced of their utility where they allowed the perpetuation of the best values of Siamese civilization within a borrowed structure. "I am convinced," he stated, "that there exists no incompatibility between such acquisition [of European (modern) science] and the maintenance of our individuality as an independent Asiatic nation."[7] Thereafter, without feeling guilty or dishonest, he could proceed to encourage Buddhist monks to assume a role in conducting modern education, to gear the teaching system to satisfy Siam's needs rather than England's or France's, and to accept the fact that some things would be done differently in Siam because this was, after all, Siam. The government could be redefined to serve new functions without destroying the state or the culture it expressed. Traditional institutions—the Buddhist monkhood, the old provincial government system, the monarchy itself—could, without creating carbon copies of Western institutions, be bent to new ends that in essence were not so very different from the ideals of Buddhist Siamese civilization.

Siam in 1910

When King Chulalongkorn died on October 24, 1910, the whole kingdom was shocked as never before. He had reigned for forty-two years, and not many could remember any other king. Court officials spent long worried nights trying to discover mourning and funeral procedures long since forgotten and imperfectly recorded. Many openly wept, and the dress and shaved heads of mourning were everywhere to be seen. The news quickly reached into the most remote corners of the kingdom, and reactions to it were colored by the pride the king's and kingdom's accomplishments had engendered, and by fear and uncertainty about what now would happen.

If by 1910 Siam was not yet a modern nation, then at least it was a modernizing nation, and securely so. In the face of foreign threats and not a little domestic opposition, Chulalongkorn had created a new structure for the state that possessed a dynamic of its own, an orientation toward change. This new Siam, however, was neither the Siam of 1850 nor the Thailand of 1950 or 1980.

First of all, the Siam of 1910 had assumed its present shape on the map, with neatly defined borders on all sides and colored an appropriate shade to distinguish it from the British colonies in Burma and Malaya that bordered it on the west and south and the French colonies in Indochina to the east. Gone were the five tiers of gradually diminishing authority of the capital that we distinguished in the early Bangkok period. They were now supplanted by a single, centralized control exercised by the Bangkok court and bureaucracy.

The kings of Luang Prabang, Sakkarin (Zakharine, 1894–1904) and Sisavangvong (r. 1904–59) continued to reign only over the handful of provinces of northern Laos, now under the superintendence of a French resident instead of a Siamese commissioner. The prince of Champassak in southern Laos, Chao Ratsadanai (r. 1900–34), was treated by the French as little more than a local dignitary. His territories and the whole of the middle Mekong valley that had been part of the old Kingdom of Vientiane now were administered by French officials supervising a bureaucracy padded by the scions of local noble families and French and Vietnamese clerks and *fonctionnaires*. Chaophraya Aphaiphubet (Baen)'s old dominions in western Cambodia had been restored to the Cambodian monarchy to be administered, again, under a French protectorate that thinly disguised control. And the sultans of the Malay states transferred to British suzerainty in 1909 one by one came to terms with the governor-general in Singapore and accepted British "advisers," though the sultan of Kedah held out as late as 1923. All these territories, then, had left the Kingdom of Siam behind and were in the twentieth century to develop along very different lines.

It should not, in some ways, be surprising that all the former vassal regions that remained in the Kingdom of Siam by the early twentieth century should have gone into rebellion early in the century. What is remarkable is that they should all have done so at the same time and that in all three cases the common people should have been involved at least as much as their rulers. The critical year was 1902. By this time, Prince Damrong's reform of the provincial administration had shifted into high gear and rapidly was sweeping away the old order in the provinces. Bangkok officials, well-dressed, confident, educated, urban young men, working out of the monthon capitals were aggressively attacking what they viewed as the evils and abuses of local ruling families in the north, the northeast, and the south. Evils and abuses there certainly were. The rural ruling families had grown fat off the sweat of peasant labor, and only a small proportion of their exactions was passed on up the hierarchy to the capital for redistribution for the common good (or to make another ruling elite wealthy). From the rational, moralistic perspective of these Ministry of Interior officials, the old system was wasteful and inefficient. But as exploitative as it may have been, the old order was an order. It gave structure to the local society, on the basis of which people knew what to expect and from which they gained some sense of identity, a sense of home and culture.

Each of the three rebellions of 1902 was different, each representing in its own way the peculiar conditions of a region. In the seven provinces of the ancient state of Pattani in the south, local governors resisted the transfer of their revenue administration to Siamese control and the appointment of Siamese officers to key positions in their administrations. The raja of Pattani, Abdul Kadir, went so far as to seek British protection, whereupon the Siamese arrested him and bundled him off to exile in faraway Phitsanulok. Without their traditional leader, the readiness of many Pattani Malays to fight for their independence weakened, at least temporarily. At about the same time, in the first months of 1902, there occurred in northeast Siam what is usually referred to as the Holy Men's Rebellion. This was a popular movement that spread over the Ubon region and also spilled across the Mekong into Laos. It was led by an Alak tribesman from the Saravane region of southern Laos who claimed supernatural powers, which he expressed primarily in Buddhist terms. Like wildfire, the prophecy spread that the "end of the world as we know it" was near; that gravel will become gold and silver and gold and silver will become gravel. Gourds and pumpkins will become elephants and horses, albino buffalo and pigs will become man-eating *yaksa*. Thao Thammikarat [a Lord of the Holy Law] will come to rule the world.[8]

From across the Mekong the "Thao Thammikarat" appeared at Khemmarat and, having recruited and armed more than a thousand followers, sacked the town. Siamese officials who with soldiers soon crushed the rebellion derided it as the superstition of ignorant peasants, but it was more than that. It briefly had strong support from some members of the old ruling families of the region and seems to have expressed a widespread feeling that the old social, political, and economic order was collapsing and being replaced by a new order that was not yet clear, but was certainly somehow "foreign."

Much the same occurred in the north in mid-1902. There it was termed the Shan Rebellion, because initially it involved mainly immigrant Shans who had come from Burma to the Phrae region to work in logging and gem mining. Several hundred Shans attacked government offices and forced Siamese officials to abandon Phrae; they then moved against Lampang. The rebels spared the local ruling elite and population, but killed Siamese. When the rising was suppressed, after about six weeks, an investigation into its causes revealed that the rebels had some support both from the local ruling elite who resented the Siamese seizure of their traditional prerogatives and from the local population who resented official abuses (like the collection of taxes in lieu of labor service while labor service was still required).

Changes indeed were occurring rapidly, and it is not surprising that they should have been resisted. In all three areas, no less than elsewhere (where, however, government intrusion into rural life had been occurring over a longer period), the old social, economic, and political order—and the three were virtually synonymous—was being undercut. The old ruling families were being displaced. They were pensioned off or simply had their revenues taken away or restricted by new accounting procedures; their sons were enticed away to schools for district officers, later to be posted in some faraway province; and the old patron-client relations that had bound together local societies simply disintegrated. Local chao müang sould no longer protect their relatives and retainers in legal cases, and with the ending of compulsory labor service in 1905, they no longer had a regular base for relations with rural populations. The old local ruling families, then, were severed from their traditional social context.

The same situation viewed from the bottom looking upward is more complex, if only because more diffuse. According to the government's first census taken around this time, there were something like thirty thousand villages in Siam. This was probably a large increase over the figure even two or three decades earlier. It is difficult to imagine it now, but the Siamese Central Plain in the late nineteenth century was nowhere near as densely settled as it is today. There were still forests closely surrounding Bangkok into the last half of the century, and even at century's end there were wild elephants roaming the countryside only twenty or thirty miles away.

A great deal of population movement occurring in the last half of the century involved the opening up of new lands for rice cultivation. Two things made this possible and encouraged it to happen. First, the opening of the kingdom to the full force of international trade by the Bowring Treaty rapidly encouraged Siamese economic specialization in the growing of rice, mainly to feed the rice-deficient portions of Asia (India and China in particular). The average annual volume of rice exported from Siam grew from just under a million *piculs* (one picul = 60 kg) per year in the late 1850s to more than 11 million piculs per year at the turn of the century; and over the same period the average price per picul doubled. During the same period, the area planted in rice rose from 5.8 million rai to more than 9 million rai.[9] This growth was achieved as a result of the collective decisions of thousands of peasant families who decided to expand the amount of land they cultivated, or clear and plant new land, or adopt more intensive methods of agriculture.

They were able to do so because of our second consideration. They were relatively freer than they had been a half-century earlier. Over the course of the Fifth Reign, as slavery ended and debt-bondage was increasingly restricted, and especially when corvée labor was abolished in 1905 (even though it persisted longer in some regions), the ties that bound rural people to the aristocracy and local ruling elites were greatly reduced. They now paid a commutation tax, a head tax, instead of rendering labor service to the government. Under these conditions, it made good sense to thousands of peasant families to in effect work full time at what they had been able to do only part time (because of the corvée) previously: grow rice for the marketplace.

Numerous changes accompanied these developments. The rural population both dispersed and grew, and was probably less homogeneous and more mobile than it had been a generation earlier. Now less under the control of local elites, the villages became more vulnerable to official arbitrariness. By the early twentieth century, as government modernization in a sense caught up with what had been happening in the countryside since the 1870s, the government intruded more and more into village life. Provincial police began to appear, along with district officers and cattle registration and land deeds and registration for compulsory military service. Village handicrafts diminished or died out completely as people bought imported consumer goods, like cloth and tools, instead of making them themselves. Certainly, more economic variation took shape in rural villages, as some grew prosperous from farming while others did not. Land too became more valuable. Private entrepreneurs in the capital, joined by members of the royal family, undertook a massive development of irrigation in the Rangsit region northeast of Bangkok, for example; the well-watered land there soon became very valuable and agricultural tenancy rose. As well as can be measured, rural standards of living improved in the Fifth Reign. But the statistical averages mean little when measured against the harsh realities of peasant life.[10]

Surely the most critical aspect of the changes in rural Siamese society in the Fifth Reign have to do with the subjective—what was happening in peoples' minds. Here we might consider three things—religion, education, and civic sense—all of which, of course, are closely related.

The reform Thammayutika sect of Siamese Buddhism founded in the mid-nineteenth century by Mongkut had, by the early twentieth, a profound effect on Siamese Buddhism. It was more rigorously intellectual and scholarly, and less ritualistic, and it lay heavy stress upon the education not only of its monks but also of the lay population. Under the vigorous leadership of Prince Wachirayanwarorot (1860–1921), who headed the sect in the last years of the nineteenth century and then became supreme patriarch of all Siamese Buddhism, it reached out effectively into the countryside. Thammayutika monasteries became especially, and disproportionately, popular in the most impoverished regions of the kingdom, particularly in monthon Ubon in the northeast and Nakhon Si Thammarat in the south. Their influence, however, was even greater than their numbers would indicate. With strong royal support, Prince Wachirayan undertook a thoroughgoing reorganization and reform of Siamese Buddhism at the turn of the century, posting ecclesiastical commissioners to all regions of the country, surveying rural monasteries and schools, and reconstituting the ecclesiastical hierarchy. Channels of communication thereby were opened through which religious practices, texts, rituals, and ideas could flow, and encouraged the rapid development of something approaching a uniform and common Buddhism for the kingdom. Institutionalized Buddhism thus reached down into all the villages and became a major vehicle for the integration of the kingdom.

At the same time Prince Wachirayan was reaching into village monasteries, he also was promoting the founding of village schools from 1898. For hundreds of years, basic education for literacy and the rudiments of religious ideas had been a primary function of village monasteries. This education, however, was very much ad hoc, centered exclusively on monk-pupil relations that suited educational content to the abilities and desires of individual students and teachers and had no systematic and little secular quality. The new schools at the turn of the century used standardized syllabi and textbooks developed by the Ministry of Public Instruction in Bangkok. They introduced rural youth, not only to basic literacy in a standardized script and language (what has come to be called "Bangkok Thai") in place of local scripts and dialects, but also to modern Western-style mathematics and science. (It is worth noting that the Buddhist monkhood in British Burma doggedly resisted such a syllabus. The difference must be that the Siamese efforts had all the prestige and power of the indigenous ruling family and government behind them, sufficiently so even to change the script in which most religious texts were written from a sort of Khmer [Khom] to Siamese.) As a generation of village youths, including both boys and girls, began to attend such schools in their local monasteries, so their integration into a unified Siamese society began. During the last decade of the Fifth Reign, the decision was made to commit the kingdom to universal compulsory primary education, though the implementation of this revolutionary decision was to take some decades.

With these religious and educational changes came the development of a new civic sense. To a certain extent it sprang naturally from the changes, from sharing in a common religious tradition and educational experience. Both constituted important aspects of new modes of social communication, those means by which a society becomes conscious of its own identity. The schools, the monasteries, and the contacts with government officials—all reinforced the idea that all inhabitants of Siam were subjects of a single king, members of a single body politic. For the time being, these ideas were expressed primarily in hierarchical terms analogous to the old patron-client relationship that pervaded the traditional society. All the inhabitants of Siam—including countless non-Siamese, as we shall see—were now clients of the same patron, the king. Obligations once owed a patron were now owed the king: loyalty, obedience, taxes, military service, education, proper behavior. In return, the king owed them security, protection, justice, compassion, help in time of need, moral example, and so on. This basic idea was, in a sense, a compromise or amalgam between the old concept of the "subject," stripped of the intermediaries that stood between the king and the peasant, and the modern concept of the "citizen." It combined elements of both, and the contradictions inherent in the combination remained to worry Siamese history subsequently.

Accompanying the internal changes within Siamese society in the Fifth Reign was a major change that occurred alongside, or atop, that society: a dramatic increase in the Chinese population. The best estimates indicate that the Chinese minority grew from about 230,000 in 1825 to 300,000 in 1850 and 792,000 in 1910; their proportion of the total population grew from less than 5 percent to 9.5 percent. Of these, by far the largest number (probably more than two-thirds) were located in the provinces immediately surrounding Bangkok and at the head of the Gulf of Siam. Most, whenever they came, had left the poverty and civil strife of rural south China to seek a better life in Siam. They worked in the market-oriented sector of the Siamese economy, as wage-laborers on the docks and in the rice mills, as agricultural laborers in the early sugar fields and later in the market-gardening communities west of Bangkok, as clerks and porters in the retail trade, and as stevedores and boatmen. Always they went to work first for other Chinese.

Increasingly, the government came to hire Chinese laborers for such tasks as canal construction, in preference to unpaid corvée labor by unwilling Siamese. Some, perhaps many, Chinese immigrants prospered; and a considerable number even entered government service. Through the nineteenth century, the rate at which they were assimilated into Siamese society was high: most Chinese immigrants were young, single males, and many took Siamese wives. Their Sino-Siamese children grew up with Siamese as their first language, and assimilation was relatively easy. These young people were among the first to respond positively to the educational opportunities that opened up by the 1880s, and they were disproportionately well represented in the bureaucracy by the turn of the century. The chief characteristic of the Chinese and Sino-Siamese minority, however, was that it was overwhelmingly urban (even Bangkokian), and in close collaboration with Western enterprise, they dominated the modern sector of the Siamese economy.

We have already suggested some of the reasons why this might have been so. In the expanding rice-export economy of the late nineteenth century, Siamese peasants were making the rational decision to specialize in rice agriculture, the occupation of their ancestors, the calling they knew best. They had little desire to work for other people for appallingly low wages, bound to the equivalent of a time clock; nor were they anxious to live in what must have seemed to them an alien city, dominated by Chinese, carrying on unfamiliar occupations. If they were ambitious, young Siamese set their sights on a career in the bureaucracy or in the Buddhist monkhood—again, traditional pursuits. It was Chinese, therefore, who literally built the modern sector of the economy of Siam. They dug the canals and constructed the railways and erected the fine new government offices and shop buildings and bridges of Bangkok. Both independently and as the employees of Western firms, they developed the network of institutions and services necessary to make the rice-export economy work: the banks, the warehouses, the wholesale and retail trading concerns, the rice mills, the barge lines that brought the rice to Bangkok, and even the brokers who traveled around the countryside buying up peasants' surplus rice for shipment ultimately to Hong Kong or Calcutta or Singapore. This had always been, since the earliest days of Ayudhya, a powerful community in Siam, but its power had been harnessed to the Siamese state by close patron-client relations. By the early twentieth century, those ties had weakened, partly because of the impersonal bureaucratization of the government and partly because of the increased size of the Chinese community and its separation from Siamese society as assimilation slowed. From the turn of the century, more Chinese women were immigrating into Siam and marrying Chinese men; their children were Chinese, not Siamese. In this social sense, then, there were at least two Siams by 1910.

A third Siam, possibly, was the new bureaucracy that Chulalongkorn and his brothers had constructed, an institution very different from the old nobility of a half or even a quarter-century earlier. The noble families of the Fourth Reign had by now lost their primacy. Their members still were active in official positions in large numbers, but they had survived as individuals rather than as members of familial factions and entourages. Some of the oldest and most powerful families may, indeed, have lost much ground in the late years of the century. Because their position was still so strong, they were slow to send their sons to modern schools, thinking such education unnecessary when jobs awaited in uncle's department or father's ministry. In the last years of the century, the minor bureaucratic families probably provided more than their proportional share of recruits to the bureaucracy, as did the Sino-Siamese families whose economic power had encouraged their rapid assimilation into Siamese society. The most important single change in the composition of the bureaucracy, however, came with the unusually active role taken by the royal family. The brothers and sons of Chulalongkorn were a majority of the ministers of state through the end of the reign; but prominent also among high officials were grandsons and great-grandsons of kings. The princes were particularly powerful within the army and navy, and by no accident, because Chulalongkorn foresaw an increased role for the military in the life of the state.

The king had assigned the bureaucracy the primary role in bringing about change as measured by Western standards, and it was therefore necessary to recruit young men who not only understood those standards but who also had come to terms with the West through modern education. The king, of course, was better able than most fathers to assure the best modern education to his male relatives. Almost all his sons, and many of his nephews, were sent to study in Europe, and their educational and social advantages over their fellows gave them qualifications for office with which few of their generation could compete. However, by the last years of the century many ministries and departments in Bangkok began to recruit commoners and others to be sent abroad for training—to the British forestry school in India, or Borough Road Teachers'

Training College in England, or German and British military academies, for example. Others studied at special training schools established for each ministry in Thailand, including a large, effective military academy. Through all these varied channels, the emphasis in recruitment was placed on educational qualifications of a formal, Western kind; and it was these recruitment standards that more than anything else defined the early twentieth-century Siamese elite.

Bangkok's ability to change the composition of the bureaucracy so thoroughly derived largely from the fact that men were being recruited to fulfill new functions in new organizations. The old provincial administration, for example, had been overwhelmingly local in its composition, dominated by the region's ruling families. The new provincial administration of Prince Damrong was first superimposed on the provinces. Accordingly, the young men went first to the new monthon administrations and only later moved out into the provincial governorships and district officers' posts. By this time the authority and functions and prerogatives of the traditional incumbents had atrophied. In addition, the specialized services (e.g., the Survey Department, Irrigation Department, Post and Telegraph Department) and the large new military establishment were wholly or partially new, competing with no pre-existing interests. Thus while Chulalongkorn was creating the new bureaucracy, assigning it functions and making it attractive to the sons of the old elite, the old order simply withered away.

What made this bureaucratic transition so effective was the degree to which central control over government was established by the king. In seizing the initiative in the eighties, Chulalongkorn did not merely re-create the First Reign partnership between crown and ministers; he also reestablished royal authority over the whole of government by breaking the old social hierarchy and creating a new one. Although in many ways, as has often been noted, Chulalongkorn then was able to stage a "revolution from above" in his program of modernization, in a very real sense the Fifth Reign revolution came from the side—at least relative to the social and political balance of the 1850s and 1860s. That segment of the elite that had had little power threw off the power of the great families. The monarchy under Mongkut had been unable to modernize, unable to lead the way to fundamental change, and it was at the mercy of the leading families and ministries for support and for the execution of state policy. By placing his own men in all the key ministries of state—the tactic that Suriyawong so successfully had employed in the Fourth and early Fifth reigns—and by choosing men without independent position and power, the king was able to subordinate the bureaucracy to his own will and with them to forge a unity and coherence of policy that made possible a consistent and forceful commitment to reform.

As always, the royal power of appointment was his single most important tool, and Chulalongkorn used this power with consummate skill. Some princes the king could appoint and forget, confident they would serve him and the nation well—men like Prince Devawongse and Prince Damrong. Other ministries changed hands often. The king had enough brothers to appoint and dismiss at will, to let them compete with one another for advancement and favor. Ministers under the old regime usually had served for life, but they had no such tenure in the Fifth Reign. Some of the highest ranking princes had the most checkered careers, not seldom being forced to early retirement after a string of poor performances in steadily less important positions. Though the king was sufficiently concerned for the future of his family and the monarchy to hope that the princes would attain an important role in the life of the state, he was committed even more to the success of modernization and the cause of national survival. He made clear to the members of his family that, all other things being equal, he would rather appoint a prince or someone of "good family," but positions would always go first to the man best qualified, whatever his social background. The extensive use of this criterion ultimately brought to power a group of men committed to the principle of meritocratic selection, and however much it was later to be strained, it was permanently established in the structure of the state.

The administration was organized to ensure close central control. However, as the king did not delegate many of his decision-making powers, a great deal ultimately depended on the dedication, and even the stamina, of the king himself. Chulalongkorn worked extremely hard at these executive functions, writing several hundred letters each day, reaching decisions—sometimes by himself, sometimes with the advice of his ministers—on matters as petty as the style of lettering to be used on a sign or as momentous as policy concerning France. When his health was poor, as during the months following the Franco-Siamese Crisis of 1893, and he withdrew temporarily from his office, the central government would be thrown into chaos. By the late nineties, however, he was sufficiently confident of the abilities of his ministers to hand over business to them and travel to Europe.

Chulalongkorn created more than new formal means of accomplishing public business by his refashioning of the bureaucracy. The civil service traditionally had been the primary organization in the Siamese social structure. Because most nonagricultural occupations performed by Siamese continued to be included within the bureaucracy, the vocational specialization and social differentiation that came with rapid modernization occurred within traditional social hierarchical patterns, and it remained under the control of the crown. In a sense, all of Siamese society potentially was harnessed to the engines of change

King Chulalongkorn giving public audience in Ayudhya on the occasion of
the fortieth anniversary of his accession to the throne.

in Bangkok. The government retained the power to command soldiers to shoot,
teachers to teach, cattle to be inoculated, and rails to be laid. Through its
command of the educational system and through increased control over the
Buddhist monkhood, it could also inculcate modern values and encourage the
acquisition of modern skills. By its setting of criteria for the recruitment of
officials in virtually every field and by its powers of promotion and dismissal, the
crown could encourage values and behavior it deemed good for the nation.

In doing so, however, the crown and the princes came out of the shadow of
palace seclusion into the full light of public view, their actions and ideas filling
the pages of the daily press. The king's willingness, and even eagerness, to speak
directly to his subjects in print and public speech and ceremony served to sweep
away the clouds of courtiers that had screened his predecessors from public
scrutiny. The high degree to which the monarchy came publicly to be identified
with the state, the society, and the success or failure of official policies lent to the
accomplishment of the work of modernization a strong forward thrust. It also
rendered the monarchy more vulnerable to criticism and public disaffection in
the event that forward momentum faltered.

8

The Rise of Elite Nationalism, 1910–1932

If King Chulalongkorn may be said to have constructed the modern Kingdom of Siam, then his two sons who followed him on the throne may be said to have made it into a nation. Chulalongkorn's reign, the Fifth Reign of the Chakri dynasty, was marked chiefly by the building of institutions, not least of all the strengthening of the monarchy and the creation of the modern army and state bureaucracy. Though in some senses, both monarchy and bureaucracy had been present in Siam for centuries, by the early twentieth century they had acquired the power and authority they had not had earlier. The state they embodied needed them in order to survive free of colonial control. Only from a longer historical perspective does their growth seem anachronistic or retrogressive—or paradoxical. Monarchy, by the end of the Fifth Reign, perhaps was more absolute than ever before, not least because it could now exert the monarch's will through a bureaucracy under his control far more effectively than ever before. Ironically, this had developed at a time when states in the West, and particularly the Atlantic democracies, were becoming less authoritarian. Moreover, for reasons that had everything to do with the difficult political situation of the Fourth and early Fifth reigns, an ever-narrowing social group was seizing political and administrative control in the last half of the Fifth Reign, as evidenced by the fact that nearly all of Chulalongkorn's ministers of state in 1910 were members of his own family, his brothers and sons.

In simplest terms, Fifth Reign modernization may be seen as a case of uneven development. Different social groups were becoming modern at different rates, the royal family faster than any because of its head start in modern education, especially its privileged access to study abroad. A generation, or half a generation, behind them was the new bureaucratic elite, who gained access to modern education a decade or so later than the royal family. Its leading members steadily advanced up the social ladder by the end of the reign. All the other elements of the society were far below them in all sorts of ways. Indeed, one might hazard the guess that the social distance—created by education, wealth, life-style, exposure to the outside world, even language—between the urban, educated elite and the peasant mass of Siamese society was never greater than it was at the end of the Fifth Reign.

Two observations may serve to characterize the history of the Sixth and Seventh reigns, the period between the death of King Chulalongkorn in 1910 and the coup d'état that ended the absolute monarchy in 1932. First, King Vajiravudh (r. 1910–25) had a great deal to do with breathing life into Chulalongkorn's state and giving it a consciousness of itself as a nation, at least at an elite level. Second, during this period the rest of the elite caught up with the royal family; it gained cohesiveness and political will—although, as we shall see, the military segment of the elite got there first. Even by the end of the period, however, the mass of the common people were still far, far behind.

King Vajiravudh and the Thai Nation

Had Chulalongkorn died thirty years earlier, the struggle over the succession to the throne might have been bitter and bloody, almost certainly involving civil war and perhaps foreign intervention and the loss of Siam's independence. By 1910, however, the Siamese had abandoned the old rules of succession to the throne and had adopted the Western pattern of designating the heir to the throne long in advance. Chulalongkorn had waited until a year after the uparat Prince Wichaichan's death and then appointed Vajirunhis as crown prince. When Vajirunhis died at the age of seventeen in 1895, Chulalongkorn named as crown prince Vajiravudh (b. 1881), his eldest son by Queen Saowapha. Vajiravudh was then in England, where he studied with tutors, underwent military training at Sandhurst, and studied history and law at Oxford, returning home only at the beginning of 1903. There established in his own palace, complete with entourage, he spent the next seven years indulging in literary pursuits and experimenting with the internal government of his household. He served as regent during Chulalongkorn's second trip to Europe in 1907. He had fifteen years to prepare for his royal duties, a luxury few other Siamese kings have had. Vella terms him a Victorian gentlemen, but he may more properly be termed Edwardian, as we shall see.[1]

Like his father, Vajiravudh underwent two coronations. The first, on November 11, 1910, was a brief, economical affair, but the second, in November 1911, was a thirteen-day extravaganza, attended by the representatives of fourteen countries, including the Japanese crown prince. It cost the Treasury in excess of 5 million baht, equivalent to about 8 percent of the state budget for that year. Profligate spending was to become a hallmark of his reign.

For all his years of preparation, Vajiravudh was not widely known or popular nor did he have extensive networks of supporters and clients prior to coming to the throne. The government and society were dominated by his uncles and his brothers, many of whom had important positions in the civil and military bureaucracy. The new king was cautious enough not to make whole-sale changes in the administration at the beginning of his reign, but he moved quickly to build up a personal following. The ways in which he did it were characteristic of a new age and a European background. In May 1911, he created two military organizations. The first was a new unit under the Ministry of the Palace to guard the royal residence, the creation of which aroused some hostility in the army which was headed by the king's brother, Prince Paribatra. The second was something completely new, the so-called Wild Tiger Corps (*Süa pa*), a nationwide mass paramilitary corps. Its chief stated function was to defend "nation, religion, and king" against all enemies, domestic and foreign, and to promote the unity of the Siamese nation. As the king himself explained:

> The aim of this national institution is to instil in the minds of the people of our own race love and loyalty towards the High Authority that controls and maintains with justice and equity the political independence of the nation, devotion to Fatherland, Nation and our Holy Religion, and, not the least of all, the preservation of national unity, and the cultivation of mutual friendship.
>
> These qualities form the strongest foundation on which our national existence will rest and not belie its name as the Nation of the Free.[2]

By recruiting members widely from the civil service (the initiation fee was high and daunted the lower classes) and ranking them in a hierarchy in-dependent of civil service status, the king went outside rigid bureaucratic hierarchies to create a personal following, subject to his own will and en-thusiasms. He thought it important to bring together people, particularly of the elite, who would otherwise remain segregated in their bureaucratic niches, to get them involved in common endeavors, and to encourage new values of patriotism, militancy, and loyalty to king and country. Here, perhaps, the king attained a sense of control over people in ways not allowed by the dry business of bureaucratized monarchy. Total membership reached approximately four thousand men by early 1912 and was complemented by a junior Boy Scout movement that endured much longer.

On February 29, 1912, King Vajiravudh was conducting Wild Tiger military maneuvers at his summer palace at Nakhon Pathom when a chartered train arrived from Bangkok carrying Prince Chakrabongse, the chief of staff of the army and acting minister of defense, who reported that a group of junior military officers was plotting a coup against the king. Over the next two days,

King Vajiravudh on the bridge of the royal yacht, the *Mahachakri*, ca. 1914.

ninety-two young men were arrested for their complicity in the plot, almost all
of whom were in their early twenties and were serving as lieutenants in the
army. Most of them had been classmates in the army academy class of 1909;
many of them seem to have been of Sino-Siamese ancestry. A few of the young
men had begun some years earlier with a personal grudge against Vajiravudh,
but this soon was transformed into a fuzzily ideological critique of the absolute
monarchy. The men had become caught up in the political excitement of their
own time, particularly the Chinese Revolution of October 1911. They considered Siam to be backward, unjust, corrupt, and even morally debased, and
they had come to blame their country's ills on the existing system of government. They were, in addition, upset by the apparent downgrading of the army
by Vajiravudh, who appeared to be creating his own with the Wild Tiger
Corps.

The conspirators were not in agreement over the course they should take.
Two groups favored creating a constitutional monarchy, but split over whether
to make Prince Chakrabongse or Prince Paribatra king. A third faction wanted
a republican form of government with Prince Rabi as president. They argued

for drastic reforms in state policies, favoring especially the promotion of rapid economic and educational development. Having met only twelve times, their plans had not gone far before the arrests of March 1–2 cut them short. Two months later, after royal clemency was extended, three conspirators received sentences of life imprisonment, twenty men were sentenced to twenty years each, and the remainder received suspended sentences.

If in retrospect the abortive 1912 coup seems minor, at the time it was not. This was not the petty rivalry of princely brothers engaged in dynastic squabbles, but a military plot by outsiders, young men of common backgrounds. It was something new in Siamese history. It represented the beginning of a new kind of politics, taking the whole of the nation as its arena and suggesting, if vaguely, an agenda of radical reform and change in the form of government. It was not immediately publicized, but news of the plot and the arrests spread quickly through Bangkok, along with a host of criticisms against the king and the government. The plot, and what it represented and provoked, was a major challenge to the new king, and it quickly forced him into taking a more active and aggressive role in his government.

In the course of 1912, Vajiravudh made some administrative and personnel changes that spoke directly or indirectly to issues raised by the abortive plot. He brought his younger half-brother Prince Rabi back into the government as minister of agriculture. He transformed the old Ministry of Public Works into a Ministry of Communications, with responsibility for railroads, highways, and posts and telegraphs, over which Chaophraya Wongsa (M.R.W. Sathan Snidvongs) presided. He put his uncle Prince Naret in charge of the revived Ministry of the Privy Seal and recalled his cousin, Prince Boworadet, a close personal friend, from the diplomatic service to take charge of those elements of the army that had been most subverted by the plotters. Another old and close personal friend, Chaophraya Aphairacha (M.R.W. Lop Suthat) was made minister of justice.

These appointments were viewed as an act on the part of the king to intervene more directly in government; they were also seen as the beginning of the decline of the princes in the highest ministerial offices. As the reign wore on, more and more of the ministries were run by others than princes, save for Prince Devawongse in Foreign Affairs, Prince Naret in Privy Seal, Prince Chanthaburi in Finance, and Prince Rabi in the Ministry of Agriculture. Almost all the rest were the great-grandsons of kings, who held the royal status of *mom ratchawong* (M.R.W.) and whose family wealth and status allowed them early to gain a European education.

In order both to quell rumors about his profligate expenditures and to devise a sounder approach to financing necessary development, the king in

March 1912 appointed a Committee to Inspect State Revenues and Expenditures, consisting of two Siamese treasury officials and three foreign advisers. The composition of the committee was intended, no doubt, to reassure the international financial world, which must have been alarmed by the 1911–12 budget incurring a deficit of than 2 million baht. As a result of the committee's work, the powers of the Ministry of Finance to draw up and monitor the annual budget were enhanced. By 1913, the state again was showing a substantial surplus of revenues over expenditures.

But Vajiravudh's most forceful reply to the challenge of 1912, and one that was maintained over most of the rest of his reign, lay in an area we might today call public relations and propaganda. Vajiravudh long had been known for his literary gifts and habits, and for his fondness for the theater. To some extent Chulalongkorn had indulged similar talents, but only privately for his own and his family's enjoyment. To Vajiravudh, however, art was for life's sake, an instrument by which people might be brought together to share a common vision of a better world and to bring that world into being. As crown prince, he had organized his courtiers and retainers into a group called the Enhancement of Knowledge Club, which published a magazine and produced theatricals espousing modern values and patterns of behavior. On becoming king, he continued these efforts, now with more resources and prestige behind him.

In his writings over a fifteen-year period, which appeared under a bewildering array of pseudonyms in a wide range of media from journals and magazines to newspapers and dramatic performances, Vajiravudh explored many ideas in several literary forms. He by no means neglected the traditional ars. He wrote a section from the *Ramayana*, as had his predecessors, in good Siamese verse, he translated Sanskrit dramas from their English versions, and he wrote scholarly studies of traditional literature. He added to Siamese literature a wholly new genre, the spoken, Western-style play, and raised the essay, particularly the political essay, to an art form. One of the most persistent themes in these writings might be termed modernity—that is, encouraging, even exhorting, people to act and live as modern people did in the West. He introduced surnames and coined names for hundreds of families; he refashioned the flag of Siam, replacing the old white elephant on a red field with the tricolor red, white, and blue; he introduced the first national holidays in honor of King Chulalongkorn (October 23) and the Chakri dynasty (April 6); he promoted team sports, particularly soccer football; he worked to improve the status of women by encouraging them to mix socially with men and by arguing for monogamy in the place of widespread Siamese polygamy; and he was an ardent supporter of modern education. He was responsible for the organization of Chulalongkorn University as a memorial to his father in 1916; and in 1921, his government finally enacted a compulsory primary education law, requiring all boys and girls between the ages of seven and fourteen to attend school (though the law at first was applied to only about 45 percent of the kingdom).

Behind all these and many other issues lay a single theme that runs through the whole reign—King Vajiravudh's idea of the "Thai nation." This is sometimes referred to as his "nationalism," and it might be useful here to distinguish between the two. King Vajiravudh's idea of the nation contained many of the ingredients of what we might call nationalism. He saw the nation as a corporate body of people, imbued with a common identity, striving for common purposes, placing the commonweal ahead of private interests. The nation should provide the primary focus of personal and group identity; it was something worth fighting and dying for. He envisioned structuring behavior and values primarily in terms of achieving the nation's goals: people should act in their personal lives in ways conducive to the nation's interest. In addition to logical concerns for national defense and the achievement of international equality (including the ending of the unequal treaties that still restricted Siam's freedom), he espoused ideas of economic nationalism—freeing the economy from foreign control and curbing Chinese domination over the internal economy. (On this subject he wrote a vitriolic essay called "The Jews of the East," which owes something to turn-of-the-century European anti-Semitism, urging Siamese to take a more active role in their own economy.) In his approach to the ultimate political issues, however, the king stopped short of nationalism in the strictest definition of the term. The distinction is a fine one, but important.

Vajiravudh's Thai nation (and he was the first to popularize this phrase) was founded on the basic triad of "nation-religion-monarch" (*chat-satsana-phramahakasat*), a trinitarian mystery in which all three elements were inextricably bound together. Allegiance to any one of the three meant loyalty to all three; disloyalty or disobedience or disrespect toward one meant disrespect toward all. (Some sophistries were engaged in to secure the allegiance of Siam's considerable Muslim and Christian minorities.)

In one critical respect, however, this definition of the nation was flawed, even self-contradictory. The structure Vajiravudh erected in support of the nation was hierarchical, involving obedience to all higher authorities in the name of the triune authority at the top. As we have seen, however, the association of the monarchy with specific programs of change and the justification of the monarchy in terms of progress toward modern goals depended on the success of those programs and their progress. When modernization did not proceed as rapidly as people wished or the king did not behave as people had been led to believe he should behave, their pursuit of what they honestly believed to be the national interest might bring them into conflict with the structure of government and the monarchy. Vajiravudh encouraged them to broaden their social circles, to learn to meet with others as equals, to reach democratically a consensus on issues that concerned them, to form clubs and associations and elect presidents and vice-presidents and secretaries, and to carry on arguments and debates in the press and in public meeting. All this would further the national will and purpose for the good of the nation. He little suspected it at the time, but it was logically impossible for him and his successors indefinitely to promote change in everything *but* political institutions. Thus, because Vajiravudh's "nation" did not allow for the nonhierarchical expression of a political will—for political activity among equals—it stopped short of "nationalism."

Certainly the nation was a central preoccupation of the Sixth Reign, and this was expressed, as it so often is, in militaristic terms. It was primarily the elite who were so involved, to begin with. It was they who bought fancy military uniforms and equipment and went on maneuvers with the Wild Tiger Corps, and it was their children who joined the Tiger Cubs at school. They were constantly reminded that Siam was in danger from the rapacious colonial West, to whom Siam had been losing territory as late as 1909, and they were worried that the French and British had not finished with them. They were exhorted to be prepared to lay down their lives for their country. When World War I began in 1914, Siam early declared its neutrality, despite the king's pro-Allies sympathies, but the sense of military danger did not diminish. Soon, the king determined to strengthen Siam's military capacity by equipping the navy with a modern warship, and a massive public campaign was carried on by the new Royal Navy League to raise money for its purchase. Military interest and military values grew as the war progressed, and pro-Allies sentiments increasingly were expressed in the press and in government actions.

Finally, in 1917, as the United States entered the war and the Allies stepped up their efforts to win neutrals to their side, the Siamese court began to worry that the victorious Allies might after the war hold Siam's neutrality against her. If they joined the war on the side of the Allies, however, they might add impetus to Siam's efforts to end the unequal treaties. Therefore, publicly stating only its moral grounds for doing so, the Siamese government declared war on the Central Powers on July 22, 1917. Astutely judging how best to reinforce the image of a modern Siamese nation, a 1,300-man expeditionary force consisting of an ambulance section, a flying squadron, and a group of automobile drivers and mechanics was dispatched to France in June 1918. (Apparently the only other Southeast Asians involved in the war were 200,000 Vietnamese employed as coolies in France.)

Though having avowedly entered the war on moral grounds, that "Right" and "Civilization" might triumph in the West, the Siamese government also sought political gains, both to avoid increasing dependence on a victorious Britain and to build a position from which to negotiate the end of the unequal treaties. Participation in the war earned Siam a place at the Versailles Peace Conference, where the Siamese delegation lobbied vigorously for full autonomy in taxation and an end to extraterritoriality and treaty constraints upon the operation of the Siamese legal system. These efforts failed in the pressure of other business on the Allied delegates, so a small group of Siamese diplomats led by Prince Charoon, the Siamese minister in Paris, worked out a negotiating strategy and a set of internal operating procedures by which to mount a concerted attack on the great powers' treaty rights.

The effort was long and arduous, and took from 1920 to 1926. Under the direction of Foreign Minister Prince Devawongse until his death in 1923, and then under his son who succeeded him, Prince Devawongs Varodaya, the negotiations were strongly supported by two Americans who served as adviser to the ministry, Eldon James and (from 1924) Francis B. Sayre (President Woodrow Wilson's son-in-law). The United States led the way in yielding to Siam's case with a new treaty at the end of 1920. This was a promising beginning, but discussions then stalled as each power waited to see what the others would yield. Finally Sayre took charge, leading a delegation that traveled around Europe negotiating with one state after another. France finally agreed, in February 1925, followed by Britain in July; within the next year all the other treaty powers had followed suit.

There were two main subjects covered by these important treaties. The first had to do with extraterritoriality. Foreigners now were placed under the jurisdiction of Siamese courts and laws. The foreign consuls retained, for a period of five years after the promulgation of all the modern law codes in Siam, a process now nearly completed, the right to evoke to their own jurisdiction any case in which their nationals were defendants. Second, by the 1920–26 treaties, Siam recovered full tariff autonomy, subject to a few limited exceptions. In the treaty with Britain, for example, import tariffs on cotton and steel goods, and on machinery, were limited to 5 percent for a period of ten years. The long battle was finally won; Siam had fully regained her sovereignty.

Meanwhile, back in Bangkok, the question of who should exercise that sovereign power, and how, was an issue growing in importance. There were a few overt incidents like the 1912 plot, perhaps the most serious of which was nipped in the bud by a series of arrests in mid-1917 (almost no details about this plot have ever come to light).[3] More generally, through most of the reign, there was a good deal of criticism of the king on a wide variety of grounds from the political to the personal. Some viewed with alarm the king's success at squeez-

ing out the old princes and replacing them with individuals of little independent
social position, and some considered that the government was becoming too
deferential to the king. Others argued that the real power in the state lay with
the king's favorites, the young men of his inner entourage for whom he had
written plays and with whom he played games and organized clubs and
societies. Some, like King Chulalongkorn before his death and Queen
Saowapha, his mother, frowned on the king's personal life and his almost total
lack of interest in the opposite sex. The common ground that most critics of the
reign shared was disapproval of Vajiravudh's style, his extravagant expendi-
ture, and his apparently frivolous preoccupation with games and plays.

To this day, Vajiravudh's reign remains controversial. It was even more so
in his own time, probably because of a combination of the king's personality
and his Westernized style. The king's preference for the company of male
favorites by itself was not politically important until people perceived that it
was affecting the distribution of power within his government and greatly
inflating royal expenditures. At that point, the king came under criticism on all
grounds, as Prince Rakronnaret had in 1848.

Politically and socially, the king initiated some important changes. By
reducing the preeminence of the princes, his brothers and uncles, and by promoting many commoners to higher positions in the still expanding government,
he encouraged the impression that he was sharing power. (Indeed, his favorites
were recruited even more widely than his top officials.) Though many could
object to the individuals whom the king promoted, they at least could agree that
government was no longer the preserve of princes that it had been a decade or
two earlier, and they could identify with the meritocratic future for Siam that
this seemed to portend. This sense of participation in government was, on a
basic level, still quite limited. Many, though, might have been encouraged by at
least the ritual sense of participation offered by the Wild Tiger Corps and their
mobilization in such common causes as the Royal Navy League and the public
ceremonial that accompanied national holidays and events like the sending of
the Siamese Expeditionary Force off to Europe in 1918. By the early 1920s, they
may have been impatient for more substantial participation.

Vajiravudh apparently devoted little thought or attention to political
changes. Vella points out that he stood with his father's ideological rejection of
constitutionalism in 1885. He rejected all calls for political reform as selfishly
motivated, disloyal, and certain to bring ruin to Siam.[4] At times even his own
high officials tried to persuade him at least to make some modifications in the
existing government. In 1917, the king's full brother Prince Chakrabongse,
then Minister of Finance, urged him to revive Chulalongkorn's Legislative
Council, a fully appointive body that would have the power to issue laws over

the monarch's signature and the right to question ministers. Vajiravudh rejected this suggestion on the ground that, being appointive, it would simply be a
rubber stamp for the king.[5] In 1921, the elderly Chaophraya Surasakmontri
(Choem Saeng-Xuto), the most famous military man of the Fifth Reign,
ventured to propose the revival of Chulalongkorn's Privy Council to advise the
monarch, but he was dismissed as being senile.[6] The furthest the king seems to
have gone was, once late in his reign, to discuss with his ministers the possibility
of appointing a prime minister, an alternative he rejected.[7]

Two issues preoccupied the last years of the Sixth Reign: economics and
finance, and the succession to the throne. The immediate postwar period was
not a happy one, economically. Rice, Siam's chief export by far, went through a
brief boom-bust cycle in 1919–21 which, combined with a monetary and
foreign-exchange crisis caused by the rise in the price of silver in postwar
markets and a disastrous crop year in 1919–20, made for economic chaos. In
sum, over the period 1919–21, the balance of trade incurred an enormous
deficit, a great deal of silver left the country, the government revenue accounts
slipped into deficit for the rest of the reign, and the kingdom repeatedly had to
borrow abroad. One major contributor to the situation, which was to persist to
the end of the reign, was the steady growth in the monarch's expenditures. The
Privy Purse and Ministry of the Palace were consuming nearly 10 percent of the
annual budget. The segment of the Wild Tiger Corps directly under the king
accounted for 1.6 million baht alone in 1924–25, out of a total royal budget of 9
million baht (the real expenditures probably were in excess 12 million baht)
and a state budget of 96.4 million baht. Numerous attempts were made to curb
the financial chaos—financial commissions, like that of 1912, were twice
appointed to recommend economies, for example—but none had much success. The economic failings of the reign, it would appear, were twofold: royal
profligacy and the inability of the king to establish and maintain effective
procedures to control public expenditures. The day of financial reckoning
might be postponed, but not for much longer.

More was involved, of course, than official balance sheets. The distribution
of the state expenditures had everything to do with the efforts government was
making to develop the country. For all its stress on education as the prerequisite
to economic and political development, only slightly more than 3 percent of the
budget was devoted to that purpose in 1924–25, while 23 percent was going to
military expenditures and more than 10 percent to royal expenditures.

Finally, the problem of the succession to the throne came to prominence
rather suddenly in the last few years of the reign. King Chulalongkorn had
fathered seventy-seven children, of whom only seven sons by his four royal
queens (including Vajiravudh) survived into the Sixth Reign. In choosing

Vajiravudh to succeed him, Chulalongkorn had indicated his preference for the succession to pass through the line of Queen Saowapha, and so Vajiravudh's younger brother Prince Chakrabongse might have been expected to be next in line for the throne. Chakrabongse, however, had married a Russian woman when in military school in St. Petersburg, which clouded his claim to the throne, and at any rate, he died in 1920. In 1924, King Vajiravudh issued a law of succession formally recognizing the primary claims of Queen Saowapha's sons in the event that he died without a son, and in the last years of his reign, he finally took several wives. Meanwhile, two of Vajiravudh's three remaining brothers died, leaving only the youngest, King Chulalongkorn's seventy-sixth child, Prince Prajadhipok, as the sole male survivor of Saowapha's line when Vajiravudh died on November 26, 1925—two days after becoming the father of a daughter. At his death, Vajiravudh left a letter naming Prajadhipok as his heir, to be the seventh king of the Chakri dynasty. All this happened very quickly. Vajiravudh was only forty-four at his death, and most of his younger brothers had been vigorously active in government before dying so suddenly between 1920 and 1925. Thus the passage of the events of 1925 came as a shock. None was more surprised, however, than the thirty-two-year-old Prajadhipok—Chulalongkorn's last son and Siam's last absolute monarch.

The Last Absolute Monarch

Prajadhipok's was the shortest, and probably the most controversial, reign in the history of the Chakri dynasty. It both began and ended under clouds of criticism and unrest, dogged almost continually by economic problems. Yet its denouement was profoundly political, involving no less than the end of the absolute monarchy and the ascension to power of segments of the new elite that had been growing since Chulalongkorn attained control of his administration in the 1880s. On the one hand, then, the short history of this reign is the story of the movement of great historical forces—of political aspirations, public opinion, social and political mobilization, economic modernization, and so on—while, on the other hand, it is very much the story of individuals and personalities and their effect upon historical events. It is not easy to assess the relative merits of each of these, but the understanding of all is crucial to the history of the period.

    The initial legacy that Prajadhipok received from his elder brother was problems, of the sort that had become chronic in the Sixth Reign. The most urgent of these was economic: the finances of the state were in chaos, the budget heavily in deficit, and the royal accounts an accountant's nightmare of debts and questionable transactions. On the successful solution of this problem depended the stability of the baht and the vitality of Siam's internationalized economy. Economic issues, in turn, had bred political problems at various levels. Ministerial bickering over the necessity to trim expenditures gave the impression of a bureaucracy out of control, of bureaucratic satrapies at constant war with one another, devoid of effective leadership. This governmental inefficiency and semiparalysis, in turn, led a substantial segment of the urban elite, virtually all of whom were employed in the bureaucracy (including the military), to lose, to some unmeasurable extent, faith in government, and at least to begin to question, if not to challenge, the fundamental tenets of their social and political system based on the absolute monarchy.

This was, indeed, the first period in Siamese history in which there may be said to have been something readily identifiable as public opinion. It was the age of the popular press, of daily newspapers and weekly magazines. In 1925 alone, there were seven Siamese, three English, and three Chinese daily newspapers published in Bangkok, and their numbers rapidly swelled in the years that followed. In the absence of any other regular mode of taking the popular pulse, the government and the educated elite seem to have regarded newspapers as the voice of public opinion. By the mid-1920s, there was no mistaking the fact that criticism of the government was increasing and that elite opinion was being both expressed and shaped in the popular press.

Prajadhipok was not prepared for his new responsibilities. He had been educated in England, at Eton and the Woolwich Military Academy, and returned to Siam most recently only in 1924 from the École Supérieure de Guerre in France, probably then expecting a staff career in the army, certainly not becoming king; but within months he was rising rapidly up the ladder of succession to the throne. He had little experience of government and may have been in some immediate awe of his older half-brothers and uncles who had long taken active roles in state affairs. His youth and inexperience weighed against him. All he had in his favor was a lively intelligence, a certain diplomacy in his dealings with others, a modesty and industrious willingness to learn, and the somewhat tarnished but still potent magic of the crown.

Virtually the first act of Prajadhipok as king entailed an institutional innovation intended to restore confidence in the monarchy and government, the creation of the Supreme Council of State. This body was an advisory council composed of five senior members of the royal family, all with considerable experience in government. Three were Prajadhipok's uncles, including Prince Damrong Rajanubhab, the long-time Minister of Interior (1892–1915); and two were his brothers, the career soldier Prince Paribatra and the prince of Chanthaburi, who had served for many years as minister of finance (1908–23). With their advice and support, the young king could begin to make rapid strides to meet the immediate financial crisis (and he set a good example by cutting royal expenditures from 10.8 to 6.8 million baht in the 1926–27 budget).[8] Within six months he reconstituted his cabinet of ministers of state. Only three of Vajiravudh's twelve ministers stayed on, and most of those who left were replaced by members of the royal family. In the short run, these appointments may have worked to the king's advantage, for they brought into the government men of talent who, on the whole, were regarded as disinterestedly honest and competent. In the long run, however, these appointments seemed to signal a return to royal oligarchy, to "government by princes." And when things did not go well, it was all the easier to blame royalty.

Once the immediate crises had passed, by mid-1926, Prajadhipok turned his attention to the nagging long-term question of political development. In July, he addressed to Francis B. Sayre, who had returned on a visit to Bangkok at the king's request, a lengthy memorandum headed "Problems of Siam," seeking advice on what Prajadhipok deemed the most important issues of the day. He mentioned nine specific questions, seeking Sayre's advice on such matters as "Must this country have a Parliamentary system one day, and is really the Anglo-Saxon type of Parliamentary Government suitable to an Eastern People?" and "Is this country ready to have some sort of representative Government?" and "Should we have a Prime Minister? . . . Should we have a Legislative Council? . . . " He closed with "Can something be done to make the Chinese become Siamese as in the old days?"[9] In the course of this document, the king expressed pessimism as to the present readiness of the kingdom for representative democracy, but he thought a useful beginning might be made with elected municipal councils. On the whole, the king evinced a sincere but cautious desire to broaden the base of Siamese politics. In the event, he received very little encouragement either from Sayre or from Prince Damrong, who also was asked to comment; and nothing came of this first flicker of interest in political change.

The king, however, was not inclined to let the matter rest. As the reign wore on, his thinking on the subject of political change became steadily less cautious. A second stage in this process occurred in 1927, when the king appointed a committee to devise a broader advisory council. As part of their deliberations, the king wrote a memorandum on "Democracy in Siam," in which he argued that

> if it is admitted that some day we may be forced to have some form of democracy in Siam, we must prepare ourselves for it gradually. We must learn and we must educate ourselves. We must learn and experiment so as to have an idea as to how a parliamentary government would work in Siam. We must try to educate the people to be politically conscious, to

realize [their] real interests so that they will not be misled by agitators or mere dreamers of Utopia. If we are to have a parliament, we must teach the people how to vote and how to elect representatives who will really have their interests at heart.[10]

He saw the immediate future as involving an advisory Committee of the Privy Council (formed in November 1927), which was much like the legislative councils established or proposed in earlier reigns, followed by experiments in municipal self-government. The former worked unspectacularly until the end of the absolute monarchy in 1932, whereas the latter never got started.

Through the late 1920s, the pressure seemed lifted. Prosperity and balanced state budgets (and even surpluses) had returned, and political criticism seemed to have died down. Below the surface, however, there was a good deal of ferment going on, for the time being confined to the young, particularly students abroad, and resident aliens.

As potential "nationalities," or self-conscious minorities, none of the minorities of Siam was an important source of challenges to the government in the period between the two world wars. The Malays of the south were for the most part quiescent, perhaps demoralized by the imposition of full Siamese control at the turn of the century. The Lao of the northeast and north were now virtually leaderless, caught up in the process of rapid integration into a not completely foreign "Thai-land." The Chinese minority, however, was in a different category, both because of its special economic role and power, and because of its geographic concentration, which was heaviest where the concentration of Siamese was highest, particularly in the Bangkok region. In the Seventh Reign, moreover, the Chinese minority reached its demographic peak—as 12.2 percent of the total population of Siam in 1932—while it was assimilating into Siamese society more slowly than ever before, owing to the increased immigration of Chinese women, the growth of Chinese education and a Chinese-language press, and heightened awareness of and identification with China and Chinese politics.[11] As we have seen, Prajadhipok was concerned in 1925 with the slowing of Chinese assimilation, and in 1927 he feared that Chinese money might dominate any representative political institutions he might create. What he actually faced, however, were anti-Japanese trade boycotts and demonstrations (and near riots), and growing politicization that included communism, though Chinese communism in Siam was relatively weak and for the most part oriented toward China. In the late 1920s, there was also some communist activity in Siam involving other ethnic groups, including the work of Ho Chi Minh among the Vietnamese minority in northeast Siam, and visits to Bangkok and Chiang Mai by the Indonesian Tan Malaka. As political influence, none of these amounted to very much during this period.

More problematic were the activities of Asian nationalists in Siam in the Seventh Reign. In addition to anti-Japanese activities among the Chinese, and communist versus Kuomintang struggles among them, Siam also became a base for Vietnamese, Lao, Cambodian, and Burmese nationalists working against colonial rule in their home countries. With these, Siamese had a certain amount of sympathy, deriving not least from the pride they took in having avoided colonialism themselves. At the same time, however, they were extremely wary of antagonizing the colonial powers who were their neighbors and attempted to maintain a policy of benign neutrality. Their exposure through the daily press to nationalist politics in neighboring countries, however, might be considered to have contributed something to their own political consciousness that was not untranslatable to domestic issues.

It was Siamese students abroad, however, who were most intensely involved in political discussions and dreams during the 1920s. These comprised a minuscule group (there were nearly four hundred abroad on government scholarships in 1924 and an indeterminate smaller number on private funds),[12] but their influence far outweighed their numbers, as most came from influential families and returned to high positions with the prestige of firsthand knowledge of the West. They had enjoyed a period of years abroad, out of reach of indigenous social controls and with the luxury to achieve the perspective that only distance can provide. The overwhelming majority studied in England and returned with an urbane skepticism that was ultimately class-consciously authoritarian and unideological. The small numbers schooled in France, however, were much more ideological and radical. These included both law students and young military officers, who at meetings in Paris in the mid-1920s talked of socialism and popular democracy. Particularly active among them were the young lawyer, Pridi Phanomyong, who in the Seventh Reign was working in the Ministry of Justice on the codification of Siamese laws and teaching law at Chulalongkorn University, and Plaek Khittasangkha, who had taken advanced military training and returned to Siam as a major on the army general staff with the title Luang Phibunsongkhram. These young men were profoundly dissatisfied with the old princely order and the absolute monarchy, and in secret they began to plot its overthrow.

Finally, we must note the rise in the late 1920s of a Siamese intelligentisia, a well-educated, urban class of intellectuals who began to express themselves in writing. This is hardly to say that Siam previously lacked intellectual life, for as we have seen the arts and letters long had flourished. There had been at least as early as the Third Reign a small strain of social criticism within Siamese intellectual life, expressed for the most part in traditional verse. Late in the Fifth Reign and early in the Sixth, a handful of mavericks, outsiders, trenchantly criticized the existing social, economic, and political order. Noteworthy among them were the turn-of-the-century journalists and essayists K. S. R. Kulap and Thianwan, both commoners who spent time in jail for their writings.

It was not until the 1920s, however, that there appeared groups, even a class, of writers and artists who could devote all their time to their work. These were found in the Seventh Reign particularly among journalists and those who wrote for the dozens of new magazines. The period is especially noteworthy for the virtually simultaneous appearance in 1928–29 of the first modern novels in Siam—by Kulap Saipradit, Prince Akatdamkoeng, and "Dokmai Sot" (M. L. Buppha Kunjara Nimmanhemin)—all of which were concerned with the conflict between Western and Siamese culture or the personal and social costs of modernization. At the same time, there was substantially increased publication of fiction and essays and books in a wide range of fields. To cite only perhaps the most unusual, Prince Sithiporn Kridakara founded the agricultural journal *Kasikon* in 1927 as part of a virtually one-man crusade to champion the cause of the Siamese farmer. He urged government support for agricultural research and policies that would recognize agriculture's unique contribution to the Siamese economy and society.

The important point here is that, by the Seventh Reign, there had come into being a community of intellectuals who were not dependent on the government for their support and could begin to come to grips with Siam's problems independently of those in power. As long as the press was relatively free, they could have some important influence on the shaping of popular opinion.

Public opinion, however, was not necessarily all that malleable. It was, for the most part, the opinions of a middle class that was either Chinese or was bound into the bureaucratic structure of authority. Although the thought of many, and particularly the young, might be shaped by intellectuals through the press, it still remained relatively passive. However much people in private must have groused about the existing order, it was, after all, the order that structured their lives, an order on which they depended for their livelihood and on the basis of which they had formed their identities as Siamese. It would take a profound shock to break their faith in the existing system.

That shock came when the Great Depression hit Siam in the early 1930s. Within a two-year period from 1930 to early 1932, the price of rice dropped by two-thirds and land values fell to as little as a sixth of what they had been before. Because rice was such a dominant component of the Siamese economy, it spiraled into a catastrophic fall. With greatly reduced cash incomes, peasants could not pay their taxes or their creditors, and they could not purchase retail goods. By early 1932, the government was faced with the necessity of cutting government expenditures by one-third. To make matters worse, a financial crisis developed as, under the prodding of the British financial adviser, Siam doggedly maintained the gold standard as the basis of its currency, while Britain abandoned it. This came to mean that Siam's rice was priced much higher than competing rice sold in currencies that had left the gold standard. It also brought about a significant outflow of gold from Siam.

The crunch came as the government prepared the budget for B.E. 2475, the financial year that was to begin April 1, 1932. Battles raged within the government, and spilled over onto the pages of the press, over matters of economic policy, over retrenchment, over salary cuts and new tax measures, over the gold standard and devaluation of the baht, and over the anticipated levels of revenues and expenditures for 1932–33. The public might well have concluded that the government was indecisive, that individual ministers (meaning, for the most part, princes) were concerned more for their own bailiwicks than for the economic welfare of the country as a whole, and that many, including the king, did not know what they were doing. Before an assembly of military officers in February 1932, Prajadhipok delivered a speech that included the following passage:

> The financial war is a very hard one indeed. Even experts contradict one another until they become hoarse. Each offers a different suggestion. I myself know nothing at all about finances, and all I can do is to listen to the opinions of others and choose the best. I have never experienced such a hardship; therefore if I have made a mistake I really deserve to be excused by the officials and people of Siam.[13]

This admission was modest and honest, but a more confident bluff might have been more reassuring to those beginning to lose faith in government's ability to cope with a most vital aspect of their existence.

Nor were the measures that government took necessarily the most politic. In addition to massive dismissals of government officials and freezes on promotions, the government instituted both salary cuts and a tax on salaries. Many were quick to point out that this was not an income tax. It affected only those— almost entirely government employees—who were remunerated by salaries and left untouched income from rents, royalties, dividends, interest, and profits on business enterprises. In other words, the Siamese middle class was hit hard, while the Chinese and the upper classes and royalty were extremely lightly taxed. The peasantry, who were given a 20 percent one-year reduction in their land tax while their cash income fell by two-thirds, were hit the hardest of all.

Why not, then, a peasant revolution? Siam's peasant farmers still were not living much above the subsistence level. With a few major exceptions, notably in the Rangsit area northeast of Bangkok, almost all peasant families still owned their own land and were able to feed themselves. What they lost was their surplus and some measure of the rice they would have eaten but now had to sell, if they could, to pay their taxes. Moreover, for all their numbers, they were leaderless. Their old access to the now-absent local nobility was gone. They could turn only to the king for aid, and thousands petitioned him for tax exemptions or for credit.

The middle class, too, was fragmented, divided into hundreds of modernized patron-client networks that riddled the bureaucracy. With few organizational and communication channels through which they could share and express their dissatisfaction, most could do little more than write complaining letters to the daily newspapers—usually signing them with pseudonyms for fear of bureaucratic punishment.

The government, and not least of all the king, was concerned, even worried about the rising degree of popular dissatisfaction. In the back of many people's minds at the time was an old prophecy, dating before 1827 and attributed to King Rama I's younger sister, Princess Narinthewi. It was interpreted to predict that the Chakri dynasty would last for 150 years. On April 6, 1932, according to the prophecy, the time would be up. Prajadhipok's response, less to the prophecy than to the political climate, was to return again to the possibility of introducing some measure of representative government. This time he turned first to Prince Devawongs Varodaya, his foreign minister, who in 1929 he had asked to study representative institutions in the Netherlands East Indies. Early in 1932, he requested that the prince submit a plan for a constitution that he might introduce on April 6. Devawongs, in turn, delegated its drafting to his American adviser, Raymond B. Stevens, and the undersecretary of the ministry, Phraya Sri Wisarn Waja. It was their plan that was submitted to the king early in March. It called for the delegation of the king's executive functions to an appointed prime minister who would preside over a cabinet responsible to a legislative assembly, the membership of which would be half elected (in indirect elections) and half appointed. The constitution under this plan was in many ways similar to that actually introduced after June 1932. Prajadhipok did not have the chance to put it into effect, however, apparently because of the opposition of certain princes, members of the Supreme Council of State. April 6 passed without incident.

Eleven weeks later, however, while the king was vacationing at the seaside, a small group of middle-level officials, numbering slightly more than one hundred, carried out a lightning-swift coup d'état at dawn on June 24, 1932. With only a handful of troops at their command, they bluffed and immobilized other military units in the capital, rounded up the chief officials of the government, and sent a delegation calling upon the king, in the name of the People's party, to agree to submit to a constitution. The king replied:

> I have received the letter in which you invite me to return to Bangkok as a constitutional monarch. For the sake of peace; and in order to save useless bloodshed; to avoid confusion and loss to the country; and, more, because I have already considered making this change myself, I am willing to co-operate in the establishment of a constitution under which I am willing to serve.[14]

The tiny group of conspirators, or "Promoters"—forty-nine military and naval officers, and sixty-five civilians—organized by Pridi Phanomyong and Luang Phibunsongkhram, had succeeded in bringing a sudden end to 150 years of absolute monarchy in Bangkok.

In the following chapter, we will examine the nature of the group that took power in 1932. Before leaving the absolute monarchy, however, we might reflect on the failures of Prajadhipok. Most would agree that Prajadhipok's chief weakness was one of personality. He is often seen as weak, as overly respectful of his elders. We note particularly his failure to follow through on his well-intentioned desire, by the end of his reign, to initiate gradual steps toward democratic reform. This particular weakness is hardly surprising, given his background and the unexpectedness of his accession to the throne, and given his sincere desire to make the most use of the undeniable talent and experience of the senior princes whom Vajiravudh had shunted aside.

The king, however, was hardly as weak, timid, or unsure of himself as some have thought. He was a hard-working, effective executive, he was intellectually equal to the demands of his office, and he was capable of overruling the opposition of his advisers and ministers. He, and those around him, simply underestimated the force of nationalism that was growing within the Bangkok elite, particularly among its younger generation. Perhaps Prajadhipok instinctively sensed it, but he was unwilling to override his closest advisers. Paradoxically, it would seem, Prajadhipok did not want to be an absolutist, and on critical issues, he hesitated to force his will on the ruling elite. Thus he shrank from using absolute power to end absolute power! As late as his death in exile in May 1941, many would have agreed with his judgment that a move toward democracy in 1932 was premature.

9

The Military Ascendant, 1932–1957

Much of the history of Thailand since 1932 revolves around the participation of the military, who seem to have had the last word on nearly every issue. In examining aspects of the past half-century of Thai history in this and the next chapter, we must necessarily pay attention to a long and in some ways dreary succession of military coups and attempted coups and to the public manifestations of behind-the-scenes mess-hall politicking. Through it all, it is important to keep in mind that the military in Thailand is and long has been a social institution, no less than a political and military one. It is perhaps rhetorically useful to argue that the military was on the rise in the first quarter-century after the overthrow of the absolute monarchy in 1932 and that from around 1957 its position gradually was being undermined. This is necessarily to adopt a social interpretation of Thai politics, to suggest that social organization and social cohesion carries major weight in the political struggle over who rules whom and how the resources of the nation ultimately are divided.

Back in the 1890s, King Chulalongkorn privately had worried about Siam's political future and guessed that the military ultimately might play a leading role in internal politics. Given the number of times when real or rumored military coups frightened the monarchy through the next thirty years, it should not have come as any great surprise when a military group seized the government in 1932. The military had considerable advantages. It had extremely high prestige as a social institution; it was the favored occupation of princes in the Fifth through Seventh reigns. In some ways it exemplified some of the strongest and most enduring values in Thai society. It was preeminently hierarchical. Like the old sakdi na system, everyone in the military knew his place exactly and even dressed according to his rank in military society. What gave the army, and especially but not exclusively the officer corps, such a high degree of social cohesion and solidarity was that they shared a single socializa-

243

tion process. They all went through a single military academy, to be shaped by the same curriculum and imbued with a core of common values that laid special stress upon the role of the military as the guardian of the nation, giving it a sense of mission. The civilian hierarchy was divided up into ministries and departments, into cliques and factions and clienteles. To a certain degree, of course, the military also was divided, particularly the army and navy from each other. But relative to their civilian rivals, the military was immeasurably more cohesive—and they also, in effect, had a monopoly on the use of physical force.

For most of the period with which we are now concerned, no civilian group had anything like the social cohesion of the military. Factions of some political significance can be detected in the legal profession (within the Ministry of Justice and the universities, but hardly outside them until relatively late) and subsequently within the political institutions that constitutional rule brought into being. They seldom seem to have had, however, much strength or public appeal. The military, on the other hand, at least had a steady succession of common soldiers, moving through the services under compulsory military training, who might develop some understanding of and sympathy for the values expressed by the soldier-politicians of the period. It was difficult for civilians to compete in politics against the strengths that the military brought into the public forum.

Army members of the group of Promoters of the Thai revolution of 1932.

One of the most striking contrasts between the 1932–57 period and all those that preceded it is the simple fact that royalty was suddenly physically absent. As we shall see, Prajadhipok soon fell out with the military and went abroad in 1934. When he abdicated in early 1935, his successor was a boy then at school in Switzerland who, except briefly in 1938, was not to return to Siam until 1946. He soon died, to be succeeded by yet another minor, who was not to have a visible role in the society until after 1957. For a quarter-century, then, Siamese society suddenly was without the royal focus that it had had for so many centuries and that to a certain extent it has since restored. This is, then, a most unusual period, dominated not by a king but rather by a handful of the Promoters of the 1932 coup. It was they who had to face and surmount the grave dangers of a world of warfare and great-power politics, challenged yet again to maintain the precarious independence of Siam.

The Early Constitutional Period

The military coup that toppled the absolute monarchy on June 24, 1932, can in no sense of the word be accurately described as a revolution, save in its longer term implications. It was accomplished by a handful of conspirators with a few hundred troops and involved only one casualty. It succeeded initially on surprise and bluff, then on the Promoters' holding of princely hostages, and finally on the sanction conferred by royal approval—all of this taking only a few hours. The public was not even aware of what was happening until it was all over, and before noon on June 24, the life of Bangkok and Siam was proceeding normally, but with new leaders at its top.

The 114 Promoters of the 1932 coup could not have succeeded as they did if they had not included in their ranks a small number of senior military men, whose membership in the group lent it credibility. It may perhaps also suggest the extent to which officials had begun to lose faith in the old order. These men, indeed, were relatively conservative, certainly compared with the youthful left-leaning civilians led by Pridi Phanomyong. It was they who dominated the first constitutional regimes until the late 1930s. The most important of these were Phraya Phahonphonphayuhasena (Phot Phahonyothin) and Phraya Songsuradet (Thep Panthumsen), both colonels by 1932. Phraya Song held a top post at the military academy in Bangkok, which gave the conspirators access to a broad range of contacts and an increasingly indoctrinated cadet corps. His tactical genius made it possible to neutralize a strong army and government with a handful of troops. Phraya Phahon was distinguished by a personal integrity that made him acceptable to all factions of the Promoters as the leader of the People's party.

Having induced the king to recognize and validate their actions, the Promoters undertook to organize a government under a provisional constitution of June 27. In order to minimize internal resistance and avoid the dangers of foreign intervention that they thought civil strife might invite, the Promoters initially stayed in the background, though they were still firmly in control. The long-term political program drawn up at the time by Pridi envisaged a three-stage process of political development. The first stage had now begun, with the adoption of a provisional constitution establishing an Assembly of seventy members appointed by the Promoters and a smaller People's Committee drawn from and responsible to it. A second stage was to begin within six months under a constitution similar to that drafted for Prajadhipok in March, with a half appointed and half indirectly elected National Assembly. A third stage of full representative government was to be inaugurated when half the population had completed primary education or within ten years, whichever came first. The general framework was defined in terms of the political leadership and tutelage of the People's party.

This party had as yet no mass membership or following, nor had it even substantial control over the army, so the first government it constituted displayed at least the façade of wide support. The first National Assembly included in its membership numerous senior officials, including some chaophraya of the old regime, amounting to about one-third of the total membership. The president of the Assembly was Chaophraya Thammasakmontri (M.R.W. Sanan Thephatsadin), a former minister of education. On the People's Committee, which handled the day-to-day administration of the government, there were eleven Promoters, including the leaders of their four chief factions, and four senior officials. Of the latter, the most important were Phraya Manopakonnithithada (Kon Hutasing), a respected judge of the Court of Appeals, and Phraya Sri Wisarn Waja, former undersecretary of the Ministry of Foreign Affairs and adviser to King Prajadhipok. Phraya Sri Wisarn was the new foreign minister, and Phraya Mano became prime minister and minister of finance.

Meanwhile, to consolidate their power while experienced hands ran the government, the People's party reorganized the army and navy to put their men in key positions and began trying to build a popular constituency. They quickly discovered that the first course was much easier than the latter, that people would not attend rallies and demonstrations unless ordered to do so, and that many now seeking to join their ranks were motivated by desire for jobs in the new government. The lack of dependable popular support clearly became evident within a few months. It left the young civilian faction within the People's party at a severe disadvantage in competing for influence with the military and with senior civilians with bureaucratic experience and networks of connections within the elite.

Once the permanent constitution of December 10, 1932, came into force the conflicts and competition latent within the ruling coalition began to erupt. One can identify at the beginning five major factions jockeying for power in the new regime. The older conservatives were divided into two groups—the senior civilians nominally led by Phraya Mano and a shadowy royalist rear guard now leaderless. The Promoters, in turn, were divided into three groups—the senior military faction of Phraya Phahon, the real force behind which was Phraya Songsuradet; the junior army and navy faction led by Luang Phibun; and the civilian faction led by Pridi Phanomyong. Through a complex series of maneuvers involving various combinations of factions, three major crises in the course of 1933 determined the contest in favor of the junior military men.

First, early in 1933, Pridi was encouraged by the leaders of the government to draft a new economic plan for the nation. What he came up with, based in part on lectures he had attended in Paris, was a vague, utopian, socialistic scheme for the nationalization of land and labor, the incorporation of all members of Siamese society into the bureaucracy as government officials, even as farmers, and a program of industrialization. The conservatives, and for the most part the military in general, pounced on the plan as communistic, enlisting even the king's aid in denouncing it. When the National Assembly, which was dominated by Pridi's faction of younger and more radical civilians, became restive, it was prorogued, and an anticommunist law was introduced. Having come under increasing fire, Pridi was urged to go into exile for a spell and left for France. The government already had outlawed all political parties, thereby forestalling any attempts to build mass-based parties that might challenge it.

Second, it then began to appear that Mano and Song were going to move against the younger military faction by denying them the direct command of troops, the result of which in the end would have been the return to full power of the senior conservatives. The junior military faction managed with difficulty to win Phraya Phahon's allegiance and, on June 20, 1933, staged a powerful coup, again bloodless, which ended Phraya Mano's government and installed Phraya Phahon as prime minister. Seven of the Promoters sat in the new cabinet, but still hesitant to take direct charge of ministries, they left these in the hands of trusted senior officials. When the National Assembly reconvened, it passed a law legitimizing the change of administration by coup d'état and at the same time adopted a decidedly anticommunist stance. Phraya Phahon's new administration seems to have been aware that its survival in power depended on an image of stability and continuity. They could not afford to antagonize the bureaucratic middle class with the specter of radicalism. Well might they have been cautious, for only four months later the kingdom came closer than it ever had before to civil war.

In the year since the overthrow of the absolute monarchy, there had been considerable grumbling, infighting, and even plotting against the new regime from a variety of motives ranging from monarchism to thwarted ambition. In October 1933, this crystallized around Prince Boworadet, a grandson of King Chulalongkorn who had been minister of war under Prajadhipok. Early that month, he suddenly appeared at the head of a provincial army revolt, having incited to rebellion the Nakhon Ratchasima garrison. Reinforced by the Saraburi and Ayudhya garrisons, he marched on Bangkok and by October 12 had seized the Don Müang airfield and was moving into the suburbs north of the city. Accusing the government of encouraging disrespect of the king and of fomenting communism, the rebels called upon the government to resign. It was a near thing. Several other provincial garrisons also revolted, but were prevented by loyal troops from joining Boworadet's forces in the attack on Bangkok. The rebels also had counted on the support of some of the army and navy units in Bangkok, but none of this materialized.

The government's military response to the rebels was organized by Lieutenant-Colonel Phibun, who as field commander mounted the counterattack on the northern fringes of Bangkok between October 13 and 16. The fighting was intense, and there were heavy casualties on both sides. Finally broken, the rebel forces retreated in the direction of Nakhon Ratchasima. As the government troops approached the city on October 25, Prince Boworadet realized that his cause was lost and fled to exile in French Indochina. There is no evidence that King Prajadhipok supported the rebellion, though it must have increased the government's distrust of him. Popular support for the government during the crisis had been considerable, especially in Bangkok where many volunteered to join the government troops. The government came out of the crisis stronger than ever before with a new, popular man-on-horseback in Phibun.

A few months later, early in 1934, King Prajadhipok, whose relations with the new regime had been growing steadily more strained, went abroad for medical treatment. From England he carried on a correspondence with the government that centered on the terms under which he could continue to serve as a constitutional monarch of Siam. In addition to requesting the continuation of some traditional royal prerogatives, such as the right to grant pardons, he was anxious to mitigate somehow the undemocratic nature of the new regime, for example, by having some voice, presumably on behalf of "the people," in the appointment of members of the National Assembly. The government would not agree, and so on March 2, 1935, King Prajadhipok abdicated. When doing so, he issued a brief public message criticizing the regime that included the following phrase, since often quoted by critics of Siam's slow political development:

> I am willing to surrender the powers I formerly exercised to the people as a whole, but I am not willing to turn them over to any individual or any group to use in an autocratic manner without heeding the voice of the people.[1]

On accepting his abdication, the National Assembly invited Prince Ananda Mahidol, the ten-year-old son of Prince Mahidol who was then at school in Switzerland, to ascend the throne, and appointed a regency consisting of two senior princes and Chaophraya Yommarat (Pan Sukhum).

Having defeated all internal challengers, the government now was put to the test of living up to the promises on which it had come to power. It had approximately five years to do so before clouds of war began to gather and overshadow its efforts.

On coming to power, the People's party had promised to allow a fully elected Assembly when the educational level of the population permitted. To its credit, it took much more aggressive steps than any of its predecessors finally to implement the law on compulsory primary education. It was money that was needed chiefly, and the government increased expenditures on education four-fold between 1933–34 and 1937–38, while total government expenditures during the same period increased only about one-third. If universal primary education still was not achieved, and would not be for some time to come in more remote areas, at least an earnest effort was being made. Subsequent census figures suggest they were largely successful. The age group of children that would have attended school in the mid-thirties had a literacy rate of over 60 percent (males, over 80 percent), and females in particular were much more likely to be literate than women only five years older.

Over the same period, the military budget doubled. The reasons for this are probably more complicated than one might think. Certainly the dominant faction in the government was feathering its own nest, giving itself promotions and improved equipment and facilities, and strengthening military conscription. They were by no means, however, completely cynical or narrow-minded in doing so. Many were convinced that the great powers still had designs on Siam, all the more so when their generally sympathetic relationship with the absolute monarchy ended. Many also were convinced that war was coming and

were caught up in the rising tide of militaristic sentiment, associated with
authoritarian and fascist regimes, that was sweeping much of the world during
this period. Many Siamese were impressed by, and fascinated with, Germany
and Italy, and even more with Japan. From the beginning of the Constitutional
Period in 1932, the younger military faction was in close touch with Japanese
officials and interests. This change in orientation for some represented realism,
for others, a sort of idealism, parallel to the political and institutional breaks
they were making with their own past. This was an age of militant nationalism
in which strong military men were depicted as leading the nation amidst a
dangerous world. The *Yuwachon* ("Militant Youth") movement spread across
the country, featuring the training and drilling of adolescent boys as a paramilitary force. Their numbers were no doubt included, along with regulars and
reserves, when Phibun in November 1938 claimed to have a million soldiers
available out of a population of 14 million.

In the field of economic policy, the government would have looked good
even if it had done nothing. It came to power at the worst point in the
Depression, and almost immediately Siam's economy improved. Going off the
gold standard on May 11, 1932, stimulated Siamese rice exports. The total
value of exports increased from a low of 134 million baht in 1931–32 to 153
million baht in 1932–33 and 204 million baht in 1938–39. Government budgets rose similarly. Expenditures went from a low of 70 million baht in 1932–33
to 111 million baht in 1938–39, while revenues jumped from 80 million baht in
1932–33 to 118 million baht in 1938–39. Leaving out capital expenditures, the
state budget ended in a surplus every year during this period, attesting to
continued financial conservatism, however radical the economic rhetoric may
at times have been. And the rhetoric was not so strong. Government policy
stressed cooperatives and government support for agricultural credit. Its chief
immediate actions publicly were to withdraw the hated salary tax, which was
replaced by an ineffective income tax, to abolish the peasants' land and
capitation taxes, and to adjust the civil service salary scales in favor of lower
ranking officials. On the whole, economic recovery from the worst of the
Depression was rapid and reflected creditably on the government.

The early days of the constitutional regime were exciting, especially for
those who had no real idea of the meaning of the words *constitution* and *democracy*.
There were those who thought *democracy* (*prachathipatai*) was Prajadhipok's
brother, or *constitution* (*ratthathammanun*) was a relation of Phraya Phahon. In
1932, there were scattered reports of junior monks challenging their seniors'
authority as "undemocratic" and schoolboys striking against school discipline,
supposing they were in step with the times. It is not surprising that electoral
participation was extremely low—under 10 percent—in the first elections of

November 1933. A probable majority of those elected (as opposed to the equal number appointed) were supporters of Pridi, who as minister of interior returned to a leading role in the government which still was led by Phraya Phahon as prime minister. The elected members, only half the Assembly, could play an important role, as they demonstrated in forcing the resignation of the cabinet in September 1934 over the issue of Siam's participation in an international scheme for stabilizing the price of rubber. (Phahon returned with a slightly reshuffled cabinet.)

Through the mid-1930s, there apparently were almost constant struggles for power both within and outside the government. The ranks of the State Council—the cabinet—were badly divided, held together only by the personality of Phraya Phahon. The chief figures were Luang Phibun, now minister of defense, and Pridi, who in 1935 became minister of foreign affairs to renegotiate treaties with the Western powers that at long last confirmed Siam's complete sovereignty. Though Pridi remained personally powerful and popular, his influence in domestic policy and economic affairs diminished, whereas Phibun's star was on the rise. Meanwhile, the National Assembly was becoming more assertive, objecting particularly to high military budgets and to the appointment of military men to civil positions. A small but important opposition developed, primarily among Pridi's followers and among representatives from the northeast. Outside government, in the bureaucracy and the military, plots were almost constantly rumored, and the ominous figure of Phraya Songsuradet, next to Phraya Mano the chief victim of the second coup of 1933, loomed over the government's shoulder.

The culmination of the struggles of the thirties came in 1937–38 when tempers heated up over a number of issues. First, through much of 1937, a scandal rocked Bangkok concerning the government's administration of crown properties, when it became known that much crown real estate had been sold at below-market prices to certain high officials. The government nearly fell in August, but the Assembly and cabinet seem to have backed down from a confrontation by agreeing to repair the damage quietly, and only three ministers lost their seats on the State Council. Three months later, the first direct elections for the Assembly were held in November, and very few of the former representatives were elected, save among the opposition members in the northeast, among the most important of whom were Liang Chaiyakan (Ubon), Tiang Sirikhan (Sakon Nakhon), and Thong-in Phuriphat (Ubon). Twenty-six percent of the population voted this time and elected 91 representatives in a National Assembly of 182. With only eleven veterans on the elected side of the Assembly, it is not surprising that they were initially quiet. But after being tested on a number of contentious issues in the course of the year, they finally asserted themselves over a budget bill in September 1938 and forced the cabinet's resignation. New elections were called for November, and on meeting in December, Luang Phibunsongkhram now became prime minister, replacing Phraya Phahon, who finally had retired from public life, no doubt weary of incessant battles with ambitious and contentious politicians and soldiers.

By 1938, old Siam already had changed considerably. The monarchy was still present in form, but hardly in practice (though King Ananda visited Bangkok for two months in 1938–39). Few any longer thought of rolling the political clock back to the absolute monarchy, and acceptance of the idea of constitutional rule was widespread. Regional and minority separatism seemed dead. The powerful monthon governments had been replaced by seventy provincial governments, and representative democracy had begun to be implemented at the local level. Popular participation and interest in national politics was growing, and there was at least the germ of opposition to military (by now the People's party was no more than a euphemism) domination of the government. In most ways, however, this was still a government of what we earlier called elite nationalism, though now of a broader elite that was beginning to reach outside the civil and military bureaucracies to solicit support.

Phibun's Nationalism and the War, 1938–1944

Luang Phibunsongkhram is one of only a handful of people who definitively put their stamp on Thai history. His first government, which ran from the end of 1938 to mid-1944, was a period thoroughly shaped by his power and personality, much as absolute kings had done a generation earlier. His ascendancy nearly coincides with World War II, and his policies had a great deal to do with the way in which Thai lived their wartime experience. Most of all, this was a period of mass nationalism, not just elite nationalism, a social and political phenomenon that was more nearly egalitarian in its implications than it could have been earlier under a monarchist psychology. In decades to come, when Thai were to speak of this first Phibun era and use the pronoun *we*, they were to signify a degree of common participation in their nation's life that was sharply distinguished from their experience of earlier decades.

Phibun was born Plaek Khittasangkha, in a humble family, near Bangkok on July 14, 1897. Sent at age twelve to the military academy, he graduated in 1914 and entered the artillery. His fine service record earned him advanced military training in France from 1924 to 1927, during which time he became a leader of the young students then beginning to plot the military overthrow of the absolute monarchy. He returned to Bangkok in 1927 to serve as a major on the army general staff and in 1928 was granted the rank and title, Luang

Phibunsongkhram. (He was later to take Phibunsongkhram as his family name.) He had become minister of defense in 1934 and rapidly became a major power in the governments of the Phahon period. As the most prominent of the younger military and a power in government, he was the target of repeated assassination attempts, and his survival added to the mystique that surrounded him. As early as 1934 he was a forceful exponent of Siam's need for strong leadership in a time of nation building and world crisis. He wrote frequently on this theme and encouraged the publication of books and articles admiring authoritarian leaders like Mussolini and Hitler, as well as the popular Thai writings of Luang Wichitwathakan (Vichitr Vadakarn), the most prolific and ardent popularizer of the constitutional regime. More than any other of his generation, Phibun was aware of the usefulness and power of the mass media. He effectively manipulated the popular press by controlling the news that was fed to them and by maintaining press censorship, and he was the first Thai public figure to use extensively the government's monopoly of radio broadcasting to shape popular support for his regime and policies.

Phibun became prime minister on December 26, 1938, presiding over a cabinet of twenty-five, of whom fifteen were military men. Quite remarkably, Phibun kept two portfolios himself—defense and interior—thus assuring himself of close control over the military and over provincial governors. Within a month he moved to quell all possible opposition by arresting some forty members of the royal family, old bureaucratic nobles, elected members of the Assembly, and army rivals, including Phraya Songsuradet, on charges of plotting against the government. After trials of dubious legality, eighteen were executed—perhaps the first clearly political executions in Siam in more than a century.[2] Phibun also moved against the monarchy, prohibiting the home display of pictures of ex-King Prajadhipok and suing him for misuse of crown property. He had amended the constitution to extend from ten years to a maximum of twenty the period of political tutelage during which half the Assembly would be appointed. All these actions confirmed and strengthened his power for the dangerous times he saw ahead.

Soon Phibun was exercising this power to build, not a new country, but a new nation (*sang chat*). The most immediately visible aspect of these attempts was the change of the name of Siam to Thailand in 1939. Phibun argued for this change on the grounds that it would signify that the country belonged to the Thai as opposed to the economically dominant Chinese, but it also had broader implications. It suggested a more than linguistic kinship with Thai- (or Tai-) speaking peoples outside the borders of old Siam, and it downplayed the central Thai-speaking (Siamese) role in the life of the nation. *Siam*, it was pointed out, first occurs historically as the name other countries (Champa, China,

Cambodia) gave the Tai of the Chaophraya valley. In the light of subsequent policies of the Phibun government, the first of these meanings was the most telling, though all in one way or another are reflected in the history of the period.

One particularly strong thrust to the Phibun government's policies was their economic nationalism, "Thailand for the Thai." The issue had become increasingly important to the elected members of the Assembly over the previous few years. In part this derived from the still frustratingly slow economic development of the countryside and the tendency to blame the apparently more prosperous Chinese, for example, with the myth of the usurious Chinese middleman and moneylender. In addition, however, there were at least two new elements in the situation that fueled anti-Chinese sentiment. The first was growing awareness of the large amounts of money remitted each year by Chinese in Thailand to their relatives in China, which constituted a formidable drain on the Thai economy. The second was the growth of Chinese nationalism in Thailand. This flared particularly when the Sino-Japanese War began in 1937 and Siam's Chinese organized anti-Japanese boycotts and thereby harmed both the Thai economy, for which Japan had become the major trading partner, and Thai foreign relations. That Thai-Chinese relations were worsening was signaled when in 1938 Luang Wichit in a public lecture compared the Chinese in Siam to the Jews in Germany and implied that Hitler's policies toward them were worth considering.

In the course of the first nine months of Phibun's government, a comprehensive series of anti-Chinese (or, as the government put it, pro-Thai) enactments were put into effect. The government formed a state corporation to compete with Chinese in the rice trade and virtually took over the salt, tobacco, petroleum, and pork business. Numerous occupations were forbidden to noncitizens. A new revenue code sharply increased taxes on the commercial (i.e., Chinese) class, and all noncitizens were required to pay an alien registration fee. Chinese schools came under close inspection to limit the use of the Chinese language to two hours a week, and all the Chinese newspapers save one were closed down. Throughout, the government was careful to explain that it was discriminating only on grounds of citizenship, not race, and some of its acts of economic nationalization affected Western multinational corporations as much as they affected Chinese enterprise (for example, tobacco and petroleum). But no one was fooled. These were anti-Chinese measures, which, from Phibun's point of view and that of many other Thai, were necessary in order to give the Thai control over their own economy and society.

As antiforeign and even xenophobic as some of these acts were, it is paradoxical that some measures taken during the same and subsequent years to define a new Thai identity were in many respects as much Western as Thai. A series of twelve Cultural Mandates were issued by the government between 1939 and 1942, "aimed at uplifting the national spirit and moral code of the nation and instilling progressive tendencies and a 'newness' into Thai life." [3] In addition to adopting the Western calendar with New Year's Day on January 1 instead of April 1, these dicta required Thai to salute the flag and know the national anthem, stay informed on current affairs, and use the national language (as opposed to local dialects or foreign languages). They were encouraged to live their lives along modern lines, to eat and sleep appropriately, and to engage in a full day of productive labor for the good of the country. They were encouraged to forswear imports and buy only Thai products; and they were required to dress in a modern fashion—the men in coats, trousers, shirt, and tie; women in skirts, blouses, hats, and gloves; and all in shoes. People were forbidden to board buses or to enter government offices to pay their taxes without wearing hats. All this, Phibun argued, was necessary in the interest of progress and civilization that the world might see that Thailand was a modern nation.

Through 1939 and thereafter, Phibun and Luang Wichit built up the cult of the leader. Phibun's photograph was everywhere, and his slogans were plastered on newspapers and billboards and repeated over the radio. Whatever the content of his leadership, Phibun was not to be ignored or avoided, and however unwilling they may or may not have been, people participated in the life of the state, even in the most trivial day-to-day ways. This participation, this common experience, was the basis upon which Phibun mobilized a population in the face of a war that most now were certain was coming. He also mobilized them in other ways as well—in stepped-up military conscription and training, through the Yuwachon military movement for adolescent boys, and through the Junior Red Cross and the Boy Scouts.

Thai mobilization bore its first, and in many ways most satisfying, fruits in the Thai war with French Indochina in 1940–41. The Thai had not yet, and perhaps still have not, forgiven the French for the Crisis of 1893 and the subsequent loss of Siamese suzerainty and control of Laos and Cambodia. The chance to avenge this defeat, and to correct a historical wrong, arose in June 1940 when France fell to Hitler's armies. The Western democracies appeared seriously threatened, perhaps even doomed. Meanwhile the Japanese were beginning to move into French Indochina, which now was controlled by a Vichy government aligned with Germany, and in September, by agreement with Vichy France, Japan secured military base and transit rights in northern Vietnam. Over the preceding four years, the Thai government had been trying to secure the retrocession to Siam of the portions of Laos west of the Mekong

River, but these negotiations broke down on the fall of France. The Phibun government now feared that the Japanese soon would extend their power into Laos and Cambodia and forestall any Thai moves to regain their lost territories. Amidst a barrage of nationalist propaganda, Thailand invaded both the disputed Lao territories and western Cambodia in November 1940. Though the country suffered a serious naval defeat in the Gulf of Siam, land forces soon occupied the contested areas. The Japanese thereupon stepped in to mediate between Thailand and Indochina and forced a settlement by which Lao Sayaboury, west-bank Champassak, and the Cambodian provinces of Battambang and Siem Reap (now renamed Phibunsongkhram province) were annexed by Thailand.

In the course of this crisis, Thailand's relations with the major Western powers rapidly deteriorated. Late in 1940, the U.S. government had halted the sale of sixteen aircraft to Thailand, and by March and April 1941, the United States was holding up petroleum supplies, relenting only in May after being assured of continued access to Thai tin and rubber. War in the Pacific clearly was coming soon, and all the major powers put Thailand's security understandably low on their priorities. The Americans decided their aircraft could better be used in the defense of the Philippines, and the British could supply no more than field guns, ammunition, and some aviation fuel. The Thai were convinced that Japan would invade Thailand next, and on August 28 the National Assembly passed a bill calling for mass popular resistance in the event of an invasion.

Late on the evening of December 7, 1941 (local time), the Japanese ambassador to Thailand appeared at Phibun's residence to inform the Thai that Japan had declared war on the United States and Britain and to request passage for Japanese armies through Thailand. Phibun was away from Bangkok, touring the new Cambodian provinces, and his foreign minister, Direk Jayanama, refused the request, while urgently summoning the prime minister back to Bangkok. A few hours later, just before dawn on December 8 (local time), the Japanese invasion began. In addition to the well-known, virtually simultaneous Japanese attacks on Pearl Harbor, the Aleutians, Midway, Guam, the Philippines, and Hong Kong, the Japanese also invaded Siam at nine points: across the land frontier in Battambang, by air against the Don Müang airfield outside Bangkok, and by amphibious landings at seven points on the gulf coast. The main Japanese attack was intended to secure the Thai airfield at Songkhla in order to provide air support for the conquest of British Malaya and Singapore. The British in Malaya had a contingency plan to check the Japanese advance by sending troops into then-neutral Thailand to stop the Japanese at Songkhla; but when they placed it into operation, a party

Field Marshal Phibun as wartime leader, conferring a
decoration on a soldier.

of Thai border police at the frontier held them back through a hard day's
fighting.[4] Elsewhere, resistance lasted only a few hours. On his return to
Bangkok at 7:30 A.M., Phibun ordered a cease-fire, his government having
agreed that to fight the Japanese would be suicide. The Thai had no choice but
to agree to allow Japanese forces passage rights through Thailand in return for
Japanese assurances of respect for Thailand's independence.

As the whirlwind of Japanese military successes followed, the military
elements, especially, in Phibun's government were convinced that Japan would
win the war, and as early as December 12 they agreed to the conclusion of a
military alliance with Japan. A month later on January 25, 1942, this was
expanded with a Thai declaration of war against the United States and Great
Britain. This was a contentious development. Why need the Thai have gone so
far as to ally themselves with Japan? Phibun and the military under his
leadership either cynically judged that Japan would win the war and

Thailand's best interests lay in going along with the tide or more adventurously judged that they might retain more independence, and better protect their citizens, by a friendly rather than adversarial relationship with the Japanese. Probably both considerations influenced their decision; those who opposed it were forced from the government. Among others, Minister of Finance Pridi Phanomyong was appointed regent for the absent King Ananda, and Foreign Minister Direk became ambassador to Japan. The Thai minister in Washington, Seni Pramoj, chose to regard his government's declaration of war against the United States as illegal and unrepresentative of the Thai people's wishes. He refused to deliver it to the U.S. government, and he soon set about organizing a Free Thai movement in cooperation with the American Office of Strategic Services.

The first year of the war was awash with excitement and enthusiasm. The long-standing Thai fascination with, and exaggerated respect for, the technologically superior, modern West was deflated as European troops were seen to be fleeing ignominiously from the colonies they had held for a hundred years or more. Japanese—Asians like themselves, Thai thought—were beating the West at their own game, and it seemed only a matter of time before the White Man's West was through. The Thai did not see themselves as victims of the Japanese, but rather as coparticipants in the shaping of a new world order in which they could participate as equals, rather than as "little brown brothers." In all of eastern Asia now, from Kamchatka to the borders of India and Australia, Thailand was the only fully independent state, an equal partner of Japan, whereas all Thailand's neighbors save French Indochina were subordinate occupied countries. In the flush of wartime military spirit, the Thai even undertook a military campaign of their own and conquered in May 1942 the Shan region around Keng Tung in northeastern Burma, completing successfully the expeditions abandoned in the late Third and early Fourth reigns. This acquisition of the "United Shan States" or "Original Thai States" was confirmed by treaty with Japan in August 1943, at which time the Japanese also turned over to Thai administration Kelantan, Trengganu, Perlis, and Kedah—the four Malay states that Chulalongkorn had transferred to Britain in 1909.

The war began to go against the Japanese with the failure of their effort to invade India in early 1944, the move by the British to the offensive on the Burma front, and the American counteroffensive in the southwest Pacific that recaptured the Philippines in early 1945. Wartime conditions had already set in in Thailand, and the euphoria of 1942 was long since gone. The Thai government had retained full control of its army and its population, and the Japanese technically were guest troops who had been loaned facilities by the Thai. The

Thai usually were able to prevent direct Japanese requisitions of goods or labor services from the Thai population, but unofficial contacts between the two sides often were bad. The Thai suffered more heavily from essential commodity shortages, increased taxation, runaway inflation, and by the middle of the war, Allied air raids. Japan could not supply Thailand's need for essential imports, and even if it had been able to, soon there was no shipping to transport them nor to carry Thailand's exports to the few markets still accessible. With inflation, rationing, and shortages came black markets, smuggling, corruption, and profiteering. Both morale and morality sagged as the war dragged on.

By mid-1944, the winds were shifting not only against Japan but against Phibun as well. There was much grumbling and not-so-quiet complaints about inflation, the Cultural Mandates, the simplified spelling (1942–44) that Phibun had introduced, and especially, the Japanese, now increasingly linked with Phibun. It was well known that the fortunes of war had turned, that the Allies had invaded France (June 1944), Italy had left the war, and the Japanese "victories" were occurring closer and closer to the Japanese home islands. On July 18, 1944, the Tojo government in Japan resigned, and only six days later the Thai National Assembly turned down two government bills and forced the resignation of Phibun as prime minister. What had happened?

When the Japanese increasingly were placed on the defensive in the war, they became all the more dependent on good relations with the Thai government, and these seem clearly to have been deteriorating by 1944. The anti-Japanese Free Thai underground, now operating under American auspices from Chungking in southwest China and from British headquarters in Ceylon and India, had successfully infiltrated even the government in Thailand. In effect it was now headquartered in Pridi's office of the Regency Council. Thai students and a few Americans and Britons had been parachuted into Thailand (and even were in hiding in Bangkok) to prepare landing strips, train commando units, and transmit intelligence back to Allied forces. For his part, Phibun also was thinking of ways, he claims, to prepare to turn against the Japanese. Part of these preparations included proposals to move the capital to remote Phetchabun, north of Bangkok, and construct a "Buddhist City," a sort of center for world Buddhism, near Saraburi—both grandiose projects in typically extravagant Phibun style. Moving to the isolated, mountain-ringed Phetchabun, Phibun later argued, would facilitate a Thai uprising against the Japanese.

The deputies in the Assembly—the same group appointed and elected in 1938 (their terms had been extended)—voted against these plans, though they could not openly be told of Phibun's plans for an uprising. They appear to have been motivated in part by the fall of Tojo, who was closely associated in their minds with Phibun, in part by their feeling that the war was turning against Japan, and in part by their feeling that Phibun was too closely identified with an authoritarian past that must now be buried for the sake of improving relations with the Allies. Even more urgent, however, was the necessity of electing a prime minister who might improve surface, formal relations with the Japanese and at the same time more adroitly shield the growing Free Thai movement. As Batson puts it, Khuang Aphaiwong was chosen "largely for his ability to dissemble with the Japanese." [5] One of the two remaining regents for the absent king resigned rather than sign the papers for Khuang's appointment, so the new government inaugurated July 31 had Khuang as prime minister and Pridi Phanomyong as sole regent—Khuang to deal with the Japanese and Pridi, through the Free Thai, with the Allies.

This was an abrupt and, at the time, surprising end to a six-year period in Thai history. Perhaps until they actually voted, the members of the National Assembly did not realize what the outcome might be. They put out of office the generalissimo of a militant nationalism that had, for the moment, gone sour and put in his place a mild-mannered, slightly awkward, but witty forty-four-year-old civilian. In the course of accomplishing this, most of the old political alliances going back to 1932 were broken. The army and navy clearly split, with the navy going to Khuang's side, and the growing rift between Phibun and Pridi opened into a chasm. Some at the time expected that Phibun, who had slunk off to military headquarters in Lopburi, might gather loyal troops and stage a coup, which he easily could have done. He wisely chose to bide his time.

Between Hot and Cold Wars

The period at the end of World War II was one of chaos and danger for Thailand. It required dramatic readjustment to a rapidly changing world, while the manifold effects of the war itself hindered the Thai ability to take effective action in their own interest. The years from 1944 to 1948 constitute a period during which the great powers continued profoundly to affect Thai life and politics. The external pressures in important ways artificially unbalanced Thai politics. In particular, American policy thrust on the shoulders of Thai civilian politicians a burden they were not prepared to carry. Nevertheless, they had to try, in order to counter with American assistance a dangerous new thrust of British and French policy.

With the impending fall of the Philippines to American forces and the rapid advance of British forces through Burma by early 1945, it became increasingly apparent that Siam soon would be on the front lines of the war. The Thai naturally were worried about an Allied reconquest (actually, conquest for the first time) of Thailand. They were well informed about Allied, and especially British, wartime thinking on the desirability of imposing postwar retribution and controls on Siam that would amount to a protectorate. Thai efforts to establish a Free Thai government-in-exile failed, whereupon they followed two complementary policies. With the Free Thai movement now well established throughout the government under Pridi's direct control, they claimed to be able to field a guerrilla force numbering in excess of fifty thousand men, in addition to virtually all the regular Thai armed forces. These they offered to turn against the Japanese whenever the Allies gave the word.

To the British they made it clear that they would immediately restore to British control the Malay and Shan territories annexed in 1942–43. They were able to refrain from making similar commitments with respect to the Lao and Cambodian provinces, since the French role in the Asian war was minimal. The Thai were worried about British designs on Siam, all the more because the predominantly British South-East Asia Command under Admiral Lord Louis Mountbatten could be expected to have primary military responsibility for the conquest of Thailand. They therefore relied very heavily on their connections with the American government through the Free Thai movement and its nominal leader, Seni Pramoj, Thai minister in Washington.

To the Americans they stressed Thai unenthusiasm for the alliance with Japan and the declaration of war against the United States and Great Britain. These actions they variously characterized as illegal (not all members of the Council of Regency had signed it, Pridi having been conveniently absent), or coerced by Japanese military pressure, or as acts of carelessness by overambitious and unrepresentative Thai militarists. They could point out that Thai troops had not actually engaged in warfare against the Allies and that they had now made a promising beginning at restoring democratic government. To the American government, without much actual interests in or previous substantial connections with Thailand, these arguments were compelling; and through the course of 1945 the U.S. State Department consistently was an advocate for Thailand against the British.

The situation suddenly changed with the unexpected surrender of Japan on August 15, 1945. The Thai acted immediately to restore the prewar status quo. As regent, Pridi termed the declaration of war illegal and null and void, and repudiated all agreements made with Japan by Phibun. Prime Minister Khuang Aphaiwong tendered his resignation on the grounds of his association with the Japanese in the past year. The National Assembly announced its intention of inviting Seni Pramoj to become premier on his return to Thailand and, in the meantime, formed a caretaker government under a prominent civilian politician, Thawi Bunyaket.

The British government immediately put heavy pressure on the Thai to accede to a long list of demands, including full restitution for all British property losses, preferential economic advantages, the right to station troops in Thailand indefinitely, and 1.5 million tons of free rice. The British felt stabbed in the back by Japan's use of Thai territory to invade Malaya and Burma, and wished to curb the Thai military they held responsible. They also wished unreasonably to punish the Thai for withholding Thai rice exports during the war and certainly did not wish to see the Thai make substantial profits on the sale of rice that could not be shipped in wartime. (They overestimated 1945 rice stockpiles by 100 percent.) The British unilaterally almost imposed these conditions on the Thai in early September, but strong American pressure forced postponements and eventually a substantial reduction in the terms when an agreement with Britain was signed at the end of December (involving only the sale, not a free gift, of Thai rice).

Terminating the state of war with France was no less difficult, as Thai feelings ran very high on the retention of the Cambodian and Lao provinces (whose populations voted in the Thai national elections in January and August 1946). Only in January 1947 did Thailand agree to restore the provinces to French Indochina in return for a French promise not to veto Thai admission to the United Nations, which was vital to Thailand's international respectability.

Through the foreign policy crises of 1946, Pridi was the power behind the Thawi and Seni governments. He had retired from the regency when the king returned in December 1945 and was formally named Senior Statesman, adviser to the government. With the apparently discredited military now withdrawn from politics in the interest of good relations with the Western powers, political parties were able for the first time to organize and contest elections. From Bangkok in November 1945, it was reported that the "British are making efforts through pro-British Siamese to organize a party with political influence but as yet have secured no outstanding leaders." [6] Regardless of their foreign support, which is impossible to gauge, at least four major parties were organizing by early 1946. The habitually antigovernment representatives from the northeast joined with Pridi's old segment of the People's party in support of Pridi. They were opposed by the Democrat party led by Khuang Aphaiwong and the Progressive (but relatively conservative) party of Kukrit Pramoj, younger brother of Seni. All the parties, with the possible exception of the Cooperative party in the northeast, had little or no mass support. They were simply loosely formalized political factions of urban, educated politicians; and both their ranks and the relations among them were rent by personal rivalries and jealousies.

The two parties supporting Pridi won a substantial majority of the elected seats in January 1946, but the Assembly then elected Khuang prime minister. A majority of the Assembly still were aligned with Pridi on policy matters, however, a situation that quickly grew intolerable for Khuang, who resigned in March. This time Pridi had to take the premiership himself. To improve the situation and create more stable political institutions, Pridi organized the drafting of a new constitution, which came into effect in May 1946. It introduced a bicameral legislature with a fully elected House of Representatives and a Senate elected by the lower house. Its membership was restricted to persons over forty with high educational qualifications or administrative or legislative experience. The outlook for democratic, civilian government appeared good, and most people now expected that stable political leadership might alleviate the lingering aftereffects of the war—inflation, shortages, widespread corruption, and still uncertain relations with the great powers.

These expectations were dashed by a series of events in 1946. First, in April, the highest Thai court halted the prosecution of Phibun and his wartime associates on the grounds that the War Crimes Act under which they were being tried, owing to Allied pressure, was retroactive and therefore unconstitutional. The legalities were not quite that simple, and there is general agreement that the ruling came at least in part as a result of popular pressure. Public opinion on the whole was favorable to Phibun. He was thought to have done the best that could be done to maintain Thai interests in the face of overwhelming Japanese pressure. Phibun and the military were, in effect, exonerated, but they were still reluctant to take an active political role in the face of possible negative reactions from the Western powers on whom Thailand so depended at this point.

Two months later, on June 9, 1946, the young King Ananda Mahidol, who had returned to Bangkok in December, was found in his bed, shot through the head with a pistol. The mysterious circumstances surrounding his death were only heightened by the government's ineptitude in handling this major crisis. They first announced the death to have been an accident. Then a government commission, including American and British doctors, appointed to investigate the affair reported that the king probably had been murdered. The three chief material witnesses were hurriedly tried and executed. Public opinion, quick to associate Pridi with antiroyalist sentiments and remembering his violent disagreement with Prajadhipok over his Economic Plan of 1933 (but forgetting his years as regent), held Pridi responsible for Ananda's death, either indirectly as head of the government in power at the time or in more sinister fashion. In August Pridi resigned as prime minister and traveled abroad. The civilian government left behind under Luang Thamrongnawasawat could not escape the regicide cloud that refused to be dispelled by evidence that did not add up and questions left unasked and unanswered. Without strong leadership, the Assembly and government floundered in the face of critical difficulties, particularly economic stagnation and extensive high-level corruption involving especially rice smuggling and profiteering.

The Thamrong government was further weakened by the fact that the by-elections held in August 1946 to fill the expanded lower house (under the new constitution) eroded Pridi's parties' control to a bare majority, which by early 1947 had disappeared as members defected from the majority party to their rivals. The legislature was falling into uncontrollable chaos, which took an ominous turn when a number of politicians were murdered. Meanwhile, Pridi had returned from abroad anxious to promote anticolonial solidarity among Southeast Asian nationalists. To this end, he founded the Southeast Asia League in September 1947. From the last years of the war, the Free Thai had had close working relations with anti-French and anti-Japanese groups in Cambodia, Laos, and Vietnam, and these connections had broadened with the rise of Pridi to power in the immediate postwar period. By 1947, the Indonesian, Lao, and Vietnamese nationalist movements had information and arms-procurement offices in Bangkok, and there was even a Mon separatist organization. Many, but especially the Thai military, believed Pridi had communist connections. Rumors spread that

> Pridi had been about to establish a Siamese republic as a cornerstone for a South East Asia Union; that radio orders had been intercepted and documents found bearing out these contentions; that agents were on their way to Switzerland to murder King Bhumipon; and that an arms cache, including many Russian weapons, had been discovered at the house of [Thong-in Phuriphat], one of Thamrong's Ministers—arms indubitably intended for the communist revolution.[7]

The cold war, whether as actual subversion or only as exaggerated fears, had come to Bangkok; and it is difficult to discern to what extent the army was acting out of cold war fears or in order, as they said, to restore order and direction to a stumbling civilian, democratic government. But act they did. On November 8, 1947, army troops seized the government, no longer styling themselves the People's party but simply the Coup Group. Pridi briefly lay hidden and then, with the assistance of the British and American naval attachés and a Shell Oil tanker, was spirited out of the country. After three weeks' hesitation, during which Phibun and the active instigators of the coup—Luang Katsongkhram, Lientenant-General Phin Chunhawan, Colonel Phao Siyanon, and Colonel Sarit Thanarat—realized that Thailand risked international disapproval, or worse, if army officers and especially Phibun ran the government, the army installed the hapless Khuang Aphaiwong as prime minister and for a time maintained the 1946 constitution.

Prime Minister Khuang Aphaiwong addressing a public meeting.

The Khuang government began well, by appointing an unusually well-qualified and experienced cabinet while preparations were made for new national elections. The army and police, however, undertook a program of rooting out leftists, which was aimed particularly at Pridi's old supporters, Free Thai activists, and ultimately opposition politicians, especially those from the northeast. In elections in January 1948, Khuang's Democrat party won a slim majority of seats in the Assembly, while a party organized by Phibun performed dismally. Phibun and the Coup Group sat back for three months and watched as the Democrats and Khuang extended their control and prepared to draft a new constitution that would further eclipse the military. Finally, threatening the use of military force again, they made Khuang resign, and Phibun became prime minister on April 8, 1948—$3\frac{1}{2}$ years since Khuang had taken over from him late in the war.

This was not a happy period in Thai history, and most would probably wish to forget many aspects of it. Almost forgotten in the series of coups, cabinet and ministerial changes, treaties, and economic crises are the things that did *not* happen. No leaders of genuine mass following arose in the period save Phibun and Pridi; and the support that each commanded was qualified—Phibun's by his wartime and authoritarian associations, and Pridi's by his leftist and possible regicide associations in the public mind. Phibun had appealed to the military and more conservative elite, Pridi to the civilian bureaucratic elite, the professional classes, and upper-level students. In neither case was there substantial mass backing, and there were nothing like mass public demonstrations in the period. We are left with the impression of a shallowly based political order involving a fragmented and fractious elite split by vague ideological orientations, attitudes toward royal authority and the economic order, and, especially, ambitions and personal interests and rivalries.

The 1944–48 period in Thai politics was artificially skewed in favor of the civilian politicians because of the exigencies of the wartime and immediate postwar situation. It was vitally necessary for Thailand to appear democratic in order to win the good will of the American government (and people) to assure U.S. assistance against first the Japanese and then the British. This imbalance on the civilian side was not righted in 1948 but rather tipped too far to the opposite extreme because of a new cold war context that seemed again to threaten the existence of independent Thailand.

Phibun's Second Government, 1948–1957

During Phibun's second government, or series of governments, between 1948 and 1957, the stakes of the political game in Thailand were much higher than they had been just a decade earlier. The kingdom was a good deal more populous, and soon much more prosperous, than it had been; the active and ambitious political elite had grown considerably; and power, which at least seemed to be more accessible and certainly had more substance, was more eagerly sought after and defended. The pattern had been established according to which, in effect, those who controlled the government made up their own rules for exercising power and for keeping others away from it. These, like the governments that had preceded them, were constitutional regimes, but with the important qualification that the constitution was subordinate to the government, not the other way around.

The political events of this period are generally well known in outline, but their details have not yet been carefully and systematically studied. They await the labors of another generation of historians not quite so close to the events and personalities. For the present, all we can do is to trace briefly this outline and then comment on what seem now to be some distinguishing features of this period.

Critically important to understanding it is its international context, particularly that of its first year, 1948. The cold war was beginning in earnest in Europe, especially with the assumption of full communist control in Czechoslovakia in February. There soon followed an upsurge in anticolonial or antigovernment insurgency in Burma, Malaya, Indonesia, the Philippines, and French Indochina. At the same time, the Civil War in China promised soon to end with a Communist victory. The onset of the cold war thus contributed immediately to the willingness of the United States and Great Britain to recognize the Phibun government in April.

Particularly in the context of his long struggle with Pridi and civilian "radicals," Phibun took seriously (but arguably exaggerated) the fears these developments inspired. He had at the same time to gain at least the appearance of popular support and to counter rivals both within the military and on the Thai political scene at large.

Phibun began much as he had in 1938 with a new anti-Chinese campaign, now given added impetus by the prominence of Chinese members in the minuscule Communist party of Thailand and by the growing depiction of overseas Chinese as a possible fifth column of subversion on behalf of a Communist China. The relative balance between pro-Communist and Kuomintang elements in Chinese society in Thailand was rapidly shifting in favor of the former at this time—in labor unions, Chinese schools, and the Chinese press and community organizations. Having already virtually halted Chinese immigration, the government again undertook a series of measures to restrict Chinese economic domination and promote Thai business. They also clamped down on Chinese associations and schools and imposed new controls on the press.

At the same time, Phibun was moving against his civilian rivals. Those identified with opposition to the government, and with Pridi, were subjected to harassment and arrest. Northeastern politicians in particular were the targets of the police. Many of these, including Tiang Sirikhan and Thong-in Phuriphat, were arrested in 1948, charged with plotting the separation of the northeast and its incorporation into a Communist-dominated Indochina. In March 1949, Thong-in and two others were shot to death "while attempting to escape" from police;[8] and the same fate befell Tiang at the end of 1952. The intimidation was sufficient to silence most politicians.

While ideas of northeastern Lao separatism during this period may have engaged the fancy of a handful of politicians and Free Thai activists, much more serious developments were occurring in the Malay provinces of the south. The efforts by Phibun's government late in the war to enforce the Cultural Mandates and to substitute Siamese for Islamic law had provoked serious resistance with strong popular support. The Khuang and Thamrong governments lessened the pressures, but new issues arose with the application in the south of the educational policies that had been aimed primarily against the Chinese—Malay schooling was forbidden. Malays in the south felt like subjects of an alien colonial regime and, in August 1947, submitted to the government a list of demands, calling for regional administrative, education, fiscal, religious, linguistic, and judicial autonomy. Luang Thamrong's government had promised the petitioners sympathetic consideration of their grievances; but Phibun's response on coming to power was the arrest and imprisonment of the chief Malay leaders in the four provinces and the outlawing of Malay and Islamic organizations. By April 1948 there was large-scale insurgency in the south, put down by government troops with massive force that included aerial bombardment.[9] There was much sympathy in Malaya for the dissidents' plight, but the onset of major and predominantly Chinese Communist insurgency against the British Malayan government in mid-1948, impinging on the border region, required cooperation between the Malayan and Thai governments and resulted in the concentration of much military force and attention in the region with Western support. This contributed to the isolation and long-term muting of Malay dissidence in the south.

Within the first year of his government, Phibun had to meet two military challenges to his power. First, in October 1948, Major-General Net Khemayothin and a number of high-ranking army officers were plotting a coup when their plans leaked out and sixty men were arrested. Early the following year, on February 26, 1949, a much more serious and violent episode occurred when the navy and marines attempted to restore Pridi to power. Fighting raged through Bangkok for three days before the Coup Group and Phibun regained control. Pridi lost much by this resort to violence, and the navy was increasingly distrusted. Meanwhile, Phibun seemed all the more justified in using draconian measures against dissidents and rivals. Police power was badly abused with the arbitrary arrest, and even torture and killing, of many citizens. Critical newspaper editors were beaten up by thugs.

But the façade of constitutional democracy remained. Thailand was now receiving such economic and military assistance from the United States, and favors from international organizations, that Phibun could not afford to jeopardize this by dispensing with the constitutional fictions that seemed so to impress the international community. The Democrat party continued to dominate both houses of the legislature, and it drafted and promulgated a new constitution in March 1949. This instrument provided that the Senate be fully appointed by the king, substantially increasing the power of the monarchy, and also gave the Senate the power to delay legislation. The military was left with no power to influence the composition of the legislature.

The *Manhattan* coup, 1951. The warship *Sri Ayudhya* under attack by the air force.

Phibun had to resort to other means to assure his control. In the June 1949 by-elections for new seats in the lower house, his government is said to have rigged many elections and financed a progovernment party that won virtually all the new seats, giving Phibun a majority in the House of Representatives. This majority he subsequently expanded to 75 of 121 votes by heavy use of patronage that involved gifts and special favors. He could still, however, do little with the upper house; nor was his position within the military itself yet completely secure.

On June 29, 1951, Phibun was participating in a ceremony aboard the dredge *Manhattan*, which the American government was presenting to Thailand as part of a major increase in its economic and military aid. The occasion was interrupted by navy officers and men who took Phibun prisoner and hustled him away to confinement on the flagship *Sri Ayudhya*. For a few hours, negotiations took place to induce the Coup Group to yield power, but these soon broke down, and by the next day, fierce fighting raged in Bangkok between the government, supported by the army, police, and air force, and the navy and marines. When the air force bombed the *Sri Ayudhya*, Phibun was able to swim away as it sank. He eventually reached friendly forces and broadcast an appeal to the navy to cease fighting. The *Manhattan* coup soon ended, but with well over 3,000 casualties including 1,200 dead, most of them civilians. As a result of the coup, the navy was cut to a quarter of its previous strength, and many arrests followed, including fifty students at Thammasat University, charged with having communist associations.

The year 1951 was a turning point in many ways. The suppression of the *Manhattan* coup marked the rise to, and confirmation in, power of Phibun's two chief rivals within the 1947 Coup Group. Major-General Phao Siyanon now became director-general of the Police Department, which was as much military as constabulary; and Major-General Sarit Thanarat, who commanded the First Army in Bangkok, soon also became deputy minister of defense. Phibun presided only uneasily over this triumvirate and gradually lost power to both his rivals.

Given the form of the 1949 constitution and the power it gave to the monarchy, the Coup Group was concerned as King Bhumibol Adulyadej prepared to return and assume his royal duties at the end of 1951. While the king was at sea, en route from Singapore to Bangkok, on November 29 the military simply announced on the state radio that

> because of the present world situation and because of Communist aggres-
> sion and widespread corruption, members of the armed forces, the police
> and leaders of the 1932 and 1947 coups d'etat had decided to put the 1932
> Constitution in force in the kingdom.[10]

The legislature was replaced by a single appointed Assembly of 123 members (106 of whom were military and police officers), to which 123 elected members were added after elections in February 1952. From the beginning, the relationship between the young king and Phibun's government was off to a bad start.

During the first fifteen years of constitutional regimes, those who might have been social critics and political activists instead joined the establishment. The next generation of intellectuals, however, were shut out of Phibun's government, and contributed to a reawakening of political ferment in Thailand in the late 1940s and early 1950s. This revived intellectual life now centered especially on Thailand's two universities, both in Bangkok: the prestigious Chulalongkorn University, long the major recruiting ground for government positions, and the newer Thammasat University, founded in 1934, which through this period was an open university with unrestricted admission, an orientation toward the study of law, and a student body drawn from lower social strata than Chulalongkorn. Thammasat had close associations with Pridi, who was mainly responsible for its founding and for a time was its rector. It should not be surprising that in this period, amidst anticolonial strife through much of Asia and the generally high prestige of communism, Marxist ideas should have had some attraction for bright youths disgruntled with their elders. They regarded Pridi as their political hero and economic mentor; and their literary interests were whetted by such authors as Kulap Saipradit, who had developed from the social critic of the twenties to a political leftist by the early fifties.

Among many important figures to come out of this environment, we might mention two, who were contemporaries at Chulalongkorn University around 1950. Chit Phumisak, who started as a brilliant literary critic and essayist in the early 1950s, was to become best known for his somewhat naive Marxist critique, *The Face of Thai Feudalism* (1957). He was imprisoned for subversion by the Sarit regime, 1958–64, and died in 1965 fighting as an insurgent in the northeast. Khamsing Srinawk, from a northeastern peasant background, supported himself as a journalist while attending Chula and wrote brilliantly satiric short stories, one of which, "The Politician," conveys well the disgust youths felt toward the political order in the fifties.[11] Significantly, neither Chit nor Khamsing seems to have made much of an impact on their contemporaries when they first wrote: the pressures for conformity were great, the dangers of overt political action possibly fatal.

The economy of Thailand improved greatly during the second Phibun regime, owing mainly to developments beyond government control. The Korean war from mid-1950 stimulated a boom in Thai commodity exports of rice, rubber, and tin; and by the best estimates the gross national product was growing at an annual rate of 4.7 percent from 1951 to 1958. At the same time, imports of manufactured goods increased even more rapidly and, in combination with the rise of a small domestic manufacturing sector—much of it in state enterprises—made available much improved supplies of consumer goods. Thai fiscal management remained conservative, as it had been since the Fifth Reign, and the Thai baht remained extraordinarily stable at around twenty to the U.S. dollar.

The major new element in Thailand's international economic and political situation was the role of the United States, which now far eclipsed the position the British once enjoyed. American policy in Asia saw Thailand as an independent state to be defended against communism and as a regional power to be wooed to the cause of containing communism in the region. Thailand was the first Asian state to send troops to fight with the United Nations in Korea, and in 1954 it became the regional cornerstone of the South East Asia Treaty Organization (SEATO). Compared to neighboring countries at the time, Thailand was powerful and stable, especially after the return of Phibun to power. With each successive Communist challenge—the establishment of a Communist regime in China (1949), the Korean War (1950–53), and the

French defeat at the hands of the Communist-dominated Viet Minh in Indochina (1954)—the United States increased its reliance on and assistance to Thailand. Between 1951 and 1957, Thailand was the beneficiary of $149 miliion in economic aid and $222 million in military aid.[12] Economic aid included work on the expansion of the port of Bangkok, and the improvement of highway and railway communications, as well as technical assistance in the fields of agriculture, education, irrigation, economic planning, and so on. Military aid among other things paid for the modern equipment and training of the air force and for a police force that reached 43,000 men in 1954, as well as for the strengthening of the army. These were substantial additions to the Thai budget, which in the early 1950s was running at about $200 million a year. One great advantage to the Coup Group was that these funds for the most part were outside parliamentary control.

Both at the time and since, there has been strong criticism of the close Thai–U.S. relationship during this period. Even the recipients of this aid would agree that it served to tip still further the political balance in Thailand in favor of the military. Not only did it render them more independent of their own political process, it also strengthened their ability to coerce the civilian population. This was especially true of the Police Department under General Phao, as we have seen; but it was also the case with the military seizure of power (and the failed coups) and the suppression of separatist and antigovernment movements. Moreover, American accounting controls over these funds could never be so efficient as to prevent large amounts ending up in the pockets and Swiss bank accounts of various Thai military figures.

But it is much too simple just to blame American policy for the corruption of Thai politics during this period. If one wishes to argue that the American government was using the Thai military to achieve U.S. anticommunist aims, or even American economic expansion aims, one must also readily admit that the Thai figures involved seem to have known exactly what they were doing. They might have had difficulty candidly explaining themselves, for their motives must certainly have been mixed. Many sincerely believed that the army was the salvation of the nation, that Communists had subverted the opposition, that Thailand had a leading role to play in holding back the spread of Communist (or Chinese or Vietnamese) power in Southeast Asia. All these ideas had been part of standard military training and indoctrination in Thailand for more than a generation.

There is still another aspect to the question, which has to do with the Thai military as a social institution. In the society of Thailand as a whole, there were roughly four institutional avenues of advancement: higher education, the military, the Buddhist monkhood, and business. The attractions of the Buddhist monkhood were limited. One had to be celibate and could never hope for more than a little money and not much more power. Business was virtually closed to Thai youths, being dominated by Chinese and imbued with values and an ethos foreign to most Thai. Historically, higher education was the means by which middle- and upper-class youths entered the bureaucracy. Entrance into universities was highly restricted until quite late and was not widely accessible until the 1960s. The army, on the other hand, recruited officers fairly widely in the society, and none of them had university education. They shared a common officers' training and resentment of wealthier citizens. By moving into politics, the military could share in the wealth of the society in ways that they could not otherwise.

Viewed in these social terms, then, the army's behavior on the political scene is more understandable, if not more praiseworthy. Ranking military officers under Phibun developed an enormous range of techniques for sharing in the nation's wealth. Officers could be appointed ministers, deputy ministers, section chiefs, and so on; they could serve as provincial governors; they might be appointed to government commissions or to act as advisers; they could thereby gain both substantially increased salaries and opportunities for graft. They could join the boards of new commercial enterprises, the capital for which was put up by Chinese or foreign businessmen. They might be granted lucrative government contracts or licenses or monopolies. The possibilities seemed endless, but a highly inventive and entrepreneurial Thai military class explored most of them.

The two leading rivals of Phibun both had very substantial private incomes, though both were of modest origins. General Phao among other things had a leading role in the illegal opium trade (while heading the Police Department), perhaps facilitated by wartime connections in the Shan states with Chinese groups which dominated a large segment of that trade. General Sarit was financed by lucrative takings from the Government Lottery Bureau. They used their funds to build personal followings and support political activities, and both of them rapidly grew into formidable rivals to a Phibun whose power and repute were waning by the mid-fifties.

By 1955, Phibun seems to have sensed that he was losing his grip and probably feared that General Phao, being more ruthless and unscrupulous than Sarit, might force him into leaving sooner rather than later. In that year, Phibun went on an extended tour of the United States and Britain, and he returned with a sudden consuming enthusiasm for democracy. Perhaps he even wanted to be loved, not just feared or respected, or perhaps he wanted to gain popular support to counter Sarit's control of the army and Phao's of the police. For whatever reasons, he began relaxing authoritarian political control. He allowed the registration of political parties and the democratization of local governments, he lifted controls on the press and speech, and he began to organize for the parliamentary elections due in early 1957. He strove to reduce Phao's power by taking over the Ministry of Interior, which ran the police, and reduced Phao's faction's control in the ministries of Finance and Defense. When the elections finally took place in February 1957, however, Phibun's Seri Manangkhasila party won just over half the seats (85 of 162) only by blatant fraud, vote rigging, tampering, and coercion.

The public outcry against "the dirtiest elections in Thai history" forced Phibun to declare a brief state of national emergency and make Sarit responsible for public order. The elections were Phibun's first big mistake, and his appointment of Sarit was his second. Instead of acting as the government's agent to suppress opposition, Sarit appeared sympathetic to student demonstrators. Asked at a rally at Chulalongkorn University about the elections, he replied, "I will say that they were dirty, the dirtiest. Everybody cheated."[13] He carefully refrained from exercising military power against civilians and quickly gained a reputation as an honest, forthright leader.

Matters came to a head in August and September 1957 as the Phibun government reeled from a succession of shocks. It showed itself as callous and inept in responding to a serious drought in the northeast and as corrupt in a timber scandal involving Phao's faction. Then the Assembly conducted a major debate on the government's policies and actions, in the course of which harsh criticism of Phao and Phibun was expressed, including allegations that Phao was against the monarchy. In the midst of all this, Sarit and his chief deputies— generals Thanom and Praphas—resigned from the cabinet. As a popular journalist explained,

> The government usually does things contrary to the popular will. . . . Field Marshal Sarit promised the people before he joined the cabinet of Phibun that the government would reform many things which people have demanded and Phibun had given his word. But now five months have passed and the government has not made the reforms which the public wanted. Therefore, Sarit had to resign.[14]

A group of appointed legislators then also resigned from the government political party, and press and popular support for Sarit boomed.

Finally, on September 13, 1957, Sarit at the head of fifty-seven army officers formally demanded that the government resign and that Phao be removed from office. On September 15, a major public rally was held to support these demands, and the crowd marched to Sarit's home to show their support for him. Late on September 16, Phibun and Phao tried to gain the highest legal authority to sanction Sarit's arrest. They were refused, and Sarit was warned. At four the next morning the army staged a well-organized, lightning coup d'état in which no blood was shed. Phibun and Phao soon fled the country, and once more the military took over. Twenty-five years had brought enormous social and economic development, but politically the kingdom seemed stuck in 1932.

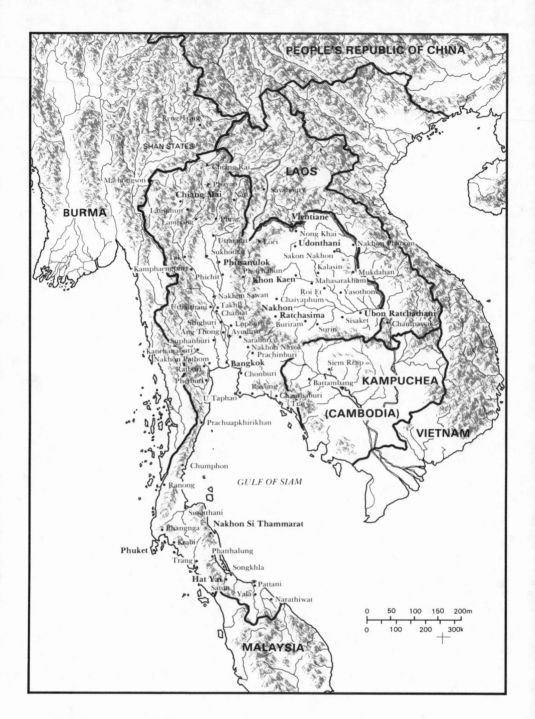

Twentieth-century Thailand.

IO

Development and Revolution, 1957–1982

At first consideration, the Thailand of the 1980s would not seem to be so different from the Thailand of Phibun—or, for that matter, from the Siam of King Chulalongkorn. All the central institutions still seem strong: the kingdom is a constitutional monarchy, the bureaucracy pervades almost every aspect of national life, the military dominates the political sphere, the economy remains predominantly agricultural with a somewhat alien urban business sector, the Buddhist monkhood is accorded special deference, and the economically disadvantaged and the cultural minorities of the outlying provinces still are imperfectly integrated into the national economy and society. The kingdom retains a paradoxical sort of national independence. It is an important participant in international affairs, yet it is still closely (and subordinately) allied economically with Japan and the Western industrial powers, politically with its ASEAN neighbors and the United States, and culturally with the West. Thailand's rulers hold up to the world an image of the country as an Asian haven of political stability and dynamic economic growth, a nation that almost miraculously has managed to maintain its distinctive cultural identity, its social hierarchy and order, and its Thai and Buddhist values, while its neighbors have slipped into seedy socialist decay or have so far modernized that they have lost their identity in a concrete maze of skyscrapers, fast-food palaces, and transistorized pop culture.

This is the same Thailand, however, that within the past decade has seen vicious political violence on the streets of Bangkok and ceaseless labor unrest with strikes and demonstrations previously unknown, involving not only a growing population of factory and other blue-collar workers but also thousands of farmers agitating for land reform and against bureaucratic insensitivity. In a country never distinguished for ideological passion, where a *mai pen rai* ("Never mind!") attitude toward public life seemed pervasive, the seventies saw a

massive outpouring of political sentiment on both the right and the left. The
Communist party of Thailand suddenly appealed to large numbers of young
Thai, not just bourgeois Chinese and intellectuals, and the Socialist party came
to seemingly permanent prominence, today regularly contesting parliamentary
constituencies. The self-assertion of the left, indeed, was so strong and its appeal
to youth so powerful as to belie the widely held impression that antiestablish-
ment ideology, and Western political thought in general, had never appealed to
Thai. When even prominent Buddhist monks took strong public stands on
political issues, voicing not only intolerance for the left but even commitment to
its physical extirpation, the polarization was complete, and gone was the old
image of the Thai nation as a single, happy, harmonious family-like community, placid in its allegiance to nation, Buddhism, and monarchy. Passions
exploded in violence, in public mistrust and suspicion, in demonstrations and
assassinations, for three chaotic years from 1973 to 1976, a period of profound
importance, the effects of which have shaped not only the Thailand of today
but also the Thailand of tomorrow and the day after.

The central problem in the recent political history of Thailand is not just to
explain how the relatively peaceful and orderly nation of the late 1950s and
early 1960s became the turbulent and confused Thailand of the eighties, nor is it
just to understand how the classical institutions of the Thai polity weakened to
the point where they failed fully to command the respect of the ruled. The
challenge also is to grapple with the question of how Thailand works—how,
indeed, the nation holds together, and how strong or weak are the bonds that
make up the society. Here we can do no more than suggest that Thailand's
successes, particularly in what might loosely be called development, while
alleviating many persistent social and economic problems, have themselves
created new problems, particularly political, to the point where revolution,
with all its associated uncertainties and ambiguities, has occurred and is
continuing to occur in Thailand.

Sarit as Paradox

Field Marshal Sarit Thanarat might be said to have come to power out of a
crisis of cultural transition. His Thai contemporaries were caught between the
older order and the new. The slow development of the Phibun era had loosened
the traditional bonds that held society together, and neither Phibun's feeble
political experiments nor new developing institutions had succeeded in forging
new ones to take their place.

At this critical moment, Sarit tried to provide his countrymen both a sense
of where they were coming from, in terms of traditional values and national

identity, and a clear vision of where they were going. In these respects he is not unlike some of his contemporaries—Nasser in Egypt, de Gaulle in France, Ayub Khan in Pakistan, and John F. Kennedy in the United States. Like some of them, his accession to power represented a generational change, in this case, the rise of a generation of leaders unique in twentieth-century Thailand. The generation of Sarit, Thanom, and Praphas is the only generation of modern Thai leaders to have been educated entirely in Thailand, as the sending of Thai students abroad had been extremely limited from the late twenties to the early fifties. This fact may account for their independent, Thai-centric ideology, for their greater respect for traditional institutions and values, for their confidence that they, better than their predecessors, could speak for the masses of their countrymen, and perhaps even for the limited receptivity they developed to some segments of public opinion. Although their commitment to traditional values and institutions enhanced their appeal to the more conservative elements in the establishment, at the same time it increasingly would work to distance them from younger, more modern-oriented members of the growing urban, civilian elite.

Field Marshal Sarit Thanarat, long-time associate and rival of Phibun and leader of the 1957 coup, was born in Bangkok on June 16, 1908, the son of an army major who among other things did Cambodian translations. He spent most of his earliest years, however, with his mother's Lao family in the Mukdahan district of Nakhon Phanom province. He returned to Bangkok for a bit of schooling, then at age eleven opted for a military career and entered the army officers' academy, from which he was graduated in 1928. His early army career seems to have been distinguished by able service in a variety of postings, all in Bangkok until 1938. He spent the war years in the Shan states, there making the important associations with Phao Siyanon and Phin Chunhawan that were to provide for his entry into politics in 1947, when he joined them in staging the coup that returned Phibun to power. Thereafter he rose rapidly, as we have seen, making his power base the critical First Army in Bangkok and rising to lieutenant-general in 1948, major-general in 1950, general in 1952, and field marshal in 1956.

In leading his coup against Phibun on September 17, 1957, Sarit emphasized that he was acting on behalf of the people and with their support. He abolished the Assembly seated by the "dirty elections" and installed an interim cabinet under Phote Sarasin, a diplomat who had just returned from service in Washington to become secretary-general of SEATO in Bangkok. While Phote reassured Thailand's American ally and prepared for December elections, Sarit went to the United States for urgent medical treatment (for cirrhosis of the liver). Following the elections, in which the government party secured a bare working majority, Phote refused to continue as prime minister, and after some prodding, Sarit's deputy, General Thanom Kittikachorn, took the post as an obvious stand-in for the absent Sarit. Thanom's problems quickly mounted. By-elections held in March gave the Democrat party thirteen new seats to the government's nine, and the Assembly proved truculent in facing budgetary problems. Even the government party would not work smoothly with the cabinet. Thanom felt helpless and would have preferred to resign.

Meanwhile, Sarit was recuperating in England and in mid-1958 was devoting much thought to the problems of Thailand. Reflecting on the self-serving and fractious behavior of legislators, on unbridled and mainly destructive press criticism, and on labor strife and demonstrations that seemed to him to be paralyzing the kingdom, Sarit concluded that drastic changes were needed in the political system. Over a period of several months, he consulted with Thanat Khoman and with the venerable Luang Wichitwathakan, now ambassadors to the United States and Switzerland, respectively, and determined that a "revolution" (*patiwat*) was needed to change Thailand. As Thanat soon was to explain,

> The fundamental cause of our political instability in the past lies in the sudden transplantation of alien institutions onto our soil without proper regard to the circumstances which prevail in our homeland, the nature and characteristics of our own people, in a word the genius of our race, with the result that their functioning has been haphazard and ever chaotic. If we look at our national history, we can see very well that this country works better and prospers under an authority, not a tyrannical authority, but a unifying authority around which all elements of the nation can rally.[1]

Sarit concluded that he must provide that authority. He returned quietly to Bangkok and, on October 20, 1958, abolished the constitution and declared martial law. More than a hundred critics of the government were arrested, including Chit Phumisak and intellectuals and journalists who had visited China, and the press was severely restricted. For the time being, Thailand was to be ruled by the decrees of the Revolutionary Council.

Sarit soon established a style of control that made his five-year government memorable and significant. He harped constantly on cleanliness and orderliness—he wished the streets to be repaired and clean, hooligans rounded up and petty crime reduced, prostitution brought under control. He viewed pedicabs as archaic and uncivilized, and banned them. He outlawed opium use and trafficking and took draconian measures against arsonists, having them publicly executed without trial almost literally on the spot of their crimes. He painted with the broad red brush of "communist" all opponents of his government, both communists and apolitical critics alike, and held them for long periods without bail or trial. Many segments of Thai society, people who increasingly had worried that the kingdom was slipping into anarchy, welcomed such authoritarian leadership and rule, while the small following of the Democrat party, primarily urban, and the considerable rural support for the northeastern politicians, were either outraged or cast politically adrift, not to surface again for fifteen years.

Sarit justified his regime on the basis of an original ideology, formulated in collaboration with Luang Wichit, that has long outlived him. As Thak Chaloemtiarana has reconstructed it,[2] this ideology or political philosophy was based on indigenous principles of authority, on a traditional type of social and political hierarchy, and on old paternalistic styles of rule, all expressed in terms of traditional Thai values. Instead of placing primary emphasis on loyalty to an abstract state or constitution, which he considered had not worked, Sarit focused primary attention upon the monarch as both the focus of loyalty for the citizen and the source of legitimacy for the government. Government, in turn, became a secular arm of the semisacral kingship and was worthy of respect and obedience by virtue of that connection. The social hierarchy, building up from the masses through the bureaucracy and government to the king, was stressed at the expense of democratic egalitarianism. The king was restored to the apex of the moral, social, and political order. Sarit attempted to redefine democracy to mean the responsiveness of the government and bureaucracy and the king to the people's needs and aspirations. This new, active responsiveness of government was to be asserted in a highly paternalistic manner. The society's leaders were to act toward members of the society as a father toward his children, solicitous of their welfare and stern in maintaining discipline.

Neither the public nor the army would have stood for a return of royal absolutism, and thus a division of labor between king and military-dominated government was necessary. Sarit restored the monarchy to an active role in Thai society, reviving public ceremonies that had been neglected since 1932, encouraging the king to appear in public, and making a major public show of allegiance to King Bhumibol Adulyadej. The king personally awarded all university degrees, for example, and made frequent tours of the provinces. The government gained authority by this association. It also gained credibility by the use it made of highly qualified experts and technicians, the vanguard of a new generation of foreign-trained Thai who took specialist jobs in cabinet and subcabinet positions. Finally, Sarit's government also attempted to legitimize its rule in democratic terms by advocating economic development in the public interest. In all of this, Sarit himself considered that his government, alone of all those since 1932, deserved the appellation "revolutionary," for he considered his regime to be devoted to a total restructuring of the social and political order.

The Sarit government's commitment to development soon could claim

King Bhumibol Adulyadej and Prime Minister Sarit Thanarat.

substantial accomplishments. More than any previous government, it attended to rural needs through highway construction, irrigation, rural electrification, and agricultural research and extension work. Particular attention was paid to the most densely populated and poorest regions of the country, and especially to the northeast, where Sarit acted out of his own family background and Lao roots. The government made concerted efforts to improve primary education and committed itself to lengthen compulsory primary schooling from four to seven years. It increased the numbers of students in secondary schools by 63 percent between 1958 and 1962, while also expanding vocational training. It increased the annual production of new teachers by 79 percent in the same period and began a major expansion at the university level by opening new universities in Chiang Mai and Khon Kaen and planning for similar expansion in the southern provinces. Coupled with all these efforts went stronger central-ized economic planning under the National Economic Development Board, with five-year development plans beginning in 1961 that particularly empha-sized infrastructure investment in irrigation, transportation, electric power, and education. Combined with liberal promotion of private and foreign invest-ment, the government's economic policies quickly achieved a high rate of growth in the gross national product, which during the 1959–69 period accelerated to 8.6 percent per year, nearly double what it had been in the previous decade. This was a very considerable achievement, supported in part by international aid and investment but ultimately dependent on Thai policy and expertise.

In a sense, of course, Sarit represented a generation and a political coalition, not just a faction within the army. His so-called revolution, his commitment to an authoritarian restructuring of the society founded on the primacy of the monarchy, gained him the support of the old bureaucratic nobility and royalists, while his advocacy of development and commitment to a free-enterprise economic order won him the support of the economic elite. He co-opted the small class of Western-educated technocrats by encouraging their participation in the expanding bureaucracy. Those who still opposed him, the rural politicians or leftist intellectuals, he silenced or eliminated.

Thai development in the period of Sarit and his immediate heirs took place in the context of an increasingly threatening international situation. The turning point came during the Laos crisis of 1960–61, in which the Thai were involved and with the outcome of which they were deeply concerned. A major impetus to the strengthening of Thai relations with the United States in the early 1950s and Thai accession to SEATO in 1954 had been the rise of Communist power in Vietnam and, especially, Vietnamese support for the leftist Pathet Lao movement of Prince Souphanouvong in Laos. The Thai in the mid-fifties countered by developing close relations with right-wing Lao elements, including General Phoumi Nosavan—who happened to be Sarit's cousin. After Laos gained full independence from France in 1953, the Pathet Lao had been shut out of government, but remained in military control of several Lao provinces bordering northern Vietnam. In 1957, however, Prime Minister Prince Souvanna Phouma negotiated a rapprochement that brought the Pathet Lao into the Lao government. The Thai military responded by briefly closing the frontier across which virtually all Laos's foreign trade flowed. Perhaps with Thai support or encouragement, the Lao right wing soon forced the Pathet Lao out and installed a government that included Phoumi Nosavan as minister of defense. At the end of 1959, after reports that North Vietnam was militarily supporting the Pathet Lao had provoked Thai attempts to gain first United Nations investigation and then SEATO intervention, both of which failed, Phoumi staged a coup d'état and installed another right-wing regime in Vientiane in April 1960. The Lao situation rapidly deteriorated into civil war, and the Thai became seriously alarmed at the growing strength of the Pathet Lao and at their military advances throughout Laos, feeling that communism now had come to their borders. They felt that SEATO had failed to function as they thought it had been intended to, and they felt betrayed when the United

Table 1   United States Economic and Military Assistance to Thailand,
              1958–1967 (millions of U.S. dollars)

Fiscal Year	1958	1959	1960	1961	1962	1963	1964	1965	1966	1967
Economic[a]	25.9	58.9	25.9	24.3	47.6	21.9	15.1	41.4	60.4	37.0
Military[b]	19.7	18.0	24.7	49.0	88.0	71.8	35.2	30.8	42.3	59.0

a. David A. Wilson, *The United States and the Future of Thailand* (New York, 1970), p. 144.

b. 1958–1960 from ibid.; 1961–1967 from U.S. Senate, Subcommittee on United States Security Agreements and Commitments Abroad, Committee on Foreign Relations, *United States Security Agreements and Commitments Abroad* (Washington, 1971, 1:633).

States abandoned the Lao right wing and supported the neutralist Souvanna Phouma, whose position at the head of a Lao government of national unity was secured by the Geneva Conference on Laos in July 1962.

Thai tolerance, if not acceptance, of this outcome was apparently obtained, first, by their receipt of a clear U.S. commitment to defend Thailand, whether or not SEATO agreed to do so, second, by the stationing of American troops in Thailand, and third, by major increases in U.S. military and economic aid. Economically, the Thai appear to have foregone economic aid in the interest of obtaining more military aid. Moreover, both economic aid and planning were redirected to accommodate security concerns, sparked by an upsurge of antigovernment insurgency, initially in the northeast. Militarily, American aid supported a military buildup in Thailand that was oriented toward Laos and then, increasingly, toward the Vietnam war.

Nor was Laos the Thai military's only concern. As Cambodian Prince Norodom Sihanouk began to draw into closer relations with Communist China in the late 1950s (in part, perhaps, to counter North Vietnam), Thailand supported the nationalist opposition against him and closed the border and broke off relations. A border dispute between the two countries involving a mountaintop temple (Preah Vihear) was submitted to the International Court of Justice at The Hague. Its decision against Thailand in 1962 seemed to the Thai to be unjust, though within the letter of international legal precedent.

Taken together, the deterioration of relations with Laos and Cambodia during this period worried the Thai military regime. Both involved areas over which the Thai felt they had strong historical claims, areas toward which they felt intuitively like "older brothers." The Thai military indeed had reconquered portions of Laos and Cambodia in 1940–41, only to be "robbed" of them by civilian politicians and great-power pressures in the immediate postwar period. Now the military in part legitimized its authority by claiming to defend Thai security against rising communist influence and control in

Indochina, yet they appeared helpless. It is just possible that in 1962 and 1963 they might have hoped to use American military training and hardware to prepare themselves for more drastic future action in Indochina should the need or opportunity arise. A more cynical assessment of their policies might lead to the conclusion that their primary preoccupation was to maintain and consolidate their military control of Thailand itself.

Sarit's health failed rapidly in 1963, and he died on December 8. Soon his family began squabbling over his estate, and it was revealed that he had left a fortune approaching $150 million, including large holdings in numerous business enterprises (like the company that held the monopoly on supplying gunny sacks for Thai rice sales), 20,000 rai (8,000 acres) of land, and numerous houses—and that, in addition to a grieving second wife, he had kept more than fifty mistresses. His reputation was suddenly, if briefly, tarnished—at least until the public experienced his successors and began to wonder whether Sarit hadn't been worth the price. He had been ruthless, privately grasping, arbitrary, and authoritarian. He had turned back the clock on parliamentary democracy and human rights, he had hitched Thailand's international position to the brightly blazing American star, and he had perhaps mortgaged the nation's future. He had established an enduring political philosophy that exaggerated traditional values and institutions, buttressing social and political hierarchy at the expense of egalitarianism and even human rights. This political legacy was difficult to overcome, however, because of Sarit's, and the military's, undeniable successes at development and his somewhat anachronistic public image as a man-on-horseback, a forceful leader, a man who got things done and cared about the quality of the lives of ordinary people.

Sarit's regime was in some important respects a paradox, for the two concepts that were central to his style and policies were contradictory. His self-proclaimed revolutionary goal was to restore a social and political order based on traditional Thai values, inherently monarchical and hierarchical. Development was intended to reinforce and justify this order, but in practice it worked to undermine it. Economic development strengthened the middle class; educational expansion contributed to the Westernization of their values, or at least to doubts about some Thai values; and close association with American policy created burning political issues. In the end, short-term strength and stability were purchased at the price of longer term instability and even political crisis.

In the Shadow of Vietnam, 1963–1973

On the death of Field Marshal Sarit, the military succession passed to General Thanom Kittikachorn, who long had been Sarit's deputy and in effect had served as his stand-in as prime minister in 1958. Thanom was generally regarded as a modest, relatively honest, and not very aggressive leader, who lacked the personality and magnetic leadership qualities of Sarit, but was more tolerant and flexible. He carried on with little change the political structure and even philosophy of Sarit through a whole decade as prime minister from 1963 to 1973. Throughout this period, as deputy prime minister and minister of the interior, General Praphas Charusathian was by his side. The alliance between these two was further cemented by the marriage of Thanom's son, Narong, with Praphas's daughter.

Three aspects of the Thanom-Praphas period seem now to have characterized it. The first has to do with the growing involvement of Thailand with the United States and the Indochina war. The second is the relentless thrust of development, the continuation of Sarit's initiatives to hasten the modernization of the kingdom. These first two in turn lead to the third, the inescapable political development of Thailand that first Sarit and then Thanom tried to halt and channel in other directions, but that ultimately led to a revolution quite different from what Sarit had intended. Many of the most strident debates of Thai public life over the past two decades have involved the country's complex relations with its neighbors and the rest of the world. On a narrow political level these debates have centered on questions involving Laos and Cambodia, or Indochina in general, on the kingdom's relations with the United States or the great powers, on its economic dealings with Japan or multi-national corporations, or on its cultural relations with the rest of the world. The debates often have been heated, with participants passionately expressing highly divergent and deeply felt views. Ultimately, what is at stake in such conflicts are fundamental issues involving the political, economic, and cultural integrity and independence of Thailand. No situation in modern Thai history better epitomizes this conflict than the issues arising from Thailand's entanglement with the United States and the Indochina war in the 1960s and 1970s.

One of the most persistent themes in the history of Thailand's foreign relations is expressed in the concern of the military with Laos and Cambodia, just as with all Thai governments since the eighteenth century. In their view, the long-term historical problem has been to integrate Vietnam into the politics of mainland Southeast Asia. This had not been a problem in earlier centuries, when Vietnam was oriented more toward China and was separated from the mainland powers by a rugged mountain barrier in the west and the buffer state of Champa along the coast to the south. But once the Vietnamese started to populate the Mekong Delta region in the eighteenth century, conflict had soon to come, as it did from Taksin's reign, first in Cambodia and then in Laos.

In their involvement in the Vietnam war, the Thai often were accused of having abandoned their traditional independence or neutrality in foreign policy in favor of close identification and involvement with a single great power, the United States. This argument distorts the past. As all readily admitted at the time, though technically evenhanded, Siam in fact had relied primarily upon Britain to blunt the more extreme imperial adventures of France. Similarly, during World War II, the Thai were closely allied with Japan and then abruptly shifted into a relationship with the United States that became ever closer in the postwar decades. The more threatened the Thai felt by developments in Indochina, the more they turned to the only great power with both the strength and the will to assist them—the United States. The first Indochina war in 1954 produced SEATO and a general multilateral commitment to come to Thailand's defense. The Laos crisis of 1960–61 produced the then secret Rusk-Thanat agreement, which committed the United States to the defense of Thailand, and it seems increasingly to have implied that the United States would defend Thailand against subversion from within, no less than invasion from abroad. The critical feature of the relationship with the United States as it developed during the period, however, is that it was by no means one-sided. The Thai were pursuing foreign policy goals of their own that were not necessarily congruent in every detail with those of the United States. They manipulated their relationship with the United States to pursue their own goals, which in the first place were to establish or maintain friendly, non-Communist, anti-Vietnamese governments in Laos and Cambodia.

The Thai military thus necessarily was drawn into the Vietnam war, which more properly must be termed the second Indochina war. In the early 1960s, when open warfare between North Vietnam and South Vietnam resumed, both Laos and Cambodia were immediately involved, though the neutralist governments in both these states attempted to disguise that fact. The North Vietnamese vitally depended on using the so-called Ho Chi Minh Trail through the mountains of southern Laos and northeastern Cambodia in order to supply their forces in the south. Both Thailand and the United States responded by intervening in Laos with very little publicity. North Vietnam and the People's Republic of China responded by supporting antigovernment insurgency in Thailand.

By mid-1964, the situation in Indochina looked increasingly threatening to Thailand and the United States. The Thai at that time agreed to a substantial upgrading of their military-base facilities and logistical systems, and from March 1964 U.S. aircraft were based at Takhli airfield in Nakhon Sawan province, 255 km. due north of Bangkok. After the Gulf of Tonkin incident in August of that year, additional U.S. aircraft were based at Khorat, while other military contingents operated out of Nakhon Phanom directed mainly against the Ho Chi Minh Trail region of southeastern Laos. The American military buildup continued from 1964 to 1968, and through most of this period and beyond, there were nearly 45,000 U.S. military (primarily air force) personnel stationed in Thailand, with nearly 600 aircraft, including B-52 bombers based at U Tapao. From these and other military installations in Thailand, the United States carried on air operations against North Vietnam and Laos, including bombing and aerial reconnaissance and supply; conducted electronic warfare with signals jamming, electronic intelligence gathering, and radar surveillance; and sent ground teams covertly into Laos and beyond.

Direct Thai involvement in the conflict also began early, with a Royal Thai Air Force contingent going to South Vietnam in mid-1964 and a naval contingent in 1965. Finally, in January 1967, the Thai agreed to send a ground combat unit to South Vietnam, and 2,200 Thai troops in Vietnam by mid-1967 grew to more than 11,000 by 1969—a force amounting to about 14 percent of the Royal Thai Army's total strength. Meanwhile, with or without American involvement and support, the Thai were conducting operations of their own in Laos. Reports from 1966 placed Thai troops in Laos, and the *Government Gazette* by then regularly named military casualties without indicating where they had been killed or wounded. None of these activities, however, seem to have provoked much controversy, as the Thai military traditionally appears to have been allowed a good deal of latitude in "military" affairs.

The effects of what they were doing, however, extended through nearly every aspect of the national life. It was not just that the economy was pumped up with American dollars and tens and even hundreds of thousands of Thai became dependent upon the American presence for their livelihood, nor was it simply that the Vietnam boom brought widespread corruption and commercial sin spawned in the hotels and honky-tonk bars and massage parlors of New Phetburi Road or Udon. The effects of this brief but intensive period ran much deeper. The economic attraction of the city, and of the service sector of the economy, worked to change social relationships even in farm families no less than it contributed to the social and economic interdependence between the ruling military elite and the Sino-Thai commercial elite. Young women and men went to the city to learn English and work as waiters and waitresses, bartenders and hotel desk clerks, prostitutes and masseuses, tour guides and souvenir shop clerks. The construction industry grew phenomenally, and roads and airstrips, hotels and coffee shops, and palatial dwellings for high-ranking foreigners and nouveau riche Thai were built. In the long run, the infrastructure for an exceptionally efficient and luxurious tourist industry would be developed, but in the short run, what was more important was the cultural and political impact of a suddenly intensive foreign presence in Thailand.

Until the late 1960s, full access to Western culture, to Western ideas, values, and fashions, was limited to a small Thai elite, but the Vietnam war period brought the outside world face to face with large segments of the population as never before. Here, the war simply accelerated what expanding educational opportunities and mass media exposure had begun a decade or so earlier. This direct exposure of much of the society to the West added force to the confrontation of Thai and Western values—noisily, for example, when aspiring musicians found a much readier market for their talents performing Western popular music than traditional Thai music, and when cassette tape audio recording could spread their achievements almost everywhere. With Western tastes and fashions came new ideas of social relationships (including, for example, sexual morality, ideas of romantic love, and the cult of youth supplanting the traditional respect accorded age) and a new questioning of existing Thai economic and political relationships. Bright university students became critical of the dominant position of Japan in Thailand's trade and in the modern sector of its economy, and, like youth elsewhere in the world, they were excited by the anti–Vietnam war movement to the point of questioning their own nation's role in that war.

Meanwhile, a combination of negative and positive factors led to the growth in the countryside of a political challenge to the ruling military government. Economists might argue about the extent to which real incomes in rural Thailand during the 1960s grew and whether the gap between rural and urban incomes diminished or increased. Ultimately, however, what mattered was what farm families *thought* was happening. As much as government efforts to improve conditions may have helped the rural poor, paradoxically they may have contributed to the farmer's consciousness—especially in the northeast— of just how badly off he was, both absolutely and by comparison with city people. And it is interesting to note that those rural people most willing to challenge the government turned out to be, not the poorest of the poor, but rather those in the best position, by virtue of their access to limited educational and economic opportunities, to see just how disadvantaged they were. It was people such as these whose disaffection turned to antigovernment insurgency.

Insurgency moved into high gear at the end of 1964 with the coalescence of the old leftist political opposition with the Communist party of Thailand in an attempt to coordinate their efforts and broaden their base. The first major threat soon came from insurgents in the northeast, directed by cadres trained in North Vietnam and Laos and involving a few thousand armed supporters, mainly northeasterners. By 1967, insurgency had spread far north to Chiang Rai and Nan provinces, where the combatants were mainly Hmong (Meo) led by Thai and Sino-Thai and probably supported and supplied from China. The following year similar forces began operating in the Loei-Phitsanulok-Phetchabun area. By this time, insurgency also was a serious threat in the mid-south (Suratthani and Nakhon Si Thammarat provinces), involving mainly Thai, and in the provinces of the extreme south, where Malay dissidents added to the military threat posed by Chinese troops of the Communist party of Malaya. The Thai now had serious internal trouble on their hand of a quantity and quality that no longer could be dismissed as it had been in the twenties—the revolutionary utopianism of a few discontented Chinese and Sino-Thai intellectuals.

By the early 1970s, the Thanom-Praphas regime faced a major security crisis. It was not simply that the army was mired in two exhausting conflicts, trying to stem a rising tide of internal insurgency while maintaining forces in Indochina. They also increasingly feared that their closest ally, the United States, was deserting them, when President Richard Nixon moved to Vietnamize the Indochina conflict, to let "Asians fight their own battles," and to reopen diplomatic relations with the People's Republic of China, a power the Thai military believed to be supporting antigovernment insurgency in Thailand. Field Marshal Thanom's response was to attempt to cash in on a decade of development, to bolster his now-aging regime with a bid for the support of those elements of Thai society that had most benefited from economic, social, and educational change. He was to find—like King Chulalongkorn in 1873–74, or Vajiravudh in 1912, or Prajadhipok in 1932, or even like Phibun in 1957—that their response lacked both gratitude and respect.

The Social and Political Costs of Development

We argued earlier that Sarit's simultaneous commitment to revolution and development was paradoxical, that development drove his revolution in a direction opposite from what he had intended. The logical opposite, as it turns out, is also true. To whatever extent Sarit and Thanom intended that development should enhance the stability and harmony of Thai society, it had just the opposite effect, to the point where we might think of Thai society in 1973 as being structurally weaker, or looser, than it had been a decade or so earlier. The processes by which this occurred are complex, and we can do no more here than to suggest their outlines.

In the starkest terms, the story of Thailand's development in the past two decades is told in a mind-numbing parade of statistics. The country's population has been soaring. From a small, underpopulated state before World War II, Thailand has become crowded and overpopulated relative to its present

Table 2   Selected Statistical Indicators, 1937–1980

	1937	1947	1960	1970	1980
Total population (000)	14,464	17,969	26,258	34,397	44,278
Median age	17.9	17.5	17.6	17.1	19.5
Urban population (000)					
Bangkok and Thonburi		782	1,703	2,496	4,711
as % of total population		4.4	6.5	7.3	10.6
					Est. 1978
Chiang Mai		38.2	65.7	83.7	105.2
Nakhon Ratchasima		22.3	42.2	66.1	87.4
Khon Kaen		14.4	19.5	29.4	80.3
Udon		13.1	30.9	56.2	76.2
Phitsanulok		13.2	30.4	33.9	73.2
Hat Yai		15.2	35.5	48.0	67.1
Songkhla		18.6	31.0	41.2	65.5
Nakhon Si Thammarat		16.7	25.9	40.7	61.0
Nakhon Sawan		17.4	34.9	48.9	55.7
Citizenship (%)					
Thailand	95.5%	97.0%	98.2%	98.9%	
China	3.7	2.7	1.6	0.9	
Literacy of those over 10 years of age					
Males	47.2%	67.4%	80.6%	88.9%	
Females	14.9	40.1	61.0	74.8	
Total	31.2	53.7	70.8	81.8	
					1980
Educational attainment of those 25 years and above					
No schooling	na	na	47.6%	33.1%	20.3%
Completed 4 years					
primary school	20.4%	na	33.5	47.5	69.0
Completed secondary					
school	0.2	1.8%	1.9	2.4	6.7
Completed university or					
equivalent	0.1	0.3	0.6	1.1	3.0
Agricultural households as percentage of all households					
			73.9%	62.9%	55.6%

SOURCES: 1937, 1947, 1960, 1970 Censuses; *Statistical Yearbook Thailand*, 1964 and 1974–1975; *Thailand Social Indicators 1978*; *Thailand into the 80's*; Correspondence, Mr. Ambhorn Arunrangsi, Secretary-General, National Statistical Office, August 20 and November 23, 1982; *Preliminary Report, 1980 Population and Housing Census* (1982).

resources. The population neared 18 million in 1947, then jumped to 26 million in 1960 and 34 million in 1970. By 1980 it had reached 44 million, and it is projected to reach nearly 60 million by 1990. The overall annual growth rate of 2.74 percent in 1974 dropped to 2.2 percent by the early eighties as a result of declining birth and death rates; but because its birth rate is still high, the population is exceptionally young—fully half the people of Thailand are under the age of twenty. This half is largely economically dependent on the other half, which must provide the funds for its upkeep and for the government's strong commitment to seven years of compulsory schooling. However, by the 1970s, scientific birth-control methods were sought equally by impoverished northeastern Thai villagers and prosperous Sino-Thai middle-class families in the cities. The recently published 1980 census results show a remarkable decline in the growth of the youngest age groups and a rise in the median age from 17.1 years in 1970 to 19.5 years in 1980.

For some years, it would appear that successive Thai governments were reluctant to undertake concerted efforts at population control. Certain influential figures are said to have argued that obedient Thai citizens would reduce the sizes of their families, while the Chinese minority would expand as a proportion of the population. However, during the past three decades, Thailand's "Chinese problem" has been steadily subsiding in importance. There has been no appreciable Chinese immigration into Thailand for thirty years, and the proportion of Chinese nationals (citizens) to Thai citizens has been dropping precipitously, from 3.7 percent of the total population in 1937 to 1.6 percent in 1960 and 0.9 percent in 1970. There are many more people who are Thai citizens but speak Chinese and identify themselves as Chinese. Their numbers, however, though they cannot be counted, are shrinking even more rapidly because of Thai educational policy, which has restricted Chinese education, and especially because of the many subtle social and economic pressures for assimilation. The ladder to success in the Thailand of the 1960s and 1970s, at a time of rapid economic growth, consisted of Thai education, Thai surnames, Thai language, and even intermarriage with Thai families.

Thailand has changed drastically over the past two decades. The most forceful changes have occurred in Bangkok, which has tripled in size and seems to be choking with congestion and air pollution. The skyline is jagged with high-rise construction—tourist hotels, government offices, apartment buildings, and commercial firms. The sprawl of the suburbs is punctuated by rambling factories producing everything from automobiles to mass-produced traditional crafts. Nor are such urban developments confined to Bangkok alone. They are found in once-sleepy provincial towns like Phitsanulok and Hat Yai, or Khorat, Khon Kaen, and Udon in the northeast.

Villages, too, have changed dramatically. For example, the remote village of Nong Sung, in the mountainous hinterland of Mukdahan district, Nakhon Phanom province in the northeast, used to be unreachable in the rainy season when the road was under water. Now it has a paved, all-weather road, piped water, electricity, refrigerators and a few television sets, a secondary school, and many dozens of village sons and daughters who have gone on to universities and teacher-training colleges and then to prestigious jobs in the government bureaucracy.

A close examination of two sets of statistics suggests how widespread such phenomena have become. First, agricultural households as a percentage of total households dropped from 73.9 percent in 1960 to 62.9 percent in 1970 and 55.6 percent in 1980. These figures may be somewhat deceptive, disguising a certain proportion of rural people who carry on agriculture in addition to other pursuits, but it should signal the fact that Thailand is no longer simply a bucolic, rural, rice-growing society. Rapidly increasing numbers of Thai now follow nonagricultural pursuits, and there has been a phenomenal increase in the diversity of Thailand's occupational structure, which now includes computer programmers and industrial chemists as well as farmers and fishermen.

Second, the country's modern manufacturing sector has undergone significant structural change. The economy of 1960 was heavily biased toward extractive activities—agriculture, forestry, and mining—and manufacturing was mainly for export. In the 1960s, under a government policy that promoted industrial development primarily to substitute locally made products for imports, the food-processing industry lost its dominant position in the industrial sector. When government development policy shifted in the 1970s toward export-oriented industry, the manufacturing sector boomed and diversified; it soon came to account for more than one-third of total export earnings and utilized a much smaller proportion of the labor force.

It is not that agriculture has ceased to perform economically. Despite its enormous population growth, Thailand continues to be one of the few steady rice-exporting countries left in the world, rice yields having been greatly improved with the onset of the so-called Green Revolution that brought improved seeds and technology to much of Asia's agriculture. At the same time, however, Thailand's farmers have diversified their crops, and by the late 1970s rice finally was surpassed by another agricultural commodity, tapioca, as Thailand's leading export, while the value of manufactured goods exported exceeded all exports of a decade earlier. Tourism cannot be classified as an export in the same way commodities and manufactured goods are, but it is the equivalent of an export because of its contribution to the kingdom's balance of payments. Earnings from tourism increased from about 250 million baht in

Table 3   Ranking of Major Exports, 1961–1978
              (by value in millions of baht)

1961			1970			1978	
1. Rice	3,598	1. Rice	2,516	1. Tapioca	10,837
2. Rubber	2,130	2. Rubber	2,232	2. Rice	10,403
3. Jute and kenaf	626	3. Maize	1,969	3. Rubber	8.020
4. Tin[a]	617	4. Tin[a]	1,618	4. Tin[a]	7,225
5. Maize	597	5. Tapioca	1,223	5. Textiles	6,863
6. Tapioca	428	6. Jute and kenaf	719	6. Maize	4,215
7. Teak	252	7. Mung beans	255	7. Sugar	3,913
8. Cement	53	8. Frozen shrimp	224	8. Electronic circuits	2,148
9. Sugar	26	9. Fluorite	222	9. Precious stones	1,709
10. Textiles	23	10. Tobacco	197	10. Frozen shrimp	1,488
11. Precious stones	21	11. Teak	156	11. Beans	1,342
12. Tobacco	16	12. Sorghum	103	12. Canned pineapple	1,195
		13. Sugar	94	13. Tobacco	1,148
		14. Cement	83	14. Frozen squid	1,019
				15. Wolfram	945

a. Ore to 1965; smelted tin thereafter.
SOURCES: 1961 from *Statistical Yearbook Thailand* (1964), pp. 323–29; 1970 and 1978 from *Thailand Into the 80's* (Bangkok, 1979), p. 206.

1961 to 2,209 in 1971 and 5,600 in 1978. On the face, these statistics are impressive. Thailand has successfully diversified its economy and reduced its dependence on a few highly vulnerable primary crops. However, in the mid-1970s, Thailand was caught in the worldwide slump in prices of primary commodities and in the catastrophic rise in the prices of petroleum and manufactured goods which the country imports in great quantities. Inflation suddenly became a very serious problem, and most affected was the burgeoning middle class that economic and educational development had created.

It is difficult to define this new Thai middle class. A standard definition by income would be misleading, even if it could be constructed. We might rather suggest its shape and size by examining a few other critical social indicators. It is predominantly urban and nonagricultural, and we have seen how these segments of the population have grown. It has arisen in Bangkok and a handful of provincial towns and cities almost entirely since 1960. For this group, modern education at the secondary level and above is the sine qua non for status and the middle-class life-style—which includes access to the mass media, especially television, sufficient income to assure quality education for one's children, and the achievement of some sense of upward social and economic mobility. Here it

Table 4   Educational Attainments, 1937–1980
           (in thousands)

	1937	1947	1960	1970	1980
Finished primary school (4th year)	1,142	2,475	7,371	12,535	26,756
Finished secondary school (10th year)	13	87	276	575	3,471
Any college or university education	5	10	95	186	868

SOURCE: Census, 1937, 1947, 1960, 1970, *Preliminary Report 1980 Population and Housing Census* (1982).

may be useful to examine the absolute numbers of people attaining various educational levels in the years since 1937.

The figures show a clear progression over recent decades. During the last twenty years, the proportion of high school graduates to primary school graduates has increased fourfold. While there were twenty-six primary school graduates to each secondary school graduate by 1960, there were only seven to one by 1980. The increase in the proportion of students gaining higher education has been just as dramatic. The increase in the relative proportion of youths continuing on to secondary and higher education certainly is important, for it reflects increased educational opportunities and changing economic and social aspirations. Just as significant, however, are the absolute numbers of such persons, which include men and women in almost equal proportions. The tenfold increase in the number of university graduates over the past two decades, from less than a hundred thousand to nearly a million, coupled with a similar rise in the number of secondary school graduates, has given Thailand's middle class a critical mass. Their size and prosperity makes them a prime target audience of mass-market advertising and the mass media. Because of their education, experience, and life-style, their values and behavior set them apart from the masses of rural society to some degree; and because their numbers are far too large fully to be absorbed into the hierarchical structure of the government bureaucracy and armed forces, they are not an integral part of the ruling establishment either. Each year their numbers swell, as enrollments in higher education continue to increase, from 107,634 in 1974 to 169,639 in 1978 and to more than 200,000 by the early 1980s.

Recent decades have been difficult and challenging for the middle class. Government employment has not been expanding as rapidly as the numbers of university graduates, and for the first time large numbers of young middle-class and aspiring middle-class Thai have had to consider entering careers in the private sector. There they find themselves more vulnerable to economic fluctuations and to judgment on the basis of their performance than they traditionally did in the civil service. They have felt relatively less secure and perhaps less certain of their social standing. These changes have shaped their political reactions and aspirations and have contributed to the volatility of Thai politics over the past decade.

This is not necessarily to argue that a Thai middle class has emerged that is fully conscious of its distinctive identity and interests. Judging only by its members' behavior, one might conclude that the growth of a middle class has strengthened a traditionalistic sort of Thai political conservatism. The members of this class have a clear interest in preserving a relatively privileged social and economic position. At the same time, their formal values—the liberal values gained from schooling and encouraged through their exposure to Western political life—increasingly have made them uncomfortable with authoritarian military rule and with those elements of Thai cultural tradition that they regard intellectually as superstitious or, by international standards, inhumane. Their interests thus lead them to value order and some modicum of hierarchy and to fear instability and any rapid, fundamental changes in the existing economic and political order. Thus, while they would support the overthrow of the Thanom-Praphas regime in 1973, they also would join the right-wing reaction against the political chaos of 1976.

The middle class has yet to act as a dominant force in Thai political life, for some of the same reasons that worked to encourage military primacy in the 1930s. The middle class of the 1970s and 1980s is, indeed, far more fragmented than their fathers' and grandfathers' generation. It is not just that their numbers are so much larger and that the private sector is so much more significant than it used to be. Even the bureaucracy and the military are impossibly large and amorphous, and to the old cleavages between separate bureaucratic organs are added new divisions between higher and lower officers, between seniors and juniors, between different educational and social backgrounds. Beneath a high degree of public conformity there lurks much rivalry, dissension, and conflict. This is true even within the army itself, where, for example, junior "Young Turks" and "Democratic Soldiers" factions have challenged the ruling group of generals. If even the army increasingly could not act as a single political entity for all its resources, then it was all the less likely that a segmented and pluralistic middle class could do so. At the same time, the growing political consciousness of the middle class has made it all the more necessary for Thailand's rulers to take both their interests and their values into account.

Much the same has occurred, though on a lesser scale and at a slower rate of development, with respect to Thailand's farmers and workers, who have been both the beneficiaries and the victims of development. At the very least, insurgency and the threat of insurgency won the government's attention to rural problems, particularly in the more remote and most impoverished regions of the country. This attention, supported by considerable U.S. and other economic aid, bore some fruit. Roads built or improved in order to enhance the government's ability to respond to military challenges in the long run made possible the increasing integration of remote villages into the national economy. Efforts to improve education and public health brought some real benefits, as did an ambitious program to improve drinking-water supplies and eradicate malaria. Irrigation projects and agricultural extension efforts hastened the Green Revolution, while improved communications and development of the economic infrastructure supported crop diversification and improved marketing of agricultural surplus. At the same time, the growth in rural income was not equally shared among Thailand's farmers, and the combination of rapid demographic growth and the exhaustion of the supply of new lands led to a decrease in the average farm size, an increase in agricultural tenancy, and the flight of youth from the farms to the already oversaturated urban labor market.

Increased government presence in the rural villages also served to heighten dissatisfaction. Villagers became more subject to military and police harassment or bureaucratic corruption and bungling; their expectations, raised by overly optimistic government promises of development, frequently were not fulfilled; and they became conscious of how far they lagged behind more prosperous regions and city dwellers. These developments heightened political consciousness and fed both insurgency and farmers' and labor unions by the early 1970s. As strong as such movements had by then become, however, they had nothing like the strength and immediacy of middle-class disaffection with the military regime. At best, rural discontent may have served to legitimize the student and middle-class commitment to political change.

Revolution and Reaction, 1973–1976

Ruling under a short provisional constitution, Sarit a decade earlier had appointed a Constituent Assembly to deliberate on a permanent constitution and thereby, perhaps grudgingly, reaffirmed a basic commitment to democratic institutions. A whole generation of the Thai middle class grew up exposed to democratic ideals in secondary and higher education, as they studied the history and institutions of Western democracies. Thanom came under increasingly heavy pressure to loosen his grip—pressure from Americans uncomfortable in their alliance with an authoritarian military regime, and pressure from a Thai middle class represented especially by the hundreds of thousands of secondary school and college students in Bangkok. In 1968, the Thanom government therefore issued a new constitution, which, like that of 1932, provided for a bicameral legislature comprising an elected lower house and an appointed Senate. Elections held in February 1969 produced a majority for the government party in the lower house, and Thanom continued as prime minister. This democratic experiment, like all those before it, failed when Thanom in effect staged a coup against himself in November 1971, dissolved Parliament, banned political parties, and again ruled under an interim constitution that restored military dominance over the government.

The reasons for the failure of this experiment were complex. The government was having difficulty getting its budgets through the lower house, and it was alarmed by what it perceived to be a collapse of national solidarity in the new atmosphere of competition among political parties, relaxed press controls, and rising political activity, particularly among the young, who demonstrated against the Thai alliance with the United States and against the government's slow pace of economic development. The military rulers of Thailand were all the more worried by the implications for Thailand's security in the U.S.–China rapprochement and the Vietnamization of the Indochina war. They feared a diminution of American support and a decreased U.S. willingness to defend Thailand against the fate beginning to overtake Cambodia and Laos. But, most of all, the Thanom-Praphas regime must instinctively have hesitated to relax military control at a time when the Thai army itself seemed to be losing its solidarity and cohesiveness. Thanom and Praphas were approaching the mandatory retirement age (sixty years), and their only clear successor was Thanom's son (and Praphas's son-in-law) Lieutenant-Colonel Narong Kittikachorn, whose support within the army was by no means strong and who was popularly regarded as corrupt.

Thanom's reinstatement of full military control, however, was by no means a solution for these problems. His strong-man approach to political crisis was one that had worked for Phraya Phahon in 1933, for Phibun in 1938 and 1947, and for Sarit in 1957–58, but it could no longer succeed in Thailand. It was not just that the military elite could not agree among themselves; the problem was more profound than that. Thai society as a whole—workers and farmers little less than students and the middle class—no longer seemed willing to accept a regime that appeared to represent only military interests in the guise of national security and the public welfare. Whether selfishly or altruistically, they expected some direct voice for their own grievances and interests, some sharing of political power well beyond what the military was willing to allow.

In the end, it was the students, that social group least wedded to the current order and most oriented toward the future, who ended the Thanom-Praphas regime. They felt betrayed. They had been led to expect political

The October revolution of 1973. Crowds assemble at the Democracy Monument
commemorating the revolution of 1932.

evolution, and their hopes were dashed by Thanom's reimposition of military
rule. They began to act on a new political consciousness and militancy and soon
gained much popular sympathy.

By mid-1973, they had become a major political force. Student demonstrations began in June over the expulsion of university students for antigovernment
publications and snowballed in October when critics calling for a constitution
in public handbills were arrested. Massive demonstrations involving between
200,000 and 500,000 persons, including university students, secondary and
technical school students, and many young members of the middle class,
demanded the release of the critics and the promulgation of a constitution. This
led to clashes with the police, and the violence escalated into attacks on police
stations and government offices. At the critical moment, Thanom was unable to
get even the army support he needed. Cooler military heads refused to send
their troops against civilian mobs and gained the support of King Bhumibol.
On October 14, 1973, Thanom and Praphas were forced to resign and hastened
out of the country to exile abroad.

In many important respects, the events of October 1973 deserved far more
the name *revolution* than either the events of 1932 or the authoritarian program

of Sarit. They brought about an end to one-man, authoritarian rule; and if they did not bring an end to the military role in politics, then they at least signaled a new consciousness of the necessity of sharing political power more widely than had ever been the case in the past. By this time, there was widespread agreement on what was wrong with the old system of government: corruption; the subordination of national interests to military self-interest; arrogant insensitivity to the interests and values of other social, economic, and cultural groups; insufficient commitment to and progress toward economic and social reform; and what was perceived as excessive dependence on and subservience to America and the West.

The vanguard of the movement was the students, who perhaps in more extreme form voiced the sentiments of many of their countrymen. They gave voice to a long, but previously always suppressed, tradition of dissent, even citing the critique of military rule given by King Prajadhipok on his abdication in 1935. They gave new popularity to the writings of the leftist literati of the forties and fifties. They had at least the good will, and perhaps the support, of even the king and elements in the army. They embarked upon an ambitious experiment of democratic reform exhilarated by the confidence that came from their conviction that the whole country shared their negative assessment of the old regime. At the same time, they underestimated the extent to which many Thai disagreed over the positive policies and ideological commitments upon which a future might be built.

The initial outcome of October 14 was a civilian government under the prime minister, Dr. Sanya Dharmasakti, a distinguished legal scholar who had been rector of Thammasat University and was president of the Privy Council and therefore close to the king. A new constitution calling for a unicameral, fully elected parliament was promulgated, and elections were scheduled for January 1975. Led or inspired by students, political organization and activities took place on an unprecedented scale, involving even strikes by urban laborers and mass demonstrations by dissatisfied farmers. Students organized political instruction in the villages, while political parties sprang up everywhere. Public expression was exceptionally free, and newspapers and magazines circulated all shades of opinion. The writings of the leftist intellectuals of the forties and fifties, like Chit Phumisak and Kulap Saipradit, were reissued, and Marxian socialism was in vogue. Bookshops were stacked with the writings of Mao, Kim Il Sung, Ho Chi Minh, Lenin, and Stalin, and one could find tracts calling for class struggle and revolution or detailing methods for making Molotov cocktails and ambushing government troops. The left, even the far left, was fully out in the open, confident that a new democratic and socialist day was at hand. The organization of labor unions and peasant associations was well under way, all initially directed toward the 1975 elections.

The elections gave no party a clear majority in Parliament. At first, the veteran politician Seni Pramoj, successor to Khuang Aphaiwong as head of the Democrat party and heir to a long political tradition, tried to govern in a coalition with two leftist parties, but this effort collapsed after two weeks. It then fell to his brother Kukrit Pramoj to organize a government. In some deft maneuvering, Kukrit managed to form a coalition of seventeen parties of the center and right, headed by his moderate Social Action party. He gained some initial successes in securing a promise of rapid American troop withdrawals from Thailand and negotiating the resumption of diplomatic relations with the People's Republic of China, both of which were popular.

Changes in Thailand's international situation contributed to souring Kukrit's easygoing and somewhat chaotic coalition. Beginning in early 1975, Communist power won dramatic victories in Indochina as Cambodia and South Vietnam collapsed and the Pathet Lao consolidated its power in Laos and abolished the six-hundred-year-old Lao monarchy. The climate of uncertainty grew on both the left and the right and exacerbated the tensions within Kukrit's already unstable coalition. Though the government's attempts to secure a complete U.S. withdrawal from Thailand were contentious, it was domestic issues that forced Kukrit, facing a non-confidence vote in Parliament, to resign in January 1976 and call for new elections he expected unrealistically to win.

The parliamentary elections of April 1976 seemed initially to promise improved stability. With the Democrats holding 114 of the 279 seats, Seni Pramoj returned to power and ruled in coalition with four parties of the center and right. The parties of the left had done poorly, and now held only 6 of their previous 37 seats. Seni, however, was hamstrung because of the conflicts within his ruling coalition; he made little progress toward solving any of the critical problems of the day, not the least of which were public order and economic reform (including rural land reform). While feuding politicians entertained or exasperated the readers of the Bangkok press, leftist university students alienated much of their following by rhetorical excesses. A counterreaction began rapidly to develop on the political right.

Quite early, the monarchy, the urban elite, and much of the middle class had become frightened by the radicalism of the students, whom they viewed as either Communist directed or inspired. Their support soon swung to a variety of new organizations of the right wing, most of which had backing in the military or the bureaucracy. These included the New Force movement (Nawaphon), based mainly on networks of personal connections in the bureaucracy, which worked to suppress the left in the name of "nation, religion, and king"; the enormously popular Village Scouts organization of youngsters and adults devoted to ferreting out communists and upholding patriotic values; and the Red Gaurs, the breakaway vocational-student faction of the 1973 student movement, which in their attacks on the left frequently resorted to violence. By 1976, political assassinations, invariably of figures on the left, were commonplace. Police harassed the electioneering of leftist parties, and even active moderates were afraid for their safety. Violence, vituperation, and incivility were now a part of public life as they never had been before in Thailand.

The political tempo accelerated to a violent climax in October 1976. Former Prime Minister Thanom had returned from exile to lead the life of a Buddhist monk (at the monastery that had been Mongkut's headquarters). His return had been welcomed by the right wing, and his respectability seemed confirmed when members of the royal family visited him. The university students were outraged at this reception of one held responsible for the violence of 1973, and daily demonstrations began, especially at Thammasat University. Quietly but directly supported by elements of the military and the government, and implicitly sanctioned by broad sectors of the ruling establishment—including economic interests and much of the middle class—the right wing struck back. On October 5, several Bangkok newspapers published photographs depicting Thammasat students hanging Crown Prince Vajiralongkorn in effigy, and an army radio station called upon patriots to join against the students and "kill communists!" Massive assaults were launched against Thammasat University, in which Village Scouts, Red Gaurs, the police, and others engaged in an orgy of violence. Students were lynched, burned alive, and beaten on October 6, brutally ending the brief democratic experiment as the military again moved in to suspend the constitution and clamp down on political expression. Many Thai were revolted by the barbarity of this episode and feared for a future that now looked very bleak for a Thailand convulsed by political violence.

The 1973–76 period imprinted the minds of virtually all Thai with vivid memories and impressions, though those mental images are filtered and tinted by individuals' values and interests, and few would interpret them unambiguously. All must have gained some heightened appreciation of the value of order, though many would disagree on the values on the basis of which that order might be constructed. The Thai political culture of the eighties owes to this period its consciousness, its dramatic definition of issues, and even its sense of national community, no matter how fragmented the community often seems to be. Much of the middle class carries from that period a renewed commitment to an at least loosely hierarchical public order structured by "nation, religion, and monarch," as well as a heightened distrust of both the military and university intellectuals. Farmers and workers are perhaps ambivalent, caught between a surer sense of what remains wrong about Thai society and skepticism as to what can now be done about it. Students and intellectuals gained an awareness of

Marxian ideology, as well as a broad repertoire of political tactics and styles they have continued to exercise. But they also suffer a barely suppressed rage at the events of October 6 and a feeling of helplessness over their apparent inability to change Thai society. Finally, since the 1973–76 period, the military's cohesion and self-confidence have been eroding, at least to the point where they are willing now to tolerate conflict and dissent to a degree unimaginable before 1973. Before they got to this point, however, they had to reach some new accommodation with a changed society and body politic. This process took them another five years.

Hesitation and Uncertainty, 1976 and After

In the wake of October 6, 1976, Thailand briefly underwent a forcible throwback to an authoritarianism more extreme, even, than the absolute monarchy had been. The military Administrative Reform Council had installed as prime minister over an appointed government a former high court justice, Thanin Kraivichien. Ironically, it turned out that this man, a civilian and a lawyer, was more authoritarian and repressive than any of his military predecessors. Rigid censorship was imposed, labor unions silenced, the ranks of bureaucrats and teachers purged of dissidents and required to undergo anticommunist indoctrination. The right wing was too exultantly triumphant, while the left wing and even many moderates were so alienated as to flee to exile or to join the insurgents in the hills. The latter included many of the student leaders of 1973–76 and a number of prominent intellectuals, including Khamsing Srinawk; the former included Dr. Puey Ungphakorn, former governor of the Bank of Thailand and rector of Thammasat University.

The military stood aside just long enough for Thanin's regime to discredit itself and then stepped back into the political fray to arrange his dismissal in October 1977. General Kriangsak Chomanand, with somewhat narrow backing in the army, became prime minister and promised yet another constitution and elections by 1979. He was able at least to stem right-wing violence, and he encouraged the return of many exiles from the hills and abroad. The gloom and despair of the Thanin period was somewhat dispelled.

By the time of the 1979 elections, however, a new kind of worry had set in with the Vietnamese invasion of Cambodia early that year. The Thai now had hostile forces on their eastern borders, hundreds of thousands of refugees from Cambodia and Laos, and various guerrilla groups attempting to operate across the border. Kriangsak's government party forged a bare majority in Parliament by drawing small parties and independents into his coalition, but his power base was weak and he was unable to effect improvements in the worsening economic stiuation or the Kampuchean crisis. He was finally forced from power by General Prem Tinsulanonda, commander-in-chief of the army, in February 1980—again by resignation rather than coup. Prem began promisingly, with a broadly based parliamentary coalition that included the Democrat party and Kukrit's Social Action party giving him more than 180 seats in the 301-member house. Few members of his large cabinet were military men, and he won considerable support by appointing respected experts to key positions managing economic policy. Prem was known to have broad military backing owing to a record untainted by corruption and distinguished by field operations against insurgency in the northeast. The king was believed also to be strongly behind him.

Prem has maintained his position longer than his immediate predecessors in the face of continuous difficulties, among the most serious of which stemmed from the Vietnamese invasion and domination of Cambodia. Intermittently, from 1980 onward, Vietnamese troops crossed the Thai frontier in force to attack Khmer partisans, and on each occasion the Thai have had to mount strong counterattacks to secure their borders. These episodes have served to reinforce the Thai sense of threat from a Vietnamese-dominated Communist Indochina.

Against this threat, the Thai have pursued a broad range of policies intended, if not to roll back the Vietnamese presence, then at least to balance Thai and Vietnamese power in these traditional buffer states. Militarily, the Thai successfully have called upon the United States for military backing in the event of more serious Vietnamese incursions, even offering permanent military bases in return for such assurances. Meanwhile, they have worked through the United Nations and the Association of South East Asian Nations (ASEAN), in which they have played a major role, to prevail upon the Vietnamese to withdraw their troops and broaden their Kampuchean government. They have sought and obtained the aid and support of China, which had been at war with Vietnam at the time of the Vietnamese invasion of Cambodia and which remained hostile to a Soviet-influenced Vietnam. They have put indirect pressure against Vietnam by briefly closing the Thai border with Laos, cutting off that nation's external trade. They have supported a wide variety of Khmer guerrilla groups and have facilitated their supply by China on Thai soil; they have continued quietly to support rightist insurgents against the Khmer and Lao governments; and they worked long and hard to pull together a unified Khmer liberation movement under their long-time nemesis, Norodom Sihanouk.

Meanwhile, Thailand has been burdened with enormous numbers of refugees from Cambodia and Laos, whose very existence has diminished the revolutionary appeal of the Thai left of a few years ago. If revolution *à la Vietnamien* (or Pol Pot or Pathet Lao) is the wave of the future, then that future is now, and it is no longer very enticing.

Certainly it became clear by the early 1980s that the end of the Indochina war had not automatically brought peace, stability, or prosperity. Serious problems remained: a dangerous international situation especially vis-à-vis Communist Indochina; high inflation and economic problems arising from skyrocketing petroleum and energy costs and global economic stagnation; and difficulty in deciding how the great powers might or might not be able to work together in the interest of peace. In addition, there were more parochial problems: rural insurgency abated, but continued to be a potent latent threat; dissident sentiments were running very high in Thailand's Muslim south; non-Thai hill peoples especially in the north were exploited and poorly integrated into the nation, if at all; the agricultural sector of the economy simply could not absorb rapid population growth; and the modern industrial sector was not expanding rapidly enough to ease growing unemployment.

In facing these problems, Thailand was laboring under an inherently conservative political and social structure. The army and bureaucracy were riddled with vested interests and factionalism. Frequently they were unable to act together in the nation's interest but rather fought among themselves in defense of selfish interests. For all of a half-century of democratic experiments, the Thai had not yet devised durable political institutions that might successfully mediate among the divergent interests of a rapidly developing and changing society. Authoritarian rule no longer worked, and for most, the attractions of the strong-man leader had long since faded. While many remained caught up in the traditional, highly structured social hierarchy in which all knew their place and politics was the business of those at the top, increasingly large numbers of the middle class now felt that politics was their business, too. Not even the army any longer believed that authority could grow out of the muzzles of the First Army's artillery; but neither could all agree blindly to accept royal authority in its place. While most would agree that there was no going back either to military dictatorship or to the chaos of 1973–76, there was no consensus as to the proper balancing of social, political, and economic interests.

For all its hesitation and uncertainty as to the future, however, the Thai state continues to display a strength and resiliency that should not surprise those familiar with the kingdom's long history. The military responses to border conflict with Vietnamese Indochina have been cautious and measured, and though the potential for conflict remains high, there is no present indication that it will get out of hand. Thai diplomats continue skillfully to court the most diverse friends and allies, East and West, Communist and non-Communist alike. Careful management and planning show signs of restoring rapid growth to the economy, aided by the undiminished confidence of foreign investors. The serious insurgency of a few years ago has abated as most of the student leaders and intellectuals who fled to the jungle in 1976 have surrendered and returned to civilian society. And finally, in April 1983, a turning point of some sort was reached with the holding of national parliamentary elections that confirmed the military and Prem's government in power.

Perhaps the most fascinating development of the sixties and seventies was the reentry of the monarchy into politics. It had begun slowly, when King Bhumibol quietly signaled his dissatisfaction with Field Marshal Phibun by refraining from attending ceremonies marking the 2,500th anniversary of Buddhism in 1957. Sarit subsequently gave the monarch a much more visible public role and helped secure the position of the monarchy at the top of the social hierarchy as the central, if still powerless, figure in the political structure. More direct involvement came in the seventies, when the king played an active role in swinging support away from Thanom and Praphas and toward the students. Soon, however, the royal family came to be closely identified with such right-wing activists as the Village Scouts, and they were at the center of the storm that ended the era of "full democracy" and brought Thanin to power. Royal support subsequently helped in the rise of Prem.

The culminating incident occurred in connection with an abortive coup in 1981, when a group of Young Turk military officers, critical of the failures of past military governments, seized government centers in Bangkok early on April 1. General Prem fled the capital in the company of the royal family and established headquarters at the provincial army base at Khorat. Soon a message from Queen Sirikit was read over Khorat Radio in effect supporting Prem's government. Royal support for Prem prevented the rebels, led by General Sant Chitpatima, from mobilizing the allegiance even of all military units in the Bangkok region. On April 3, Prem was able to retake Bangkok at the cost of only two wounded. Again, the monarchy was out in the open, exposed, identified with one politico-military group at the expense of another.

There are many reasons for this development and many ways in which it enhanced the strength and stability of Thailand, at least up to a point. For many years, most people saw the king as being, if not above politics, then as involved in Thai politics generally for the interests of all Thai. When he intervened, it was usually to restrain excesses, whether of the extreme left or the extreme right. He legitimized the holders of political power so long as they exercised that power within vaguely defined permissible limits. He also was perceived to be an ultimate resort in time of crisis, accessible equally to individual petitioners and general public opinion.

All this occurred within the framework of the traditional social hierarchy. His power is moral and social, and it might be abused by him, by others in his name, or by his successor. Those who wish to see radical changes in Thailand increasingly are impatient with monarchy, which they view as hopelessly identified with the authoritarian military structure and a corrupt and inefficient bureaucracy. Those who would not discard the system, but work within it, look to the king not only to define political limits but also to assist them in pressing government to respond more rapidly and effectively to their needs and demands. With these pressures from both the right and the left, Thailand's political future in highly ironic fashion depends in some important respects on the monarch. Because of this fact and because two generations of royal monogamy have reduced the potential candidates for succession to the throne, the Succession Law recently was changed to allow women to succeed to the throne; both Prince Vajiralongkorn and Princess Sirindhorn have been designated as heirs presumptive.

More than two decades ago, Thailand's military regime embarked on a course of revolution and development. A generation now is coming of age that is both the creation and the heirs of those policies. The next group of Thailand's leaders is different in many ways. They are highly educated men and women, many of whom were trained abroad. Their values and experience make them much more comfortable with mass politics and at home in a complex international situation in ways that Sarit's generation could not be. They bear, perhaps, the scars of past conflict, the emotional and political consequences of the 1973–76 period, but they also possess a stronger sense of political and social values than their elders. Certainly they carry with them not only a commitment to development, in all the varied senses of that term, but also an ambitious vision of a modern Thailand. Although many of them might be uncomfortable with the term *revolution*, their very existence as a group—as a large, urban, well-educated, and prosperous middle class—is a product of a real revolution in the Thai social and political order, the full consequences of which may take generations to evolve.

Appendix A

KINGS OF SUKHOTHAI

1. Sri Indraditya	?1240s–?1270s
2. Ban Müang	?1270s–?1279
3. Ramkhamhaeng	?1279–1298
4. Lö Thai	1298–1346–47
5. Ngua Nam Thom	1346–47
6. Mahathammaracha I (Lüthai)	1346–47–1368–74?
7. Mahathammaracha II	1368–74?–1398?
8. Mahathammaracha III (Sai Lüthai)	1398–1419
9. Mahathammaracha IV	1419–1438

Appendix B

KINGS OF LAN NA

1.	Mangrai (from 1292 in Chiang Mai)	1259–1317
2.	Chai Songkhram	1317–1318
3.	Saen Phu	1318–1319
4.	Khrüa	1319–1322
5.	Nam Thuam	1322–1324
6.	Saen Phu (second reign)	1324–1328
7.	Kham Fu	1328–1337
8.	Pha Yu	1337–1355
9.	Kü Na	1355–1385
10.	Saen Müang Ma	1385–1401
11.	Sam Fang Kaen	1401–1441
12.	Tilokaracha	1441–May 24, 1487
13.	Yot Chiang Rai	1487–1495
14.	Müang Kaeo	1495–1526
15.	Ket Chettharat	1526–1538
16.	Chai	1538–1543
17.	Ket Chettharat (second reign)	1543–1545
18.	Queen Chiraprapha	1545–1546
19.	Setthathirat (of Lan Sang)	1546–1551
20.	*Thao Mae* Ku (Queen)	1551
21.	Mekuti (perhaps same as no. 20?)	1551–1564
22.	Queen Wisutthithewi (under Burmese suzerainty)	1564–1578
23.	(Burmese) Tharawaddy Prince	1578–1607
24.	(Two sons of no. 23?)	1607–1613
25.	Thadogyaw	1613–1615
26.	Si Song Müang	1615–1631
27.	Phraya Thipphanet	1631–1659

310

28. (Ruler of Phrae)   1659–1672
29. Ingsemang (Burmese)   1672–1675
30. Chephutarai (Burmese)   1675–1707
31. Mangraenara (Burmese)   1707–1727
32. Thep Sing (rebel)   1727
33. Ong Kham   1727–1759
34. Chan   1759–1761
35. Khi Hut   1761–1762
36. Abhayagamani (Burmese)   1762–1768
37. Moyagamani (Burmese)   1768–1771
     Revolt of Lan Na   1771–1774

CHAO OF CHIANG MAI

1. Kavila (1775–1781 in Lampang)   1781–1813
2. Thammalangka   1813–1821
3. Kham Fan   1821–1825
4. Phutthawong   1825–1846
5. Mahawong   1846–1854
6. Kavilorot   1856–1870
7. Intanon   1871–1897
8. Suriyawong   1901–1911
9. In Kaeo   1911–1939

Appendix C

KINGS OF AYUDHYA

1.	Ramathibodi	1351–1369
2.	Ramesuan	1369–1370
3.	Borommaracha I	1370–1388
4.	Thong Chan	1388
5.	Ramesuan (second reign)	1388–1395
6.	Ramaracha	1395–1409
7.	Intharacha	1409–1424
8.	Borommaracha II	1424–1448
9.	Borommatrailokanat	
	(ruling in Ayudhya)	1448–1463
	(ruling in Phitsanulok)	1463–1488
10.	Borommaracha III	
	(in Ayudhya)	1463–1488
11.	Intharacha II	1488–1491
	(nos. 10 and 11 are the same)	
12.	Ramathibodi II	1491–1529
13.	Borommaracha IV	1529–1533
14.	Ratsada	1533–1534 (5 months)
15.	Chairacha	1534–1547
16.	Yot Fa	1547–June 1548
17.	Khun Worawongsa (usurper)	June–July 1548
18.	Chakkraphat	July 1548–January 1569
19.	Mahin	January–August 1569
20.	Maha Thammaracha	August 1569–June 1590
21.	Naresuan	June 1590–April 25, 1605
22.	Ekathotsarot	April 25, 1605–October 1610/November 1611

23. (Si Saowaphak   1610–1611?)
24. Song Tham (Intharacha)   1610–11–December 13, 1628
25. Chettha   December 13, 1628–August 1629
26. Athittayawong   August–September 1629
27. Prasat Thong   September 1629–August 7, 1656
28. Chai   August 7–8, 1656
29. Suthammaracha   August 8–October 26, 1656
30. Narai   October 26, 1656–July 11, 1688
31. Phra Phetracha   July 11, 1688–1703
32. Süa   1703–1709
33. Phumintharacha (Thai Sa)   1709–January 1733
34. Borommakot   January 1733–April 13, 1758
35. Uthumphon   April 13, 1758–May 1758
36. Suriyamarin   May 1758–April 7, 1767

KING OF THONBURI

Taksin   late 1767–April 6, 1782

KINGS OF BANGKOK, CHAKRI DYNASTY

1. Phra Phutthayotfa (Rama I)   April 6, 1782–September 7, 1809
2. Phra Phutthaloetla (Rama II)   September 7, 1809–July 21, 1824
3. Phra Nangklao (Rama III)   July 21, 1824–April 3, 1851
4. Mongkut (Rama IV)   April 3, 1851–October 1, 1868
5. Chulalongkorn (Rama V)   October 1, 1868–October 23, 1910
6. Vajiravudh (Rama VI)   October 23, 1910–November 26, 1925
7. Prajadhipok   November 26, 1925–March 2, 1935
                                    (abdicated)
8. Ananda Mahidol   March 2, 1935–June 9, 1946
9. Bhumibol Adulyadej   June 9, 1946–

Appendix D

PRIME MINISTERS OF THAILAND, 1932–1982

1. Phraya Manopakonnitithada (Kot Hutasing) — August 28, 1932–June 20, 1933
2. Phraya Phahonphonphayuhasena (Phot Phahonyothin) — June 21, 1933–December 16, 1938
3. Luang Phibunsongkhram (Plaek Phibunsongkhram) — December 16, 1938–July 24, 1944
4. Khuang Aphaiwong — August 1, 1944–August 17, 1945
5. Thawi Bunyaket — August 31, 1945–September 17, 1945
6. M.R.W. Seni Pramoj — September 17, 1945–January 31, 1946
7. Khuang Aphaiwong — January 31, 1946–March 18, 1946
8. Pridi Phanomyong — March 24–August 21, 1946
9. Luang Thamrongnawasawat (Thawan Thamrongnawasawat) — August 23, 1946–November 8, 1947
10. Khuang Aphaiwong — November 10, 1947–April 8, 1948
11. P. Phibunsongkhram — April 8, 1948–September 16, 1957
12. Phot Sarasin — September 21, 1957–December 26, 1957
13. Thanom Kittikachorn — January 1, 1958–October 20, 1958
14. Sarit Thanarat — February 9, 1959–December 8, 1963
15. Thanom Kittikachorn — December 9, 1963–October 14, 1973
16. Sanya Dharmasakti — October 14, 1973–February 15, 1975
17. M.R.W. Seni Pramoj — February 15–March 6, 1975
18. M.R.W. Kukrit Pramoj — March 14, 1975–January 12, 1976
19. M.R.W. Seni Pramoj — April 20, 1976–October 6, 1976
20. Thanin Kraivichien — October 8, 1976–October 20, 1977
21. Kriangsak Chomanand — November 11, 1977–February 28, 1980
22. Prem Tinsulanonda — March 3, 1980–

Notes

Chapter 1

1. I am grateful to Dr. Anthony Diller, of the Australian National University, for help in shaping the ideas in this section.

2. G. H. Luce, trans., *Man Shu (Book of the Southern Barbarians)* (Ithaca, N.Y.: Cornell Southeast Asia Program, 1961), pp. 83–84.

Chapter 2

1. "Tamnan Suwanna Khom Kham" [Chronicle of Suwanna Khom Kham], in *Prachum Phongsawadan* [Collected chronicles], pt. 72 (Bangkok, 1961), p. 46 (hereafter cited as *PP*); French translation in Camille Notton, *Annales du Siam*, vol. 1 (Paris, 1926), p. 121.

2. "Tamnan Singhanawati" [Chronicle of Singhanawati], in *PP*, pt. 61 (Bangkok, 1973), p. 75; French translation in Notton, *Annales*, vol. 1, p. 186.

3. Than Tun, "A History of Burma Down to the End of the Thirteenth Century," *New Burma Weekly*, Jan. 3, 1959, p. 25.

4. Li Fu-i, *Ch'e-li hsüan-wei shih hsi k'ao ting* [A revised study of the genealogy of Ch'e-li pacification chieftaincy] (Ch'e-li, 1947), pp. 1–3, 44; read with the assistance of Dian Murray.

Chapter 3

1. G. H. Luce, "The Early *Syam* in Burma's History," *Journal of the Siam Society* 46, pt. 2 (Nov. 1958): 161 (hereafter cited as *JSS*), quoting contemporary Chinese sources.

2. *Tamnan phün müang Chiang Mai* [Chiang Mai local chronicle] (Bangkok, 1971), p. 13 (hereafter cited as *TPMCM*); French translation in Notton, *Annales*, vol. 3 (Paris, 1932), p. 28.

3. Quoted from a variant text of the Chiang Mai chronicles by Notton, *Annales*, vol. 3, p. 49, n. 2.

4. A. B. Griswold and Prasert na Nagara, "The 'Judgments of King Măṅ Rāy': Epigraphic and Historical Studies, no. 17," *JSS* 65, pt. 1 (Jan. 1977): 153. Griswold and

Prasert translate *phrai* as "citizen," while I prefer "freeman" and have changed the translation accordingly.

5. Griswold and Prasert, "The Inscription of King Rāma Gaṃheṅ of Sukhodaya (1292 A.D.): Epigraphic and Historical Studies, no. 9," *JSS* 59, pt. 2 (July 1971): 205–08.

6. Ibid., pp. 207–08.

7. Ibid., p. 216.

Chapter 4

1. Paul Pelliot, trans., *Mémoires sur les coutumes du Cambodge de Tcheou Ta-Kouan*, Oeuvres posthumes de Paul Pelliot, vol. 3 (Paris, 1951), pp. 32, 34.

2. Pelliot, *Mémoires*, p. 30; translation from J. Gilman d'Arcy Paul, *Notes on the Customs of Cambodia by Chou Ta-kuan* (Bangkok, 1967), p. 37.

3. Richard D. Cushman, trans., "The Royal Chronicles of Ayutthaya," unpublished ms., p. 22. All Western writers on Ayudhya's history record the date of its foundation as A.D. 1350. The Siamese texts all say 712 of the *chulasakkarat* era—a year that began on March 28, 1350, and ended on March 27, 1351. The year 712 began on the fourth day of the waning moon of the fifth month, so the sixth day of the waxing moon of the fifth month did not occur that year until March 4, 1351.

4. Jeremias van Vliet, *The Short History of the Kings of Siam*, trans. Leonard Andaya (Bangkok, 1975), p. 61.

5. Ibid.

6. A. B. Griswold and Prasert na Nagara, "A Declaration of Independence and Its Consequences: Epigraphic and Historical Studies, no. 1," *JSS* 56, pt. 2 (July 1968): 207–49.

7. *TPMCM*, p. 72; French translation in Notton, *Annales*, vol. 3, p. 153.

8. G. E. Harvey, *History of Burma* (London, 1925; reprint, 1967), p. 106.

9. Cushman, "Royal Chronicles," p. 136.

10. Ibid., pp. 74–75.

11. Ibid., p. 136; emphasis added.

Chapter 5

1. Cushman, "Royal Chronicles," p. 298.

2. "Report from the Council at Batavia (Jakarta) to the Dutch East India Company, Jan. 21, 1657," in *Records of the Relations between Siam and Foreign Countries in the 17th Century*, vol. 2 (Bangkok, 1916), p. 20.

3. George Vinal Smith, *The Dutch in Seventeenth-Century Thailand* (DeKalb, Ill., 1977), p. 35.

4. ibn Muhammad Ibrahim, *The Ship of Sulaiman*, trans. John O'Kane (London, 1972), pp. 94–97.

5. van Vliet, *Short History*, pp. 87–88.

6. Smith, *Dutch*, p. 35.

7. Paul le Boulanger, *Histoire du Laos français* (Paris, 1931), p. 109.

8. Quoted in *Kingdom of Laos: The Land of the Million Elephants and of the White Parasol*, ed. René de Berval (Saigon, 1959), pp. 63–64.

9. *Phraratchaphongsawadan chabap phraratchahatlekha* [Royal autograph edition of the royal chronicles (of Ayudhya)], ed. Prince Damrong Rajanubhab (Bangkok, 1962), 2:218; cf. Cushman, "Royal Chronicles," pp. 1016–17.

10. *Koun-hpaung-hset maha-yazawin-taw-kyi* [Royal chronicles of the Konbaung era (of Burma)] (Rangoon, 1967), 1:382.

11. Somdet Phra Wannarat, of Wat Phra Chetuphon, *Saṅgītiyavaṃsa: phongsawadan rüang sangkhayana phra tham winai* [Saṅgitiyavaṃsa: Chronicle of the great councils] (Bangkok, 1923), pp. 409–10.

Chapter 6

1. Sarasin Viraphol, *Tribute and Profit: Sino-Siamese Trade, 1652–1853* (Cambridge, Mass., 1977), p. 144, citing a writing by King Mongkut, dated 1853, from the Thai National Library.

2. François Henri Turpin, *History of the Kingdom of Siam*, trans. B. O. Cartwright (Bangkok, 1908), pp. 178–79; original French ed., 1771.

3. Letter from King Mongkut to Sir John Bowring, n.d., printed in Sir John Bowring, *The Kingdom and People of Siam* (London, 1857; reprint, Kuala Lumpur, 1969), 1:65–66.

4. "M. Coude to the Directors of the Foreign Missions Seminary, 1780," in Adrien Launay, *Histoire de la Mission de Siam, 1662–1811; Documents historiques, II* (Paris, 1920), p. 301.

5. Craig J. Reynolds, "The Buddhist Monkhood in Nineteenth Century Thailand," Ph.D. diss., Cornell University, 1972, p. 33.

6. Journal of M. Descourvieres, [Thonburi], Dec. 21, 1782; in Launay, *Histoire*, p. 309.

7. *Kotmai tra sam duang* [Three Seals Laws], 5 vols. (Bangkok, 1962–63), 1:5.

8. *Latthithamniam tangtang* [Customs and practices], 2 vols. (Bangkok, 1961–62), 1:495–96.

9. *Kotmai tra sam duang*, 1:5.

10. Chaophraya Thiphakorawong (Kham Bunnag) and Prince Damrong Rajanubhab, *Phraratchaphongsawadan Krung Rattanakosin ratchakan thi 1 ... ratchakan thi 2* [Royal chronicles of the First and Second Reigns of the Rattanakosin era] (Bangkok, 1962), p. 222.

11. David Porter Chandler, "Cambodia before the French: Politics in a Tributary Kingdom, 1794–1848," Ph.D. diss., University of Michigan, 1973, p. 76.

12. Prince Chula Chakrabongse, *Lords of Life: The Paternal Monarchy of Bangkok, 1782–1932* (New York, 1960), p. 118.

13. Thiphakorawong and Damrong, *Phraratchaphongsawadan*, pp. 432–36.

14. Sir Thomas Stamford Raffles, *Substance of a Memoir on the Administration of the Eastern Islands* (n.p., 1819), p. 5.

15. Chaophraya Thiphakorawong, *Phraratchaphongsawadan Krung Rattanakosin ratchakan thi 2* [Royal chronicle of the Second Reign of the Rattanakosin era] (Bangkok, 1961), pp. 201–02.

16. "Diary of Capt. Henry Burney, Jan. 5, 1826," in *The Burney Papers*, 4 vols. (Bangkok, 1910–14; reprint, Farnborough, Hants., 1971), 1:87–88.

17. Quoted in Chandler, "Cambodia before the French," p. 150.

18. Prince Wachirayanwarorot, *Tamnan Wat Bowonniwetsawihan* [History of Wat Bowonniwet] (Bangkok, 1922), p. 18.

19. Letter of D. B. Bradley, March 28, 1851, in *Straits Times* (Singapore), July 8, 1851; quoted in William L. Bradley, "The Accession of King Mongkut," *JSS* 57, pt. 1 (Jan. 1969): 156.

20. Chaophraya Thiphakorawong, *Phraratchaphongsawadan Krung Rattanakosin ratchakan thi 3 . . . ratchakan thi 4* [Royal chronicles of the Third and Fourth Reigns of the Rattanakosin era] (Bangkok, 1963), p. 366.

Chapter 7

1. I am grateful to Noel Battye for calling this information—taken from American missionary archives—to my attention.

2. Wong Lin Ken, "The Trade of Singapore, 1819–1869," *Journal of the Malayan Branch, Royal Asiatic Society* 33, no. 4 (Dec. 1960): 278; and James C. Ingram, *Economic Change in Thailand 1850–1970* (Stanford, 1971), pp. 332–35. During the third quarter of the century, the baht was valued at about eight to the pound sterling; and a picul was approximately sixty kg.

3. King Mongkut to President Franklin Pierce, Feb. 14, 1861; in Abbot Low Moffat, *Mongkut, the King of Siam* (Ithaca, 1961), p. 89.

4. Chula, *Lords of Life*, p. 261.

5. Ibid., p. 263.

6. *Straits Times* (Singapore), May 16, 1957.

7. *Bangkok Times*, Jan. 26, 1898.

8. John B. Murdoch, "The 1901–1902 'Holy Man's' Rebellion," *JSS* 62, pt. 1 (Jan. 1974): 57.

9. Ingram, *Economic Change*, p. 38.

10. Lauriston Sharp and Lucien M. Hanks, *Bang Chan: Social History of a Rural Community in Thailand* (Ithaca, N.Y., 1978).

Chapter 8

1. Walter F. Vella, *Chaiyo! King Vajiravudh and the Development of Thai Nationalism* (Honolulu, 1978), p. 9.

2. *The Souvenir of the Siamese Kingdom Exhibition at Lumbini Park B.E. 2468* (Bangkok, 1927; reprint, 1976?), p. 167, quoting from a speech delivered by Vajiravudh at his coronation in 1911.

3. Benjamin A. Batson, "The End of the Absolute Monarchy in Siam," Ph.D. diss., Cornell University, 1977, p. 22; *Bangkok Times*, June 25, 1932.

4. Vella, *Chaiyo!*, pp. 60–75.

5. Chula, *Lords of Life*, p. 290.

6. Stephen L. W. Greene, "Thai Government and Administration in the Reign of Rama VI (1910–1925)," Ph.D. diss., University of London, 1971, p. 326.

7. M. C. Wibun Sawatwong, *Khwamsongcham* [Memoirs] (Bangkok, 1943), pp. 28–29.

8. Batson, "Absolute Monarchy," p. 50.

9. The memorandum, written in English, is reproduced in full in Benjamin A.

Batson, comp. and ed., *Siam's Political Future: Documents from the End of the Absolute Monarchy*, rev. ed. (Ithaca, 1977), pp. 13–22.

10. Reproduced in ibid., pp. 48–50; quotation from p. 49.

11. G. William Skinner, *Chinese Society in Thailand: An Analytical History* (Ithaca, 1957), p. 183.

12. Batson, "Absolute Monarchy," p. 72.

13. *Bangkok Times*, February 13, 1932, in Batson, *Siam's Political Future*, p. 80. I have amended the translation of the fourth sentence on the basis of the original Thai text, from Batson, p. 73, n. 6.

14. Kenneth Perry Landon, *Siam in Transition: A Brief Survey of Cultural Trends in the Five Years Since the Revolution of 1932* (Chicago, 1939; reprint, New York, 1968), p. 10.

Chapter 9

1. Batson, *Siam's Political Future*, p. 102.

2. I am indebted to Benjamin A. Batson for this information.

3. Thamsook Numnonda, *Thailand and the Japanese Presence, 1941–45* (Singapore, 1977), p. 23.

4. S. Woodburn Kirby, *The War against Japan*, vol. 1 (London, 1957), p. 186.

5. Benjamin A. Batson, "The Fall of the Phibun Government, 1944," *JSS* 62, pt. 2 (July 1974): 110.

6. *Foreign Relations of the United States, Diplomatic Papers*, 1945, vol. 6 (Washington, 1969), p. 1375.

7. John Coast, *Some Aspects of Siamese Politics* (New York, 1953), p. 42.

8. Charles F. Keyes, *Isan: Regionalism in Northeastern Thailand* (Ithaca, 1967), pp. 33–34.

9. Ibrahim Syukri, *Sejarah Melayu Kerajaan Patani* [History of the Malay Kingdom of Patani] (Pasir Puteh, Kelantan, ca. 1961), from a manuscript translation by John N. Miksic and Conner Bailey.

10. *Bangkok Post*, Nov. 30, 1951; cited in Frank C. Darling, *Thailand and the United States* (Washington, 1965), p. 92.

11. A selection of Khamsing's short stories is available in English translation as *The Politician and Other Stories* (Kuala Lumpur, 1973).

12. David A. Wilson, *The United States and the Future of Thailand* (New York, 1970), p. 144.

13. *Sayam Nikon* (Bangkok), March 3, 1957; translated in Thak Chaloemtiarana, *Thailand: The Politics of Despotic Paternalism* (Bangkok, 1979), pp. 108–09.

14. Thai Noi and Kamon Chantarason, *Watoelu khong Chomphon Plaek* [The Waterloo of Field Marshal Plaek (i.e., Phibun)] (Bangkok, 1957), p. 3; translated in Thak, *Thailand*, p. 118.

Chapter 10

1. *Bangkok Post*, March 10, 1959; quoted in Thak, *Thailand*, p. 156.

2. Thak, *Thailand*, pp. 152–71.

Suggestions for Further Reading

The bibliography of Thai history begins only a century ago, when printing in Thailand began and interest in the country's history arose. A full listing of all the materials relevant to the serious study of this subject would require at least another full volume in itself. Here I can do little more than suggest some of the most useful and important works on Thai history, confining myself primarily to those available in Western languages.

General

Much of the best work is quite recent and for the most part is not yet published in book form. It consists of academic dissertations, most of which are available through University Microfilms in Ann Arbor, Michigan. Dissertations characteristically include exhaustive bibliographies of their subject. Articles on Thai history appear regularly in the *Journal of the Siam Society* (hereafter *JSS*) (Bangkok, 1904–) and the *Journal of Southeast Asian Studies* (Singapore, 1970–). One good guide to the field is Charles F. Keyes, *Southeast Asian Research Tools: Thailand* (Honolulu, 1979).

Two especially good geographical references are Robert L. Pendleton, *Thailand: Aspects of Landscape and Life* (New York, 1962), and Larry Sternstein, *Thailand: The Environment of Modernisation* (New York, 1976). Among the most important of the general introductions to Thailand are Frank J. Moore, *Thailand: Its People, Its Society, Its Culture*, rev. ed. (New Haven, 1974); the old army "area handbook," *Thailand: A Country Study* (Washington, 1980); and Thailand, Office of the Prime Minister, *Thailand Into the 80's* (Bangkok, 1979), which has superb color illustrations.

A few intrepid souls have attempted to write general histories. The first was W. A. R. Wood, *A History of Siam* (London, 1926; reprint, Bangkok, 1959), which covered the Bangkok period in just eight pages and is now badly outdated. Rong Syamananda, *A History of Thailand* (Bangkok, 1973) and M. L.

Manich Jumsai, *Popular History of Thailand* (Bangkok, 1972) are quite brief and uncritical.

The Beginnings of Tai History

Frank M. LeBar, Gerald C. Hickey, and John K. Musgrave, *Ethnic Groups of Mainland Southeast Asia* (New Haven, 1964), provide an excellent ethnographic survey of the Tai peoples with a good bibliography and fold-out map. Materials on the prehistory of the region and the Tai peoples are widely scattered and deserve to be brought together. Wilhelm G. Solheim II, "Northern Thailand, Southeast Asia, and World Prehistory," *Asian Perspectives* 13 (1973): 145–62, and Chester F. Gorman and Pisit Charoenwongsa, "Ban Chiang: A Mosaic of Impressions from the First Two Years," *Expedition* 18, no. 4 (1976): 14–26, are representative of a great deal of exciting work in this field. The most recent linguist to have ventured speculation in print on the subject of linguistic development is James R. Chamberlain, "A New Look at the History and Classification of the Tai Languages," in *Studies in Tai Linguistics in Honor of William J. Gedney*, ed. Jimmy G. Harris and James R. Chamberlain (Bangkok, 1975), pp. 49–66.

Two articles suffice to sort out the "Nan-chao problem": F. W. Mote, "Problems of Thai Prehistory," *Sangkhomsat parithat* 2, no. 2(Oct. 1964): 100–09; and Hiram Woodward, "Who Are the Ancestors of the Thais? Report on the Seminar," *Sangkhomsat parithat* 2, no. 3 (Feb. 1965): 88–91. G. H. Luce translated the contemporary account of Nan-chao by the Chinese official, Fan Ch'o, the *Man Shu (Book of the Southern Barbarians)* (Ithaca, N.Y., 1961). The early history of Nan-chao is treated in Charles Backus, *The Nan-chao Kingdom and T'ang China's Southwestern Frontier* (New York, 1982).

For an overview of mainland Southeast Asia in the ninth and tenth centuries, one could hardly do better than G. Cœdès, *The Indianized States of Southeast Asia*, trans. Susan Brown Cowing (Honolulu, 1968). A provocative map of the region in this period is in Georges Maspero, "La géographie politique de l'Indochine aux environs de 960 A.D.," in *Études asiatiques publiées à l'occasion du vingt-cinquième anniversaire de l'École Française d'Extrême-Orient* (Paris, 1925), 2:79–125.

The Tai and the Classical Empires, A.D. 1000–1200

Cœdès, *Indianized States*, provides good, general background. H. G. Quaritch Wales, *Dvaravati, The Earliest Kingdom of Siam (6th to 11th Century A.D.)* (London, 1969), is an excellent overview, but needs revision in the light of more recent archeological excavations and finds. The *Camadevivamsa* chronicle of Haripunjaya is among those translated by Camille Notton, *Annales du Siam*, vol. 2 (Paris, 1926–32; Bangkok, 1939); and the *Jinakalamali* chronicle is available in English translation by N. A. Jayawickrama, *The Sheaf of Garlands of the Epochs of the Conqueror*

(London, 1968). On chronicle sources in general, with an extensive bibliography, see David K. Wyatt, "Chronicle Traditions in Thai Historiography," in *Southeast Asian History and Historiography: Essays Presented to D. G. E. Hall*, ed. C. D. Cowan and O. W. Wolters (Ithaca, 1976), pp. 107–22.

Angkor's history is stiffly summarized in L. P. Briggs, *The Ancient Khmer Empire* (Philadelphia, 1951).

The early history of the Tai of the Yonok country must remain highly conjectural until its problematic sources have been worked over more carefully. The most important of the chronicle materials are translated in the first volume of Notton, *Annales du Siam*; but he appears to have used a much abridged version of the *Singhanavati* chronicle, and his rendering of dates is highly suspect. G. H. Luce, *Old Burma—Early Pagan*, 3 vols. (Locust Valley, N.Y., 1970), is the classic synthesis of Pagan's history, now importantly supplemented by Michael Aung Thwin, "The Nature of State and Society in Pagan: An Institutional History of 12th and 13th Century Burma," Ph.D. diss., University of Michigan, 1976. Material on early Shan history is in vol. I, pt. 1, of James George Scott and J. P. Hardiman, *Gazetteer of Upper Burma and the Shan States* (Rangoon, 1900).

A Tai Century, 1200–1351

The basic Ahom chronicle is the *Ahom Buranji*, trans. and ed. Golap Chandra Barua (Calcutta, 1930). The text appears badly edited, and the translation is neither literal nor complete. For secondary sources, see Sir Edward Gait, *A History of Assam*, rev. and enlarged by B. K. Barua and H. V. S. Murthy (Calcutta, 1963); and N. N. Acharrya, *The History of Medieval Assam (from the Thirteenth to the Seventeenth Century)* (Gauhati, 1966). On the fall of Pagan, an especially useful analysis, based on Burmese sources, is Paul J. Bennett, "The 'Fall of Pagan': Continuity and Change in 14th-Century Burma," in *Conference under the Tamarind Tree: Three Essays in Burmese History* (New Haven, 1971), pp. 3–53. Good Shan materials are included in Scott and Hardiman, *Gazetteer*, and in Sao Saimong Mangrai, *The Padaeng Chronicle and the Jengtung State Chronicle Translated* (Ann Arbor, 1981).

G. H. Luce's magisterial two-part article, "The Early Syam in Burma's History," *JSS* 46, pt. 2 (Nov. 1958): 123–214, and 47, pt. 1 (June 1959): 59–101, ties together much of northern Southeast Asia during this period, based particularly on Chinese-language sources.

The Kingdom of Lan Na still awaits serious scholarly attention by those willing to undertake study of the Tai Yuan language and script. Notton, *Annales*, vol. 3, is a translation of one version of the Chiang Mai chronicle, while the published central Thai version differs from it on many points. Many other texts await critical study, including early chronicles from all the various principalities in the quadrangle defined by Chiang Mai, Nan, Chiang Hung, and Keng Tung.

In their monumental series of articles, "Epigraphic and Historical

Studies," beginning in *JSS* 56, pt. 2 (July 1968), A. B. Griswold and Prasert na Nagara systematically have established and translated the texts of the earliest Tai inscriptions of Sukhothai and its neighbors, improving considerably on the earlier work of G. Cœdès, done in the 1920s. They have stimulated some critical discussion, also in the pages of the *JSS*, especially by M. C. Chand Chirayu Rajini and Michael Vickery. Griswold's *Towards a History of Sukhodaya Art* (Bangkok, 1967) is an especially genial work.

Ayudhya and Its Neighbors, 1351–1569

The most important primary sources on the history of the Kingdom of Ayudhya are the various versions of the Ayudhya chronicles, of which only two very short versions are available in translation: O. Frankfurter, trans., "Translation of Events in Ayuddhya 686–966," *JSS* 6, pt. 3 (1909): 1–21 (reprinted in *Selected Articles from the Siam Society Journal*, vol. 1 [Bangkok, 1954], pp. 38–64), translates the chronologically reliable Luang Prasoet version; and David K. Wyatt, "The Abridged Royal Chronicle of Ayudhya of Prince Paramanuchitchinorot," *JSS* 61, pt. 1 (Jan. 1973): 25–50. Michael Vickery, "The '2/k 125 fragment': A Lost Chronicle of Ayutthaya," *JSS* 65, pt. 1 (Jan. 1977): 1–80, is an important text and translation of a recently discovered fragment dealing with the early fifteenth century. Richard D. Cushman is in the process of preparing a full composite translation of all the versions of the Ayudhya chronicles, an early draft of which runs to more than 1,200 pages. A Dutch resident in Ayudhya in the 1630s compiled a history of Siam based on Thai sources: Jeremias van Vliet, *The Short History of the Kings of Siam*, trans. Leonard Andaya (Bangkok, 1975).

Early Ayudhya history is the subject of a provocative synthesis, Charnvit Kasetsiri, *The Rise of Ayudhya: A History of Siam in the Fourteenth and Fifteenth Centuries* (Kuala Lumpur, 1976). In addition to several of their "Epigraphic and Historical Studies," A. B. Griswold and Prasert na Nagara shed fascinating light on the Ayudhya–Lan Na wars in their study of the poem *Yuan phai*, "A Fifteenth-Century Siamese Historical Poem," in *Southeast Asian History and Historiography*, ed. Cowan and Wolters, pp. 123–63. The general problem of manpower control was first laid out by Akin Rabibhadana, *The Organization of Thai Society in the Early Bangkok Period, 1782–1873* (Ithaca, N.Y., 1969), which, despite its title, has much to say about Ayudhya and its laws. H. G. Quaritch Wales, *Ancient Siamese Government and Administration* (London, 1934; reprint, New York, 1965), remains a useful reference.

For Lan Na in this period there is little available in Western languages beyond Notton's translation of the Chiang Mai chronicle, and Jayawickrama's translation of the *Jinakalamali*; but see *The Nan Chronicle*, trans. Prasert Churatana, ed. David K. Wyatt (Ithaca, N.Y., 1966). Paul le Boulanger, *Histoire du Laos français* (Paris, 1931), is a very uncritical history of Laos, as is Maha Sila Viravong, *History of Laos* (New York, 1964), which is a poor translation of a Lao original. A more useful Lao work deserves translation: Chao Khamman Vongkotrattana, *Phongsavadan sat Lao* [History of the Lao nation], 2d ed. (Vientiane, 1973). Fascinating Lao legends of the history of the middle Mekong region are translated in Charles Archaimbault, *Contribution à l'étude d'un cycle de légendes lau* (Paris, 1980). See also *The That Phanom Chronicle: A Shrine History and Its Interpretation*, trans. and ed. James B. Pruess (Ithaca, N.Y., 1976). Comparable material from the south, spanning both this and the earlier period, is in *The Crystal Sands: The Chronicles of Nagara Sri Dharrmaraja*, trans. and ed., David K. Wyatt (Ithaca, N.Y., 1975).

The Empire of Ayudhya, 1569–1767

The sources dealing with the seventeenth century suddenly become much fuller as contemporary European visitors appear on the scene. In addition to chronicles already cited, there are important collections of primary European documents, both published by the Thai National Library: *Records of the Relations between Siam and Foreign Countries in the 17th Century Copied from Papers Preserved at the India Office*, 5 vols. (Bangkok, 1915–21); and *Dutch Papers: Extracts from the "Dagh Register," 1624–1642* (Bangkok, 1915). Among the most useful accounts of foreign visitors are the following: *Peter Floris: His Voyage to the East Indies in the Globe, 1611–1615*, ed. W. H. Moreland (London, 1934); "Translation of Jeremias van Vliet's Description of the Kingdom of Siam," trans. L. F. van Ravenswaay, *JSS* 7, pt. 1 (1910): 1–108; the same author's *Historical Account of Siam in the 17th Century*, trans. W. H. Mundie (Bangkok, 1904), and see F. H. Giles, "A Critical Analysis of van Vliet's Historical Account," *JSS* 30, pt. 2 (1938): 155–240, and 30, pt. 3 (1939): 271–380; Nicholas Gervaise, *Histoire naturelle et politique du royaume de Siam* (Paris, 1689), trans. H. S. O'Neill as *The Natural and Political History of the Kingdom of Siam* (Bangkok, 1928); Claude de Beze, *1688, Revolution in Siam*, trans. E. W. Hutchinson (Hong Kong, 1968); the marvelous Simon de la Loubère, *A New Historical Relation of the Kingdom of Siam* (London, 1693), reprinted as *The Kingdom of Siam* (Kuala Lumpur, 1969); and the recently discovered Persian account, *The Ship of Sulaiman*, trans. John O'Kane (London, 1972).

Among secondary works, we might begin with O. W. Wolters's account of Sino-Siamese relations in the 1590s, "Ayudhya and the Rearward Part of the World," *Journal of the Royal Asiatic Society* (1968): 166–78. The seventeenth century is now much clearer thanks to George Vinal Smith, *The Dutch in Seventeenth-Century Thailand* (DeKalb, Ill., 1977). E. W. Hutchinson, *Adventurers in Siam in the Seventeenth Century* (London, 1940) is the standard account of Narai's dealings with the West. Maurice Collis, *Siamese White* (London, 1936) reads as a thrilling adventure story, and as history, it is reasonably accurate. Luang Sitsayamkan (Sit Hoontrakul), *The Greek Favourite of the King of Siam* (Singapore, 1967), is a good account of Phaulkon.

The 1688–1767 period is poorly covered in the available literature. A major exception is Busakorn Lailert's University of London dissertation, "The Thai Monarchy in the Ban Phlu Luang Period, 1688–1767" (1972), on which all scholars of this period must rely.

On Lan Na and Lan Sang there is nothing to be added to the sources mentioned above.

The Early Bangkok Empire, 1767–1851

The historiography of Thailand changes dramatically with the beginning of the Bangkok Era, for the sources become much more plentiful and include extensive archives. The number of scholars who have worked in this field is correspondingly high. Here we can do no more than indicate the most important recent scholarship in Western languages, most of which is available only in dissertation form. For an overview of source materials, see David K. Wyatt and Constance M. Wilson, "Thai Historical Materials in Bangkok," *Journal of Asian Studies* 25 (1965–66): 105–18, which is now considerably outdated.

Among the works dealing with the early Bangkok period as a whole, we already have drawn attention to Akin, *The Organization of Thai Society*. The only general overview of modern Thai history is Prince Chula Chakrabongse, *Lords of Life: A History of the Kings of Thailand*, rev. ed. (London, 1967), which is excessively hagiographical and personal. Sarasin Viraphol, *Tribute and Profit: Sino-Siamese Trade, 1652–1853* (Cambridge, Mass., 1977), is nicely complemented by Jennifer Wayne Cushman, "Fields from the Sea: Chinese Junk Trade with Siam during the Late Eighteenth and Early Nineteenth Centuries," Ph.D. diss., Cornell University, 1975. Lorraine Marie Gesick, "Kingship and Political Integration in Traditional Siam, 1767–1824," Ph.D. diss., Cornell University, 1976, speaks most directly to questions concerning kingship and the organization of the Thai empire. Craig J. Reynolds has written extensively about Thai Buddhism and about intellectual life in the Bangkok period. Here we note especially his 1972 Cornell Ph.D. dissertation, "The Buddhist Monkhood in Nineteenth Century Thailand" and his seminal article, "Buddhist Cosmography in Thai History, with Special Reference to Nineteenth-Century Culture Change," *Journal of Asian Studies* 35 (1975–76): 203–20. David K. Wyatt, "Family Politics in Nineteenth Century Thailand," *Journal of Southeast Asian History* 9, no. 2 (Sept. 1968): 208–28, deals with the definition of the ruling elite; and Lysa Hong, "The Evolution of the Thai Economy in the Early Bangkok Period and Its Historiography," Ph.D. diss., University of Sydney, 1981, assesses economic change. Relations with Chiang Mai and Lan Na are treated by Nigel J. Brailey, "The Origins of the Siamese Forward Movement in Western Laos, 1850–92," Ph.D. diss., University of London, 1968, the first chapter of which goes back to the Thonburi period. Siam's relations with Cambodia are the subject of David P. Chandler, "Cambodia before the French:

Politics in a Tributary Kingdom, 1794–1848," Ph.D. diss., University of Michigan, 1973, based on Cambodian, Thai, and Vietnamese sources. Laos is dealt with in David K. Wyatt, "Siam and Laos, 1767–1827," *Journal of Southeast Asian History* 4, no. 2 (Sept. 1963): 13–32.

Apart from coverage in works already mentioned, especially Gesick and Reynolds, there is little currently available on the reign of Taksin, apart from Jiri Stransky, *Die Wiedervereinigung Thailands unter Taksin 1767–1782* (Hamburg, 1973), and Jacqueline de Fels, *Somdet Phra Chao Tak Sin Maharat, le roi de Thonburi* (Paris, 1976).

The reign of King Rama I still would repay a great deal more scholarly labor. The First Reign Chronicle by Chaophraya Thiphakorawong (Kham Bunnag) has begun to appear in a translation by Chadin and the late Thadeus Flood, *The Dynastic Chronicles, Bangkok Era, The First Reign*, vol. 1 (Tokyo, 1978). Klaus Wenk, *The Restoration of Thailand under Rama I, 1782–1809* (Tucson, 1968), is a useful summary that does not go far beyond the chronicles. A different view of the period is presented in David K. Wyatt, "The 'Subtle Revolution' of King Rama I," in *Moral Order and the Question of Change: Essays on Southeast Asian Thought*, ed. A. B. Woodside and D. K. Wyatt (New Haven, Conn., 1982), pp. 9–52.

Little material is available on the Second Reign, save John Crawfurd's important *Journal of an Embassy from the Governor-General of India to the Courts of Siam and Cochin China* (London, 1828; reprint, Kuala Lumpur, 1971).

The reign of King Rama III begins with the confrontation between Siam and Britain represented in the Burney Mission, on which see *The Burney Papers*, 4 vols. in 5 (Bangkok, 1910–14; reprint, Farnborough, Hants., 1971), a still relatively untapped gold mine of information yielding much data up through the 1840s. The late Walter F. Vella's first book was *Siam under Rama III* (Locust Valley, N.Y., 1957), and it has withstood well the researches of another quarter-century. Nicholas Tarling, "Siam and Sir James Brooke," *JSS* 48, pt. 2 (Nov. 1960): 43–72, is the first in a series of that author's detailed treatments of Anglo-Siamese relations. On the succession crisis at the end of the reign, see William L. Bradley, "The Accession of King Mongkut," *JSS* 57, pt. 1 (Jan. 1969), 149–62.

Mongkut and Chulalongkorn, 1851–1910

The Fourth and Fifth reigns are among the most heavily studied by scholars, who have utilized a wealth of documentary materials in Bangkok and abroad. In addition to general works cited in the previous section, a large number of important works are available that span considerable lengths of time. Economic change has been particularly well treated by James C. Ingram, *Economic Change in Thailand, 1850–1970* (Stanford, 1971). G. William Skinner, *Chinese Society in Thailand: An Analytical History* (Ithaca, N.Y., 1957), is both durable and valuable. Three related collections of documents deserve special notice: Chatthip Nartsupha and Suthy Prasartset, *The Political Economy of Siam 1851–1910* (Bangkok, 1981), *The Political Economy of Siam 1910–1932* (Bangkok, 1981), and *Socio-Economic Institutions and Cultural Change in Siam, 1851–1910* (Singapore, 1977). Rural society is viewed from the perspective of economic history by David H. Feeny, *The Political Economy of Productivity: Thai Agricultural Development, 1880–1975* (Vancouver, 1982); by David Bruce Johnston, "Rural Society and the Rice Economy in Thailand, 1880–1930," Ph.D. diss., Yale University, 1975; and in a marvelously readable sort of local and ethnohistory, by Lauriston Sharp and Lucien M. Hanks, *Bang Chan: Social History of a Rural Community in Thailand* (Ithaca, N.Y., 1978).

The bibliography of the Fouth Reign is treated exhaustively by Constance M. Wilson, "Towards a Bibliography of the Life and Times of Mongkut, King of Thailand, 1851–1868," in *Southeast Asian History and Historiography*, ed. Cowan and Wolters, pp. 164–89. Wilson's own massive dissertation, "State and Society in the Reign of Mongkut, 1851–1868: Thailand on the Eve of Modernization," Cornell University, 1971, is the best full account of the period, especially strong in economic materials. The external relations of the kingdom are the subject of Neon Snidvongs, "The Development of Siamese Relations with Britain and France in the Reign of Maha Mongkut, 1851–1868," Ph.D. diss., University of London, 1961.

Of the contemporary sources of the period, we need to call attention particularly to Sir John Bowring, *The Kingdom and People of Siam*, 2 vols. (London, 1857; reprint, Kuala Lumpur, 1969); and to Bishop Jean-Baptiste Pallegoix, *Description du royaume Thai ou Siam*, 2 vols. (Paris, 1854; reprint, Farnborough, Hants., 1969). Both are highly evocative and comprehensive accounts of Siam on the eve of major change. The standard Thai record of the reign is more bland, but useful in tracing internal developments: Chaophraya Thiphakorawong, *The Dynastic Chronicles, Bangkok Era, The Fourth Reign, B.E. 2394–2411 (A.D. 1851–1868)*, trans. Chadin Flood, 5 vols. (Tokyo, 1965–74).

Of the secondary sources available for the Fourth Reign, too recent to be included in Wilson's bibliography, note especially William L. Bradley, *Siam Then: The Foreign Colony in Bangkok before and after Anna* (Pasadena, 1981); and Milton E. Osborne, *River Road to China: The Mekong River Expedition 1866–1873* (New York, 1975), on the Lagrée-Garnier explorations.

Contemporaries' accounts of Siam in the Fifth Reign vary considerably in their quality. Among the best are J. G. D. Campbell, *Siam in the Twentieth Century* (London, 1902); A. Cecil Carter, *The Kingdom of Siam* (New York, 1904), prepared for the St. Louis Exposition; James McCarthy, *Surveying and Exploring in Siam* (London, 1900); and *Twentieth Century Impressions of Siam*, ed. Arnold Wright (London, 1908), which is especially useful for its illustrations.

Among the scholarly monographs of the past two decades are Pensri (Suvanij) Duke, *Les relations entre la France et la Thailande (Siam) au XIXème siécle d'apres les archives des affaires etrangères)* (Bangkok, 1962); David K. Wyatt, *The Politics of Reform in Thailand: Education in the Reign of King Chulalongkorn* (New Haven, Conn., 1969); Tej Bunnag, *The Provincial Administration of Siam 1892–1915* (Kuala Lumpur, 1977); and Chandran Jeshurun, *The Contest for Siam 1889–1902: A Study in Diplomatic Rivalry* (Kuala Lumpur, 1977). Recent doctoral dissertations deserve to be equally available: David B. J. Adams, "Monarchy and Political Change: Thailand under Chulalongkorn, 1868–1885," University of Chicago, 1977; Ian G. Brown, "The Ministry of Finance and the Early Development of Financial Administration in Siam, 1885–1910," University of London, 1975; Noel Alfred Battye, "The Military, Government, and Society in Siam, 1868–1910: Politics and Military Reform during the Reign of King Chulalongkorn," Cornell University, 1974; Stephen J. Zack, "Buddhist Education under Prince Wachirayan Warorot," Cornell University, 1977; Thamsook Numnonda, "The Anglo-Siamese Negotiations 1900–1909," University of London, 1966; and M. R. Rujaya Abhakorn, "Ratburi, an Inner Province: Local Government and Central Politics in Siam, 1868–1892," Cornell University, 1984.

Finally, two memoirs make fine but very different reading on this period. Prince Wachirayan was Chulalongkorn's brother, a Buddhist monk, and one of the leading intellectuals of the reign: *Autobiography: The Life of Prince-Patriarch Vajiranana of Siam, 1860–1921*, trans. Craig J. Reynolds (Athens, Ohio, 1979). W. A. R. Wood was British consul, an amateur historian, and a long-time resident of Thailand: *Consul in Paradise: Sixty-Nine Years in Siam* (London, 1965).

The Rise of Elite Nationalism, 1910–1932

The Sixth Reign, that of King Vajiravudh, is admirably treated in Walter F. Vella, *Chaiyo! King Vajiravudh and the Development of Thai Nationalism* (Honolulu, 1978). Vella might, however, have made productive use of two useful doctoral dissertations: Stephen L. W. Greene, "Thai Government and Administration in the Reign of Rama VI (1910–1925)," University of London, 1971; and Peter Brian Oblas, "Siam's Efforts to Revise the Unequal Treaty System in the Sixth Reign (1910–1925)," University of Michigan, 1974.

Of contemporary accounts, W. A. Graham, *Siam*, 2 vols. (London, 1924), is to its era what Pallegoix and Bowring were to theirs, a comprehensive description. Malcolm Smith, *A Physician at the Court of Siam* (London, 1946), makes for delightful reading.

The last absolute monarch, King Prajadhipok, is known now mainly through the extensive writings of Benjamin A. Batson. Note particularly his Cornell Ph.D. dissertation, "The End of the Absolute Monarchy in Siam," 1977, and his *Siam's Political Future: Documents from the End of the Absolute Monarchy* (Ithaca, N.Y., 1977). A contemporary journalist's impressions are in Andrew A. Freeman, *Brown Women and White* (New York, 1932).

The Military Ascendant, 1932–1957

For this period, the major addition to previously cited works is a fine collection of documents edited by Thak Chaloemtiarana, *Thai Politics: Extracts and Documents 1932–1957* (Bangkok, 1978), which is extremely useful as a translated Thai voice. The same author's *Thailand: The Politics of Despotic Paternalism* (Bangkok, 1979), includes a long introduction that goes back to 1932. In addition to the two Batson works already cited, necessary as background to the 1932 coup and its aftermath to 1935, there are a number of useful specialized works. E. Thadeus Flood, "Japan's Relations with Thailand, 1928–1941," Ph.D. diss., University of Washington, 1967, adds a new dimension to the study of the period. Thawatt Mokarapong, *History of the Thai Revolution, a Study in Political Behavior* (Bangkok, 1972), is especially good on the events of 1932 itself, while Pierre Fistié, *Sous-développement et utopie au Siam, le programme des réformes présenté en 1933 par Pridi Phanomyong* (Paris and The Hague, 1969), considers the sources and shape of Pridi's socialist thought. Of contemporaries, Kenneth P. Landon, *Siam in Transition, a Brief Survey of Cultural Trends in the Five Years since the Revolution of 1932* (Chicago, 1939; reprint, New York, 1968), wrote from long experience in the country; while Virginia Thompson, *Thailand, the New Siam* (New York, 1941; reprint, New York, 1967) wrote an enormous volume relatively well on the basis of minimal firsthand experience. Nicholas Tarling, "King Prajadhipok and the Apple Cart: British Attitudes towards the 1932 Revolution," *JSS* 64, pt. 2 (July 1976): 1–38, explores one aspect of Siam's diplomatic relations in this period.

The regime of the first Phibun government, 1938–44, includes the Indochina war of 1940–41 and most of World War II and is immeasurably complex. On the Indochina war, *Thailand's Case* (Bangkok, 1941) was stated by Luang Wichit Wathakan; and the war was described by a contemporary journalist, M. Sivaram, *Mekong Clash and Far East Crisis* (Bangkok, 1941). A more recent view is that of E. Thadeus Flood, "The 1940 Franco-Thai Border Dispute and Phibun Songkhram's Commitment to Japan," *Journal of Southeast Asian History* 10, no. 2 (Sept. 1969): 304–25. On the Phibun government and the world war, see Charnvit Kasetsiri, "The First Phibun Government and Its Involvement in World War II," *JSS* 62, pt. 2 (July 1974): 25–88; two pieces by Thamsook Numnonda, "Pibulsongkram's Thai Nation-Building Programme during the Japanese Military Presence, 1941–1945," *Journal of Southeast Asian Studies* 9, no. 2 (Sept. 1978): 234–47, and *Thailand and the Japanese Presence, 1941–45* (Singapore, 1977); and the extremely important memoirs of Direk Jayanama, *Siam and World War II*, trans. Jane Godfrey Keyes (Bangkok, 1978). Benjamin A. Batson, "The Fall of the Phibun Government, 1944," *JSS* 62, pt. 2 (July 1974): 89–120, is definitive. John B. Haseman, *The Thai Resistance Movement during the Second World War* (DeKalb, Ill., 1978) is generally disappointing; and one can still gain much from firsthand accounts: Sir Andrew Gilchrist, *Bangkok Top Secret* (London, 1970); Peter Kemp, *Alms for Oblivion* (London, 1961); and Nicol Smith and Blake Clark, *Into Siam, Underground Kingdom* (Indianapolis, 1946).

The diplomatic crisis at war's end is best studied in selections from the U.S. diplomatic documents, published in *Foreign Relations of the United States, Diplomatic Papers, 1945*, vol. 6 (Washington, 1969). Three articles cover that crisis from varying perspectives: Nicholas Tarling, "Atonement before Absolution: British Policy towards Thailand during World War II," *JSS* 66, pt. 1 (Jan. 1978): 22–65; James V. Martin, Jr., "Thai-American Relations in World War II," *Journal of Asian Studies* 22, no. 4 (1963): 451–67; and Herbert A. Fine, "The Liquidation of World War II in Thailand," *Pacific Historical Review* 34, no. 1 (1965): 65–82. Frank C. Darling, *Thailand and the United States* (Washington, 1965), traces the relationship up to the 1960s.

The postwar period, down to 1957, is still very difficult to unravel. Thak's coverage in *Thai Politics 1932–1957* and in the early chapters of *Thailand: The Politics of Despotic Paternalism* is, so far, the best available. Additional Thai voices may be heard through translations of recollections in Jayanta Kumar Ray, *Portraits of Thai Politics* (New Delhi, 1972). Two contemporary outside observers were the journalist Alexander MacDonald, *Bangkok Editor* (New York, 1949), and Edwin F. Stanton, the first American ambassador to Thailand, *Brief Authority* (New York, 1956). The memoirs of Pridi Phanomyong (Pridi Banomyong), *Ma vie mouvementée et mes 21 ans d'exil en Chine populaire* (Paris, 1974), are as interesting for what they do not say as for what they do.

Development and Revolution, 1957–1982

On this most recent period, serious historical scholarship has hardly begun. Thak's study of the Sarit regime is a fine beginning, but the source materials are hardly available to allow scholarship to proceed with certainty beyond that period. There are bits and pieces, not least dealing with Thailand's relationship with the United States, in published official documents of both governments. Political scientists have at least provided the historian with views of the structure within which developments have taken place. Fred W. Riggs, in *Thailand: The Modernization of a Bureaucratic Polity* (Honolulu, 1966), has, for example, some insightful analysis of the relations between the Thai military and the business community; and William J. Siffin, *The Thai Bureaucracy: Institutional Change and Development* (Honolulu, 1966), is useful and informative. Three recent books on politics are useful in providing the immediate background to the present. Clark D. Neher, ed., *Modern Thai Politics: From Village to Nation*, rev. ed. (Cambridge, Mass., 1979), is a fine and up-to-date collection of articles on a range of contemporary topics. John L. S. Girling, *Thailand: Society and Politics*

(Ithaca, N.Y., 1981), is concerned primarily with the structure and patterns of Thai political relationships and their roots in changing Thai society. David Morell and Chai-anan Samudvanij, *Thailand: Reform, Reaction and Revolution* (Cambridge, Mass., 1981), is exceptionally well informed and required reading for an understanding of the turbulence of the mid-seventies.

Index

All toponyms mentioned in the book are included on the maps, and map references are given in this index at the conclusion of the relevant entries.

333